PHYSICAL ANTHROPOLOGY

ORIGINAL READINGS IN METHOD AND PRACTICE

Edited by

Peter N. Peregrine
Lawrence University

Carol R. Ember
Human Relations Area Files

Melvin Ember
Human Relations Area Files

Prentice
Hall

UPPER SADDLE RIVER, NEW JERSEY 07458

Library of Congress Cataloging-in-Publication Data

Physical anthropology: original readings in method and practice/edited by Peter N. Peregrine,
Carol R. Ember, Melvin Ember.
    p. cm.
Includes bibliographical references.
ISBN 0-13-093979-X
    1. Physical anthropology.   I. Peregrine, Peter N. (Peter Neal).   II. Ember, Carol R.   III. Ember, Melvin.

GN60 .P49 2001
599.9—dc21   2001052110

AVP, Publisher: Nancy Roberts
Editorial assistant: Lee Peterson
Marketing manager: Chris Barker
Editorial/production supervision: Kari Callaghan Mazzola
Prepress and manufacturing buyer: Ben Smith
Electronic page makeup: Kari Callaghan Mazzola and John P. Mazzola
Interior design: John P. Mazzola
Cover director: Jayne Conte
Cover design: Kiwi Design

This book was set in 10/12 Palatino by Big Sky Composition
and was printed and bound by Von Hoffman Graphics.
The cover was printed by Phoenix Color Corp.

 © 2002 by Pearson Education, Inc.
Upper Saddle River, New Jersey 07458

Printed in the United States of America
10 9 8 7 6 5 4 3 2 1

ISBN 0-13-093979-X

Pearson Education LTD., London
Pearson Education Australia PTY, Limited, Sydney
Pearson Education Singapore, Pte. Ltd
Pearson Education North Asia Ltd, Hong Kong
Pearson Education Canada, Ltd., Toronto
Pearson Educación de Mexico, S.A. de C.V.
Pearson Education—Japan, Tokyo
Pearson Education Malaysia, Pte. Ltd
Pearson Education, Upper Saddle River, New Jersey

CONTENTS

Preface   v

PART I   EVOLUTION
---

1   Evolutionary Genetics   1
Robert B. Eckhardt

2   Genes, Bodies, and Species   14
Jonathan Marks

3   Paleoanthropology and Evolutionary Theory   29
Ian Tattersall

PART II   PRIMATE EVOLUTION
---

4   Explaining Primate Origins   42
Matt Cartmill

5   Why Are Primates So Smart?   53
Joan B. Silk and Robert Boyd

6   Miocene Apes   68
David R. Begun

7   Chimpanzee Hunting Behavior and Human Evolution   90
Craig B. Stanford

PART III   HUMAN EVOLUTION

8   Australopithecus Afarensis and Human Evolution   103
         Scott W. Simpson

9   "Robust" Australopithecines, Our Family Tree,
         and Homoplasy   124
         Henry M. McHenry

10   The Natural History and Evolutionary Fate
         of Homo Erectus   140
         Andrew Kramer

11   Neandertal Growth: Examining Developmental Adaptations
         in Earlier Homo Sapiens   155
         Nancy Minugh-Purvis

12   Testing Theories and Hypotheses about Modern Human
         Origins   174
         David W. Frayer

PART IV   MODERN HUMAN VARIATION

13   Natural Variation in Human Fecundity   190
         Peter T. Ellison

14   What Accounts for Population Variation in Height?   204
         J. Patrick Gray and Linda D. Wolfe

15   Growth and Development of Turkana Pastoralists   219
         Michael A. Little

16   The Concept of Race in Physical Anthropology   239
         C. Loring Brace

PART V   PHYSICAL ANTHROPOLOGISTS AT WORK

17   Paleoanthropology and Life History, and Life History
         of a Paleoanthropologist   254
         Timothy G. Bromage

18   The Evolution of a Physical Anthropologist   264
         Katharine Milton

PREFACE

Which would you rather read: (A) "Fragments of the cranium were exposed by heavy surface erosion," or (B) "I found the skull after a huge rainstorm washed away the soil covering it"? If you answered B, then this book is for you. Most collections of articles that are used in undergraduate courses are made up of works patched together from material written by anthropologists for other anthropologists or, in some cases, for a popular audience. Rarely are works included that were written explicitly for college students. This is a problem, for often works written for scholars are too detailed and jargon-laden for students to digest easily, while works written for a popular audience contain little information that would be new to students who have already been exposed to physical anthropology. This book, on the other hand, is composed of chapters written explicitly for college students. The chapters are not reprints of articles published elsewhere, but were composed for you, a student of physical anthropology, to help you appreciate the methods, practices, and experiences of some of the top physical anthropologists working today.

How do the chapters in this book differ from those in other collections? Usually when we read an article or book chapter about a piece of research, we find out about the results—what the researchers think they have discovered, what they think they know. Rarely do we get to understand the process. Where do ideas come from? How does an idea get transformed into a research project? What was exciting about the research? What was disappointing? What is the person behind the process like? These questions are rarely addressed in scholarly writing, and they are often absent even in popular accounts of research. Here these questions are central, for the anthropologists who wrote the chapters in this collection wanted to help you understand the process of discovery. They wanted you to understand not only what they found, but also how they went about finding it, and what the experience was like. Most of all, they wanted to excite you about physical anthropology—not only about the findings in physical anthropology, but also about the process of doing physical anthropology itself.

The purpose of this collection is to make research in physical anthropology more alive for students like you who are just beginning to get to know physical anthropology. While the articles in the first four parts focus on "standard" topics in physical anthropology courses, they are not dry expositions on methods and data; rather, each article brings the experiences and insights of an active scholar to the practical matters of doing physical anthropological research. The authors all provide examples from their own research to give you a better sense of what physical anthropologists actually do in the field and laboratory.

Part I, "Evolution," introduces basic concepts of biological evolution and evolutionary theory. Part II, "Primate Evolution," examines the evolution of the primate order and some of the theories about primate origins. Part III, "Human Evolution," explores our australopithecine and early human ancestors, and considers how and why modern humans evolved. Part IV, "Modern Human Variation," considers both the nature and causes of physical variation among contemporary peoples. The authors of the chapters in these four parts try to convey a feeling for the research process by focusing on a particular topic or issue. If the issue is one that scholars disagree about, the authors convey a feeling for the dynamics of research and the excitement of debate, the variety of questions asked by physical anthropologists, and the diverse methods they use to answer them.

Part V, "Physical Anthropologists at Work," is a bit different from the parts that precede it, as it includes two autobiographical articles. We left it up to these two authors to choose what they wanted to write about. After all, we want you to get a feeling for how physical anthropologists vary, not just how their research varies. In these ways, we hope you will come to appreciate that physical anthropology is not just an unemotional set of methods and data, but rather a bunch of hard-working, insightful people who employ those methods and data to answer particular questions about human evolution and variation.

ACKNOWLEDGMENTS

The chapters collected here were composed between 1995 and 2000 by a diverse group of scholars who set aside their research projects and teaching loads to take the time to write these engaging pieces. The task was easy for some, difficult for others, but enjoyable for all. We want to thank all the authors for their efforts in producing these fine works for undergraduate students. We also want to thank the people at Prentice Hall, particularly Nancy Roberts and Sharon Chambliss, who have been tremendously supportive and helpful throughout the process of getting this work into print. Before appearing here many of the chapters were part of the *Research Frontiers in Anthropology* series, published by Simon & Schuster Custom Publishing, and our thanks go to Pat Naturale, Stephanie Mathiessen, and Kari Callaghan Mazzola for their help in the initial production of these works. Finally, we want to thank you, the reader, for taking the time to explore the product of our collective efforts.

Peter N. Peregrine
Carol R. Ember
Melvin Ember

EVOLUTIONARY GENETICS

ROBERT B. ECKHARDT

Like most adults in our society, college students are usually only partially and imperfectly informed by the media about important new scientific developments and discoveries at the frontier of research. This unsatisfactory situation occurs because, as a rule, even in our supposedly "information-based society," consumers—whether they are television viewers, readers of daily newspapers, subscribers to the glossy weekly or monthly news magazines, or even the somewhat captive audiences of college textbooks—are not usually given information in the form of raw data or detailed analyses. Instead, potential consumers of knowledge typically are given conclusions: brief accounts that summarize findings without presenting the full array of evidence and reasoning that would enable an intelligent person to evaluate the reported results. Such a mode of media operation is unfortunate for several reasons. Adults in general and students in particular should be committed to acquiring the tools of critical thought, the essential building blocks of reasoning and synthesizing ability. Thus equipped, they could proceed from assessing basic information to making informed and intelligent judgments during the entire span of their lives as citizens: that is, as voters, parents, schoolboard members, and the like. Without these conceptual tools, citizens are handicapped intellectually, and what they don't know certainly *can* hurt them.

Even if some field of scientific research is at the cutting edge, dull reporting can reduce its impact on the general population, while sharp reporting can heighten its positive influence. This is nowhere more true than in the case of knowledge about human genetics and evolution. Misinformation can reinforce prejudices, while ignorance of genetic influences on physical and mental health can maintain the general quality of life at a level far lower than what is already attainable.

Another reason for rejecting any approach from authority (which says, in effect, "Here's the answer; take it or leave it") rather than from genuine understanding ("Here is the evidence we have and here is how we reasoned from the data to our conclusions—and, by the way, here are a few complications that you might want to consider") is that any dogmatic approach is by definition unscientific. More specifically, an authoritarian approach to knowledge about the natural world lends false support to critics of evolutionary biology who would like to persuade everyone that belief in evolution in particular, or even the scientific method in general, is "just another kind of religious belief." Oddly enough, fundamentalist critics of an evolutionary worldview are sometimes aided in their dubious, anti-intellectual endeavor by scientists who are so eager to gain wide acceptance of their theories that they link aspects of evolutionary biology to familiar but unsuitable biblical metaphors. Let's start by looking at one example of this sort before returning to the basic and straightforward principles that make it possible to understand the dynamics of genetic change in evolution.

SCIENCE IN THE NEWS: "Y" NOT SUPPORT FOR EVE?

A recent *Science News* report carried the title "Lineage of Y Chromosome Boosts Eve Theory."[1] What does this mean, and what is the significance of the scientific work reported? The background to this story begins in 1987 when a group of molecular biologists headed by Berkeley's Allan Wilson (now deceased) proposed, as summarized in the *Science News* report, that "... all humans evolved from one woman, dubbed Eve, or more likely from a small group of women, living about two hundred thousand years ago in Africa...." The original "Eve" hypothesis appears to have been an attempt to draw attention to the ability of molecular biologists to analyze DNA sequences extracted from tiny particles in the cell's cytoplasm called *mitochondria*.

Mitochondrial DNA (abbreviated *mtDNA*) preserves an ancient system of heredity that is substantially independent of the genetic system in the cell's nucleus, from which it differs chiefly in two properties. First, mtDNA is transmitted almost exclusively to children from their mothers. Second, mtDNA appears to accumulate mutations at a higher rate than the DNA of nuclear genes. Maternal transmission of mtDNA occurs because the unfertilized eggs produced by women contain abundant cytoplasm and cytoplasmic particles such as mitochondria, while sperm derived from fathers contribute chiefly nuclear genes. On fertilization, the nuclear genome combines the maternal and paternal chromosomes and their genes, while the cytoplasm as a rule contains exclusively maternal mitochondria. Because there is no recombination of mitochondrial genomes, mutation is the only source of change in mtDNA. And since as a general rule the mutations occur sequentially, they can be used to trace descent through female lineages.

Wilson and his coworkers combined the observations of maternal transmission and change due exclusively to mutation with a further convenient assumption, that mutations accumulate in mtDNA at a relatively constant rate. From this combination of observations and assumptions the Berkeley group theorized that it would be possible not only to trace all of the mitochondrial diversity that they observed in living humans back to one ancestral gene sequence, but to assign a date for when the mitochondrial lineages started to diverge from a common female ancestor. They made some calculations that placed this divergence temporally somewhere in the range of one hundred thousand to two hundred thousand years ago—geographically in Africa because they believed that continent exhibited the greatest mitochondrial diversity.

When it appeared that these interpretations were becoming accepted, further speculations were offered: These included migration routes that the hypothetical descendants of hypothetical Eve might have followed as they spread across the world, and how Eve's proposed descendants could have eliminated all earlier human populations already living in Europe and Asia (another essential assumption, since areas of the Old World outside Africa had yielded thousands of fossils from previous human populations, some of them as much as a million years old). Wilson and coworkers theorized that the previous humans could have been eliminated if Eve's descendants introduced new infectious diseases, competed more successfully for limited resources, or directly killed off the competition. Some enthusiasts of the replacement theory even reconstructed what "Eve" probably looked like and proposed that her people were the first to have human speech—even though the fractional mitochondrial genomes studied contain no known genetic sequences that encode information that might influence the development of physical appearance or behavior.

At this point we might return to the recent *Science News* story and ask, "But what does the Y chromosome have to do with any of this?" The direct answer is, "Nothing whatsoever." The Y chromosome is part of a separate hereditary system, one contained in the nucleus, not the cytoplasm. In contrast to mtDNA, a Y chromosome is not transmitted to females but exclusively from male to male. And in the 1995 study referred to at the beginning of this section, *no differences at all* were found among the thirty-eight males in whom the Y chromosome genes were studied.[2] This *absence* of Y gene diversity in the human sample might make some of us feel that any basis for calculating a time of divergence was missing—particularly because it was the abundant *presence* of genetic diversity in mtDNA that served as the genesis of the Eve story. If you find all of this a bit puzzling and are willing to admit this confusion, read on, because you may have the makings of a research scientist.

Like much of what is sometimes called "supermarket science," consisting of headlines that scream from the tops of tabloid newspapers on grocery store display racks—"UFOs Taught Me to Type" and "Two Women Give Birth to Same Baby"—the "mitochondrial Eve" story contained at least some verifiable points. But the mitochondrial Eve story jumbles together several different

areas of genetic investigation that can be understood more easily if they are
kept distinct, at least at the outset.

EVOLUTIONARY GENETICS: UNTANGLING THE DOUBLE HELIX

On first consideration, evolutionary genetics might seem to be simply a re-
dundant phrase of the same sort as "green plant" or "tall basketball player."
But on close examination these verbal linkages are not mere repeats after all.
Not all plants are green (for example, mushrooms and other fungi), not all
professional basketball players are tall, and so perhaps it is not such a surprise to find that not all areas of genetic research are evolutionary in content
or methodology. In order to make sense out of recent research in molecular genetics or other areas of evolutionary biology, it is useful to sort out different
areas of knowledge that come together under the heading of evolutionary genetics: the genetics of transmission, the genetics of development, and the genetics of replacement.

GENETICS OF TRANSMISSION: THE MATERIAL BASIS OF HEREDITY

Two of the most widely known, central discoveries in the history of genetics
deal predominantly with the normal and predictable transmission of hereditary characteristics. These central discoveries are the laws of gene segregation and independent assortment formulated by Gregor Mendel, and the
double-stranded helical model establishing DNA as the chemical carrier of
genetic information formulated by Watson, Crick, Wilkins, and their associates. These findings establish the physical and biochemical bases of genetic
transmission, but by themselves do not explain (or make it possible to measure directly) the genetic changes that are essential features of evolution.
Knowledge of gene structure and transmission provide the foundation for
understanding the evolutionary process, but they are not sufficient for representing the dynamic aspects of change through time. Because the discoveries
by Mendel and by Watson, Crick, and their associates can be found in any elementary textbook of biology, they will not be repeated here. The dynamics
of change, which are not nearly so widely known or understood, will be the
principal focus of our attention.

GENETICS OF DEVELOPMENT

In contrast with gene transmission, developmental genetics is concerned with
gene expression. In humans and other complex organisms, a central mechanism of gene expression begins with a process in which messenger RNA
(mRNA) is copied along a section of one strand of DNA in the nucleus. The
mRNA segment corresponding to one gene is then edited by enzymes that

excise functionally superfluous segments of the mRNA, called *introns*, and splice back together the information-containing segments, called *exons*. Subsequently, this edited strand of mRNA moves from the nucleus to the cytoplasm, where it interacts with other cell components (ribosomes, transfer RNA molecules, amino acids) to form a protein (technically, a *polypeptide*) that serves a particular structural or enzymatic function. Since each cell can contain tens of thousands to hundreds of thousands of nuclear genes, the proteins produced from different mRNA templates can interact with each other, as well as with environmental influences, in many complex ways. These interactions shape the biochemical activities that determine cell structure and function throughout the life cycle, the general term for the course of events from spore or fertilized egg through production of another spore or gamete that can begin the next generation.

Some biologists would limit the term development only to the highly noticeable changes that occur during the juvenile stages of the life cycle in multicellular organisms. However, a better case can be made for being more inclusive, and viewing development as a set of biochemically-based processes that have been present from the very beginning of life, but have become increasingly complex during the course of evolution.

The simplest existing single-celled organisms (*prokaryotes*) lack a separate nucleus, and their single closed loop of double-stranded DNA may include as few as several dozen genes, with the biochemical interactions among their products comprising the full extent of gene expression. The other extreme is encountered in *eukaryotes*, the term for organisms based on cells with cytoplasm separated from a nucleus in which genes are distributed among several chromosomes. Although there are some single-celled eukaryotes, this category also includes humans along with other multicellular animals, as well as the more complex plants. In these larger organisms the total number of cells in a single individual can range into the billions and trillions. During the course of their development, the expression of thousands of genes in each nucleus leads to differentiation by structure and function into numerous varieties of cells, tissues, and organs. To introduce a point that we will return to later, development itself has responded to natural selection by becoming more diverse and, in some organisms, far more complex than in others. As a result, within each life cycle multicellular organisms can have numerous molecular cycles, organelle cycles (one example of which is mitochondrial replication), and cell cycles.

Thanks to the tremendous progress made in molecular biology and molecular genetics, today we know vastly more about development than we did only a few decades ago. Nonetheless, it is important to realize that there are still some important limitations to a strictly reductionist molecular approach. One of these limits is intrinsic, resulting from a built-in feature of biological organization: Not all DNA products are synthesized anew each generation; some (such as the mitochondria and some of the structures involved in cell division) are carried over, already formed and structurally intact, from previous life cycles. Another limitation of the molecular approach, this one more a property of biologists than biology, is the tendency of some researchers to equate all evolutionary change with alterations in nucleotide sequences. But if not all aspects of development arise directly from the instructions coded in DNA or RNA sequences, it follows that it is impossible to reconstruct or interpret evolution solely from the information encoded in any series of nucleotides.

This last limitation is particularly important to our understanding of human evolution, as our detailed knowledge of human gene sequences remains limited to certain portions of the genome. At present we are confronted by a frustrating paradox: Most of the gene sequences that we know in detail have very little direct influence on the external features that are so familiar to us in everyday life: size, shape, color, behavior. This is because these aspects of appearance or *phenotype* result from interactions of the products of genes at many loci with each other and with environmental agents. And most of the detailed sequence information that we have is for individual genes with little known influence, if any, on external form. This paradox places a severe limitation on molecular approaches to reconstructing the course of human evolution, since molecular sequence information derived from living populations on the one hand, and morphological features preserved in the fossil record on the other hand, are effectively decoupled.

This is not to say that developmental geneticists are entirely at a loss to explain the hereditary basis of complex morphological features such as the body build, shape, and limb proportions of living people, or the sizes, shapes, and other details of bones from members of present and past populations. In fact there has long been a domain of genetic research referred to as *quantitative genetics* that has developed a set of powerful statistical techniques useful in investigating the interplay of multiple genes with each other and with environmental factors (such as nutrition, exercise, climate, and disease) to produce complex traits of the human skeleton and other organ systems.

Scientifically, quantitative genetic research has deep roots.[3] Its techniques were developed initially by Sir Francis Galton, Charles Darwin's first cousin, in 1889. Galton was trying to understand the transmission of human stature as an example of a continuously-distributed phenotypic characteristic. By an accident of history, however, Galton's work was ignored, possibly because it was done between Gregor Mendel's unrecognized discovery of the basic principles of gene transmission in 1866 and the rediscovery of those principles in 1900 by another generation of geneticists. As a result of this accident, Galton's empirical work was carried out in the absence of a major theoretical insight that might have enabled scientists to avoid decades of delay and confusion in the study of human heredity.

Even after Mendel's work was rediscovered, the *biometricians* (so called because they measured biological structures) who followed Galton's pioneering efforts did not see how Mendel's work related to theirs. Mendel had studied traits that exhibited discontinuous variation of the sort that falls into discrete, non-overlapping categories (differences in seed shape or color). Anthropologists and human geneticists still study many discontinuous traits today, in the form of the *genetic polymorphisms* such as ABO and other blood groups. In contrast, the biometricians studied continuous variation of the sort that cannot be subdivided into categories in any non-arbitrary way (such as attempting to divide a roomful of people into two categories: tall and short). In addition to stature, there are many such features that are of intense interest to those who are studying the genetics of the evolutionary process. Indeed, in complex organisms a great many anatomical and physiological characteristics that can be measured rather than categorized are expressed as continuous, metric, or quantitative traits. The genes that underlie these traits still remain largely unidentified.

Why do some traits fall into a few easily-studied discrete categories while others present a nearly infinite, smoothly graded array of phenotypes influenced by genetic loci that are poorly known? The core of the answer is that genes differ greatly in the relative magnitudes of their phenotypic effects. A *major gene* or allele is one that produces a pronounced phenotypic effect that is detectable against the background provided by other genetic loci. *Minor genes* are those with influences that are too slight to be identified individually by conventional techniques. Traits (such as stature) that reflect the joint action of several such genes at different loci (commonly five to ten) are referred to as *polygenic characteristics*. These polygenes of minor effect appear to be more easily influenced by environmental factors than are major genes.

There are long-standing limitations on the study of polygenic traits due to our limited ability to recognize minor gene variants and to localize them to known chromosomal regions. As will be discussed later in this chapter, this situation is already changing. As a result, we are entering an era of expanding knowledge of the very numerous genetic loci with alleles that make contributions that are individually slight but cumulatively significant in their effects on features of structure, function, and behavior.

GENETICS OF REPLACEMENT

The term replacement can refer to the substitution of one genetic alternative, or *allele*, for another at a given locus, or of one entire population by another. At one extreme both processes coincide, since gene substitution can occur when one closely related population supplants another. Documented examples of complete large-scale population replacement are exceedingly rare, however. The more general cases comprise situations in which a population in a given location undergoes genetic change over a series of generations. These genetic changes occur through a variety of mechanisms, including mutation, gene flow, genetic drift, and natural selection.

A *mutation* is any heritable change in the structure or amount of genetic material in a cell. Although mutations are rare events, they are important because ultimately they are the source of all genetic variation. The physical and chemical alterations in the genetic material that result from mutation take place on a continuum of effects from slight to great, from the molecular level to alterations in whole sets of chromosomes. At the molecular level are *point mutations*. In the most common form of these, a *base substitution*, one nucleotide replaces another. Less common are *additions* and *deletions* of nucleotides, which can alter the reading of larger stretches of genetic material. *Chromosome mutations* can produce even greater scale changes in genetic material, altering not only molecular sequences but also the size or shape of a chromosome when viewed under a microscope. Larger still in the extent of genetic material changed are *genome mutations*, shifts in chromosome numbers that add or delete one or more entire chromosomes.

Gene flow is the term given to the transfer of alleles from one gene pool to another through interbreeding between members of the two populations. Gene flow can therefore supplement mutation in introducing genetic variation into any given population. Unlike mutation, though, gene flow generally decreases differences between populations, making them more alike genetically. Gene flow usually occurs as the result of normal mate exchanges between adjacent populations, and can take place with little or no population movement. Although *migration* commonly is used as a synonym for gene flow, the term migration really is better used to refer to the mass movement of large groups of people, followed by widespread mating that unites the elements of what previously had been two distinct populations into a single new group or hybrid population. Migration and hybridization are documented in historical times and thus seem to be common events. However, for most of human prehistory, when people lived as hunters and gatherers, migration probably was far rarer than simple flow of genes from population to population.

Genetic drift refers to any random change in gene frequency between one generation and the next. Drift occurs because of random events—accidents. The smaller the population, the greater the chance for *sampling error*—the chance that a small group is not representative of a larger group from which it is drawn. For example, all of the offspring born to any real set of parents is much smaller than the total number that might have been produced if all of the hundreds of eggs released by a female during her reproductive lifespan had been fertilized by a like number of sperm—and those few hundred sperm would be but a tiny percentage of the millions of sperm produced by a male during his reproductive life. Drift also can occur as a result of *founder effect*, which occurs when one small group of people buds off from a parent population and moves to a new, previously uninhabited area. Under these circumstances there is a very good chance that the departing subgroup will have a sampling of genes differing in various ways from the larger parent stock.

Natural selection takes place when some genotypes in a population produce more surviving offspring than do others for some reason that is non-random—that is, for a reason that is causally related to their hereditary characteristics. This mechanism, first proposed by Charles Darwin over a century ago, is based on abundant observations that, for generation after generation in species after species, more offspring are produced than there are parents of the preceding generation. The resultant population pressure, inferred Darwin, virtually guarantees that there must be competition for resources—food, shelter, mates, and so on—and hence for survival and reproduction. Darwin combined this inference with another observation, that hereditary variation is abundant. Certain of these inherited variants might give their possessors an advantage over other individuals, he reasoned, allowing them to survive longer and produce more offspring. These descendants, in turn, would reproduce the advantageous inherited characteristics of their particular parents. The result, put in more modern terms, would be a highly non-random compounding of advantageous genes at much higher rates than their less advantageous alleles.

In sum, mutation, gene flow, genetic drift, and selection can bring about evolutionary changes in populations, altering the frequency of any allele at any locus, or of numerous genes at various loci. Each of these forces of evolution can act either in isolation or, as must be more common, in interaction with each other to determine the frequencies of genes in populations.

One common misconception among individuals with little knowledge of genetics is that it is difficult to explain evolutionary change. Perhaps this is why so many people uncritically reject previous human groups (such as Neanderthals) as possible ancestors. They are "too different" to have evolved into beings such as ourselves. This reaction ignores the vast stretches of time available for evolutionary change (in the case of Neanderthals, at least tens or hundreds of thousands of years—many hundreds of generations). Such a reaction also overlooks the array of evolutionary forces just outlined in this section. In fact, the chief difficulty that evolutionary biologists have in explaining genetic change is an "embarrassment of riches" in the sense that there are usually several alternative explanations for any particular change that we can detect.

This abundance of potential causes of change can be illustrated by adding to the preceding list of evolutionary forces a relatively rare mechanism that has come to light only very recently: *horizontal gene transfer*, which is defined as the passage of genetic information from one genome to another—specifically between two different species.[4] The "horizontal" part of this term is used to distinguish certain cases of genetic transmission from the far more common "vertical transfer" of genes from parent to offspring by mating and fertilization. Horizontal gene transfer is made possible by the existence of *retroviruses*. These relatively rudimentary microorganisms can infect a higher organism of one species and incorporate some of its chromosomal DNA into the viral genome. The viral infection subsequently can be transmitted to a member of some other species, at which point the viral genome becomes incorporated into that of the new host.

One striking example of horizontal gene transfer has resulted in the presence of a baboon virogene (that is, a viral gene found in baboons and other Old World monkeys) in six species of cats that are related to the domestic cat (*Felis catus*), even though the gene is absent from more distant felids such as lions, leopards, and bobcats.[5] Details of the virogene sequence in primates and felids make it likely that the transfer was from the monkeys to the cats. This inference about direction is made because numerous Old World primate species contain the gene, while it is present in only a few species of cats from the Mediterranean area. The time of transfer can even be pinpointed because the virogene sequence in cats resembles most closely that of a few closely-related baboon species that diverged from other primates five to ten million years ago.

The case of horizontal gene transfer has been included in this section, rather than in the earlier material on the genetics of transmission because, from the standpoint of a species population on the receiving end of the virally-mediated horizontal transfer, the outcome is a complex form of gene flow that involves at least three species (donor, viral transmitter, and recipient) and mimics mutation in its outcome. From the example given, we can see that well-documented mechanisms of evolutionary genetics can be verifiable scientifically and even be logical in their own way—yet still be astonishing. Let's face it: Horizontal gene transfer sounds like something that would be invented by a fiction writer such as Michael Crichton or Steven Spielberg. But, clearly, off-the-wall events have taken place in the history of life on earth. To return to the earlier example of mtDNA, a large body of evidence now makes it all but certain that the mitochondria found almost universally in eukaryotic cells are descended from ancient bacterial invaders that established a symbiotic relationship with the host cells: energy in exchange for shelter and protection.

RE-EXAMINING THE "MITOCHONDRIAL EVE"

New scientific breakthroughs are exciting, and the ability to obtain sequence data from human mtDNA and from a Y chromosome intron certainly helps to extend our knowledge about the evolutionary genetics of human populations. This is not the same, however, as saying that these data equally support all interpretations that have been based on them. By now, readers of this chapter have sufficient basic knowledge to understand a critical reanalysis of the mitochondrial Eve hypothesis, some of it based on my own research and some of it on a paper written by the population geneticist Alan Templeton in 1993.[6] The essential points of our reanalyses are varied, but all stem directly from basic principles of evolutionary genetics as outlined earlier.

In terms of the genetics of transmission, we know that all allelic variants in a population must trace ultimately to a common ancestral gene. Because mtDNA is maternally inherited in humans and other primates, all human mtDNA must trace back to a common female ancestor. This ancestor could be called mitochondrial Eve if imagination fails to bring forth anything more original and less misleading in its associations. By the same logic, gorillas must have their own common ancestral mother; calling her an Eve as well might upset or at least confuse people who thought that they had at least some vague mental grasp of the original mitochondrial Eve story.[7]

The genetics of development make clear that the intrinsic nature of the mtDNA and Y chromosome intron data provide absolutely no direct way to reconstruct any aspect of the physical appearance or behavior of mitochondrial Eve or similar theoretical constructs. The difficulty is not that the reconstructed populations lived an indefinitely long time ago or that only a limited number of living humans have been sampled. The problem is that the mitochondrial and Y chromosome sequences that have been studied have no direct influence on the development of anatomical features of the bones and teeth that make up the bulk of the human fossil record. Nevertheless, some researchers appeared to believe that they were solving problems in developmental genetics when they were actually extrapolating metaphorically from the genetics of transmission and the genetics of replacement.

Statistics based on the genetics of replacement suggest that the common human mitochondrial ancestor may indeed have lived in Africa, but this conclusion is in no way certain; in fact, the African root was accepted after a single computer program run of a single type. Later analyses by Templeton and others identified over a thousand different arrangements of the mtDNA data, many of which pointed to a non-African origin. In addition, there were flaws in the statistics originally used to establish the dates of one hundred thousand to two hundred thousand years ago (or several other variants on this range) for the common mitochondrial ancestor. The common mitochondrial ancestor and directly antecedent populations could have lived long before the origin of modern humans, perhaps as much as half a million to a million years ago.[8] Finally, the Y chromosome intron data from humans show no variation whatsoever, thus providing no logical basis for calculating a divergence time in the range of one hundred thousand to two hundred thousand years ago (or for that matter, any other time); corresponding Y chromosome intron data from other primates exhibit a pattern in which either the rate of molecular change is not constant, or the suggested species branching patterns are incorrect—in any case, theories of modern human origins based on the Y chromosome intron data stand up no better than did the previous mtDNA data.[9]

This chapter has reviewed much of what has been written about the mitochondrial Eve episode, and reading through it one is reminded of a remark made long ago about another discipline, by Wolfgang Pauli: "Some physics papers are so bad that they are not 'even' wrong." Rather than end on a negative note, however, I prefer to emphasize to readers of this chapter that much exciting and important work remains to be done. Fortunately, it should be possible for evolutionary genetics to move forward from its present situation. There may be problems, but there are also many more possibilities.

Until recently, for instance, the study of quantitative genetics was eclipsed by some spectacular advances in molecular genetics (not to mention some wild theories). Recently this gap has been closed by research on *quantitative trait loci*; these studies combine powerful mathematical and molecular techniques in ways that now make possible the study of individual gene effects on quantitative characters.[10] Such approaches hold the promise of eventually linking evolutionary genetics with direct studies of morphological characteristics having real time depth in the fossil record. This avenue or work is not as forbidding as it sounds. Comparative studies of many species show that there has been a high level of conservation of gene sequences and of genomic organization. We know, for example, that humans and chimpanzees share 98 percent to 99 percent of their genes in common despite our lineages having been separated for at least five million years. When we know much more detail about the contents of these genomes, we may be able to reconstruct the genomic organization of some of our more recent human ancestors, which so far are known only from the fossil record.

Another avenue of approach is a longer shot in terms of payoff, although more direct: recovery of ancient DNA from the fossil bones themselves. Some progress has been made along these lines in other organisms, and many molecular laboratories are making further attempts. Don't bet against an eventual payoff on these long odds.

NOTES

1. T. Adler, "Lineage of Y Chromosome Boosts Eve Theory," *Science News* 147 (May 27, 1995): 326.

2. Robert L. Dorit, Hiroshi Akashi, and Walter Gilbert, "Absence of Polymorphism at the ZFY Locus on the Human Y Chromosome," *Science* 268 (May 26, 1995): 1183–1185.

3. Robert B. Eckhardt, "Human Quantitative Genetics: A Century of Research," in Praveen Kumar Seth and Swadesh Seth, eds., *Human Genetics: New Perspectives* (New Delhi, India: Omega Scientific Publishers, 1994), pp. 21–34.

4. Wen-Hsiung Li and Dan Graur, *Fundamentals of Molecular Genetics* (Sunderland, MA: Sinauer Associates, 1991), pp. 199–201.

5. R. E. Benveniste, "The Contributions of Retroviruses to the Study of Mammalian Evolution," in R. I. MacIntyre, ed., *Molecular Evolutionary Genetics* (New York: Plenum, 1985).

6. Alan R. Templeton, "The 'Eve' Hypotheses: A Genetic Critique and Reanalysis," *American Anthropologist* 95 (1993): 51–72.

7. R. R. Hudson, "Gene Genealogies and the Coalescent Process," *Oxford Studies in Evolutionary Biology* 7 (1990): 1–44.

8. Robert B. Eckhardt and Terry W. Melton, "Human mtDNA Diversity is Compatible with the Multiregional Continuity Theory of the Origin of Homo sapiens," *American Journal of Physical Anthropology*, Supplement 16 (1993): 83.
9. Dorit, Akashi, and Gilbert, "Absence of Polymorphism at the ZFY Locus on the Human Y Chromosome."
10. James Cheverud and Eric Routman, "Quantitative Trait Loci: Individual Gene Effects on Quantitative Characters," *Journal of Evolutionary Biology* 6 (1993): 463–480.

Suggested Readings

Falconer, Douglas Scott. *Introduction to Quantitative Genetics*. Harlow, England: Longman Scientific and Technical Publications, 1989. This is the classic work in the field of quantitative genetics. It is distinguished by leavening mathematical treatment with highly readable text.

Li, Wen-Hsiung, and Dan Graur, *Fundamentals of Molecular Evolution*. Sunderland, MA: Sinauer Associates, 1991. This book provides a highly readable and reasonably current coverage of research progress in molecular evolutionary biology.

Medawar, Peter B. *Advice to a Young Scientist*. New York: Basic Books, 1979. This slim volume is not concerned with evolutionary genetics, but it is one of the most important books that can be read by anyone contemplating a career in the biological sciences.

Simpson, George Gaylord. *This View of Life*. New York: Harcourt, Brace and World, 1964. The view of life referred to in the title of this timeless volume is that of an evolutionist, and the author was one of the leading evolutionary biologists of this century. Simpson's views are carefully thought through and written with extreme clarity.

Wallace, Bruce. *The Search for the Gene*. Ithaca, NY: Cornell University Press, 1992. One authority in the field suggested that this book "… might be read by undergraduates with a little spare time who … want to explore some of the background to what is certainly one of the most exciting scientific stories of our century."

GENES, BODIES, AND SPECIES

JONATHAN MARKS

This chapter is about the biological hierarchy through which changes in DNA ultimately become differences between species. The idea of *hierarchy* is an old and fairly nebulous one in evolutionary biology, generally invoked to differentiate between what geneticists study and what anatomists or natural historians study.[1] What geneticists study—genes and chromosomes—is of course so small that you can't see it with the naked eye, while what anatomists study can be sliced and weighed. Likewise, what geneticists study *causes* what anatomists study—that is, genes "code for" bodies.

And yet, such a biological hierarchy is certainly intended to convey something more than simply gross size of the subject matter—big things versus little things! After all, non-genetic information has a major role in the form of the end products of biological development. And genes only "code for" bodies in a very crude way, for bodies also constitute the manner by which the genes are passed into the next generation—so there is an important sense in which bodies make genes as much as genes make bodies.

The object of this chapter is to link together the small and the large through modern evolutionary theory, and to explore the relationships among genes (or cells), phenotypes (or bodies), and populations (or species). The point will be that cells, organisms, and species are all "individuals"— that is to say, singular entities bounded in space and time and composed of interacting parts; as opposed to "classes," or sets of objects, transcending time and space and composed of members sharing a specific quality or essence.[2] Each of these kinds of individuals can be studied in a particular fashion, and we will explore the manner in which that is so, and the different kinds of evolutionary knowledge that is accessible from each kind of individual.

GENETICS: CELLS AS INDIVIDUALS AND GENES AS MACHINE CODE

Cells were recognized in the nineteenth century as the most fundamental form of life. Reproduction and development, whose relationship to one another had previously been very unclear, were now seen to be related through the processes of cell division. While the body at all stages was composed of cells, reproduction and development were the results of two different kinds of cell division. Mitosis was the process by which cells divided into two identical cells, and the body thereby grew; and meiosis was the process by which sperm and egg cells were produced to transmit genetic information into the next generation of organisms. Each sperm or egg has half the amount of genetic information of ordinary cells, and the genetic information they carry differs. Thus, ordinary cells have two copies of each gene and are thus *diploid*, while sperm and egg have one copy of each gene and are thus *haploid*. In addition, ordinary cells all carry a set of identical genetic information, while the genetic information carried within each sperm or egg cell is unique and thus distinct from every other sperm or egg.

Cell generations, then, are similar to those of larger organisms. Cells originate, persevere, and die. They exist in space and have a duration in time. They reproduce. They interact with others like themselves and with the physiological environment in which they exist. They are autonomous biological units.

Another powerful recognition came half a century later, as biologists grappled with the precise nature of the genetic information itself. In a book called *What is Life?* published in 1944, physicist Erwin Schrödinger suggested that the genetic information could be considered as a kind of code that the cell's mechanism effectively decodes. This idea of the *genetic code*, evoking powerful images of language and machinery, has subsequently become one of the most powerful metaphors in science.[3]

The units of genetic information themselves came to be known early in the twentieth century as "genes."[4] The development of population genetics in the 1930s provided a powerful theoretical model for the processes of evolution, based on a mathematical abstraction, the *gene pool*—a hypothetical summation of all the hereditary elements in a population—a pool in the sense of office pool, not swimming pool.

By focusing on the gene pool, population genetics established a fundamental way of thinking about evolution, a way that completely avoided the recognized biological units: cells and organisms. Population genetics modeled evolution as changes in the gene pool, in which organisms were simply represented by genotypes, transient pairs of genes, each of whose lifespan was far shorter than that of the gene pool itself. The proportions of each genotype were mathematically predictable from the proportions of each gene by a relation that has come to be known as the Hardy-Weinberg Law.[5]

The Hardy-Weinberg Law has two parts. The first part tells us that, given two genetic variants (alleles) in a gene pool, one with a frequency of p and the other with a frequency of q, the ordinary processes of organismal reproduction will sort these alleles into diploid genotypes in fixed proportions. One homozygote (an organism with two identical alleles) will exist with a frequency of p^2, the other with a frequency of q^2, and the heterozygote (an organism with one of each allele) will exist in the population with a predictable frequency of $2pq$. In other words, if 30 percent of the alleles in a gene pool are A1, and 70 percent are A2 (A1 and A2 being two hypothetical variants of the A gene), then we would expect to find 9 percent of the *organisms* to be A1A1 homozygotes, 49 percent to be A2A2 homozygotes, and 42 percent to be A1A2 heterozygotes. The second part of the Hardy-Weinberg Law tells us that these proportions remain constant every generation, as long as no other forces are acting on the population aside from reproduction.

Evolution, then, according to population genetics, is simply a violation of this genetic equilibrium. Studying evolution involves asking a single fundamental question: What causes the proportions of genotypes and genes *not* to remain constant?

Empirically this question can be studied using genetic markers, bits of genetic material whose transmission can be tracked in populations, even though they may not be functionally significant. After all, this is a corpus of statistical theory that eliminates phenotypes, bodies, and organisms from the picture. The function of a gene—what it does, and its effect on the body—is thus irrelevant here.

So what alters the gene pool? Preferential mating with relatives (*inbreeding*) makes a population more homozygous, but doesn't directly affect allele frequencies. Differential reproduction of particular genotypes (*selection*) will directly affect allele frequencies; as will the introgression of genetic material from another population (*gene flow*). Finally, since real populations are finite in size, the laws of chance dictate random deviations from the predicted mathematical constancy (*genetic drift*). Each of these forces has specific effects: Since the environment is what permits different genotypes to reproduce more or less efficiently than their alternatives, selection permits populations to track their environments genetically; thus selection makes populations different from one another adaptively. Gene flow, on the other hand, makes populations more similar to one another, for it reflects the genetic contact between populations. And finally, genetic drift also makes populations different from one another, but in a non-adaptive way.

Thus, "the spread of genes" is a classic way of visualizing evolution, assuming a direct translation from genetical variant to physical/anatomical variant, and modeling the ways in which a population is altered through time upon the emergence of these new genetic variations. But recently, the precise nature of these genetic variations has come to be examined in greater depth, and has revealed a system of far greater complexity than such simple modeling had considered.

THE GENOME AS INFORMATION

The image of genes as blueprints or machine code for the body is immensely powerful. It lies behind the program begun in the 1980s called The Human Genome Project, in which great public and private resources were mustered to generate a comprehensive vision of the blueprints: the DNA sequence of each chromosome. A genome is, formally, the genetic structure of a single reproductive cell: a haploid genetic complement, one of each chromosome.

The chromosomes are visible structures whose purpose seems to be to guide a great mass of DNA through cell division by condensing it into a manageable number of regular structures. Thus, chromosomes are only visible during cell division; at other times the DNA is loose in the cell nucleus, although "anchored" to the nuclear membrane at certain points.

Humans have twenty-three pairs of chromosomes, so the Human Genome Project's goal was to reproduce the detailed linear sequence of each of them. Once we have the gene sequences, and the knowledge that the gene sequence is like machine code for the production of organisms, we will have, as the Human Genome Project's purple prose said, "The Book of Man" or "The Holy Grail of Biology."[6, 7]

This misses a crucial part of genetic physiology, however. As we noted earlier, a normal human body cell is diploid; only gametes are haploid. In fact, the human body is constrained to have two, *and only two*, sets of instructions in its cells. While many domestic plants have multiple sets of chromosomes, a condition known as polyploidy, mammalian cells simply can't work that way. A human with three sets of chromosomes (sixty-nine total) is triploid and cannot survive.

Moreover, having one copy (monosomy) or three copies (trisomy) of any specific chromosome is also bad. This is known as the problem of dosage: You need two doses of DNA, not one and not three. Having one copy of a particular chromosome (making forty-five total) is not compatible with life, unless that chromosome is the X chromosome, which still results in a characteristic pathological condition known as Turner's Syndrome. Having three copies of a particular chromosome (forty-seven total) is slightly better, but not much. One can live normally with an extra Y chromosome (because there is very little on that chromosome): One can also survive, but again with distinctive pathological phenotypes, with an extra X chromosome (Klinefelter's Syndrome) or chromosome 21 (Down's Syndrome). The X chromosome can tolerate variation in number more readily than other chromosomes because it has relatively few genes and has its own special mechanism for regulating dosage—since normal males have one X and normal females have two Xs. Chromosome 21 seems to be able to tolerate trisomy because it is so small and has only about 200 genes, rather fewer than chromosome 22, which is about the same size.

The point is that normal development depends not just on the DNA sequence, but specifically on the interactions of *two* DNA sequences. Using the metaphor of DNA as a blueprint or code, it may be easy to miss the importance of the dosage of DNA required; the complex interactions between two *sets* of instructions that seem to add up to more than the sum of their parts.

They say that when the only tool you have is a hammer, everything tends to look like a nail. Unfortunately we don't really have tools for understanding the interaction between two genomes that results in a normal, healthy organism. But we do have the ability to study the structure of an individual genome in its finest detail, and so we do. From the standpoint of evolution, this leads us to the process of mutation. Mutation is a change in the genetic material; alleles differ from one another ultimately because of mutation, and consequently mutation is the source of all genetic differences between organisms and between species. Since the 1980s, our increasing knowledge of the genome has greatly affected our view of mutation.

The genome is composed of DNA, a long series of elementary subunits known as adenine, guanine, cytosine, and thymine, abbreviated A, G, C, and T. These are known as nucleotides or bases. When we speak of a "DNA sequence" we mean simply a long, specific arrangement of those four bases: for example, AAGCTATATCCAGCA.

The human genome is essentially 3.2 billion of those letters, divided among twenty-three chromosomes. Genes are simply particular regions of the genome that have some kind of function. Here, however, is where a major conceptual revolution in the past quarter-century has occurred. Where it used to be thought that the genes were arrayed like beads on a string—the genome being the string and the genes being the beads—it is now clear that (1) the beads are simply "special cases" of string; and (2) there are very few beads.[8] In other words, the genes are simply functional bits of genome; and genes are rare within the genome. The human genome sequence, published in early 2001, shows that less than 25 percent of the genome consists of genes (30,000 genes, each on average 27,000 bases long), and even within each gene less than 10 percent is actually functional. The Human Genome Project reports that only between 1–2 percent of the DNA actually comprises *coding sequence*.[9]

Moreover, there are complex patterns of redundancy within the genome. These patterns of redundancy are themselves products of the mutational machinery, and contribute to the perpetuation of that redundancy. For example, the most basic kind of mutation is the substitution of one base for another, such as AAGCT to AAGCC. However, a different mutational process called *strand slippage* can insert or delete additional bases, such as altering AAGAG-GCT to AAGAGAGAGAGGCT. That of, course, creates a fundamental pattern of redundancy of bases. It may also increase in intensity over the generations, as an auto-catalytic process. This has now been found to be the cause of a significant class of genetic diseases, which includes Huntington's chorea and fragile-X syndrome.

Another kind of redundancy is created by a widespread "rubber-stamping" process in the genome, whereby one DNA sequence is simply copied next to itself. If this DNA sequence includes a functional gene, it will produce two functional genes next to each other, where formerly there was only one. Three things can happen to this new copy over many generations: (1) It can continue to do the same thing, so the body now has twice as much gene product, which, if beneficial, would then be preserved; (2) if its presence makes no difference to the body, it can degrade by mutation to a state of nonfunction, now called a *pseudogene*; (3) rather than becoming nonfunctional, mutations can alter the properties of the second gene product so that it does something different, which again might be beneficial.

And indeed we find that genes in the genome are found in clusters, some copies of which do identical things, some of which do slightly different things, and some of which do nothing at all. The genes coding for hemoglobin, the best-known genetic system, are located in two clusters, one at the tip of chromosome 11 and the other at the tip of chromosome 16. The one at the tip of chromosome 16 codes for the alpha component of hemoglobin, a protein that is 141 amino acids long, and has two identical genes, side-by-side, churning out the raw material for alpha-globin. There is also, however, a gene just a little ways away, which also makes a 141-amino-acid-long protein, but only does so early in embryonic life, when the needs for gas transport in the tissues are considerably different. And there are also DNA stretches that bear strong similarities to the functional genes but do not themselves do anything: pseudogenes, the result of archaic duplications of DNA that didn't help and didn't hurt, a genetic experiment that neither succeeded nor failed, but whose record remains.

Other portions of the genome appear to be immensely long stretches of simple sequences—just a few letters repeated millions of times, the result of a process (or processes) of massive tandem duplication.

Still other kinds of mutation involve the movement of specific DNA bits from one place to another, known as transposition, or the creation of several copies of a particular DNA bit, and the integration of these DNA copies in many places throughout the genome, known as retrotransposition. The most famous of these DNA segments is known as *Alu*, and consists of a fairly specific stretch of DNA about 300 bases long and intercalated seemingly at random through the genome, over a million times.

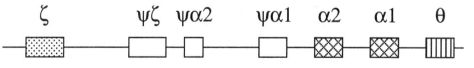

FIGURE 2-1

Schematic diagram of the alpha-globin gene cluster at the tip of human chromosome 16. From left to right, zeta is a functional gene in embryonic life; three pseudogenes are inactive; the two alphas contain identical coding sequences and are functional throughout the entire lifespan; and theta is of unknown function. The entire region covers about 30,000 bases.

Since the genome is far more complex than had been thought by an earlier generation, our ideas about the genome have had to be revised, particularly in relation to evolution. We have tended to conceptualize mutation as a simple process of nucleotide substitution in functional genes in our formal models, but it is now clear that the genome is a dynamic landscape, and can tolerate considerable change without apparent adverse effect. With mutation being the basic source of biological novelty, the implication is that the sources of novelty for evolution are considerably more diverse than considered by earlier generations of geneticists. How do we use this new information to understand the biological history of species?

REPRESENTATION

From the standpoint of evolution, these different parts of the genome can convey different kinds of information. It is axiomatic, for example, that since most of the genome is nonfunctional, it is not affected by natural selection. Thus, most mutations have no effect on the phenotype and are not weeded out by natural selection, while those that alter the structure of genes generally do so adversely and are consequently eliminated. Thus inter-genic DNA evolves most rapidly, and genic DNA most slowly.

However, in the time since, say, human and chimp have been separate species, very few changes have occurred in the genome. We are over 98 percent genetically identical to chimpanzees and (at least to a first approximation) 100 percent genetically identical to each other; consequently it is hard to use DNA to study the relationships among human beings. However, a particularly rapidly evolving part of the genome is found outside the cell nucleus and is known as mitochondrial DNA or mtDNA. Here, humans and chimpanzees are 9 percent different, and two random humans are 0.2 percent different from each other. Consequently this can be used as a genetic marker for studying the relationships among groups of people.

Genetic markers can be tricky, however. Most of the genome doesn't vary from person to person, and what does vary is often the product of complex mutational processes in the cell and complex population dynamics over the eons. Therefore simple explanations of the patterns are unlikely to be correct. For example, the very first genetic marker was the ABO blood group, now known to be caused by a single gene on chromosome 9, whose product adds a sugar to a molecule coating the surface of a red blood cell. Type A adds one sugar, type B adds a different sugar, and type O adds none. Simple enough.

The distribution of the three alleles, however, is far from simple. All populations of the world have all three of them but in different proportions, with O being universally the most common. Clustering human populations on the basis of the frequencies of these alleles puts very different peoples together who share the same frequencies by accident, such the Poles and Chinese. Moreover, in spite of the fact that most people are type O, chimpanzees are overwhelmingly type A, and gorillas are overwhelmingly type B. It is simply not clear just what is going on, or how can we make easy evolutionary sense of it.

It is also important to bear in mind that these are genetic markers, and not genes *for* physical attributes, such as skin color or facial contour—which even today we have no access to.

By the 1970s it was evident that one could pool several different genetic markers and use high-powered statistics to determine which populations had the most similar clusters of allele frequencies, and might therefore be considered closest relatives. It turned out, however, that the results were always very unstable, and highly sensitive to just which genetic markers were used, just what computer algorithm was used, the demographic history of the population (whether expanding, contracting, or interbreeding), and even the specific people chosen to represent the population, and the specific populations chosen to represent the region.[10]

In one infamous anecdote, a geneticist drew blood from pygmies in central Africa but rejected anyone he thought was too tall; thus the test tubes he brought back from the field didn't reflect the real population, but rather his preconceptions of what the population should have been. Other studies generalized extravagantly about "Africans" from two or three local tribes. Thus, representation is a key issue: An accurate relationship between the samples the geneticist has and what or whom those samples are supposed to reflect cannot be taken for granted.

The problem of representation is crucial when we begin to appreciate that populations are composed of diverse organisms that may, and usually do, have complex histories. Looking, for example, at the relationships among human populations, one is always laboring under the shadow of gene flow. Two human populations may be genetically similar because they diverged recently, or because they have interbred. Human populations are also fluid and symbolically-defined: Marriage, adoption, raiding, alliance, and trade all serve to make the boundaries between them far less distinct genetically than culturally. Thus, if one wished to study the genetic relationships among the Germans, Swiss, and Italians, there may be no real scientific answer to such a scientific-sounding question. The answer you get will depend crucially on who is selected to represent those populations, given that Switzerland lies geographically in between Germany and Italy and has a long and complex social history in relation to them.

The important point is that all comparisons are not equal, nor are all evolutionary conclusions based on genetic data self-evident. Simply the choice of specimen, from which the DNA is ultimately isolated, may have a major effect on the conclusions of a study, if the hierarchical relationships between person, population, and cell are ignored. On the other hand, this problem might seem to be mitigated if you study the relations among different species.

Above the species level, gene pools can only diverge; there can be no inter-species breeding (that is generally what we mean by species, after all). Thus, the relations among humans, chimpanzees, and gorillas might at face value seem an easier question.

SPECIATION

Population genetics is a classically *transformationist* field, tracking a single gene pool as it changes through time. The diversity of life, however, is a product of divergence, as well as descent. How does one evolutionary lineage become two, so that divergence, presumably by a combination of genetic drift and natural selection, can occur?

The multiplication of lineages is the proliferation or reproduction of species, a series of processes known collectively as speciation. This can be considered analogous to the mitosis of cells or the reproduction of (asexual) organisms—the generation of two individuals or biological units where formerly there was but one.

Speciation requires the division of the gene pool, or more precisely it requires the segregation of organisms into populations that are not in genetic contact with one another. The maintenance of genetic contact (gene flow) acts in opposition to speciation. Once the population is divided into two or more segments, they diverge through time genetically both at random (via genetic drift), and in conjunction with their new environments (natural selection). The key question, however, is how the organisms of those populations ultimately come to regard one another as *different*—that is to say, not as potential mates. Dogs, after all, can be exceedingly promiscuous with other dogs, even with dogs that look quite different, but one never sees them mate with cats.

What is it that permits an organism to recognize another as a potential mate, and thereby worthy of reproductive attention and effort, so that it doesn't squander its time, resources, and energy? How does a rhesus monkey know it's a rhesus monkey and not a pig? And more importantly, how does it recognize another rhesus monkey as a potential mate?

The processes of species formation involve not just genetic divergence, but the development of new specific mate recognition systems.[11] These may be visual, olfactory, or behavioral signals, but they comprise a crucial part of the evolutionary process. Often, one population becomes physiologically incapable of reproducing with another population before they recognize each other as being different species—they may be fertile at different times of the year, or recognize different mating signals, or simply have physically incompatible genitalia. Or it may be that the structure of the chromosomes of one population has changed, so that they may mate and hybridize, but the hybrid is infertile—precisely the situation that exists between horse and donkey.

Three sets of changes, all ultimately genetic, but not easily related to one another, occur together during speciation. The first are the clocklike genetic changes all through the genome, so that regardless of the function (if any) of a particular DNA segment, it can be used as a record of the biological history of the cell, organism, and species it came from. The second are the physical changes to the body, itself a responsive and reactive system. And the third are the physiological, reproductive signals that unite a reproductive community, and distinguish it from others. Species that have been separated for a long period of time are different in all three ways; but recent divergences, or even incomplete divergences, yield important insights into the manner by which molecular, anatomical, and reproductive divergences or incompatibilities are generated in populations separately, but in parallel.

Since these kinds of changes occur together, although at different rates, the relationships of closely related species are no more easy to disentangle with molecular data than they are with classical anatomical data. Returning to the question of chimpanzees, gorillas, and humans, we find that some molecular data appear to link chimps and people, some link chimps and gorillas, and most yield thorough ambiguity. We are consequently obliged to regard the relationships among chimps, gorillas, and humans as a three-way-split or trichotomy.[12]

A question arises when we study the relationships among groups of organisms, whether they are parts of one species, or of several: Is one representative sufficient? Can a single specimen stand as a synecdoche (a metaphor in which the part substitutes for the whole) of a biological group?

Actually we can show quite easily the inadequacy of such an assumption at the level of the species. Imagine a single ancestral species, broadly distributed geographically. Perhaps they are protochimpanzees in equatorial Africa. One group fissions off to the west, and over a few hundred thousand years they become a species of protogorillas. Another group fissions off to the east and over a similar span of time they become protohominids. To ask which pair of species a few million years later are closest relatives is a nonsensical question: The protochimpanzees would be the ancestors of all three living forms (gorillas, chimps, and humans), the early gene pools of the species would have overlapped extensively, and the relations of their modern descendants would be ambiguous.[13] Indeed, the answer you obtained might depend very specifically on which specimens you chose to represent the species: The chimpanzees from one region might turn out to be slightly more closely related to protogorillas and those from another might be slightly more closely related to protohumans. After all, according to this simple model, they were ancestral to both.

And once again, we find that at places where genetic diversity has been sampled in the apes, it is generally considerably greater than anticipated (especially considering that the apes are all endangered, and living in small ranges in Africa), and also considerably larger than in humans, who have nevertheless expanded to fill up the entire planet.[14]

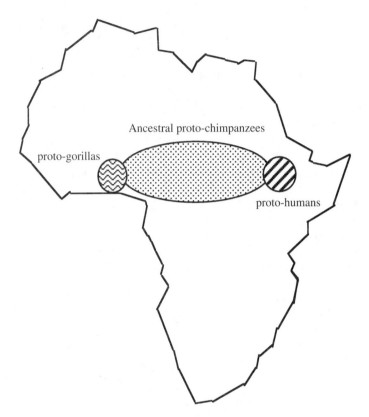

FIGURE 2-2

If an ancestral population of protochimpanzees gave rise to both protogorillas in the west and protohumans in the east at around the same time, the phylogenetic relationships among them would be vague from modern species in precisely the way we find them to be. And it wouldn't matter whether you looked at DNA or bodies—the problem would be modeling the biological history adequately.

So, just like the problems of understanding the relationships among human populations if the hierarchical relations of cell, body, and population are ignored, there exists a similar set of problems that accrue if one tries with comparable naivete to understand relationships among species.

SEEING EVOLUTION: THE EYE OF THE BEHOLDER

The processes of evolution to a molecular geneticist involve principally mutation and genetic drift. Random changes to the DNA occur at a calculable rate, and since most of the genome has no function, the changes are generally either unexpressed or neutral (functionally equivalent to their alternatives), and will thus be unaffected by selection. Even in functional regions there is considerable "slop"—insulin derived from the pancreas of a pig, while structurally different, nevertheless still functions well for a human.

The action of selection here is principally to weed out genetic variations that function poorly. Thus, given the structure of a protein and its physiological necessities, randomly altering its structure (by mutation) is far more likely to compromise its function than to improve it. Imagine opening the hood of your car and randomly hitting your engine with a hammer (the equivalent of mutation). While it is theoretically conceivable that you might improve the engine's performance, it is exceedingly unlikely. Most likely you'll screw it up; and if you're lucky you just won't do any serious damage.

A geneticist therefore finds two DNA sequences from different species to differ in very specific ways. Because of the constant pressure of genetic mutation, differences will always be there, but you expect to find the most differences in functionless regions, and proportionately fewer in regions with important genes; and within each gene, you expect to find more differences in specific regions that compromise the structure and function of the protein product the least.

In other words, one expects to find difference when comparing DNA regions across species; when "too much" similarity is found, that is taken as evidence for strong constraints on the particular DNA region, indicative of functional importance. That is precisely how the *homeobox*—a stretch of 180 nucleotides in a small class of genes involved in early embryonic development—was discovered: It was there, almost intact, in the genomes of flies and mice. Since flies and mice have little else in common, this suggested an exceptional physiological importance for the region.

Morphologists see evolution, in the classical sense, quite differently. They anticipate stability of structure, because they work with adapted bodies, not with sloppy genes. Therefore they expect related organisms to be *similar* to one another, and attempt to explain the *differences* by recourse to selection. This is precisely the opposite of what the geneticists do, expecting divergence of DNA sequence and explaining the situation in which sequences are more similar than anticipated!

A geneticist and a morphologist look at the same animals: orangutans (*Pongo pygnaeus*), chimpanzees (*Pan troglodytes*), and humans (*Homo sapiens*). The geneticist finds that most of the genome differs by about 2 percent between humans and chimps, and by about 5 percent between either of them and the orangutan. But certain regions are identical: The geneticist thus frames questions such as, "Why haven't mutation and drift caused this region to diverge more through time? Why is this region so important? What does it do that constrains it from tolerating any change?" The morphologist, by contrast, sees two creatures with hairy bodies, long arms, and small brains, and asks, "Why has the other species lost body hair, changed limb proportions, and expanded its brain?" The morphologist does *not* ask, "Why does the orangutan and chimpanzee *retain* body hair, long arms, and small brains?" The answer is simple: Those features work. The morphologist expects preservation of functional body systems due to adaptation, and in contrast the geneticist expects decay of DNA sequences due to the constant pressure of mutation.

The geneticist and the morphologist thus see different patterns in their data, see change occurring at different rates, in different modes, and ask different evolutionary questions to explain their findings. While genes, bodies, and species all evolve together (obviously!), it is frequently difficult to unify them into a coherent evolutionary narrative. This is not altogether surprising: The big question in genetics is the complex relationship between genotypes (i.e., genetic constitutions or DNA sequences) and phenotypes (the outward appearances of organisms).

In the simplest case, early geneticists following Mendel found that one phenotype was dominant over another, but a pea heterozygous for a gene (Aa) looked indistinguishable from a pea homozygous for one of the genes (AA). Thus, from what the pea looks like, you cannot tell what alleles it has.

In more complex cases, a phenotype results from the interaction of several genes operating in physiological systems. Not only that, but the developing body is reactive and sensitive to the conditions of growth. Thus, someone may be short-statured because of a particular combination of alleles, or because of nutritional stress during childhood. The body is thus developmentally plastic: A given genetic background may result in different physical forms under different circumstances. The body is sensitive to the conditions of life; it is adaptable.

More than that, the body is also pulled in the opposite direction. Not only does the body change in harmony with the circumstances of growth, but in other ways the body is also very *in*sensitive to genetic variation or environmental shock. The developmental geneticist C. H. Waddington called this property *canalization*—the tendency of the genetic system to be buffered, so that the same phenotype may result from different genetic backgrounds or in different environments.[15]

In other words, the same genotype can produce different phenotypes, and the same phenotype can be the product of different genotypes. With such a level of disconnect between genes and bodies, it's no wonder that molecular and morphological specialists see their subject matter in such different ways.

CONCLUSIONS

The ultimate source of all evolutionary difference is mutation, the change in DNA, located in cells. Mutation is a more complex process than earlier generations conceived it to be. The genome is a complex landscape, only being mapped now, and the study of *comparative genomics* is in its infancy.

The fundamental changes that occur initially in a cell ultimately accrue to the body the cell is a part of. Mutations that aid in the survival and reproduction of those bodies—or at least don't hurt them—are perpetuated, and thus become disproportionately represented in the gene pool. New species arise when the gene pool is partitioned, and organisms cease to identify each other as potential mates.

Cells, organisms, and species are the units of contemporary biology—molecular or cellular biology in the first case, physiology and anatomy in the second, and systematic biology in the third. Their connections are real, but sometimes difficult to understand; and it has often been easier to ignore the other levels than to grapple with the complexity they impart to the study of evolution. The marvel is that somehow, the same history of life is inscribed into species in each of their manifold components. It is etched into each body and each cell; the trick is to decode it.

NOTES

1. M. C. King and A. C. Wilson, "Evolution at Two Levels in Humans and Chimpanzees," *Science* 188 (1975): 107–116.
2. D. Hull, "Units of Evolution: A Metaphysical Essay," in U. L. Jensen and R. Harré, eds., *The Philosophy of Evolution.* (Brighton: Harvester Press, 1981), pp. 23–44.
3. S. Sarkar, "Decoding "Coding"—Information and DNA," *BioSystems* 46 (1996): 857–864.
4. This was in honor of Darwin, who paradoxically had nothing to do with it. Darwin had proposed a theory of heredity called "pangenesis," which never gained wide acceptance. Darwin himself, of course, became a biological icon for his theory of evolution by natural selection. Decades later, while searching for a name for the elementary particles of heredity first characterized by Mendel, the evolutionary geneticist Hugo De Vries proposed the Darwinian "pangenes." The second syllable stuck. E. F. Keller, *The Century of the Gene* (Cambridge, MA: Harvard University Press, 2000).
5. William B. Provine, *The Origins of Theoretical Population Genetics*, 2d ed. (Chicago: University of Chicago Press, 2001).
6. W. Bodmer and Robin McKie, *The Book of Man* (London: Little, Brown, 1994).
7. Daniel J. Kevles and L. Hood, eds., *The Code of Codes* (Cambridge, MA: Harvard University Press, 1992).
8. J. Marks, "Beads and String: The Genome in Evolutionary Theory, in E. J. Devor, ed., *Molecular Applications in Biological Anthropology* (New York: Cambridge University Press, 1992), pp. 234–255.
9. J. C. Venter, et al., "The Sequence of the Human Genome," *Science* 291 (2001): 1304–1351.
10. J. Marks, *Human Biodiversity: Genes, Race, and History* (Hawthorne, NY: Aldine de Gruyter, 1995).
11. L. R. Godfrey and J. Marks, "The Nature and Origins of Primate Species," *Yearbook of Physical Anthropology* 34 (1991): 39–68.

12. J. Marks, "Blood Will Tell (Won't It?): A Century of Molecular Discourse in Anthropological Systematics," *American Journal of Physical Anthropology* 94 (1994): 59–80.
13. Amos S. Deinard, "The Evolutionary Genetics of the Chimpanzees" (Ph.D. Thesis, Department of Anthropology, Yale University, 1997).
14. G. Ruano, Jeffrey A. Rogers, Anne C. Ferguson-Smith, and Kenneth K. Kidd, "DNA Sequence Polymorphism within Hominoid Species Exceeds the Number of Phylogenetically Informative Characters for a HOX2 Locus," *Molecular Biology and Evolution* 9, no. 4 (1992): 575–586.
15. C. H. Waddington, "Evolutionary Adaptation," in S. Tax, ed., *Evolution after Darwin* (Chicago: University of Chicago Press, 1960), vol. 1: 381–402.

SUGGESTED READINGS

Lewontin, R. *The Triple Helix: Gene, Organism, and Environment* (Cambridge, MA: Harvard University Press, 2000).

Marks, J. *Human Biodiversity: Genes, Race, and History* (Hawthorne, NY: Aldine de Gruyter, 1995).

Marks, J. *What it Means to Be 98% Chimpanzee* (Berkeley: University of California Press, 2002).

Monod, J. *Chance and Necessity* (New York: Knopf, 1971).

Simpson, G. G. *The Meaning of Evolution* (New Haven: Yale University Press, 1951).

PALEOANTHROPOLOGY
AND EVOLUTIONARY THEORY

IAN TATTERSALL

Nothing in recent years has affected the interpretation of the human fossil record more profoundly than have theoretical notions of how the evolutionary process works. Paleoanthropologists generally learn these fundamental concepts early in their careers and rarely, if ever, reexamine them thereafter, even as they pass them along to their students—a practice that manifests itself in the extraordinary parochialism that our particular branch of paleontology continues to exhibit. The past couple of decades have been a time of extraordinary ferment in the fields of evolutionary theory and phylogenetic reconstruction—ferment that has been fully reflected in the literature of other fields of vertebrate paleontology. From reading the bulk of the paleoanthropological literature, however, you'd never guess it.

Let's start at the beginning and look at how evolutionary theory developed, before examining a couple of examples from the human fossil record. Back in the mid-nineteenth century, Charles Darwin defined evolution as "descent with modification." This formulation recognizes the two fundamental aspects of evolutionary process. The first of these is that life has a genealogical history (phylogeny), through which all organisms alive today are interrelated by descent from a single common ancestor that existed in the remote past. The second aspect—modification—involves physical change over time. It is the interaction of these two elements that has resulted in the pattern we see in nature: All the species of organisms are groupable on the basis of their morphological (anatomical) characteristics into a vast hierarchical series of sets within sets. This pattern had been noted long before Darwin wrote his great book *On the Origin of Species*. Indeed, a hundred years before Darwin's 1859 publication of his evolutionary views, the great Swedish naturalist Linnaeus had used the hierarchy of living things as the basis for the system of classifying living things that we use today. In the Linnaean system species are grouped into genera, genera into families, families into orders, orders into classes, and so forth. It was not until Darwin's time, however, that it was realized that this pattern resulted from common descent. Members of the same order, for instance, share a single common ancestor—members of the same family share a more recent common ancestor, and members of the same genus share an even more recent common ancestor.

Darwin based his notion of evolution on two fundamental observations: first, that in every species individuals vary among themselves in heritable characteristics and, second, that in every generation more individuals of each species are born than ever survive to reproduce themselves. From this emerged the concept of "natural selection," by which the individuals best adapted to their environments multiply more successfully than those more disadvantaged—and pass their favorable characteristics on to their offspring, so that these favorable traits will become more common in each succeeding generation. In essence, natural selection is nothing more than differential reproductive success, mediated by the environment; and though the differences between individuals of the same species are normally slight, over the generations the continual pressure of natural selection will lead to the accumulation of substantial change. Variation will always be there, though, so that if circumstances change, the blind forces of natural selection can shift direction and drive the lineage along another adaptive pathway.

Although Darwin titled his book *On the Origin of Species*, he actually paid scant attention to the implied question of how the natural diversity of species originates. In large part this may have been due to the fact that, in Victorian England, he faced a substantial problem in getting his evolutionary notions accepted. This problem lay in the entrenched belief, grounded in Christian theology, that species are static and unchanging, remaining forever as designed by the Creator. In order to destroy this notion of immutability, Darwin concentrated on showing that species responded instead to the pressures of natural selection by changing over time—changing so much, indeed, that in the end they evolved themselves out of existence, becoming new species in the process. While in a sense this idea did explain how new species might arise, it did nothing to address the question of the multiplication of species, that is, the origin of the diversity of species that is such a conspicuous feature of the living world. Paleoanthropologists, obsessed with tracing the history of the single species *Homo sapiens* back into the distant past, have, however, continued to be entranced by the notion of gradual change.

Darwin formulated his evolutionary theories in the absence of any understanding of the processes of heredity. For his purposes, the simple fact that physical variations are inherited was enough. But with the rapid development of the science of genetics in the early years of the twentieth century, notions of how the evolutionary process worked began to multiply. Darwin's ideas of evolution revolved around the gradual accretion of tiny changes; but the Dutch botanist Hugo deVries, for example, discovered that large-scale changes could occur in evening primroses. This suggested to him that new species could arise by sudden major disruptions of the hereditary material in a single individual, and hence it was unnecessary to invoke natural selection in the origin of species. By the 1930s, however, a general agreement on the mechanics of evolution emerged under the rubric of the "Modern Synthesis," expounded most importantly in three books by the geneticist Theodosius Dobzhansky (1937), the systematist Ernst Mayr (1942) and the paleontologist George Simpson (1944).[1]

This formulation had the elegant simplicity of all great ideas, essentially reducing the entire spectrum of evolutionary phenomena to the working of natural selection on the inherited variation that occurs within populations. Dobzhansky identified three levels at which the evolutionary process acts: (1) in the origin of genetic novelties; (2) in the ordering of those novelties in "molding the genetic structures of populations into new shapes"; and (3) in the "fixation of the diversity already attained on the preceding two levels."[2] The first level is accounted for by genetic mutations and recombinations. Where "normal" variation (as occurs among viable, nonmalformed individuals) is involved, such genetic changes usually result in rather minor differences, on the order of those with which Darwin was concerned. Natural selection then acts on these at the second level. Together these two processes explain the phenomena of "microevolution," the genetic and physical changes that occur in populations. This much was pure Darwinism, integrated with the new knowledge of genetics.

Dobzhansky, though, was also concerned with discontinuities in nature, which is where his third level of the evolutionary process enters in. Larger-scale differences among organisms—the phenomenon of "macroevolution"—were also to be accounted for. How? Ultimately, Dobzhansky and his colleagues decided that macroevolution and microevolution are essentially the same thing: that large-scale evolutionary changes, at the species level and higher, consist simply of the accumulation of tiny generation-by-generation changes over long periods of time. Simpson, the paleontologist, explained this by borrowing the geneticist Sewall Wright's metaphor of the "adaptive landscape," whereby populations balance atop peaks of optimal adaptation, while natural selection prunes off individuals who fall into the valleys between them.[3] By noting that environments change, and altering the metaphor to that of a "choppy sea," Simpson visualized peaks splitting apart and carrying fragments of the population away from each other on separate adaptive courses. Under such circumstances, relatively rapid change and macroevolutionary innovation might be expected.

Before long the architects of the Synthesis were ready to share their insights with the paleoanthropologists, who had stood very much to one side while all this rethinking was going on. Basic to the Synthesis was the realization that species do not consist of individuals all of whom conform more or less to a basic archetype, but rather are made up of clusters of variable individuals and populations bound together by reproductive continuity. The forays of the synthesists into paleoanthropology reflected this fundamental observation. As early as 1944 Dobzhansky weighed in with the suggestion that in the light of population variability, Asian *Homo erectus* should be viewed as belonging to our own species *Homo sapiens*.[4] Six years later Mayr argued in the same vein that the australopithecines should be included in the genus *Homo*.[5] Neither Dobzhansky nor Mayr was at all familiar at first hand with ranges of morphological variation in primate species; but their suggestions came as a breath of fresh air to paleoanthropologists, burdened as they were at the time by a plethora of genus and species names that almost matched the available fossils in number. The upshot was that, while few followed Dobzhansky and Mayr all the way in adopting these sweeping conclusions, paleoanthropology fell completely under the sway of the evolutionary views of the Synthesis—where it remains, for the most part, today. Human evolution became viewed as a stately progression, under the benevolent hand of natural selection, from the benighted australopithecines to enlightened *Homo sapiens*. Adopting this view of things was easier for paleoanthropologists than for paleontologists in other fields (who were confronted daily with unequivocal evidence for species diversity in the fossil record), because paleoanthropologists had basically only one goal: to trace the history of *Homo sapiens* as far back in the fossil record as possible. Nobody bothered, it seems, to explore whether the existence today of only a single species of *Homo* might actually be an exception rather than the rule.

Accepting the dictates of the Synthesis also involved abandoning the idea of species as discrete entities and looking on them instead as ephemeral groupings that evolved regularly and imperceptibly from one into another. Gaps in the fossil record became viewed as convenient places to recognize species boundaries (which would otherwise have been theoretically impossible), with the astonishing result that paleoanthropologists began to congratulate themselves on the incompleteness of their data base! Species were recognized as the "units of evolution," and the importance of being able to give them names was acknowledged—for how otherwise could the fossil record be discussed? But the more complete the fossil record became, the more difficult and arbitrary the recognition of species within it would become. In essence, time and change were seen as virtually synonymous, a proposition that was particularly easy to accept in paleoanthropology because of the undeniable trend in human evolution toward increasing brain size with time. As long as this notable trend was there for all to see, the examination of other morphological features in human fossils became somehow secondary.

The Synthesis was not, of course, entirely without its critics. Even as it was being formulated, alternative theories were being proposed by scientists such as the geneticist Richard Goldschmidt and the paleontologist Otto Schindewolf.[6] Both of these biologists came up with "saltationist" notions—the idea of sudden "jumps"—to account for the undeniable morphological gulfs that do exist between major groups: genera, families, and so forth. A lot of effort was expended by the architects of the Synthesis in rejecting such claims, and the upshot was that Goldschmidt and Schindewolf's theories never gained much ground. But the observations their ideas proposed to explain are valid ones, and evolutionary theory eventually had to come to terms with them.

The triumph of the Synthesis made the geneticists and systematists the guardians of evolutionary mechanisms, leaving the paleontologists with little more than an intellectual mopping-up operation to perform: to demonstrate, on the basis of fossils, that life had indeed evolved as predicted by theory. Perhaps it was inevitable, then, that the eventual challenge to the Synthesis as the all-embracing account of how evolution worked came from the direction of paleontology. For a long time, the failure of the fossil record to supply the expected intermediates between long-known species was simply ascribed to that record's legendary incompleteness. But in 1972 two invertebrate paleontologists, Niles Eldredge and Stephen Jay Gould, pointed out that this incompleteness might not be simply a deficiency or a convenience, depending on how you looked at it.[7] They suggested that perhaps the gaps in the record were telling us something about how evolution actually took place.

Eldredge and Gould argued that, in fact, the fossil record carries a strong signal of stability rather than of gradual change. They demonstrated that the fossil records of interest to them (North American trilobites—ancient sea-bottom-dwelling invertebrates—and Bermudan land snails) simply failed to show the expected pattern of gradual change over time. Instead, species tended to turn up suddenly in the record and to linger there, essentially unchanged, often for very long periods of time—several million years in some cases. At any one locality they would eventually be replaced, as abruptly as they had appeared, by distinct but closely related species that had evolved someplace else. Species thus reemerged as entities that are bounded in time as well as in space—entities that have births, lifespans, and extinctions. Finding this to be a general pattern in the fossil record, Eldredge and Gould thus proposed the mechanism of "punctuated equilibrium" as an alternative, or at least as a supplement, to "phyletic gradualism," their term for the pattern predicted by the Synthesis. Under punctuated equilibrium the life of a species is mostly characterized by "stasis" (nonchange), and most evolutionary innovation comes right at the beginning of their histories, at and around the speciation events in which they arise.

To explain speciation, Eldredge and Gould turned to a notion that had been most fully explored by Ernst Mayr, who, despite ultimately capitulating to gradualism, had been, like Dobzhansky, greatly concerned by the origin of discontinuities in nature. Mayr developed what is known as the Allopatric Model of speciation, which depends on the fact that all widespread species exist as series of local populations that generally show some degree of differentiation from each other. Such local populations are able to interbreed with each other in areas where they are in contact, but if they are separated long enough by some geographical or ecological barrier, genetic differences often arise between them that lead to some degree of genetic incompatibility. Once complete incompatibility is established, there will be two species where there was only one before—and they will already differ somewhat because of the preexisting differentiation between them.

Under the Synthesis this process of speciation was seen as a more or less passive result of adaptation to different habitats, and thus as a long-term phenomenon. But Eldredge and Gould pointed out that, on the geological scale, speciation is a short-term event, taking only tens of thousands of years at most, as opposed to the hundreds of thousands or millions of years for which species tend to persist in the fossil record. It should also be emphasized in this connection that the kinds of genetic changes involved in speciation are not necessarily those that are active in the production of microevolutionary change: Species may accumulate a large amount of genetic and morphological diversity without speciating (witness all the varieties of dogs, all of which can potentially interbreed) while speciation can take place in the presence of minimal change. While microevolutionary change is susceptible to being studied in the laboratory, modeled mathematically, and is thus, in principle, quite well understood, the actual mechanisms of speciation remain pretty obscure. Speciation, indeed, probably involves a whole set of different genetic mechanisms that have only one thing in common—that they disrupt reproductive continuity.

It should be mentioned that, apart from eliciting unfounded accusations of antiadaptationism from traditionalists, Eldredge and Gould's contribution revived an earlier debate about whether environmental influences could act upon entire groups of organisms ("group selection"), as opposed to simply influencing the reproductive success of individuals. In an important book published in 1966, the biologist George Williams argued that natural selection, as propounded by Darwin, could only act in situations where at any moment in time individual variations existed that could result in differing degrees of success.[8] In particular, he opposed the notion that any form of selection could be "for the good of the species." Out of Williams' fundamentalist position, which placed the spotlight squarely on individual variation, there ultimately sprang the zoologist Richard Dawkins' yet more extreme notion of the "selfish gene."[9] In Dawkins' view, selection acts not directly on the morphological characteristics of organisms (through which they actually interact directly with the environment), but rather on the genes through which they are inherited. He sees organisms simply as the vehicles for the genes themselves: It is the genes that compete for success, rather than the organisms that carry them.

At about the same time, the geneticist William D. Hamilton devised the theory of "kin selection," whereby apparently altruistic behaviors (those that do not benefit the individuals who indulge in them, or indeed may harm them) may actually assist in propagating the actor's genes.[10] This happens when such actions promote the success of related individuals with similar gene combinations. Put together with the selfish gene notion, the idea of kin selection resulted in the formulation of the theory of sociobiology, the ramifications of which are enormous. Basic to the theory, however, is that the behavior of individuals in cooperative societies influences the success of those societies as a whole. The individual is not seen as a single economic entity, but rather as a member of a group upon which the overall success of his or her own survival and reproduction depends. The validity of all this rests, of course, on the extent to which behavior is genetically determined. In the insect societies that stimulated the original sociobiological notions, behavior does seem to have a highly significant genetic component, but the situation is far less clear-cut among humans and other primates.

Another aspect of group selection is of more immediate importance in the consideration of human physical evolution. This is the fact that species compete with one another for ecological space. Such competition has long been recognized as a major factor in evolution, but the revival by Eldredge and Gould of the notion that species are "real," spatiotemporally bounded, units placed it back at the center of the discussion of evolutionary mechanisms. For example, long-term evolutionary trends—such as the human increase in brain size—are considered under the Synthesis to be the result of equally long-term directional selection acting within lineages to perfect adaptation to existing environments or to accommodate to changing ones. But if species are real units with histories that are marked more by nonchange than by change, then such trends are more likely to reflect the preferential survival of species as a whole. Species—particularly closely-related species that have reestablished contact with each other following allopatric speciation—compete among themselves, just as individuals do, for ecological resources and for survival. The differential success of this competition among them, summed up over many speciation events, may well result in the kind of long-term change in the fossil record that we perceive as trends.

Distinctive evolutionary trends are actually not all that numerous, and in any given lineage they normally encompass protracted shifts in only one or two major characteristics, such as brain size. Major innovations—upright bipedalism in hominids, for example—normally tend to show up relatively abruptly in the fossil record, perhaps not surprisingly since it is difficult to imagine the advantage of "intermediate" conditions between two different adaptive states. The rarity of trends in any but very general characteristics also coincides well with what we know about how environments change through time. The gradualist interpretation of evolutionary change under natural selection depends on steady ecological pressures acting over long periods of time; but our increasingly fine appreciation of how past climates and ecologies have shifted indicates that rather rapid oscillations were the rule. Not only do rapid fluctuations of this kind make long-term directional selection vanishingly improbable, but they underline the importance of species origination and extinction in the evolutionary process.

Hence climatic fluctuation, with the geographical and ecological fragmentation of populations that it entails, has a couple of important consequences. First, it provides ideal conditions for the origin of new species (when continuous populations are fragmented) and for competition between the resulting new species when conditions return to those that prevailed before. And second, when conditions change on a short-term basis, it is very unlikely that species will accommodate to the new conditions by adaptive change. Ecological zones shift with climate, and it's far more likely that when they do their component species will move along with them—or become extinct if favorable conditions disappear totally. None of this implies that the changes that we do pick up in the fossil record may not be adaptive or that adaptation does not lie squarely at the center of the evolutionary process. It does. But it also means that we have to look more carefully at the level at which the adaptive process takes place.

Most species have more than local distributions. They are, indeed, normally spread over a variety of more or less distinct habitats. Among other things, this means that we cannot define them on the basis of their "ecological niche," or even on their ecological role, which will vary from place to place and from ecological community to ecological community. More often than not, we find that local populations within a species differ somewhat (though generally subtly) among themselves in morphology—as indeed do those of *Homo sapiens*. The differences that develop among such local populations are largely under the control of natural selection; and to the extent that they are, they will be adaptive. This process of adaptation is facilitated by the small size of local populations, for small gene pools are less stable than large ones are, and genetic shifts are thus more likely to occur within them. Thus, while Eldredge and Gould in their original formulation of punctuated equilibrium suggested that most evolutionary change takes place at speciation (when gene pools are evidently in a state of disequilibrium of some kind), it actually appears that most, if not all, adaptive change in fact occurs *within* species—during the acquisition of geographical variation—and *before* speciation takes place.

The importance of speciation in this context is that, to return to Dobzhansky's terminology, it "fixes" the diversity attained at his first two levels of the evolutionary process. As long as speciation does not intervene, any genetic novelties acquired within a local population of a species are at risk of being lost if, through interbreeding, the local gene pool is reabsorbed into that of the species population at large. Differentiation within a species is thus ephemeral up to the point of speciation. What speciation does is to produce a new bounded entity that incorporates the genetic novelties present in what was formerly merely a local population of the parent species.[11] When such fixation has been achieved, the novelty can be lost only by extinction. In the meantime, it has achieved a historical reality, and, if advantageous, it will be passed on to descendant species.

This scenario of evolutionary change is based on what we know about how adaptive (or nonadaptive) genetic novelties arise in populations of living organisms. This is hard to observe in the fossil record, which is why Eldredge and Gould concluded that change usually takes place at a later stage—at and around speciation events. The reason for this is that the morphological differences that distinguish closely related species (those within the same genus, and particularly parent and daughter species) are normally very small—much smaller than is usually appreciated. This is particularly true of distinctions in the skeleton and teeth: precisely those body parts that provide us with the fossil record from which we usually reconstruct evolutionary histories. It is thus far from easy to recognize species in the fossil record. I have argued that because of the minor nature of the morphological distinctions between parent and daughter species, our tendency will be to underestimate the number of species actually represented in the fossil assemblages before us.[12]

I should emphasize that even though the episodic pattern of evolution predicted by the punctuated equilibrium notion seems to fit the facts of the fossil record and to accommodate what we know of past environmental changes better than the gradual change predicted by the Synthesis, species are not static entities. As I have recently suggested,[13] they probably vary over time in very much the way that they vary in space. However, it is very misleading to look at species as unitary things that vary in a consistent way. Species are agglomerations of local populations, each a dynamic genetic entity, that are bound together by a common reproductive thread. Every such local population is an engine of genetic—and hence at least potentially of evolutionary—change and is doing business slightly differently from other populations of the same species. It is the accumulation of such geographic variations (a process of diversification, certainly not of linear change) that in my view lies at the heart of evolutionary innovation and reflects the true role of species in the evolutionary process. It's important, however, to remember that the sorting of species (differential survival) over time by ecological factors (which include competition between parent and daughter species, or between daughter species of the same parent) is certainly influenced by environmental changes that may be entirely random with respect to the specific adaptations developed in local populations.

All of this stands in stark contrast to the models of evolution that exist in the minds of most paleoanthropologists when they attempt to discern evolutionary events in our own lineage from the evidence of the human fossil record. For, as I've already said, paleoanthropology as a whole is pretty firmly wedded to the principles of the Synthesis. These envision a gradual progress through time; and since we are starting historically from the desire to trace the history of the single species *Homo sapiens* back into the distant past—rather than to discover the position of our species in the diverse family Hominidae—this has been a perspective that paleoanthropologists have found particularly congenial. However, this is hardly enough to allow us to conclude that human evolution has proceeded along lines that differ from those of all other mammal species. For "culture" (whatever that may be) can hardly be considered a significant distinguishing factor during the long period before humans, as Eldredge[14] recently put it, declared independence from local ecosystems with the adoption of settled agriculture (which has indeed effectively changed the rules whereby we interact with nature). Like all paleontologists, paleoanthropologists should at least be on the lookout for species diversity in the human fossil record. But this is something that, mesmerized by the Synthesis, practitioners of our science until very recently have been notably reluctant to do.

The most classic modern example of this has been the development of the so-called "Single Species" hypothesis. Stemming ultimately from C. Loring Brace's stylish attack in the mid-1960s on the exclusion of Neandertals from direct human ancestry,[15] and elaborated most notably by Milford Wolpoff,[16] this notion was based on the idea that human culture made the human "ecological niche" so broad as to exclude the possibility that (since the days of the australopithecines) more than one human species had existed anywhere in the world at any one time. By extension, this meant that human phylogeny consisted of a temporal succession of species that could only arbitrarily be delimited one from another. When this dogma had been laid to rest definitively by discoveries in Kenya (in brief, there is incontrovertible evidence for the existence of multiple hominid species in the East Turkana region in the period between about 1.9 and 1.5 myr ago),[17] the philosophy behind it was resuscitated in the form of the "Multiregional Continuity" hypothesis, first articulated by Thorne and Wolpoff.[18]

The Multiregional Continuity notion, which contrasts with the idea favored by many paleoanthropologists that *Homo sapiens* had its origin in a single geographical center (Africa is the current favorite), sees human evolution worldwide from the time of *Homo erectus* of the middle Pleistocene as a matter of the regional development of a series of distinct lineages, leading to the major geographical groups of today. Each of them possessed, from the beginning, a suite of characteristic features, and each distinctive lineage remained part of the same species by regular genetic interchange. How differentiation and continuity are simultaneously maintained remains unexplained (see, however, the chapter by Frayer in this book for an alternative viewpoint); but the obvious problem of how distinct lineages could evolve separately from one ancestral species into the same descendant species has recently been resolved by the simple expedient of sinking the remarkably different *Homo erectus* into *Homo sapiens*.[19]

This last device is special pleading at best, and it illustrates dramatically the extent to which paleoanthropologists have been beguiled by the splendidly simple elegance of the Synthesis—which, as we have seen, attained that simplicity by blinding itself to the complexities of the evolutionary process. In viewing evolutionary change uniquely as a result of natural selection acting on local populations, and hence dismissing species as ephemera, the Synthesis effectively circumvented the complex question of discontinuities among species and higher taxa. For although all innovations in evolution appear to have the same root in local population dynamics, microevolution and macroevolution are emphatically not the same thing. Speciation—a non-adaptive mechanism—has to be factored into the equation, and it appears that major discontinuities in nature arise from the accumulation of minor discontinuities that are "fixed" by this process, with the subsequent loss of intermediates through extinction.

Viewing the evolutionary process in this way means that we have to take very seriously the possibility that species diversity in the human evolutionary past was considerably greater than received paleoanthropological wisdom suggests. This is not, moreover, merely a product of theoretical considerations; for, while conventional estimates place a mere three species intermediate between *Australopithecus afarensis* and *Homo sapiens*, the morphological gulf that separates us from the earliest known hominid species is far greater than this minimal taxonomic separation implies. Of course, our ability to discern the actual species diversity represented in the human fossil record will depend on the development of more reliable means than we have at present for recognizing fossil species; but the fact that this diversity is currently underestimated is already abundantly clear.

Pending the availability of better techniques of species recognition, it is nonetheless evident that paleoanthropologists need—however regrettably—to rethink the value of the generous liberal spirit that has led to the conventional inclusion of virtually all large-brained fossil hominids in *Homo sapiens*. For example, nobody disputes that the Neandertals are quite possibly our closest known relatives in the fossil record and thus in nature. Nonetheless, however large their brains, it makes no sense to classify such anatomically distinct forms in our own species when the morphological differences between the Neandertals and ourselves so greatly exceed those that we see between close relatives (species classified within the same genus) in the living primate fauna. In my view the likelihood is small that Neandertals and modern humans could have interbred effectively. Brain size has without doubt been an important factor in human evolution, but it is hardly a criterion for species membership. After all, most other living primate species have close but genetically distinct relatives of similar brain size.

I do not pretend that this brief survey is in any sense a definitive review of the evolutionary process. If science advances at all, what we believe today is bound to be found eventually to be incorrect or, more likely, incomplete. The Synthesis is a case in point. It was a magisterial achievement that swept away a vast panoply of mythology; but it was not, in the end, a comprehensive account of how evolution works. Nonetheless, half a century after it was formulated, paleoanthropology still labors under its simplifying assumptions.

Most paleoanthropologists probably, and most textbook-writers certainly, continue to favor the view of hominid evolution as a stately succession of gradually modifying species—which in turn implies that their job is essentially one of discovering and describing what amount to successive links in a single long chain. Even where a certain degree of diversity is recognized in the human fossil record (as, for example, by the proponents of Multiregional Continuity), the tendency is still to dismiss such diversity as "merely" intraspecific—and thus as epiphenomenal, rather than as historical reality to be accounted for.

Yet there has clearly been much more to our evolution than a simple, long uphill slog. The history of our kind has evidently been like that of most others, marked by numerous speciations and extinctions and mediated by fluctuating environments and frequent competition between closely related species. The intricate evolutionary pattern thereby produced requires analysis rather than mere discovery. As our science absorbs the lessons of evolutionary complexity that other branches of paleontology have already learned, we can look forward to a new perspective on our own origins.

NOTES

1. Theodosius Dobzhansky, *Genetics and the Origin of Species* (New York: Columbia University Press, 1937); Ernst Mayr, *Systematics and the Origin of Species* (New York: Columbia University Press, 1942); George Gaylord Simpson, *Tempo and Mode in Evolution* (New York: Columbia University Press, 1944).
2. Dobzhansky, *Genetics and the Origin of Species*, p. 13.
3. Sewall Wright, "The Roles of Mutation, Inbreeding, Crossbreeding, and Selection in Evolution," *Proceedings of the Sixth International Congress of Genetics* (Menasha, WI: Brooklyn Botanic Garden, 1932), vol. 1: 356–366.
4. Theodosius Dobzhansky, "On Species and Races of Living and Fossil Man," *American Journal of Physical Anthropology* 2 (1944): 251–265.
5. Ernst Mayr, "Taxonomic Categories in Fossil Hominids," *Cold Spring Harbor Symposia on Quantitative Biology* 15 (1950): 109–118.
6. Richard Goldschmidt, *The Material Basis of Evolution* (New Haven: Yale University Press, reprint 1982); Otto Schindewolf, *Grundfragen der Palaontologie* (Stuttgart: Schweizerbart, 1950).
7. Niles Eldredge and Stephen Jay Gould, "Punctuated Equilibria: An Alternative to Phyletic Gradualism," in Thomas J. M. Schopf, ed., *Models in Paleobiology* (San Francisco: Freeman, Cooper & Co., 1972), pp. 82–115.
8. George Williams, *Adaptation and Natural Selection: A Critique of Some Current Evolutionary Thought* (Princeton: Princeton University Press, 1966).
9. Richard Dawkins, *The Selfish Gene* (New York: Oxford University Press, 1976).
10. William Hamilton, "The Genetical Theory of Social Evolution, I and II," *Journal of Theoretical Biology* 6 (1964): 1–52.
11. Ian Tattersall, "Species Recognition in Human Paleontology," *Journal of Human Evolution* 15 (1986): 165–175; Douglas Futuyma, "On the Role of Species in Anagenesis,"

American Naturalist 130 (1987): 465–473; Douglas Futuyma, "History and Evolutionary Processes," in Matthew Nitecki and Doris Nitecki, eds., *History and Evolution* (Albany: State University of New York Press, 1992), pp. 103–130.

12. Tattersall, "Species Recognition in Human Paleontology," pp. 165–175.

13. Ian Tattersall, "How Does Evolution Work?" *Evolutionary Anthropology* 3 (1994): 2–3.

14. Niles Eldredge, *Dominion* (New York: Henry Holt & Co., 1995).

15. C. Loring Brace, "The Fate of the "Classic" Neanderthals: A Consideration of Hominid Catastrophism," *Current Anthropology* 5 (1964): 3–43.

16. Milford Wolpoff, *Paleoanthropology* (New York: Knopf, 1980).

17. Ian Tattersall, *The Fossil Trail: How We Know What We Think We Know about Human Evolution* (New York: Oxford University Press, 1995).

18. Alan Thorne and Milford Wolpoff, "Regional Continuity in Australasian Pleistocene Hominid Evolution," *American Journal of Physical Anthropology* 65 (1981): 337–349.

19. Milford Wolpoff, "*Homo Erectus* in Europe: An Issue of Grade, or Clade, or Perhaps No Issue at All," *Mitekufat Haeven* Supplement 1 (1992): 137.

SUGGESTED READINGS

Eldredge, Niles. *Time Frames*. New York: Simon & Schuster, 1985. An account of the development of evolutionary thought and, specifically, of the notion of punctuated equilibria.

Eldredge, Niles. *Unfinished Synthesis*. New York: Oxford University Press, 1985. An inquiry into the nature of biological hierarchies and their incorporation into evolutionary theory.

Futuyma, Douglas J. *Evolutionary Biology*. Sunderland, MA: Sinauer, 1979. A general overview of evolutionary thought.

Mayr, Ernst. *Animal Species and Evolution*. Cambridge, MA: Harvard University Press, 1966. A classic statement of the "Modern Synthesis" of evolutionary theory.

Tattersall, Ian. *The Fossil Trail: How We Know What We Think We Know about Human Evolution*. New York: Oxford University Press, 1995. A history of the discovery of the human fossil record and of the development of human evolutionary thought.

Explaining Primate Origins

Matt Cartmill

The Primates are an order of mammals that includes human beings and their close animal relatives—apes, monkeys, tarsiers, lemurs, and so on. Most primates live in trees, and many of them have strikingly humanlike hands and faces. Scientists who study primate evolution agree that these two facts must be connected in some way. The details, however, are a matter of debate.

Most of the things that make apes, monkeys, and other primates look humanlike can be grouped under five headings:

1. Grasping extremities: Primates have soft, moist, pudgy palms and soles covered with fingerprint ridges. The first ("big") toes, and often the thumbs as well, are splayed apart from the adjacent digits and oppose them in grasping tree branches and other objects. (Our own oddly specialized feet no longer fit this description, but our hands do.)

2. Claw loss: The first toes of primates, and usually the other digits as well, are tipped with flattened, shield-shaped nails instead of the pointed claws seen in primitive mammals.

3. Visual specializations: The organs of vision, including the retina of the eye and the visual parts of the brain, are unusually well developed in primates. The optic axes of the two eyeballs are parallel in primates—that is, both eyes point in the same direction. The eye sockets, which are enclosed in complete bony rings or cups, are drawn together toward the middle of the face. In the skulls of some small primates (tarsiers, slender lorises, and the smaller monkeys), the left and right eye sockets are so close together that they actually contact each other in the midline.

4. Reduced olfaction: The organs of smell are smaller and simpler in primates than they are in most other mammals. This is particularly true of "higher," or anthropoid, primates (monkeys and apes), and tarsiers. These animals also lack the wet, dog-like nose tip found in typical "lower" primates (lemurs and lorises).

5. Brain enlargement: Primates have bigger brains overall than most other mammals have. This is especially true of anthropoids, and superlatively true of our own species.

The first Darwinian explanations of these primate peculiarities were put forward in the early twentieth century by two British anatomists, G. Elliot Smith and F. Wood Jones. Both interpreted the distinctive primate traits as adaptations to life in the trees.

Smith, who was an expert on the comparative anatomy of the brain, thought that arboreal life placed a premium on brains in general and on the visual apparatus in particular. A keen nose, he argued, is of little use to a tree-dwelling mammal. However, such animals need sharp eyes in running and leaping from branch to branch, and they must have quick wits to plan and follow complex, three-dimensional paths through the treetops. Smith concluded that these demands of arboreal life had launched our primate ancestors on an inexorable course of brain enlargement and improvement, leading by successive evolutionary stages from primitive lemurs through tarsiers, monkeys, and apes to *Homo sapiens*.[1]

Jones saw human bipedalism as another product of arboreal life. In animals that run around on the ground, Jones argued, the forelimbs do pretty much the same job as the hind limbs. But the two sets of limbs tend to take on separate functions in a tree-climbing animal: The hind limbs typically support and propel the body from below, while the forelimbs explore and reach for new supports above. Jones thought that this tendency had worked throughout primate evolution, shifting the job of locomotion increasingly back to the hind feet and increasingly freeing the hands for the more delicate work of touching, grasping, and handling objects. As the hands took over these manipulatory functions from the snout, the face shrank, drawing the eyes together in the midline. Like Smith, Jones thought the resulting evolutionary trends had produced a progressively humanlike series of primates, from lemurs to tarsiers to human beings.[2]

The theories of Smith and Jones were worked up into a grand synthesis by another British anatomist, W. E. Le Gros Clark, whose ideas about primate and human evolution dominated the textbooks from the late 1920s through the 1960s. Le Gros Clark's studies of tree shrews had convinced him that these southern Asian mammals are primates, closely related to the lemurs of Madagascar. But tree shrews lack the grasping hands and feet, flattened nails, and forward-pointing eyes found in lemurs and other primates. Le Gros Clark concluded that these and other typical primate traits had evolved independently in many different primate groups. It was not a particular suite of traits that distinguished primates from other mammals, Le Gros Clark argued, but *tendencies* to *develop* such traits. The primate evolutionary trends, he wrote, are the "natural consequence of an arboreal habitat, a mode of life which among other things demands or encourages prehensile functions of the limbs, a high degree of visual acuity, and the accurate control and co-ordination of muscular activity by a well-developed brain."[3]

The "classical primatological synthesis" put together by Le Gros Clark, which defined the order Primates in terms of shared trends rather than shared traits, began to fall apart in the late 1960s. It was generally thought at that time that the order's earliest fossil representatives were *Plesiadapis* and other "archaic primates" that had lived around sixty million years ago during the Paleocene epoch, at the dawn of the Age of Mammals. The molar teeth of these animals were strikingly similar to those of true, lemurlike primates known from the early Eocene epoch, some eight million years later. But as more fossils of these "archaic primates" came to light, it became evident that their primatelike features were not the same ones found in tree shrews. Unlike tree shrews and true primates, *Plesiadapis* and its relatives had no bony rings around their eyes. On the other hand, their cheek teeth were more primatelike than those of tree shrews, and the bony shell (tympanic bulla) enclosing their middle ear appeared to be formed as an outgrowth from the petrosal bone, as in all living primates, rather than from a separate entotympanic bone as in tree shrews.

These new findings were interpreted as reasons for throwing the tree shrews out of the primate order. New "cladistic" philosophies of biological classification, which began to dominate zoological systematics in the 1960s, insisted that every animal group had to be defined by *synapomorphies,* or novel traits that first appeared in the group's last common ancestor. By 1970 the features of the teeth and ear region shared by archaic and modern primates were generally accepted as synapomorphies that defined the primate order, and the resemblances shared by Malagasy lemurs and tree shrews were dismissed as traits that had evolved separately in the two groups (which no longer counted for anything in the new philosophy of systematics). Le Gros Clark's explanations of the shared primate evolutionary trends became increasingly irrelevant to the new conception of Primates, and the grand vision of primate evolution that he had put together was gradually abandoned.

RECENT EXPLANATIONS

Several new accounts of primate origins have been put forward to fill the vacuum left by the collapse of the classical synthesis. Until recently the main contenders were the conflicting stories offered in various versions over the past two decades by Frederick S. Szalay and myself. Szalay's account offered to explain primate origins in terms of the synapomorphies shared by modern and archaic primates, whereas my explanations centered on the traits peculiar to "primates of modern aspect."[4] Both these accounts are now being challenged by new findings and interpretations.

In Szalay's view, primates evolved from a tree-shrewlike arboreal "archontan" ancestor through a shift to a more herbivorous diet. He inferred this shift from various specialized features of molar morphology, including lower cusps and broader crushing surfaces, that are shared by archaic and modern primates.[5] Szalay has argued that *Plesiadapis* and other archaic primates may have had somewhat divergent and thumblike first toes, but he thinks that perfected grasping extremities and flattened nails first appeared in the ancestral "euprimates" (modern or non-archaic primates) as adaptations for a more acrobatic "grasp-leaping form of locomotion.[6]

I arrived at a very different account of euprimate origins by studying non-primate mammals that live in trees.[7] Most of these tree-dwellers do not look much like euprimates. Their organs of smell are well developed, and almost all of them have sharp, sturdy claws. Many of them—for example, squirrels—have eyes that face more or less sideways. Nevertheless, they have no difficulty running around and feeding in trees. From these facts I concluded that arboreal life does not automatically select for primatelike features, and that some additional factor must have been responsible for producing the distinctive characteristics of euprimates.

The forward-facing eyes of primates had been explained by Le Gros Clark as an adaptation for stereoscopic vision, "particularly for the accurate judging of distance and direction in arboreal acrobatics."[8] I rejected this analysis. It seemed to me that shoving the eyes together in the middle of the face would enlarge the field of stereoscopic vision but decrease parallax (the separation between the two eyes and the amount of difference between the pictures they see), thus reducing the distance at which stereoscopic vision can work. Optic convergence, I argued, must have evolved in animals that needed a wide field of stereoscopic vision at close range.

Marked optic convergence is also seen in cats and many other predators that rely on vision in tracking and nabbing their prey. Noting the predatory habits of small prosimian primates like *Miaocebus*, *Loris*, and *Tarsius*, which track insect prey by sight and seize them in their hands, I interpreted optic convergence as a hunting adaptation in the ancestral primates as well. Grasping extremities and claw loss, I suggested, had also originated as predatory adaptations, facilitating stealthy locomotion among the slender twigs of the forest canopy and undergrowth where insects are most abundant—and where sharp claws, which help in climbing thick trunks, are of little use. I saw olfactory reduction as a side effect of the shoving-together of the two eye sockets, which necessarily constricts the space available for the organs of smell and their connections to the brain. All these distinctive euprimate traits, I concluded, could be explained in this way as adaptations for an ancestral habit of "visually directed predation," and I urged that *Plesiadapis* and other archaic primates, which showed no signs of such adaptations, be removed from the primate order.

Although R. D. Martin and a few other people have long agreed with this last point,[9] the informed consensus during the 1970s and 1980s favored Szalay's views on the primate affinities of *Plesiadapis* and its relatives. During the past few years some cracks have started to appear in that consensus. J. R. Wible and H. H. Covert concluded in 1987 that many of the so-called archaic primates have no demonstrable relationship to either *Plesiadapis* or euprimates, and that the closest euprimate relatives are probably tree shrews after all.[10] More recently, R. F. Kay and K. C. Beard have both concluded, from different evidence, that at least some of the archaic primates are probably more closely related to colugos (flying lemurs) than they are to euprimates.[11] If these conclusions hold up in the long run, Szalay's adaptive account of euprimate peculiarities will not be refuted, but the details of his historical account will have to be revised.

Those details are important to Szalay, who sees the causes of evolutionary events as highly contingent and case-specific, constrained by the morphological and ecological details of the evolving species and the evolutionary baggage that it has carried over from its differently adapted ancestors.[12] On the other hand, I have always argued that particular evolutionary events cannot be explained except as instances of some more general regularity, and that "the only evolutionary changes we can hope to explain are parallelisms."[13] An explanation that applies to only one case—for example, Szalay's description of the prehensile foot of euprimates as an adaptation to a "grasp-leaping" habit unique to euprimates—explains nothing. Adaptive explanations must be general enough to predict similar adaptations in other cases, and they must be rejected if those predictions are not borne out.[14]

My own account of primate origins was itself vulnerable to attack on these grounds. Just as not all arboreal mammals have grasping extremities and reduced olfaction, not all visual predators have eyes that point in the same direction. Cats, tarsiers, and owls do; mongooses, tupaiine tree shrews, and robins do not. Therefore, visual predation per se cannot explain optic convergence in the ancestral primates. Some other factor must be involved.

This flaw in my theory was patched up by J. Allman, who suggested that rotating the eyes forward serves not so much to enhance stereoscopy as to allow an animal to see what lies in front of it more clearly.[15] The image projected by a spherical lens is sharpest directly behind the center of the lens. Images that pass through the lens more obliquely get blurred.[16] This means that an animal whose eyes face sideways cannot clearly see things directly in front of it. This does not matter so much in diurnal animals, because their pupils constrict in bright light and thus act like a pinhole camera to help focus the blurred image. However, a nocturnal animal with a wide-open iris encounters more serious problems with spherical aberration. This fact, Allman argued, explains why nocturnal visual predators like owls and cats—and early primates—have tended to swing their eyes around to the front, while diurnal ones like mongooses have been able to remain more walleyed and retain a more panoramic visual field.

My theory also does not satisfactorily explain why the ancestral primates converted their claws into flattened nails. Paul Garber's fieldwork on *Saguinus oedipus*, Panamanian tamarins,[17] shows that these small monkeys feed chiefly on insects among the twigs and vines of the forest understory, just like my hypothetical primate ancestor. But all their digits (save the divergent first toe) are tipped with sharp claws. Their claws afford them a second mode of feeding, in which they cling squirrel-fashion to large tree trunks while eating gummy sap oozing from holes in the bark. Their claws evidently do not hinder movement and foraging on thin branches, and they allow *Saguinus* and its relatives to do things that more typical, clawless primates cannot do. All this makes it hard to argue that adaptation for visual predation on insects in the undergrowth would have favored the reduction of claws in the ancestral primates.

Robert W. Sussman has criticized my theory on other grounds, and has put forward some alternatives of his own. In 1978 Sussman and botanist Peter H. Raven suggested that early primates might have been adapted for feeding on flowers and nectar, like some bats or the little Australian marsupial *Tarsipes*, and that this might explain the evolution of flattened nails and grasping feet in the ancestral primates. "These adaptations," Sussman and Raven argued, "would have allowed the Eocene prosimians far greater access to fruits and flowers, as well as to many plant-visiting insects, making them much more efficient at locomoting and foraging in the small terminal branches.... It [was] probably this improved ability to feed in terminal branches that was the most important impetus for the major adaptive shift seen in these Eocene primates."[18]

The main difficulty with this early version of Sussman's theory lies in the dental anatomy of the oldest fossil euprimates, the adapids and omomyids of the early Eocene. The molar teeth of these prosimians display a wide variety of adaptations for eating insects, fruit, or leaves, but none of them show the marked reduction of the posterior teeth characteristic of dedicated nectar-eaters like *Tarsipes*. The nectar-feeding theory also does not account for the visual specializations characteristic of primates. The ancestral primates may occasionally have eaten flowers or nectar, as some Malagasy lemurs do today, but positing such a habit does not seem to help explain their distinctive anatomical characteristics.

Sussman's latest ideas on the subject leave nectar largely out of the picture and concentrate on fruit. In a recent article, he argues that most of the small nocturnal prosimians that I had pointed to as model visual predators eat more fruit than insects, and that this was probably true of the ancestral primates as well.[19] Sussman sees the grasping extremities of primates as an adaptation for eating fruit. Grasping feet, he suggests, allow these animals to cling and feed uninterruptedly among the thin twigs where most fruit grows, instead of having to scurry back to perch and eat on larger, safer supports as squirrels do when they are harvesting nuts. The origin and radiation of the primates, Sussman suggests, may have been a side effect of a great radiation of fruit-bearing plants in the Eocene, which provided new evolutionary opportunities for specialized fruit-eaters.

There are still some problems with Sussman's revised theory. Comparative anatomy suggests that the ancestral marsupials, back in the era of the dinosaurs, had grasping feet with divergent, clawless first toes, like those of opossums and other tree-dwelling marsupials today. The diversification of fruit-bearing plants occurred much later, after the dinosaurs had become extinct, and thus cannot explain the evolution of primate-like feet in the first marsupials. Sussman's account also fails to explain the characteristic visual specializations of primates. It makes sense to think that a visually predatory animal would find it useful to have a wide field of sharp stereoscopic vision directly in front of it, to make sure of hitting its prey accurately on the first strike; but such specializations are not obviously needed when the prey is a banana. On the face of it, my theory might seem to do a better job than Sussman's in accounting for the peculiarities of the primate visual apparatus.

However, comparative functional anatomy provides some support for both Sussman's and my theories. The forward-facing eyes of nocturnal visual predators like owls and cats have clearly evolved as predatory adaptations. Yet similar specializations occur among some non-predatory tree-dwellers. Some of these animals, such as kinkajous (*Potos*) and African palm civets (*Nandinia*), are carnivores that have turned secondarily to a diet of fruit, and these creatures probably inherited their forward-facing eyes from visually predatory ancestors. But that explanation does not fit the case of the "flying foxes" of the Old World tropics. Unlike the small-eyed, sonar-guided, insect-eating bats of the temperate zone, these big fruit-eating bats have large, moderately convergent eyes, and the visual parts of their brains are strikingly primatelike in many features.

Sussman admits that his theory "does not explain the unique visual adaptations of primates and fruit bats," but the similarities between the two groups demand an explanation of some sort. The only explanation put forward so far is that proposed by the neuroanatomist J. D. Pettigrew, who argues that fruit bats are not really bats but primitive primates that have evolved wings.[20] If so, then they might have inherited their primatelike traits from a visually predatory primate ancestor. However, no one has yet urged this possibility, mainly because most sources of evidence to date still link all the bats together as a monophyletic group with no particular ties to primates.[21] The importance of such phylogenetic questions in debates about the origin of primate peculiarities underscores the point, made by Szalay and other evolutionary biologists, that the sequence of adaptations through which an evolving lineage passes has to be taken into account in trying to figure out why that lineage retained or developed certain traits.

Several people have looked to the primatelike features of marsupials as a key to explaining primate origins. Almost all arboreal marsupials have grasping hind feet with clawless, divergent first toes; and some small Australian marsupials like *Cercartetus* and *Tarsipes* have reduced claws on their other toes and fingers as well. Most marsupial tree-dwellers have moderately convergent eyes. The vaguely prosimian appearance of such small, undergrowth-haunting marsupials as the "pygmy possum" *Cercartetus* and the little South American mouse opossum *Marmosa* is one of the things that led both Sussman and me to think that the ancestral primate was also a diminutive shrub-layer forager.

Another South American opossum, *Caluromys derbianus*, furnishes an important natural experiment bearing on some of these questions. *Caluromys* differs from typical opossums in many primatelike features, including its relatively large brain and eyes, bony postorbital processes, short snout, small litters, increased lifespan, and high basal metabolic rate. Its orbits are more frontally directed than those of other American opossums (that is, they face more toward the end of its nose and less toward the top of its head). Knowing more about the habits of *Caluromys* might therefore be expected to shed new light on primate origins.

In 1988 Tab Rasmussen undertook a field study of *Caluromys* to try to determine the adaptive significance of its primatelike specializations.[22] He concluded that *Caluromys* fits my theory as well as Sussman's. About half of its food consists of fruits it gathers in the terminal branches, where its prehensile feet allow it to cling and feed like a primate. But the other half of its diet consists of insect prey, which it locates visually and seizes with its hands. On large branches, *Caluromys* stalks its prey deliberately; but when clambering around in thin terminal branches, where it is clumsier and more noisy, it just opportunistically grabs whatever insects its movements happen to stir into flight. On the basis of these observations, Rasmussen argues that early primates may have climbed out into the terminal branches in search of fruit (as Sussman thinks), and developed their visual peculiarities to help them catch the insects that they encountered there (as my theory implies). The currently available facts thus continue to support my earlier contention that "the last common ancestor of the extant primates, like many extant prosimians … subsisted to an important extent on insects and other prey, which were visually located and manually captured in the insect-rich canopy and undergrowth of tropical forests."[23]

We need to find out more about the adaptations and behavior of other arboreal mammals to sort out and test the explanations that have been offered for the evolution of grasping feet and flattened nails in the first primates. We might learn a lot by studying the behaviors of arboreal frugivores with typical mammalian feet (like *Potos* and *Nandinia*) and seeing how they differ in their details from the behavior of shrub-layer foragers with primatelike grasping extremities and reduced claws (like *Tarsipes* and *Cercartetus*). It would also help if we knew something about the order in which the various primate peculiarities were acquired. If the first primates had grasping feet and blunt teeth adapted for eating fruit, but retained small, divergent orbits like those of *Plesiadapis*, Rasmussen's account would gain added plausibility. If they had convergent orbits and the sharp, slicing molar teeth of insect-eaters, that would support my ideas. The oldest fossil primates we know of at present resemble modern primates in both their foot bones and their eye sockets, and so they do not help to answer this question. We can only hope that new fossil finds will help us to tease apart the various strands of the primate story, and give us some clearer insights into the evolutionary causes behind the origin of the primate order to which we belong.

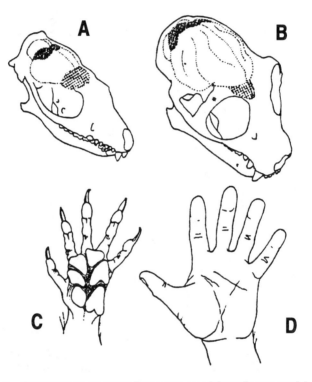

FIGURE 4-1   DIFFERENCES BETWEEN PRIMATES AND MORE PRIMITIVE MAMMALS

A. Skull of the hedgehog *Erinaceus*. The brain (stippled outline) is small, the visual part of the cortex (dark tone) is restricted, and the olfactory bulbs (hachure) are large. The eye sockets face as much sideways as forward, and are not encircled in bone. **B.** Skull of the prosimian primate *Otolemur*. The brain is enlarged, the visual cortex is expanded, and the olfactory bulbs are reduced. The eye sockets are larger and face more toward the front of the head than those of *Erinaceus*, and they are enclosed by a complete bony ring (asterisk). **C.** Hand of the treeshrew *Tupaia*. All five digits are about equally divergent, and all are tipped with long, pointed claws. The palm bears separate, protruding pads like those on the feet of a dog. **D.** Hand of a primate (*Homo*). The pads are fused together into a broad, soft surface. The first digit (thumb) diverges widely from the other four, and all digits are tipped with flattened, shieldlike nails.

Source: Reprinted with permission from Matt Cartmill,[24] © 1992 Wiley-Liss, Inc.

NOTES

1. G. E. Smith, *The Evolution of Man* (London: Oxford University Press, 1924).

2. F. W. Jones, *Arboreal Man* (London: Arnold, 1916).

3. W. E. Le Gros Clark, *Early Forerunners of Man* (Baltimore: William Wood, 1934), pp. 284–288; W. E. Le Gros Clark, *The Antecedents of Man* (Edinburgh: Edinburgh University Press, 1959), p. 43.

4. Matt Cartmill, "Basic Primatology and Prosimian Evolution," in F. Spencer, ed., *A History of American Physical Anthropology, 1930–1980* (New York: Academic Press, 1982), pp. 147–186.

5. Frederick S. Szalay, "Paleobiology of the Earliest Primates," in R. H. Tuttle, ed., *The Functional and Evolutionary Biology of Primates* (Chicago: Aldine-Atherton, 1972), pp. 3–35.

6. Frederick S. Szalay and E. Delson, *Evolutionary History of the Primates* (New York: Academic Press, 1979), p. 99; Frederick S. Szalay, A. L. Rosenberger, and M. Dagosto, "Diagnosis and Differentiation of the Order Primates," *Yearbook of Physical Anthropology* 30 (1987): 75–105; Frederick S. Szalay and S. G. Lucas, "Cranioskeletal Morphology of Archontans, and Diagnoses of Chiroptera, Volitantia, and Archonta," in R. D. E. MacPhee, ed., *Primates and Their Relatives in Phylogenetic Perspective* (New York: Plenum, 1993), pp. 187–226.

7. Matt Cartmill, "Arboreal Adaptations and the Origin of the Order Primates," in R. H. Tuttle, ed., *The Functional and Evolutionary Biology of Primates* (Chicago: Aldine-Atherton, 1972), pp. 97–122; Matt Cartmill, "Rethinking Primate Origins," *Science* 184 (1974): 436–443.

8. W. E. Le Gros Clark, *History of the Primates: An Introduction to the Study of Fossil Man* (Chicago: University of Chicago Press, 1959), p. 48.

9. R. D. Martin, *Primate Origins and Evolution: A Phylogenetic Reconstruction* (Princeton, N J: Princeton University Press, 1990).

10. J. R. Wible and H. H. Covert, "Primates: Cladistic Diagnosis and Relationships," *Journal of Human Evolution* 16 (1987): 1–22.

11. K. C. Beard, "Gliding Behaviour and Paleoecology of the Alleged Primate Family Paromomyidae," *Nature* 345 (1990): 340–341; R. F. Kay, R. W. Thorington, Jr., and P. Houde, "Eocene *Plesiadapi* Form Shows Affinities with Flying Lemurs, Not Primates," *Nature* 345 (1990): 342–344.

12. Frederick S. Szalay, "Arboreality: Is It Homologous in Metatherian and Eutherian Mammals?" *Evolutionary Biology* 18 (1984): 215–258.

13. Matt Cartmill, *A View to a Death in the Morning: Hunting and Nature through History* (Cambridge, MA: Harvard University Press, 1993), p. 226.

14. Matt Cartmill, "Human Uniqueness and Theoretical Content in Paleoanthropology," *International Journal of Primatology* 11 (1990): 173–192; Matt Cartmill, review of "Wonderful Life" by S. J. Gould, *American Journal of Physical Anthropology* 84 (1991): 368–371.

15. John Allman, "Evolution of the Visual System in the Early Primates," *Progress in Psychobiology and Physiological Psychology* 7 (1977): 1–53.

16. A. Hughes, "The Topography of Vision in Mammals of Contrasting Life Style: Comparative Optics and Retinal Organization," in F. Crescitelli, ed., *The Visual System in Vertebrates* (Berlin: Springer-Verlag, 1987), pp. 613–756.

17. Paul Garber, "Locomotor Behavior and Feeding Ecology of the Panamanian Tamarin (*Saguinus oedipus geoffroyi*, Callitrichidae, Primates)," *International Journal of Primatology* 1 (1980): 185–201.
18. Robert W. Sussman and Peter H. Raven, "Pollination by Lemurs and Marsupials: An Archaic Coevolutionary System," *Science* 200 (1978): 731–736.
19. Robert W. Sussman, "Primate Origins and the Evolution of Angiosperms," *American Journal of Primatology* 23 (1991): 209–223.
20. J. D. Pettigrew, "Phylogenetic Relations between Microbats, Megabats, and Primates (Mammalia: Chiroptera and Primates)," *Philosophical Transactions of the Royal Society of London* 325 (1989): 489–559.
21. R. D. E. MacPhee, ed., *Primates and Their Relatives in Phylogenetic Perspective* (New York: Plenum, 1993).
22. D. Tab Rasmussen, "Primate Origins: Lessons from a Neotropical Marsupial," *American Journal of Primatology* 22 (1990): 263–277.
23. Cartmill, "Rethinking Primate Origins."
24. Matt Cartmill, "New Views on Primate Origins," *Evolutionary Anthropology* 1 (1992): 105–111.

SUGGESTED READINGS

Conroy, Glenn C. *Primate Evolution*. New York: Norton, 1990. Chapters 2 and 3 offer a readable, well-illustrated sketch of the important facts about "archaic primates" and the earliest true primates.

Fleagle, J. G. *Primate Adaptation and Evolution*. San Diego, CA: Academic Press, 1988. A general survey of primate evolution for the beginning student.

WHY ARE PRIMATES SO SMART?

JOAN B. SILK AND ROBERT BOYD

Primates are unusual, if not unique, in the relatively large size of their brains and the complexity of their social behavior. Monkeys and apes have larger brains in relation to their body size than members of any other taxonomic group, except the toothed whales and dolphins. Humans, of course, carry these evolutionary trends to even greater extremes.

One of the central questions of human evolution is: Why has evolution made humans so smart? Understanding the nature and causes of the cognitive abilities of our closest living relatives, the nonhuman primates, will help us to answer this question. We begin this chapter by considering the selective factors favoring intelligence and behavioral complexity within the primates and then examining evidence regarding the extent of cognitive complexity in nonhuman primates.

WHAT IS INTELLIGENCE?

Intelligence is notoriously difficult to define for humans. Many researchers avoid the term entirely, referring instead to specific cognitive capacities that humans possess. It is even more difficult to define and assess the degree of intelligence of members of other species, partly because we know so little about their mental processes. Considerable ink has been spilled over the question of whether other animals have mental representations, thoughts, or consciousness.

In this chapter, we define intelligence as the ability to solve problems in complex situations by flexible means. It is important to emphasize that intelligence and evolutionary success are not necessarily synonymous. If they were, then we would have no basis for distinguishing between a bird that recalls thousands of locations at which it has stored seeds for the winter, a whale that finds its way from a beach in southern Argentina to summer fishing grounds in the Arctic Circle, a wildebeest female that manages to protect her calf from a hungry pride of lions, or a chimpanzee that leads his companions away from a hidden cache of prized food and returns to eat it in privacy. While a capacious memory, impressive navigational abilities, and effective parenting strategies clearly contribute to the fitness of these organisms, they may be based upon fixed stimuli or invariant rules that regulate behavior. Intelligence implies something more about the flexibility of the means used to solve problems. Therefore, our definition emphasizes the ability to cope with complexity and to incorporate novel solutions into existing behavioral repertoires.

HYPOTHESES FOR THE EVOLUTION OF INTELLIGENCE IN PRIMATES

There is now considerable debate about the primary factors that favored the evolution of relatively large brains and enhanced cognitive capacities among nonhuman primates. Some researchers argue that ecological factors associated with locating and processing inaccessible food items are principally responsible for the elaboration of cognitive skills and the increase in brain size within the primates. Others have suggested that social demands associated with life in large and stable groups provided the primary selective force favoring cognitive complexity and intelligence among nonhuman primates. We will review the rationales for each of these positions, and then consider the empirical data that bear on each.

The challenges associated with exploiting ephemeral and patchily distributed foods may have favored greater cognitive abilities. Fruit trees in tropical forests are patchily distributed and bear ripe fruit for relatively short periods of time. Despite these difficulties, trees present an advantageous feature to consumers—they do not move. Once an animal has located a food source, it will become a dependable, but seasonal, resource over the lifetime of the individual. It would be advantageous for primates to form a detailed mental map of the sites at which fruit may be found and to be able to find their way from one food source directly to another. University of California, Berkeley anthropologist Katharine Milton argues that it would not be useful to code information about the location and quality of food items genetically because the status of food sources changes rapidly over time.[1] Instead, individuals that can plan routes efficiently, anticipate the availability and quality of various food resources, and keep track of changing conditions of food sources may be at a distinct advantage.

Another ecological hypothesis contends that primates are smart because they exploit complex packages of food that require considerable ingenuity to process. Sue Parker of California State University at Sonoma and Katherine Gibson of the University of Texas have argued that specific features of some primate species' preferred foods may have favored enhanced cognitive abilities.[2]

They note that many primates eat things that must be peeled, cracked, excavated, or extracted before they are consumed. For example, some primates eat hard-shelled nuts that must be cracked open with stones or smashed against the tree trunk. Others dig up roots and tubers or extract insect larvae from bark or wood pith. Although these *extractive* foods are often difficult and time consuming to obtain and to process, they are valuable to primates because they tend to be rich sources of protein and energy. At the same time, extractive foods require complicated, carefully coordinated techniques to process. For example, when the aye-aye forages, it taps, probes, listens, and peers into the darkness. Then, as it locates a promising site, it extends its long middle finger underneath the bark of trees and scrapes out insect larvae.

Other scientists hold that primate intelligence evolved in order to solve social problems. In contrast to these ecological models, a number of primatologists believe that social challenges may have provided the most important selective factor favoring the evolution of intelligence in primates. As we have seen, life in social groups means that animals face competition and experience conflict. At the same time, social life provides opportunities for affiliation, cooperation, nepotism, and reciprocity. Nicholas Humphrey of Cambridge University was among the first to voice these ideas. He wrote the following:

> The life of social animals is highly problematical. In a complex society, such as those we know exist in higher primates, there are benefits to be gained for each individual member both from preserving the overall structure of the group, and at the same time from exploiting and out-maneuvering others within it. Thus, social primates are required from the very nature of the system that they create and maintain to be calculating beings; they must be able to calculate the likely behavior of others, to calculate the balance of advantage and loss—and all this in a context where the evidence on which their calculations are based is ephemeral, ambiguous, and liable to change, not least as a consequence of their own actions. In such a situation, "social skill" goes hand in hand with intellect, and here at last the intellectual faculties required are of the highest order. The game of social plot and counter-plot cannot be played merely on the basis of accumulated knowledge, any more than can a game of chess.[3]

This view that the challenges of social life have promoted the evolution of intelligence in primates is now generally known as the social intelligence hypothesis.

TESTING MODELS OF THE EVOLUTION OF INTELLIGENCE

Robin Dunbar, a primatologist at University College London, pointed out that it is possible to evaluate these models of the evolution of intelligence in primates because they generate specific predictions about the patterning of variation in intelligence or cognitive abilities among living primates.[4] For example, Parker and Gibson's idea can be tested by seeing whether species that have to process complex, packaged foods are more intelligent than species that feed on simpler foods. The main obstacle to making such tests is the lack of a reliable operational criteria to assess and to compare cognitive abilities, ecological features, and social complexity among primate species.

The assessment of cognitive abilities is particularly problematic since we do not know exactly how the brain processes information or solves problems. However, Dunbar believes that the volume of the brain's neocortex provides the most useful anatomical measure of cognitive capacity in primates for two reasons. First, the evolutionary changes that have occurred in the primate brain have mainly involved changes in the size and structure of the forebrain, particularly the neocortex. Second, the neocortex seems to be the thinking part of the brain, the part of the brain most closely associated with problem solving and behavioral flexibility. To assess cognitive capacities, then, Dunbar uses the *neocortex ratio*, the ratio of the size of the neocortex to the rest of the brain.

The ecological hypotheses for the evolution of intelligence suggest that specific characteristics of the diet or the environment of particular primate species will be correlated with their cognitive abilities. For Milton's model, this means that the patchiness of food resources that a species uses should be associated with the degree of intelligence it possesses. Frugivores, which utilize a dispersed, patchy, and ephemeral food supply, would need greater cognitive skills than folivores, whose foods are more uniformly distributed. Thus, we might predict that we would find a consistent relationship between the proportion of fruit in the diet and the neocortex ratio. It is also possible that the size of the area contained in the mental map places the greatest demands upon the brain. Frugivores typically have larger home ranges and longer day journeys than folivores. Thus, the neocortex ratio and home-range size or day-journey length might be positively correlated. From Parker and Gibson's model, we would predict that extractive foragers would have relatively larger neocortex ratios than those that feed upon more readily accessible foods.

The social intelligence hypothesis suggests that there would be a correlation between the complexity of social life and the neocortex ratio. Dunbar suggests that group size may be taken as a rough index of social complexity because primates in social groups recognize, associate, and interact with all the other members of their groups. Animals somehow keep track of their relationships with other members of their groups, particularly when they participate in social interactions that are regulated by nepotism or by reciprocity. Similarly, the decision to act aggressively or submissively, or to intervene in conflicts involving others, may depend in part upon an individual's ability to remember or assess the dominance ranks of other group members. As groups grow larger, the number of pairs grows rapidly, making it considerably more difficult to keep track of social relationships. Thus, Dunbar predicts that there should be a positive correlation between the size of social groups and the neocortex ratio.

Dunbar compiled data on neocortex ratio, ecological parameters, and group size in a variety of primate species to test this series of predictions. He found that the neocortex ratio is more consistently related to group size than to any of the ecological variables that he examined. That is, primates that live in large social groups tend to have larger neocortex ratios than those that live in smaller social groups. On the other hand, neither the amount of fruit in the diet, the length of the day journey, nor the tendency to use extractive foraging techniques are consistently associated with variation in the neocortex ratio.

These data provide support for the idea that social challenges played an important role in the evolution of greater cognitive capacities in nonhuman primates. However, there are two reasons to be cautious in drawing conclusions from these data: First, we cannot be sure that the neocortex ratio is a valid measure of cognitive ability. Second, it is always problematic to infer causal relationships from correlations. The correlation between group size and neocortex ratio may be a spurious result that arises because both group size and neocortex ratio are causally related to a third variable that has not yet been identified. Thus, we turn to other lines of evidence.

SOCIAL KNOWLEDGE VERSUS ECOLOGICAL KNOWLEDGE

One of the primary predictions that can be derived from the social intelligence hypothesis is that the cognitive abilities of monkeys and apes should be better suited to solve social challenges than to solve ecological problems. The problem with assessing this idea empirically is that it is very difficult to determine objectively what monkeys know about the world. Unlike psychologists working with human subjects, we cannot ask monkeys what they are thinking. At the same time, we cannot simply infer monkey knowledge or conceptual understanding from their actions. To see why this might be problematic, consider the following example. An observer watching a female macaque notes that she does not respond when her infant screams. How can the observer determine whether this means that the mother is (a) unaware that her infant is in distress, (b) unable to recognize her own infant's scream, or (c) reluctant to intervene unless her infant is truly at serious risk? To distinguish among these three possibilities, the observer must be able to demonstrate that mothers can distinguish between calls given in different contexts, that mothers can recognize their own infant's calls and can differentiate them from the calls of other infants, and that mothers can assess the nature and magnitude of the risks their infants face. As daunting as these tasks seem, several researchers, studying primates in laboratory and field situations, have developed methods for answering these kinds of questions. As a result of this innovative experimental work, we are beginning to get some idea of what monkeys know about their world.

KNOWLEDGE OF SOCIAL RELATIONSHIPS

One of the most striking things about primates is the interest that they take in one another. Newborns are greeted and inspected with interest. Adult females are sniffed and visually inspected regularly during their estrous cycles. When a fight breaks out, other members of the group watch attentively. Current evidence from the field and laboratory suggests that monkeys know a lot about one another.

One piece of this evidence comes from a playback experiment done with vervet monkeys in Amboseli National Park, Kenya, by Dorothy Cheney and Robert Seyfarth at the University of Pennsylvania.[5] Seyfarth and Cheney were among the first to apply experimental methods, originally used in studies of bird song and communication, to study the form and function of vocalizations in free-ranging primate groups. The first step in their research was to tape record vocalizations given by vervet monkeys in a broad range of situations. Then Seyfarth and Cheney assessed the relationships between the acoustic properties of the calls and the context in which the calls were given. This allowed them to identify a number of distinct calls, and to develop hypotheses about the functional significance of the calls. These hypotheses were then tested in carefully designed playback experiments. In these naturalistic experiments, tape recorded calls are played back to selected individuals from a hidden speaker, and the responses of the listeners are recorded on film or, more recently, on videotape. When they hear the tape recorded calls, monkeys look intently in the direction of the hidden speaker, approach the hidden speaker, or ignore the call. The duration of the monkeys' gaze in the direction of the hidden speaker is used to gauge the level of their interest in the tape-recorded call.

One of Cheney and Seyfarth's experiments provides information about the understanding of maternal relationships. In the experiment, the tape-recorded scream of a juvenile vervet was played to several female vervets. After the call was played, the mother of the juvenile stared in the direction of the speaker, or approached it, longer than other females did. This suggests that mothers recognized the call of their own infants. What is particularly interesting, however, is that the other females that heard the tape recorded scream, looked at the juvenile's mother. This suggests that other females understood who the juvenile belonged to and that they were aware that a special relationship existed between the mother and her offspring.

Additional evidence that monkeys may understand this type of kin relationship comes from more controlled laboratory experiments conducted by Verena Dasser working with a captive group of long-tailed macaques in Zürich, Switzerland.[6] In these experiments a young female was the primary subject. In each trial she was shown one of several slides of a single mother-infant pair, and then a slide of another pair of animals in the group. These were all members of her social group, and she knew them all well. She was trained to pick out the particular mother-offspring pair in each trial. Then she was presented with slides showing novel mother-offspring pairs from her group, and others displaying a pair of unrelated animals. These new mother-infant pairs included some mothers with young infants, and some mothers with considerably older offspring. If, *and only if*, she understood the nature of the relationship between the mother and offspring that served as her exemplar in training, then she would choose the novel mother-infant pair rather than the pair of unrelated individuals. Another monkey was trained in a very similar procedure. Both of these young females picked out the mother-offspring pair in nearly every trial and they seemed to have a clear understanding of what made those pairs of animals different from other pairs. Their performance in these experiments is particularly remarkable because the mother-infant pairs shown in the slides consisted of offspring of diverse ages and of both sexes. In some cases, the subject of the experiment had not even observed the mother interacting with her offspring as an infant.

Monkeys may also have some understanding of other kinds of social relationships among members of their groups. The evidence for this also comes from Cheney and Seyfarth's work on vervet monkeys. When monkeys are threatened or attacked, they often respond by threatening or attacking a lower ranking individual that was not involved in the original incident. We call this phenomena *redirected aggression*. Cheney and Seyfarth noticed that vervets do not randomly target other group members. Instead, they selectively redirect aggression toward the maternal kin of the original aggressor. So, if female A threatens female B, then B threatens AA, a close relative of A. If monkeys were simply blowing off steam or venting their aggression, they would choose a target at random. Thus, the monkeys seem to know that certain individuals associate regularly together.

These three lines of evidence suggest that monkeys are able to classify some pairs of individuals in special ways. But we do not know what cues the animals use to make such classifications, or exactly what mental rules they may use to assess relationships. Perhaps monkeys simply keep track of association patterns and realize that some pairs of individuals spend more time together than others. They may also have learned that particular pairs of monkeys that spend a lot of time together are likely to groom and to support one another. Their responses may be based upon complicated, learned associations, but they may have no special notion of kinship.

PARTICIPATION IN COALITIONS

In a coalition, one or more individuals intervene in an ongoing dispute between two other individuals. Thus, at least three individuals are involved. Moreover, very different kinds of interactions are going on simultaneously.

Consider the simplest case in which one monkey, the aggressor, attacks another monkey, the victim. Then the victim solicits support from a third party, the ally, and the ally intervenes on behalf of the victim against the aggressor. In this case, the ally behaves altruistically toward the victim, giving support to the victim at some potential cost to itself. At the same time, however, the ally behaves aggressively toward the aggressor, imposing harm or energy costs upon the aggressor. Thus, the ally simultaneously has a positive effect upon the victim and a negative effect upon the aggressor. Under these circumstances, decisions about whether or not to intervene in a particular dispute may be quite complicated. Consider a female that witnesses a dispute between two of her offspring. Should she intervene? If so, which of her offspring should she support? When a male bonnet macaque is solicited by a higher ranking male against a male that frequently supports him, how should he respond? In each case, the ally must balance the benefits to the recipient, the costs to the opponent, and the costs to itself.

As complicated as these calculations may be, they do not necessarily prove that primates are smarter than other animals. Many animals form alliances in defense of their territories. Moreover, parental support of offspring is not limited to primates. Swans, for example, routinely defend their young. However, Sandy Harcourt of the University of California, Davis, who has compared the pattern of coalition formation in primates and in other animals, has concluded that primates use alliances in different ways from other animals.[7] He noted that primates seem to assess differences in competitive ability among other members of their group, and cultivate relationships with powerful individuals. For example, in many species monkeys direct grooming up the dominance hierarchy. In some of these species, grooming is exchanged for support in antagonistic encounters. In some cases, primates compete actively over access to powerful individuals. Thus, female macaques and vervets sometimes supplant one another from grooming high-ranking individuals. Furthermore, primates seem to attempt to prevent the formation of alliances among their rivals. Perhaps the best example of this involved a male chimpanzee that attempted to disrupt the development of a coalition relationship between two lower-ranking males.

CAPACITY FOR DECEPTION

Andrew Whiten and Richard Byrne of the University of St. Andrews in Scotland compiled and catalogued instances of deception in nonhuman primate species.[8] Since there is little published information about deception, they distributed a survey among primatologists in which they solicited information about deceptive behavior among nonhuman primates. From the responses, they found evidence of a range of deceptive strategies employed by monkeys and apes. Four examples follow.

Concealment Hans Kummer, of the University of Zurich, observed hamadryas baboons in Ethiopia. Once he watched as an adult female hamadryas baboon spent twenty minutes inching toward a spot behind a rock. Once she reached this spot, she began to groom a subadult male. This was an interaction that was normally not tolerated by the resident adult male.

Distraction In the mountains of South Africa, Bryne and Whiten observed a young male chacma baboon attack a juvenile that screamed repeatedly. Screams are one means of recruiting support. As several adults came into view giving aggressive vocalizations, the attacker stood bipedally and stared intently into the distance as if a predator had been spotted. The adults paused and followed his gaze. Although no predator was detected, the aggressive interaction was terminated.

Creating a False Image In a large outdoor compound at Arnhem Zoo in the Netherlands, Frans de Waal saw a male chimpanzee sitting with his back to a rival male. The male heard his rival give an aggressive vocalization and he grinned submissively. He used his fingers to push his retracted lips together over his teeth, altering his facial expression. He repeated this three times before the fear grin was eliminated. Then he turned to face his rival.

Manipulation of a Conspecific Using a Social Tool Robin Dunbar studied gelada baboons in the Ethiopian highlands. He described an incident in which an infant gelada baboon was unsuccessful in its efforts to nurse. The infant moved near the group's dominant male and then vocalized, hit the male's back, and pulled on the long mane of hair around his shoulders. The male ignored the infant, but the infant pulled on his hair again. The male then turned and struck at the infant. In the commotion, the mother looked up. The infant approached, and the mother allowed it to nurse.

Whiten and Byrne argue that the significance of these anecdotes, and others that they have compiled, is that each requires considerable behavioral flexibility on the part of the actor. The acts are normal parts of the animal's behavioral repertoire, but the behaviors are used in unusual ways and contexts to achieve what seem to be specific objectives that are beneficial to the actors. Thus, when a baboon suddenly looks intently toward the horizon in the midst of an aggressive contest, it uses a standard part of its behavioral repertoire. Such behavior generally means that a predator has been sighted, and it is not a standard element in antagonistic encounters. In this case, it has the effect of distracting the baboon's opponents and terminating the conflict.

It is important to point out that deception among primates differs from the kinds of deception seen in other animals. Other animals feign injury to lure potential predators away from vulnerable young, mimic the phenotypes of foul-tasting species, or camouflage themselves to blend in with their surroundings, but they do not show much flexibility in their deceptive behavior. Moreover, all of these forms of deception are principally directed at members of other species. Primates seem to be unusual in the flexible and tactical nature of their deception, and in their capacity to deceive familiar conspecifics.

A number of researchers remain skeptical about the existence of deception among nonhuman primates, and believe that each of the anecdotes catalogued by Whiten and Byrne has a simpler explanation. It is very difficult to prove that a given incident is the result of a conscious intention to deceive conspecifics. Behaviors like hiding from the dominant male while grooming a subordinate male or distracting aggressors by feigning concern about a predator, may be random innovations that happen to work, not goal-directed strategies.

PROBLEM SOLVING IN NONSOCIAL DOMAINS

While the social intelligence hypothesis predicts that primates would be good at solving social problems, it also predicts that their ability to solve these problems is more fully developed than their ability to solve technical or ecological ones. Several lines of evidence suggest that this is the case.

We turn again to the Amboseli vervets. Cheney and Seyfarth compared the abilities of monkeys in social and nonsocial contexts by challenging vervets with two parallel tasks: one related to a social dilemma and the other related to a non-social situation. In one experiment, they played to subjects in one group the taped intergroup *wrr* call of a female in another group, from one of two locations. In one set of trials, the call of a female from neighboring group A is played from B's range. In another set of trials, the call of a female from neighboring group A is played from the center of A's range. The monkeys responded much more strongly when the call came from the wrong range. These results suggest that monkeys knew to which groups their neighbors belonged and where they should be found. Aberrant calls were greeted with what appeared to be concern and intense interest.

The researchers performed a parallel experiment to see if monkeys would make similar responses to the calls of other species. The tape-recorded calls of a hippopotamus and of black-winged stilts, two species that are normally found near the water, were played to the vervets. The calls of each species were played from two different locations. In one set of trials, calls were played from the direction of the swamp, the appropriate place for the animals that made the calls. In another set of trials, the calls were played from the direction of the open grassland, an inappropriate place for hippopotomi or black-winged stilts. Since vervets have probably never seen hippopotomi or black-winged stilts on the savanna, they were expected to be more attentive to calls coming from the inappropriate location. In fact, the vervets did not seem to distinguish between calls coming from the swamp or from the savanna.

These negative results do not necessarily mean that monkeys do not know that hippopotomi or black-winged stilts should be in the water. They might know but not care, since hippopotomi and stilts have little importance in their daily lives. Intergroup encounters might be a much more salient stimuli than the calls of animals that neither eat vervets nor compete with them for resources. However, the marked contrast between responses to intergroup calls from the wrong territory and responses to hippopotomi and black-winged stilts from the wrong habitat is suggestive. Monkeys are apparently more concerned, if not more knowledgeable, about their social world than about their environment.

Another set of experiments conducted on the Amboseli vervets is consistent with this view. Pythons and leopards often prey upon vervets in Amboseli. Vervets give alarm calls and seem very worried when they encounter these creatures. It seems likely that there would be important selective advantages associated with learning to avoid pythons and leopards. Thus, Seyfarth and Cheney were curious about whether monkeys would associate certain visual cues with the likely presence of a predator. To test this idea, they took advantage of the fact that pythons and leopards leave clear visual signs of their presence. Python tracks have a distinctive form. They look like long straight indentations in the dust. A human tracker would immediately know that a python was nearby if he or she saw such a track. Similarly, leopards often drag their kills into trees before they eat them in order to prevent scavengers from stealing them. There is no other way for an antelope carcass to get into a tree, since antelopes do not climb trees. If you came upon an antelope carcass in a tree, you would immediately look over your shoulder for the leopard that made the kill. So Cheney and Seyfarth used this information to conduct two experiments. In one experiment, they created a life-like python track and watched the monkeys' responses when they approached the track. In the other experiment, they placed a life-like stuffed antelope carcass in the crook of a tree. The vervets made no vocal or behavioral response when they came upon the python track or when they saw the antelope carcass in the tree. They showed none of the same concern that they would show if they confronted the python or leopard itself. It seems that the monkeys are unable to associate visual information about a predator's presence with the idea that the predator might also be nearby.

DIFFERENCES IN COGNITIVE ABILITIES AMONG HUMANS AND OTHER PRIMATES

Experimental studies of primate cognition conducted in the laboratory suggest that there are some ways in which nonhuman primate cognitive capacities are fundamentally different from those of humans. In particular, monkeys appear to lack a sense of self-awareness and a capacity for empathy, pretense, and perspective taking. Monkeys apparently cannot distinguish between their own knowledge or view of the world and that of others. To understand what this means, consider the following situation. A female monkey watches as a python slithers into the leaf litter at the base of an acacia tree, but she gives no sign that anything is amiss as two group members begin to descend the trunk of the same tree. Why doesn't the monkey give an alarm or communicate her concern? The answer, we think, is that the knowledgeable monkey is unaware that her companions' understanding of the situation is different from her own. The ability to understand the mental states of other individuals is called a *theory of mind*.

While monkeys consistently fail tests that rely on the presence of a theory of mind, apes are more successful in these kinds of experiments. Chimpanzees can solve some nonverbal cognitive problems that three-year-old human children can solve, but are usually unable to solve problems that only older children can solve. Chimpanzees, and perhaps other great apes, may have a rudimentary theory of mind.

The question of whether or not monkeys and apes can attribute mental states to others, or have a theory of mind, might seem both methodologically intractable and of no real practical importance. However, a number of researchers believe that a theory of mind is an essential prerequisite for complex deception, imitation, and teaching. For example, deception is based upon manipulating another individual's belief about the world. Take, for example, a low-ranking animal that comes unexpectedly upon a very desirable food item. He may know from past experience that older and stronger animals routinely take such items from him. It would make sense, then, to carry the food item away surreptitiously, to hide it and return to it later, or to lead ignorant group members away from the area. But to execute this deception, the finder must first understand that his knowledge differs from the knowledge of nearby group members, and then come up with a way to effectively take advantage of this discrepancy. A similar argument can be made for teaching. Female chimpanzees have been seen demonstrating the fundamental elements of nut cracking to their offspring. In teaching, the instructor first has to realize the limits of the pupil's knowledge. The pupil, in turn, has to grasp the intent of the instructor and the objective of the behavior. Both imitation and teaching play an important role in the transmission of complex behavior patterns in humans, and underlie the human capacity for culture. It may be no coincidence that convincing examples of complex deception, imitation, and tool use are restricted to the great apes.

EXAMINING THEORY OF MIND IN CHILDREN, MONKEYS, AND APES

Readers may be surprised, skeptical, or extremely dubious about our conclusions about nonhuman primate ability to distinguish between their own knowledge of the world and other primates' knowledge of the world. How can we know this for any organism that we cannot question directly? It turns out that cognitive psychologists have devised a number of extremely clever ways to address these issues that do not require language. Several experiments deal with *attribution*, the capacity to assess the knowledge or mental states of others.

To give you a concrete example of what is meant by attribution, we will briefly outline the classic experiment on attribution. A young child is shown a matchbox and is asked what it contains. The child normally answers that it contains matches. The child is shown that the matchbox actually contains something else, such as M & Ms. Then a newcomer enters the room and the child is asked what the newcomer will think is in the matchbox. Children below the age of three or so invariably say that the newcomer will think that the matchbox contains M & Ms. Older children say that the newcomer will think that the matchbox contains matches. These results suggest that young children cannot distinguish what they know about the world from what others know about the world, but acquire this ability as they mature.

This test cannot be applied directly to monkeys and apes, but other tests can. Cheney and Seyfarth conducted a series of experiments designed to assess attribution in monkeys.[9] One of these experiments compared the behavior of mothers when their offspring were aware of the presence of desirable food items, and when they were ignorant of the food's proximity. In one set of trials mothers and their offspring were seated side by side and both could see into the test area as apple slices were placed into a food bin. In the other set of trials, only the mother could see the apple slices being placed in the food bin. Next the juvenile was released into the test area. Mothers of ignorant offspring did not behave any differently from mothers of knowledgeable offspring; they did not call more often, orient more toward the food bin, or otherwise seem to communicate their knowledge to their offspring. As a result, knowledgeable offspring found the food items significantly sooner than ignorant offspring did. These results suggest that mothers did not differentiate between what they knew and what their infants knew, though other explanations for the mothers' behavior are not precluded. For example, mothers might be aware of their infants' mental state but not use this information to alter their behavior. However, this interpretation is weakened by the fact that, in a parallel experiment, mothers also failed to warn ignorant offspring about the presence of a frightening and potentially dangerous situation. Certainly there should be strong selection favoring alerting offspring to the presence of danger.

David Premack of the University of Pennsylvania has conducted an ingenious series of experiments to assess the chimpanzee's ability to attribute mental states.[10] In one experiment, Sarah, a chimpanzee that was involved in research on language and cognition, was shown videotapes of an actor in a cage who was faced with a variety of dilemmas. In one case, the actor could not reach a bunch of fruit hanging from the top of the cage. In another, he could not reach fruit just beyond the bars of the cage. Then Sarah was given a series of photographs. One of the photographs depicted the solution to the problem (such as standing on a chair) and the others depicted irrelevant actions (such as reaching sideways with a stick). Sarah routinely chose the photograph that represented the appropriate solution to the problem. Premack argued that Sarah's choice of the correct solution means that she may have understood the actor's intention and desire to get the fruit. To do this, she may have attributed a state of mind to the actor. On the other hand, as Premack acknowledged, it may be that Sarah understood the problem and knew how to solve it, but did not actually attribute a state of mind to the actor.

Sarah could not solve all the attribution problems put to her, but young human children cannot solve all the attribution problems that Sarah can solve. These data do not prove that apes have a theory of mind, or that monkeys do not. But they do provide suggestive evidence regarding this question, and they do indicate that such questions are amenable to objective, scientific investigation.

CONCLUSIONS

Research on the cognitive abilities of nonhuman primates is just beginning to provide information that will help us to understand why primates are so smart. We are not yet sure whether the social intelligence hypothesis will be verified or whether the tentative conclusions that we have drawn from the limited data now available will be confirmed. As this field of research continues to produce new insights, our view of the cognitive abilities of nonhuman primates will surely change. These developments will, in turn, shape our theories of the evolution of the cognitive abilities in human ancestors.

NOTES

1. K. Milton, "Foraging Behaviour and the Evolution of Primate Intelligence," in R. Byrne and A. Whiten, eds., *Machiavellian Intelligence* (Oxford: Oxford Science Publications, 1988), pp. 285–305.
2. K. Gison, "Cognition, Brain Size, and the Extraction of Embedded Food Resources," in J. Else and P. C. Lee, eds., *Primate Ontogeny, Cognition, and Social Behaviour* (Cambridge: Cambridge University Press, 1986), pp. 93–104.
3. N. K. Humphrey, "The Social Function of Intellect," in P. P. G. Bateson and R. A. Hinde, eds., *Growing Points in Ethology* (Cambridge: University of Cambridge Press, 1976), pp. 303–317.
4. R. I. M. Dunbar, "Neocortex Size as a Constraint on Group Size in Primates," *Journal of Human Evolution* 20 (1992): 469–493.
5. D. L Cheney and R. M. Seyfarth, *How Monkeys See the World* (Chicago: Chicago University Press, 1990).

6. V. Dasser, "A Social Concept in Java Monkeys," *Animal Behaviour* 36 (1988): 225–230.
7. A. H. Harcourt, "Coalitions and Alliances: Are Primates More Complex Than Non-Primates?" in A. H. Harcourt and F. B. M. de Waal, eds., *Coalitions and Alliances in Humans and Other Animals* (Oxford: Oxford University Press, 1992), pp. 445–471.
8. A. Whiten and R. Byrne, "The Manipulation of Attention in Primate Tactical Deception," in R. Byrne and A. Whiten, eds., *Machiavellian Intelligence* (Oxford: Oxford University Press, 1988), pp. 211–223.
9. Cheney and Seyfarth, *How Monkeys See the World*.
10. D. Premack, "'Does the Chimpanzee Have a Theory of Mind?' Revisited," in R. Byrne and A. Whiten, eds., *Machiavellian Intelligence* (Oxford: Oxford Science Publications, 1988), pp. 160–179.

SUGGESTED READINGS

Byrne, R. *The Thinking Ape*. Oxford: Oxford University Press, 1995.
Byrne, R., and A. Whiten, eds. *Machiavellian Intelligence*. Oxford: Oxford University Press, 1988.
Cheney, D. L., and R. M. Seyfarth. *How Monkeys See the World*. Chicago: University of Chicago Press, 1990.
Harcourt, A. H., and F. B. M. de Waal, eds. *Coalitions and Alliances in Humans and Other Animals*. Oxford: Oxford University Press, 1992.

MIOCENE APES

DAVID R. BEGUN

PRELUDE: A CASE HISTORY

July in Catalonia can be ideal if you are on the beach, or it can be unbearable if you are in a building with no air conditioning, you have nothing to do, and you are seven. That was my son André's problem one summer day in 1991. He was patiently waiting for me to finish planning for our 1991 field season at the Miocene hominoid locality of Can Llobateres, about twenty kilometers northeast of Barcelona. When I suggested that we take a trip to the site late that afternoon, André was thrilled. We drove to the site to look over the area. I wanted André to run around a bit, and I gave him a pick to poke around with. I was also looking for the type of sediment we knew from previous work to be most likely to contain fossils. The hard green clays of Can Llobateres are the richest in ape fossils, and I wanted to find a new layer of this sediment. André and I had a great time chopping dirt and I did find some green sediment that looked very promising. The next day the field season began officially. My Spanish colleague and I, along with André and a team of excavators, arrived the next morning, and after setting up I showed my colleague the area I considered most promising. Our picks rose together as we prepared to clear away the layer of overburden covering the fossiliferous sediment. As they struck on both sides of the mark I had made the previous day, a tooth popped out. My colleague's pick had hit an upper jaw, or maxilla, dislodging the first premolar tooth. As we watched the tooth roll down the slope, we realized we had something significant. Looking at the spot from which the tooth had come, we saw broken bone. When we finished three days later, we had a nearly complete face, by far the most intact specimen of *Dryopithecus* (discussed later) ever recovered from Spain.

Discoveries in paleoanthropology are often a combination of luck and homework. In the case described above, we were lucky to clean a section right where a beautiful specimen was buried. But we also knew that apes had been found at Can Llobateres, and we knew from the nature of the sediments where our chances of finding good fossils were greatest. Sediments reveal details of the environments in which they were deposited. We knew that fossil apes are associated most often with fine grained sediments indicative of very slow moving water, such as that of a river delta, floodplain, or lake margin. In fact, the goals of our project at Can Llobateres were not only to find fossil apes, but also to collect as much information as possible about the environment in which they lived and died, and their geologic age. This information is combined with data on the anatomy of the fossils to tell us how those organisms lived, what they ate, and how they moved around in their environment.

Our research at Can Llobateres is just one example of many projects on Miocene apes in the past few years. This chapter summarizes research on Miocene apes, its implications for our understanding of ape and human evolution, and the prospects for future work in Miocene ape paleobiology. I will focus on those Miocene apes that are relatively well known and whose general relations to other apes and to humans are reasonably clear.

Background

Before discussing Miocene apes, a few terms must be defined. Hominoids, or the Hominoidea, is a superfamily in the Order Primates that includes all living apes and humans. The Hominoidea is divided into families, the exact number of which is controversial. Most researchers studying Miocene hominoids recognize two families. One is the Hylobatidae (hylobatids), including the gibbons and siamangs (genus *Hylobates*) of Southeast Asia. The other is the Hominidae (hominids), including the great apes and humans. The great apes include the orang-utan (*Pongo pygmaeus*) from Indonesia, and the African apes—the chimpanzee (*Pan troglodytes*), the bonobo, sometimes called the pygmy chimpanzee (*Pan paniscus*), and the gorilla (*Gorilla gorilla*). Many researchers, and most text books, continue to separate the great apes and humans taxonomically by recognizing a third family, the Pongidae (pongids) for the great apes. This reflects tradition and a bit of anthropocentrism that often prevents anthropologists from seeing the remarkable similarities between humans and great apes. In fact the overwhelming majority of evidence indicates that African apes and humans are more closely related to one another than either are to orangs. To many paleoanthropologists, this means that African apes should not be placed in a separate family from humans. However, since orangs, African apes, and even the earliest members of the human lineage, *Australopithecus*, all look very similar, at least from the neck up, and since all are so different from hylobatids, two hominoid families separating the lesser apes and the great apes and humans is most practical, and most in agreement with current interpretations of hominoid relations (see later discussion).

Living hominoids share a set of characteristics that distinguish them from other living anthropoids, or higher primates. Their cheek teeth, or molars, have a distinctive arrangement of cusps. Their brains are also somewhat larger than expected for an anthropoid of their size range. But most dramatically, hominoids can be distinguished from other living anthropoids by their postcranial skeleton. All hominoids have skeletons bearing the hallmarks of a suspensory arboreal animal, even those who, like humans, no longer frequent the trees. Hominoids have rather loose but powerful, outwardly facing shoulders, highly specialized elbows to maximize stability in a wide range of positions, mobile wrists capable of adopting a wide range of positions, and long and powerful fingers. All hominoids lack an external tail, and all have specific attributes of the vertebral column, pelvic basin, hip joint, ankle, and foot related to arboreality and more vertical postures.

Apes use these characteristic features to grasp branches and support their body weight from above, unlike most arboreal primates, which move about on top of branches. Humans retain these features because they allow the wide range of arm and hand positions that are crucial to the human way of life, one that is dependent on intensive and elaborate manipulation of the environment.

Hominids (great apes and humans) share many additional characteristics that set them apart from other hominoids (hylobatids). Hominids are all large in body size and relative brain size compared to other hominoids. They have very enlarged front teeth, or incisors, and most have a greatly elongated front part of the palates or upper jaws. They share many other more subtle traits in the dentition and skull, and a large number of features of the postcranium not found in the hylobatids or other primates.

The early history of research on Miocene hominoids has been described in detail elsewhere.[1] Through the 1960s the story of hominoid evolution seemed relatively straightforward. Early Miocene hominoids such as *Proconsul* were thought to be directly related to the great apes (see Table 6-1). Earlier researchers had recognized a closer evolutionary relationship between African apes and humans than between African and Asian great apes.[2] But this view was later abandoned, prematurely as we shall see, and the great apes were lumped together as the descendants of *Proconsul*.[3]

At this time most fossil apes were placed in the genus *Dryopithecus*, a taxon named in 1856 for a lower jaw from France.[4] Many other names had been used for a wide variety of great ape-like Miocene specimens from Europe, Africa, and South Asia, including for example *Sivapithecus* from India and Pakistan, and *Proconsul* from Kenya and Uganda.[5] These and many other names were later subsumed under *Dryopithecus*.[6] One group of fossil apes was excluded from *Dryopithecus*. These specimens were most often referred to the genus *Ramapithecus*, and looked more human, mostly by virtue of the thick covering of enamel on their cheek teeth (molars). Figure 6-1 (on page 73) shows the consensus classification and phylogeny (evolutionary tree) of hominoids as of 1969. It reflects the then accepted division of great apes and humans into "pongids" and "hominids," with the "dryopithecines" as ancestors of the former, and the "ramapithecines" ancestral to the latter.

Table 6-1   Fossil Hominoid Taxa and Chronology

Taxa are listed opposite their localities. First occurrences are listed in their entirety; subsequent occurrences are abbreviated. Localities within a row are contemporaneous if separated by a comma or placed in relative stratigraphic position if separated by a period. This table illustrates the incredible diversity of Miocene hominoid taxa. Many remain unnamed (Hominoidea indet.), but when these are combined with named taxa approximately thirty genera of hominoid can be identified. Given that this probably represents a small percentage of the total number of forms that actually existed (known fossils greatly underrepresent taxonomic diversity in the past) and considering the fact that only five genera of hominoid exist today, the Miocene can truly be considered the golden age of apes.

MA	Locality	Taxa
26	Lothidok (Kenya)	Hominoidea (new genus and species)
21	Meswa Bridge (Kenya)	*Proconsul sp.*
20		
19	Tinderet series (Kenya-Kuru, Legetet, Chamtwara, Songhor), Napak (Uganda),	*Proconsul africanus, Xenopithecus koruensis, Limnopithecus legetet, Limnopithecus evansi, Kaleopithecus songhorensis, Micropithecus clarki, Proconsul major, Dendropithecus macinnesi, Rangwapithecus gordoni, Nyanzapithecus vancouveringorum* (N.B. Not all occur at each locality)
17	Rusinga Island, Mwfangano Island (Kenya)	*Proconsul nyanzae, Proconsul hesloni, D. macinnesi, L. legetet, N. vancouveringorum*
	Kalodirr, Buluk (Kenya)	*Afropithecus turkanensis, Turkanapithecus kalakolensis, Simiolus enjiessi*
	Ad Dabtyah (S. Arabia), Sindhi (Pakistan)	*Heliopithecus leakeyi, Dionysopithecus sp.*
16	Sihong (China).	*D. shuangouensis, Platodontopithecus jianghuaiensis,* Hominoid indet.
15	Kipsarimon (Kenya)	2 Hominoidea indet.
	Maboko, Majiwa, Kaloma, Nachola (Kenya).	*Nyanzapithecus pickfordi, Mabokopithecus clarki, "Kenyapithecus africanus," Micropithecus leakeyorum*
	Pasalar (Turkey), Devinsk Nová Ves (Slovakia)	*Griphopithecus darwini*
13	Çandir (Turkey).	*Griphopithecus alpani*
	Fort Ternan (Kenya).	*Kenyapithecus wickeri,* 3 Hominoidea indet.
12	St. Gaudens, La Grive (France).	*Dryopithecus fontani*
	St. Stefan (Austria), Can Vila, Can Mata, Castel de Barbera, Sant Quirze (Spain), Chinji (Pakistan).	*Dryopithecus cf., D. fontani, Sivapithecus indicus*

TABLE 6-1, CONT.

11	Ngorora (Kenya).	Hominoidea indet.
10	Can Ponsic, El Firal (Spain).	*Dryopithecus crusafonti*
	Can Llobateres, Polinya (Spain), Melchingen, Trochtelfingen, Ebingen, Wissberg, Eppelsheim (Germany), Yassioren (Turkey).	*Dryopithecus laietanus, Dryopithecus cf, D. brancoi Ankarapithecus meteai*
9	Rudabánya (Hungary), Mariathal (Austria), Salmendingen (Germany), Udabno (Georgia).	*D. brancoi*
	La Tarumba (Spain).	*D. laietanus*
	Ravin de la Pluie, Xirochori, Nikiti (Greece), Nagri (Pakistan, India).	*Ouranopithecus macedoniensis, Sivapithecus sivalensis, Sivapithecus parvada*
8	Pygros (Greece), Baccinello VI (Italy).	*Graecopithecus freybergi, Oreopithecus bambolii*
7	U-level, Hari Talyangar (Pakistan), Samburu (Kenya), Shihuiba (Lufeng, China).	*S. sivalensis, Gigantopithecus giganteus,* Hominoidea indet., *Lufengpithecus lufengensis*
6	Lukeino (Kenya), Hari Talyangar (Pakistan).	Hominoidea indet., *Gigantopithecus bilaspurensis*
5	Lothagam (Kenya).	cf. *Australopithecus*

Three more recent developments in paleoanthropology have completely undermined this view of hominoid evolutionary history. Interpretations or hypotheses in paleoanthropology, as in other sciences, are subject to testing made possible by new discoveries and new techniques for generating data. A field in which ideas are always changing in the face of new discoveries is exciting and dynamic; method is more important than interpretation. A field in which interpretations never change, hypotheses are never falsified, and theories are unaffected by new data, is not much of a science at all.

Of the three recent developments, two fall into the category of new techniques, while the third is categorized as new discoveries. The first development, relatively new to paleoanthropology but with a long history in biology, is molecular systematics. Since the turn of the century, researchers have been attempting to reconstruct evolutionary history using molecules rather than morphology.[7] In the 1960s a number of researchers had concluded on the basis of work on proteins that humans were more closely related to African apes than to orangs,[8] as Huxley had suggested a century earlier on the basis of

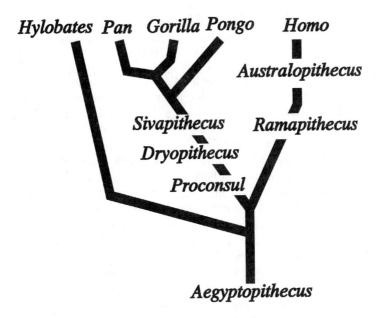

FIGURE 6-1 EVOLUTIONARY RELATIONS AMONG FOSSIL
AND LIVING HOMINOIDS, AS INTERPRETED CIRCA 1968

Aegyptopithecus, now known to be a primitive anthropoid, was then thought to be an early hominoid, broadly ancestral to all later forms. Most authors placed *Sivapithecus*, *Dryopithecus*, and *Proconsul* in the same genus, *Dryopithecus*, and thought that these were ancestral to living great apes. *Ramapithecus*, now recognized to be a synonym of *Sivapithecus*, was thought by most to be the first "hominid." See text for details.

anatomical comparisons. The antiquity of the split between apes and humans was also dramatically different according to the molecular evidence. Sarich and Wilson estimated that the split could not have occurred more than three to five million years ago,[9] whereas most paleoanthropologists at the time, recognizing *Proconsul* as a great ape ancestor, placed the split sometime before the evolution of this form, at least twenty million years ago. Though Sarich's molecular clock is not widely cited today, his estimate is probably much closer to the truth than the estimate based on *Proconsul*. Modern research in molecular systematics now shows, based mostly on DNA sequencing, how very closely related we are to the African apes and maybe more specifically to the chimpanzee.[10]

The second development, again new to paleoanthropology but with a longer history in paleobiology, is cladistics. Cladistics or phylogenetic systematics is an approach to biological classification that is explicitly evolutionary.[11] All organisms must be classified according to their evolutionary interrelationships. Organisms placed together in a group, or taxon, must be more closely related to the other forms in that taxon than to any organism in another taxon. So, for example, African apes and orangs cannot be grouped to the exclusion of humans, because African apes are more closely related to humans than they are to orangs. This is the main reason the taxon Pongidae is no longer used by many. Taxa like the Pongidae are paraphyletic, meaning they fail to include some lineages, like humans. Including humans with the great apes changes the name of the taxon to Hominidae, because Hominidae was named first. Cladistic methodology provides an explicit protocol for determining ancestor-descendant relationships.[12] The main effect of the application of this method in the analysis of Miocene hominoids has been a thorough re-evaluation of the evolutionary significance of the characteristics used to reconstruct evolutionary relations. Characteristics once thought to indicate a close evolutionary relationship among the great apes, such as large, elongated faces, large canine teeth, very elongated forelimbs, short hindlimbs, and others, are now recognized as primitive characteristics that were also present in the ancestors of humans. Therefore they do not distinguish the human lineage from that of the apes. In contrast, other characteristics, such as well-developed brow ridges, elongated crania, a reduced number of wrist bones, and other details of cranial and postcranial anatomy found only in African apes and humans, suggest that these forms share a period of common ancestry not shared by the orang. Cladistic methods allow researchers to distinguish characteristics indicative of a close evolutionary relationship, or derived characteristics, from those that are more primitive. This type of revision has lead to substantial changes in interpretation of the pattern of relationships among Miocene apes.

The third development of importance to Miocene hominoid research has been new discoveries. The old view of a dichotomy between the "ramapithecines" and the "dryopithecines" has been completely rejected on the basis of new discoveries of both groups. As described later in this chapter, new fossils from Pakistan show that *Ramapithecus* and *Sivapithecus* are in fact the same genus. New discoveries of *Proconsul*, *Dryopithecus*, *Sivapithecus*, and completely new forms reveal the pattern of hominoid diversity in the Miocene to be very different from the simple tree that was the consensus in 1969. Figure 6-2 is a revision of Miocene hominoid classification based on the developments noted earlier. For the rest of this chapter, I will describe these new discoveries and their implications for the evolutionary history of the great apes and humans.

CURRENT ISSUES AND INTERPRETATIONS IN MIOCENE HOMINOID RESEARCH

The earliest well-documented Miocene hominoid is *Proconsul*, from sites in Kenya and Uganda up to about twenty Ma (mega-annum, or millions of years ago). One of the most important of these localities is Songhor in southwestern Kenya, near Lake Victoria. Songhor is thought to be about nineteen Ma.[13]

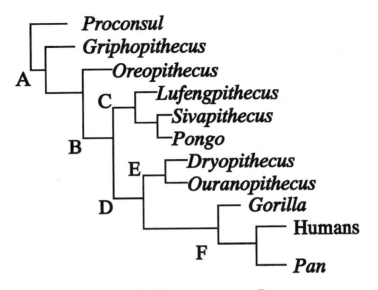

FIGURE 6-2   ONE INTERPRETATION OF RELATIONS
AMONG FOSSIL AND LIVING HOMINOIDS

Instead of arranging taxa in an evolutionary tree, most researchers today prefer dendrograms such as this one, which arrange taxa based on relations but avoid speculations about ancestors and descendants. Note, for example, that *Proconsul* is not ancestral to other forms; it simply branched off first. The common ancestor of *Proconsul* and other hominoids is represented by node A, which is not a named taxon but a hypothetical ancestral form sharing characteristics of both *Proconsul* and other hominoids. In this phylogeny, *Sivapithecus*, *Lufengpithecus*, and *Pongo* share a common ancestor at C not shared by any other taxon. They are thus most closely related to one another, and related in the same way to all other taxa, with which they are linked at B. Similarly, *Dryopithecus* shares a common ancestor with *Ouranopithecus* at E, and both share an ancestor with the African apes and humans at D. Humans (including *Australopithecus*) share a common ancestor with chimps (*Pan*) at F, and are therefore more closely related to chimps than either are to gorillas. See text for discussion.

Many fossil hominoids are known from Songhor and nearby sites, including species of *Proconsul*, *Rangwapithecus*, and other smaller forms of very unclear evolutionary affinities (see Table 6-1 on pages 71–72).[14] Most are probably related to *Proconsul*, but some, like *Dendropithecus*, may represent a different kind of hominoid, or may not be a hominoid at all.

The specimens from Songhor, apart from a small number of more complete jaws, are fragmentary and include only a few postcranial remains. However, a bit later in time, between about 17.2 and 17.8 Ma, additional similar-looking primates are found at a site on nearby Rusinga Island, in Lake Victoria.[15] Many of these specimens are more complete and provide most of the information we have about the anatomy and evolutionary relations of *Proconsul*.

The Rusinga specimens attributed to *Proconsul* are slightly different from specimens from the older sites, but are currently assigned to the same genus. Based mostly on the evidence from Rusinga, we know that *Proconsul* was a monkey-like arboreal quadruped.[16] Its limbs were roughly equal in length, and its forelimbs lacked most of the characteristics of modern hominoids related to their suspensory locomotor capabilities. *Proconsul* does have a number of features that seem to foreshadow hominoid postcranial anatomy. *Proconsul* elbows, for example, include a specialized ridge similar to but less well developed than a ridge in modern hominoid elbows, designed to maintain maximum stability through the range of motion at the joint. Subtle aspects of the wrists and fingers also suggest mobility and grasping capabilities similar to that seen in living hominoids, but again less well developed than in modern forms.[17] The hip joints and innominate, or pelvic bones, of *Proconsul* also suggest some enhanced ranges of mobility foreshadowing the hominoid condition, as do some details of the anatomy of the feet.[18] Most important, the anatomy of the sacrum, the final section of the vertebral column before the tail, indicates that *Proconsul* was like hominoids in lacking an external tail.[19] Thus, *Proconsul* may have been a more deliberate climber, venturing out on smaller branches and branch ends, and often adopting more vertical postures than living monkeys.

The anatomy of *Proconsul* jaws and teeth suggest that it was a generalized frugivore, or fruit eater, but probably taking in some leaves as well.[20] The incisors are not as large as in modern great apes, which use these teeth for processing foods with tough coverings, but were similar to those of the frugivorous gibbons and many Old and New World monkeys. These forms generally have diets of 50 to 75 percent fruits, grains, nuts, bark, roots, and other plant parts excluding leaves. The pattern of microwear on the molars of *Proconsul* also indicates a diet similar to that of modern frugivores.[21] The brain of *Proconsul* is known from one specimen, a skull from Rusinga Island. It is very primitive looking in overall morphology and size, and was no more advanced than the brains of living monkeys. In fact in some ways it resembles the brains of living prosimians.[22]

All in all, with its generalized monkey-like morphology but subtle ape-like features, *Proconsul* is a good representative of the ancestor of living apes, and possibly of living hominids. It may be that *Proconsul* was already somewhat specialized in its own direction and is not directly related to modern forms, but the common ancestor of modern hominoids must have been very similar to *Proconsul*.

Contemporary with the latest specimens of *Proconsul* from Rusinga is another set of taxa from northern Kenya. These are the somewhat enigmatic forms *Afropithecus*, *Turkanapithecus*, and *Simiolus*.[23] These forms are known from the sites of Kalodirr and Buluk, in the Lake Turkana region of northern Kenya, the same region that has proven so rich in fossil humans. A fragmentary jaw and some isolated teeth from Saudi Arabia originally attributed to *Heliopithecus* may also be *Afropithecus*.[24] Although contemporary with *Proconsul*, these three species are very different in their cranial and dental anatomy from other early Miocene forms, which makes their correct placement among the hominoids very difficult.

Simiolus is a very small form with unusual cresty teeth and a primitive postcranial skeleton, lacking a number of characteristics that in *Proconsul* foreshadow the hominoid condition.[25] It may not even be a true hominoid but a descendant of a branch that diverged before the hominoids evolved. *Turkanapithecus* is close in size to the smallest species of *Proconsul*. The best specimen of *Turkanapithecus* is a partial skeleton with most of the face and teeth and a number of associated postcranial bones.[26] *Turkanapithecus* has a more projecting mid-face, the region of the nose, than *Proconsul*, and this is reminiscent of more primitive "pre-hominoids" like the thirty-three-million-year-old genus *Aegyptopithecus* from the Fayum deposits of Egypt.[27] Other aspects of the anatomy of *Turkanapithecus* are more similar to *Proconsul*, especially the postcrania, which are very similar in both forms.

Afropithecus is close in size to the largest species of *Proconsul*, but has a distinctive cranial morphology, with a mixture of features resembling *Aegyptopithecus* and *Proconsul*.[28] The upper incisor region or premaxilla of *Afropithecus* is superficially more like that of modern hominoids, being slightly elongated and large, to house the large, thick, upper incisor teeth. Unlike *Proconsul*, *Afropithecus* molars have thick layers of enamel,[29] an extremely hard material that coats the teeth of all primates and of most other vertebrates. This is more like the molars of later more advanced hominoids. The postcrania of *Afropithecus* is nearly indistinguishable from that of *Proconsul*.[30] *Afropithecus* was probably an arboreal quadruped that moved above branches, like modern monkeys, but was a strong climber and spent more time in vertical postures than do living monkeys. The dietary adaptations of *Afropithecus* were probably also similar to those of *Proconsul*, though the thicker enamel of the former suggests a more varied diet that included hard or tough objects, such as nuts and fruits with durable coverings, or foods that tend to wear teeth rapidly, such as those obtained from terrestrial sources that incorporate some grit. *Turkanopithecus*, with its more cresty molars, may have relied more heavily on foods that require extensive cutting and chopping, such as leaves, which must be finely chopped to liberate the few nutrients they contain.

The mixture of primitive and more advanced, or derived, characteristics of *Turkanopithecus*, and especially *Afropithecus*, makes it difficult to place these taxa in a phylogenetic or evolutionary scheme. It may be that both are more primitive hominoids than *Proconsul*, as suggested by the facial similarities with *Aegyptopithecus*, or it may be that *Afropithecus* is derived, given the more modern appearance of its teeth. More fossil material is needed to resolve the enigmatic relations of these relatively newly described Miocene hominoids.

At the end of the early Miocene, about 16.5 Ma, few fossil hominoids are known from East Africa. A small number of fossils similar in morphology to smaller possible relatives of *Proconsul* are known from China and Pakistan.[31] But the record of Miocene apes is relatively barren at that time until about fifteen Ma, at which time a rich record of primates is known from Maboko Island and other nearby localities in western Kenya, close to the early Miocene sites of Rusinga and Songhor. Some of the earliest specimens of true Old World monkeys are known from Maboko, as is a prosimian and several hominoids.[32]

Maboko occurs at the beginning of the middle Miocene, which lasts from about 16.5 Ma to about 11.5 Ma. Along with the early Miocene hominoids that persist at Maboko is a new type of hominoid. This form has thick enamel, like *Afropithecus* and *Sivapithecus*, but more modern looking molars, with less strongly developed cingula than in *Proconsul* and *Afropithecus*. It is most like *Kenyapithecus*, first described from the somewhat younger site of Fort Ternan, also in western Kenya.[33] *Kenyapithecus* is more advanced than early Miocene hominoids in molar morphology but retains many primitive features also found in *Proconsul*, both cranially and, especially, postcranially. However, one important set of differences in the postcranial anatomy of *Kenyapithecus* suggests that it may have been more terrestrial than most other hominoids. Certain characteristics of the shoulder joint in *Kenyapithecus* from Maboko are more like those of terrestrial monkeys such as baboons than are the shoulders of *Proconsul* and other hominoids.[34] The possibility of increased terrestriality in *Kenyapithecus* combined with its thickly enamelled molars suggests a greater dependence on terrestrial sources of food, which tend to contain more grit and therefore tend to wear teeth more rapidly. More will be known about the cranial and postcranial anatomy of *Kenyapithecus* when a large new sample from the Nachola area, west of Baragoi, in northern Kenya is analyzed.[35]

Dentally and postcranially similar hominoids are also known from Europe and Turkey at sites contemporaneous with Fort Ternan. The sites of Çandir and Pasalar, both in Turkey, Devinska Nová Ves (formerly Neudorf) in Slovakia, and Klein Hadersdorf in Austria, have produced cranial and postcranial remains very similar to those of Maboko and Fort Ternan.[36] These forms, called *Griphopithecus*,[37] may, together with *Kenyapithecus*, be the earliest members of the lineage that includes the living great apes and humans. However, the precise placement of this group of hominoids represents a major puzzle in hominoid evolutionary studies. *Griphopithecus* and *Kenyapithecus* have molars and premolars that look more like those of modern great apes than do those of early Miocene forms or those of hylobatids. Yet hylobatids and all late Miocene hominoids (discussed later) have postcranial attributes in common with great apes, all of which reflect the importance of suspensory postures in the trees.[38] So there is a conflict between the evidence for the limbs and the evidence of the teeth.

The earliest substantial evidence of modern hominoid cranial and postcranial anatomy comes at the end of the middle Miocene and the beginning of the late Miocene. In the early Miocene form *Proconsul*, aside from relatively subtle changes in fore and hindlimb anatomy and the less subtle absence of a tail,[39] modern hominoid postcranial anatomy is not present. At Moroto, a site in Uganda from the middle Miocene, about fourteen Ma,[40] a lumbar vertebra is known that looks more modern than any attributed to *Proconsul*, suggesting the presence of a great ape with a short, stiff lower back and a broader torso, like modern forms.[41] By the end of the middle Miocene and into the late Miocene, modern great ape anatomy becomes even more evident. Two forms appear at nearly the same time, one in South Asia (India and Pakistan) and one in Europe. The South Asian hominoid is *Sivapithecus*, and its European contemporary is *Dryopithecus*. *Sivapithecus* is known from many specimens from sites in the Potwar Plateau region of India and Pakistan.

The sample of *Sivapithecus* was formerly divided into several different forms (as discussed earlier) but is now universally accepted as two genera, *Gigantopithecus* for a small number of large to gigantic specimens and *Sivapithecus* for the vast majority of the material. *Sivapithecus* and *Gigantopithecus* are probably closely related to one another, based on considerable similarities in dental morphology.[42] But only *Sivapithecus* is well known from cranial and postcranial morphology, so I will focus on this form here. The face of *Sivapithecus*, known from several palatal specimens and a remarkably complete face, GSP 15,000, is extremely similar to the faces of modern orangs. This is true in details of the structure of the palate or upper jaw, the zygomatics or cheek bones, the orbits and the region between the orbits, and in the forehead or frontal bone. In fact, it was the discovery of GSP 15,000, more than any other development (discussed earlier), that convinced most paleoanthropologists that *Sivapithecus* was not a "dryopithecine" but an early member of the lineage of the orang.[43] Other discoveries of smaller jaws and teeth from the Potwar plateau convinced most researchers that Len Greenfield had been correct in recognizing that *Ramapithecus* was simply small individuals of *Sivapithecus*.[44] Greenfield concluded that specimens called *Ramapithecus* differed from *Sivapithecus* only in size and in having smaller canines with a different morphology. Because the canines of *Sivapithecus* all looked very similar to those of male great apes, and the canines of *Ramapithecus* all looked very much like those of female great apes, Greenfield concluded that all specimens of *Ramapithecus* were in fact females of *Sivapithecus*, the taxon that had been named first. With the publication of GSP 15,000 it became widely accepted that *Sivapithecus* (now including *Ramapithecus*) was a close relative of the orang, and had nothing directly to do with the origins of the human lineage.

The interpretation of *Dryopithecus* has also changed considerably due to new discoveries. *Dryopithecus* is now known from cranial and postcranial characteristics to be much more modern-looking than *Proconsul*, with which it was once grouped (see earlier discussion). Three partial crania and large numbers of jaws, teeth, and limb bones from various sites in Europe (see Table 6-1 on pages 71–72) show that *Dryopithecus* has characteristics of the palate, jaw joint, mid face, frontal, and braincase only found in African apes and humans, and one other Miocene hominoid, Ouranopithecus, from the late Miocene of Greece.[45]

Ouranopithecus is much larger than *Dryopithecus* and has many of the same features found in *Dryopithecus* but in exaggerated form. The Greek form also has many unique features of the face and teeth, and even shares a few traits, such as extremely thick enamel and very small canines, with early humans. Some have suggested that the similarities to humans indicate a close relationship,[46] while others have suggested close affinities to gorillas.[47] However, for a number of reasons, it appears more likely that the similarities to australopithecines occur convergently (that is, they were acquired independently), while the similarities to gorillas are superficial and based on the similar sizes of *Ouranopithecus* and gorillas.

If the characteristics that link *Dryopithecus* and *Ouranopithecus* to African apes and humans indicate a close evolutionary relationship, then these European forms may be more closely related to African apes and humans than are *Sivapithecus* and the orang. This is almost exactly the opposite of the interpretation of these genera thirty years ago, based on a smaller number of fossils, that linked a South Asian form to humans and linked *Dryopithecus* to a side branch of the great apes.

Dryopithecus and *Ouranopithecus* both have short faces and poorly developed brow ridges compared to African apes and fossil humans, but both are very similar to African apes and humans in the details of these areas. Given these differences, the view that *Dryopithecus* and *Ouranopithecus* are more closely related to African apes and humans than is *Sivapithecus* is controversial. *Sivapithecus*, after all, has an elongated premaxilla, the front part of the upper jaw, like all great apes, though it is structurally distinct from all but the orang. The issue will probably not really be resolved until African relatives of the African apes and humans are found in the time period between about ten to five Ma. If these relatives more closely resemble *Dryopithecus* and *Ouranopithecus*, which I consider more likely, the Asian forms would have branched off first. If the African relatives share a similar premaxilla with *Sivapithecus* and the orang, that would suggest the European forms diverged first.

Sivapithecus, *Ouranopithecus*, and *Dryopithecus* are all quite distinct from one another in the morphology of their jaws and teeth. *Dryopithecus* has more lightly built jaws and teeth with sharper, more pointy cusps, similar to modern chimps, which are frugivorous in their dietary preferences. *Sivapithecus* and *Ouranopithecus* have more massive jaws, and teeth with lower, more rounded cusps and thick layers of enamel, as in the more primitive forms *Kenyapithecus* and *Afropithecus*. In both forms this suggests the inclusion of harder, tougher, or more gritty objects in the diet, requiring higher bite forces to crack or deform, and/or thicker enamel in response to more rapid wear. These characteristics, which are present in early humans (australopithecines) as well, have also been interpreted as indications of a closer relationship to great apes and humans than to *Dryopithecus*. However, since similar anatomical characteristics also occur in the clearly more primitive early and middle Miocene forms, it seems more likely that these are simply traits that have changed relatively frequently during hominoid evolution. Even among australopithecines, other fossil humans, and modern great apes, the spectrum of jaw and teeth morphology is tremendous, and it is not obvious which type of morphology gave rise to which. In the final analysis, hominid jaw and tooth morphology are reliable indicators of diet, but not for reconstructing evolutionary relationships. In terms of the jaws and teeth, hominids are mostly what they eat.

The postcranial anatomy of *Dryopithecus* and *Sivapithecus* is not so well documented as in *Proconsul* (and is almost unknown for Ouranopithecus), but the forelimbs and feet are reasonably well known. Both taxa are modern hominoid-like in the morphology of their fingers and elbows, which indicate well developed suspensory capabilities and wide ranges of joint mobility with maximum stability.[48] Wrist and foot bones also indicate mobility of the type typical of modern hominoids, but most tend to retain certain characteristics of more primitive hominoids like *Proconsul*, suggesting that suspensory arboreality may not have been quite so well developed as in modern forms. The hamate, a bone of the wrist, is more similar to modern hominoids in *Dryopithecus* than in *Sivapithecus*, mostly due to the configuration of the hamate hook, which is more strongly developed in *Dryopithecus* and modern hominoids and is probably associated with more powerful wrist and finger flexion. The shaft of the humerus is also more like modern hominoids in *Dryopithecus*, being slightly curved backwards in side view.[49] This is also thought to be indicative of suspensory arboreality. In *Sivapithecus* the humeral shaft is bent forwards in side view and has very powerful attachment sites for the muscles of the shoulders.[50] This is most similar to large monkeys such as baboons, and may be related to more terrestriality in *Sivapithecus*. Both *Dryopithecus* and *Sivapithecus* were probably basically arboreal. *Dryopithecus* seems to have been more hominoid-like, being highly arboreal and suspensory, but also probably retained the monkey-like ability to walk atop the branches. *Sivapithecus* probably ventured to the ground more often, but did not knuckle-walk, as do the African apes when on the ground. Like *Dryopithecus*, *Sivapithecus* was also partly monkey-like, but more similar to terrestrial than arboreal monkeys.

Three other large bodied Miocene hominoids are known, but their relations to other Miocene forms and to living hominoids are even less clearly understood. *Otavipithecus* is only known from a single lower jaw fragment and a few limb bone fragments. It is of middle Miocene age, and shares characteristics with both early and middle Miocene forms. It is interesting that *Otavipithecus* comes from Namibia in southern Africa, and is the first Miocene hominoid from this far south.[51] The other two Miocene hominoids are from the late Miocene and are represented by very large samples of fossils, but remain poorly understood because of their unique combinations of anatomical features. These are *Oreopithecus* from the late Miocene of Italy and *Lufengpithecus* from the late Miocene of China. Both these forms existed between seven and eight Ma, and are the latest surviving Miocene hominoids, along with the last surviving populations of *Sivapithecus*.

Oreopithecus, from Monte Bamboli in Tuscany, is known from more post-crania than any other Miocene hominoid except *Proconsul*. Many jaws and teeth are also known, as are fragments of the cranium. *Oreopithecus* has been called a hominoid by some and a monkey by others.[52] Cranially, *Oreopithecus* is very primitive, with a short face, like gibbons and *Proconsul*, and a very small brain for its body size.[53] Dentally, *Oreopithecus* is highly specialized, with a unique combination of characteristics resembling both hominoids and Old World monkeys. It has small canines, like some hominids, but long teeth with very tall, transversely aligned, pointy cusps, like monkeys. Also like monkeys, their upper and lower molar teeth greatly resemble one another. The dentition of *Oreopithecus* is more functionally than structurally similar to that of Old World monkeys. Both morphologies are probably associated with folivory, or leaf eating, but the differences in the number and position of cusps and cutting ridges, or crests, in each indicate separate origins. Similar kinds of folivore-type teeth are also found in other primates such as New World Monkeys and prosimians.

The postcranial anatomy of *Oreopithecus* is another matter. Much of one skeleton of an *Oreopithecus* individual is known, and a number of isolated pieces from other individuals are known as well. These all indicate a highly advanced suspensory hominoid with forelimb adaptations to hanging and swinging below branches comparable to that of living apes.[54] It is clear that *Oreopithecus* was more advanced in modern hominoid-like postcranial anatomy and behavior than any other Miocene hominoid. More detailed analysis of the entire skeleton of *Oreopithecus* is necessary to reveal whether it is similar in most details to living hominoids, and therefore probably closely related to them, or whether it differs in a large enough number of structural details to suggest an independent evolution of suspensory behaviors in *Oreopithecus*, as seems to be the case with the dentition and diet.

Lufengpithecus is represented by over one thousand specimens, mostly individual teeth, but also several large cranial specimens and a small number of postcrania, from the site of Lufeng, in Yunnan Province, China.[55] The postcrania include scraps of forelimb material that appear to closely resemble great apes, much like *Dryopithecus* and *Sivapithecus*.[56] Not enough is known to determine what differences, if any, from great apes characterized the postcrania of *Lugfengpithecus*. The teeth of *Lufengpithecus* are very much like many hominids in overall morphology. The postcanine teeth are most like the orang, which, like *Lufengpithecus*, has wrinkled or crenulated enamel on its molars and premolars.[57] The incisors, however, are very similar to those of *Dryopithecus* and *Ouranopithecus* in being quite tall-crowned and narrow. Certain parts of the face, especially around the nose, eyes, and forehead, closely resemble *Sivapithecus* and the orang, while others, particularly the premaxilla and the space between the orbits, are very different from other Asian forms.[58] So *Lufengpithecus*, like *Oreopithecus*, presents an intriguing combination of characteristics from a diversity of hominoids, making the placement of both in the evolutionary framework of the Hominoidea very difficult at present.

CONCLUSIONS

The results of the past twenty-five years of research in Miocene hominoids has produced some dramatic changes in interpretations of hominoid evolution. Hominoid evolution is much more complicated than was once thought, with at least twenty-five different genera known from between about twenty to six Ma. This increase in recognized hominoid diversity may prompt cries of "splitting," but in fact is more in line with the known diversity of primates in other superfamilies, like Old World Monkeys (*Cercopithecoidea*) or New World Monkeys (*Ceboidea*). Living hominoids are but a mere shadow of the former diversity of this group.

Several trends are now apparent in hominoid evolution. Dietary changes are relatively subtle, and involve increased specialization of the front teeth (incisors and canines), probably to increase the ability to process a wider diversity of foods. Modern hominids use their front teeth as tools for removing the various protective coverings of the foods they consume. This ability seems to have developed in the late Miocene. A few hominoids, such as *Oreopithecus* and *Ouranopithecus*, became very specialized in their diets, with unusually enhanced folivore morphology in the former and with huge jaws and teeth suggesting enhanced omnivory in the latter. A more dramatic trend is in the evolution of positional behavior. Monkey-like above branch arboreality imposes limits on the size of animals living in the trees and the ease with which they can move within the canopy. Ape-like below branch arboreality and enhanced limb mobility allows access to smaller branches, where much of the food is. Larger animals have a more difficult time balancing above branches, but can remain in the trees if they can effectively position themselves below branches. The trend to below branch arboreality and increasing body size is apparent from more monkey-like *Proconsul* to more ape-like *Dryopithecus* and *Oreopithecus*. The late Miocene witnesses the appearance of many new and specialized forms of positional behavior. Although no living hominoid moves about in the same way as did any fossil form, all have much in common in their postcranial anatomy. This suggests that the changes in the postcranial skeleton of late Miocene hominoids was extremely successful and flexible, and has led to the development of such diverse patterns of positional behavior as brachiation, knuckle-walking, and bipedalism characteristic of modern hominoids.

The other major conclusion from recent research in Miocene hominoids concerns our understanding of the relations among living hominoids and the place humans occupy among them. There is now widespread agreement among morphologists and molecular systematists that humans are more closely related to African apes than either are to orangs. Furthermore, it is also becoming apparent that humans and African apes are very closely related to one another, such that the precise order in which each diverged from their common ancestor is very unclear. Molecular systematists have been saying with increased frequency that humans and chimps are most closely related among hominids,[59] though many continue to hold that it is just too close to call.[60] Most paleoanthropologists who focus on morphology believe that chimps and gorillas are closest, citing such specialized similarities as knuckle-walking and thinly enamelled teeth.[61] But as we have seen in this review, the significance of these characteristics is not so clear-cut. Enamel thickness is a poor indicator of evolutionary relationships because it changes so often in response to dietary requirements. Knuckle-walking, which is unique to African apes among living forms, is commonly considered to be a recent specialization of the African apes. A more controversial, but in my mind more likely, view is that knuckle-walking characterized our ancestors too. After all, humans do share unusual features of the hand and wrist only with African apes, such as fewer wrist bones, more stability of the joints of the wrist, and shorter hand and finger bones. One real possibility is that humans retain these characteristics because we evolved from a knuckle-walker that needed them to ensure wrist and hand stability while walking on the knuckles. When humans shifted to two feet we lost many features still found in knuckle-walkers, while others were suitable to the tasks important to early bipeds, such as enhanced manipulation.

If humans evolved from knuckle-walkers, a strong possibility given that all three of the closest relatives of humans (chimps, gorillas, and bonobos) are still knuckle-walkers, this tells us something about the history of human descent from the trees. Humans apparently went through a two step process, first becoming sometime terrestrial knuckle-walkers, like living African apes, and then committing themselves more completely to the ground. As knuckle-walkers, the common ancestors of chimps and humans probably exploited resources similar to those exploited by living chimps today. Living chimps and humans still exploit the greatest range of resources of any primate; they are able to range over long distances and in diverse habitats, and they can to use tools to help process foods that would otherwise be unavailable to them. Humans probably diverged from chimps when they became committed to the more completely open ecology of the grassland, requiring a more efficient mode of long distance terrestrial locomotion (bipedalism) and perhaps also an enhanced ability to manipulate the environment with their hands, which bipedalism made possible. These positional changes, which are apparent in the very first humans, *Ardipithecus ramidus*,[62] precede most other changes that today separate humans from other animals. The brain, for example, changed very little, at least in external morphology and relative size, until comparatively late in human evolution, after the appearance of the genus *Homo*. Obligate terrestriality was really the major impetus in human origins, and it appears to have a long history going back to our common ancestors with the African apes. Research on Miocene hominoids has produced many new insights into human evolution in the past twenty years, and we can expect many more in the years to come. Much new fossil material is already known and is being studied. These new data will provide grist for the mill in the continuing endeavor to unravel the mystery of human origins.

Notes

1. Elwyn L. Simons and David R. Pilbeam, "Preliminary Revision of the Dryopithecinae (Pongidae, Anthropoidea)," *Folia Primatologica* 3 (1965): 81–152.
2. Thomas H. Huxley, *Evidence as to Man's Place in Nature* (London: Williams and Norgate, 1863).
3. David R. Pilbeam, "Tertiary Pongidae of East Africa: Evolutionary Relationships and Taxonomy," *Peabody Museum of Natural History* 31 (1969): 1–185.
4. Eduard Lartet, "Note sur un grand singe fossile qui se rattache au groupe des singes superieurs," *Comptes Rendus de l'Academie de Sciences* 43 (1856): 219–223.
5. Guy E. Pilgrim, "New Siwalik Primates and Their Bearing on the Question of the Evolution of Man and the Anthropoidea," *Records of the Geologica Survey of India* 45 (1916): 1–74; A. T. Hopwood, "Miocene Primates from Kenya," *Zoological Journal of the Linnean Society* 38 (1935): 437–464.
6. Simons and Pilbeam, "Preliminary Revision of the Dryopithecinae (Pongidae, Anthropoidea)," pp. 81–152.
7. G. H. F. Nutall, *Blood Immunity and Blood Relationships* (London: Cambridge University Press, 1904).
8. Vincent M. Sarich and Alan C. Wilson, "Immunological Time-Scale for Hominoid Evolution," *Science* 158 (1967): 1200–1203; Morris Goodman, "Man's Place in the Phylogeny of the Primates as Reflected in Serum Proteins," in Sherwood L. Washburn, ed., *Classification and Human Evolution* (Chicago: Aldine Press, 1963), pp. 204–234; Morris Goodman, "The Chronicle of Primate Phylogeny Contained in Proteins," *Symposia of the Zoological Society of London* 33 (1973): 339–375.
9. Sarich and Wilson, "Immunological Time-Scale for Hominoid Evolution."
10. Jonathan Marks, "Genetic Relationships among the Apes and Humans," *Current Opinion in Genetics and Development* 2 (1992): 883–889; Jonathan Marks, C. W. Schmid, and V. M. Sarich, "DNA Hybridization as a Guide to Phylogeny: Relations of the Hominoidea," *Journal of Human Evolution* 17 (1988): 769–786; J. Rogers, "The Phylogenetic Relationships among *Homo, Pan,* and *Gorilla*: A Population Genetics Perspective," *Journal of Human Evolution* 25 (1993): 201–216; Goodman, "The Chronicle of Primate Phylogeny Contained in Proteins"; Morris Goodman, B. F. Koop, J. Czelusniak, D. H. A. Fitch, D. A. Tagel, and J. L. Slightom, "Molecular Phylogeny of the Family of Apes and Humans," *Genome* 31 (1989): 316–335; S. Horai, Y. Satta, K. Hayasaka, R. Kondo, T. Inoue, T. Ishida, S. Hayashi, and N. Takahata, "Man's Place in Hominoidea Revealed by Mitochondrial DNA Genealogy," *Journal of Molecular Evolution* 34 (1992): 32–43; B. F. Koop, D. A. Tagel, M. Goodman, and J. L. Slightom, "A Molecular View of Primate Phylogeny and Important Systematic and Evolutionary Questions," *Molecular Biology and Evolution* 6 (1989): 580–612; M. Ruvolo, "Molecular Evolutionary Processes and Conflicting Gene Trees: The Hominoid Case," *American Journal of Physical Anthropology* 94 (1994): 89–113.

11. W. Hennig, *Phylogenetic Systematics* (Chicago: University of Illinois Press, 1966).

12. Daniel R. Brooks and Deborah A. McClennan, *Phylogeny, Ecology, and Behavior* (Chicago: University of Chicago Press, 1991); E. O. Wiley, D. J. Siegel-Causey, D. R. Brooks, and V. A. Funk, *The Compleat Cladist: A Primer of Phylogenetic Procedures* (Lawrence: Museum of Natural History, University of Kansas, 1989).

13. Martin Pickford, "Geochronology of the Hominoidea: A Summary," in J. G. Else and P. C. Lee, eds., *Primate Evolution* (Cambridge: Cambridge University Press, 1986), pp. 123–128.

14. Peter Andrews, "A Revision of the Miocene Hominoidea from East Africa," *Bulletin of the British Museum of Natural History (Geology)* 30, no. 2 (1978): 85–224; Terry Harrison, "The Phylogenetic Relationships of the Early Catarrhine Primates: A Review of the Current Evidence," *Journal of Human Evolution* 16 (1987): 41–80.

15. Alan Walker and Mark F. Teaford, "The Hunt for Proconsul," *Scientific American* 260 (1989): 76–82.

16. Michael D. Rose, "Miocene Hominoid Postcranial Morphology: Monkey-Like, Ape-Like, Neither, or Both?" in Russel L. Ciochon and Robert S. Corruccini, eds., *New Interpretations of Ape and Human Ancestry* (New York: Plenum, 1983), pp. 405–417; Alan C. Walker and Martin Pickford, "New Postcranial Fossils of *Proconsul Africanus* and *Proconsul Nyanzae*," in Russel L. Ciochon and Robert S. Corruccini, eds., *New Interpretations of Ape and Human Ancestry* (New York: Plenum, 1983), pp. 325–351.

17. K. Christopher Beard, Mark F. Teaford, and Alan Walker, "New Wrist Bones of *Proconsul Africanus* and *Proconsul Nyanzae* from Rusinga Island, Kenya," *Folia Primatologica* 47 (1986): 97–118; Michael D. Rose, "Kinematics of the Trapezium-1st Metacarpal Joint in Extant Anthropoids and Miocene Hominoids," *Journal of Human Evolution* 22 (1992): 255–266; David R. Begun, Mark F. Teaford, and Alan Walker, "Comparative and Functional Anatomy of *Proconsul* Phalanges from the Kaswanga Primate Site, Rusinga Island, Kenya," *Journal of Human Evolution* 26 (1994): 89–165.

18. Carol V. Ward, Alan Walker, Mark Teaford, and Isiah Odhiambo, "A Partial Skeleton of *Proconsul Nyanzae* from Mfangano Island, Kenya," *American Journal of Physical Anthropology* 90 (1993): 77–111; Begun, Teaford, and Walker, "Comparative and Functional Anatomy of *Proconsul* Phalanges from the Kaswanga Primate Site, Rusinga Island, Kenya."

19. Carol V. Ward, Alan Walker, and Mark Teaford, "*Proconsul* Did Not Have a Tail," *Journal of Human Evolution* 21 (1991): 215–220.

20. Peter Andrews and Lawrence Martin, "Hominoid Dietary Evolution," *Philosophical Transactions of the Royal Society of London B* 334 (1991): 199–209.

21. Mark F. Teaford and Alan Walker, "Quantitative Differences in the Dental Microwear between Primates with Different Diets and a Comment on the Presumed Diet of *Sivapithecus*," *American Journal of Physical Anthropology* 64 (1984): 191–200.

22. W. E. Le Gros Clark and Louis S. B. Leakey, "The Miocene Hominoidea of East Africa," in *Fossil Mammals of Africa* (London: The British Museum of Natural History, 1951); Walker and Pickford, "New Postcranial Fossils of *Proconsul Africanus* and *Proconsul Nyanzae*"; Dean Falk, "A Reconsideration of the Endocast of *Proconsul Africanus*: Implications for Primate Brain Evolution," in Russel L. Ciochon and Robert S. Corruccini, eds., *New Interpretations of Ape and Human Ancestry* (New York: Plenum, 1983), pp. 239–248; Alan Walker, Dean Falk, Richard Smith, and

Martin Pickford, "The Skull of *Proconsul Africanus*: Reconstruction and Cranial Capacity," *Nature* (October 6, 1983): 525–527.

23. Richard E. F. Leakey, Meave G. Leakey, and Alan Walker, "Morphology of *Afropithecus Turkanensis* from Kenya," *American Journal of Physical Anthropology* 76 (1988): 289–307; Richard E. F. Leakey, Meave G. Leakey, and Alan Walker, "Morphology of *Turkanopithecus Kalakolensis* from Kenya," *American Journal of Physical Anthropology* 76 (1988): 277–288; Richard E. F. Leakey and Meave G. Leakey, "A New Miocene Small-Bodied Ape from Kenya," *Journal of Human Evolution* 16 (1989): 369–387.

24. Peter J. Andrews and Lawrence Martin, "The Phyletic Position of the Ad Dabtiyah Hominoid," *Bulletin of the British Museum of Natural History* 41 (1987): 383–393.

25. Leakey and Leakey, "A New Miocene Small-Bodied Ape from Kenya"; Michael D. Rose, Meave G. Leakey, Richard E. F. Leakey, and Alan C. Walker, "Postcranial Specimens of *Simiolus Enjiessi* and Other Primitive Catarrhines from the Early Miocene of Lake Turkana, Kenya," *Journal of Human Evolution* 22 (1992): 171–237.

26. Leakey, Leakey, and Walker, "Morphology of *Turkanopithecus Kalakolensis* from Kenya."

27. Elwyn L. Simons, "New Fossil Apes from Egypt and the Initial Differentiation of Hominoidea," *Nature* 205 (1965): 135–139; John G. Fleagle and Richard F. Kay, "New Interpretations of the Phyletic Position of Oligocene Hominoids," in Russel L. Ciochon and Robert S. Corruccini, eds., *New Interpretations of Ape and Human Ancestry* (New York: Plenum, 1983), pp. 181–210.

28. Leakey, Leakey, and Walker, "Morphology of *Afropithecus Turkanensis* from Kenya"; Meave G. Leakey, Richard E. F. Leakey, Joan T. Richtsmeier, Elwyn L. Simons, and Alan Walker, "Similarities in *Aegyptopithecus* and *Afropithecus* Facial Morphology," *Folia Primatologica* 56 (1991): 65–85.

29. Andrews and Martin, "Hominoid Dietary Evolution."

30. Carol V. Ward, "Torso Morphology and Locomotion in *Proconsul Nyanzae*," *American Journal of Physical Anthropology* 92 (1993): 291–328.

31. Raymond L. Bernor, Lawrence J. Flynn, Terry Harrison, S. Taseer Hussain, and Jay Kelley, "*Dionysopithecus* from Southern Pakistan and the Biochronology and Biogeography of Early Eurasian Catarrhines," *Journal of Human Evolution* 17 (1988): 339–358.

32. Monte L. McCrossin and Brenda R. Benefit, "Recently Recovered *Kenyapithecus* Mandible and Its Implications for Great Ape and Human Origins," *Proc. National Academy of Science* 90 (1993): 1962–1966.

33. Louis S. B. Leakey, "A New Lower Pliocene Fossil Primate from Kenya," *Annual Magazine of Natural History* 13 (1962): 689–696.

34. Brenda R. Benefit and Monte L. McCrossin, "New *Kenyapithecus* Postcrania and other Primate Fossils from Maboko Island, Kenya," *American Journal of Physical Anthropology Supplement* 16 (1993): 55.

35. H. Ishida, M. Pickford, H. Nakaya, and Y. Nakano, "Fossil Anthropoids from Nachola and Samburu Hills, Samburu District, Northern Kenya," *African Study Monographs Supplementary Issue* 2 (1984): 73–85.

36. David R. Begun, "Phyletic Diversity and Locomotion in Primitive European Hominids," *American Journal of Physical Anthropology* 87 (1992): 311–340; Berna Alpagut, Peter Andrews, and Lawrence Martin, "New Miocene Hominoid Specimens

from the Middle Miocene Site at Pa-alar," *Journal of Human Evolution* 19 (1990): 397–422; Peter Andrews and Hans Tobien, "New Miocene Locality in Turkey with Evidence on the Origin of *Ramapithecus* and *Sivapithecus*," *Nature* 268 (1977): 699–701.

37. O. Abel, "Zwei neue menschenaffen aus den leithakalkbildingen des Wiener Bekkens," *Sitzungsberichte der Akademie der Wissenschaften Wien, mathematisch-naturwissenschaftliche Klasse III, Abteilung* 1 (1902): 1171–1207; Begun, "Phyletic Diversity and Locomotion in Primitive European Hominids."

38. Rose, "Miocene Hominoid Postcranial Morphology: Monkey-Like, Ape-Like, Neither, or Both?"; Michael D. Rose, "Another Look at the Anthropoid Elbow," *Journal of Human Evolution* 17 (1983): 193–224; Begun, "Phyletic Diversity and Locomotion in Primitive European Hominids."

39. Ward, Walker, and Teaford, "*Proconsul* Did Not Have a Tail."

40. D. Allbrook and William W. Bishop, "New Fossil Hominoid Material from Uganda," *Nature* 197 (1963): 1187–1190; William W. Bishop, J. A. Miller, and F. J. Fitch, "New Potassium-Argon Age Determinations Relevant to the Miocene Fossil Mammal Sequence in East Africa," *American Journal of Science* 267 (1969): 669–699.

41. Ward, "Torso Morphology and Locomotion in *Proconsul Nyanzae*."

42. Jay Kelley and David Pilbeam, "The Dryopithecines: Taxonomy, Comparative Anatomy, and Phylogeny of Miocene Large Hominoids," in Daris R. Swindler and J. Erwin, eds., *Comparative Primate Biology, vol. 1: Systematics, Evolution, and Anatomy* (New York: Alan R. Liss, 1986), pp. 361–411.

43. David R. Pilbeam, "New Hominoid Skull Material from the Miocene of Pakistan," *Nature* 295 (1982): 232–234.

44. Leonard O. Greenfield, "On the Adaptive Pattern of *Ramapithecus*," *American Journal of Physical Anthropology* 50 (1979): 527–548.

45. David R. Begun, "Miocene Fossil Hominids and the Chimp-Human Clade," *Science* 257 (1992): 1929–1933.

46. Louis de Bonis and George Koufos, "The Face and Mandible of *Ouranopithecus Macedoniensis*: Description of New Specimens and Comparisons," *Journal of Human Evolution* 24 (1993): 469–491.

47. David Dean and Eric Delson, "Second Gorilla or Third Chimp?" *Nature* 359 (1992): 676–677.

48. Rose, "Miocene Hominoid Postcranial Morphology: Monkey-Like, Ape-Like, Neither, or Both?"; Rose, "Another Look at the Anthropoid Elbow"; Mary E. Morbeck, "Miocene Hominoid Discoveries from Rudabánya: Implications from the Postcranial Skeleton," in Russel L. Ciochon and Robert S. Corruccini, eds., *New Interpretations of Ape and Human Ancestry* (New York: Plenum, 1983), pp. 369–404; Begun, "Phyletic Diversity and Locomotion in Primitive European Hominids."

49. Begun, "Phyletic Diversity and Locomotion in Primitive European Hominids."

50. David R. Pilbeam, Michael D. Rose, John C. Barry, and S. M. I. Shah, "New *Sivapithecus Humeri* from Pakistan and the Relationship of *Sivapithecus* and Pongo," *Nature* 348 (1990): 237–239.

51. Glenn C. Conroy, Martin Pickford, Brigitte Senut, and John Van Couvering, "*Otavipithecus Namibiensis*, First Miocene Hominoid from Southern Africa," *Nature* 356 (1992): 144–148; Glenn C. Conroy, Martin Pickford, Brigitte Senut, and Pierre Mein, "Additional Miocene Primates from the Otavi Mountains, Namibia," *Comptes Rendus de l'Academie de Science Paris Serie II* 317 (1993): 987–990.

52. Terry Harrison, "A Reassessment of the Phylogenetic Relationships of *Oreopithecus Bambolii*," *Journal of Human Evolution* 15 (1987): 541–583; Fredrick Szalay and Eric Delson, *Evolutionary History of the Primates* (New York: Academic Press, 1979).

53. Terry Harrison, "New Estimates of Cranial Capacity, Body Size, and Encephalization in *Oreopithecus Bambolii*," *American Journal of Physical Anthropology* 78 (1989): 237.

54. Estaban E. Sarmiento, "The Phylogenetic Position of *Oreopithecus* and Its Significance in the Origin of the Hominoidea," *American Museum Novitates* 2881 (1987): 1–44.

55. R. Wu, "A Revision of the Classification of the Lufeng Great Apes," *Acta Anthropologica Sinica* 6 (1987): 265–271.

56. Yipu Lin, Shangzun Wang, Zhihui Gao, and Lidai Zhang, "The First Discovery of the Radius of *Sivapithecus Lufengensis* in China," *Geological Review* 33 (1977): 1–4.

57. Kelley and Pilbeam, "The Dryopithecines: Taxonomy, Comparative Anatomy, and Phylogeny of Miocene Large Hominoids."

58. Jeffery H. Schwartz, "*Lufengpithecus* and Its Potential Relationship to an Orang-Utan Clade," *Journal of Human Evolution* 19 (1990): 591–605.

59. Brooks and McClennan, *Phylogeny, Ecology, and Behavior*; Wiley, Siegel-Causey, Brooks, Funk, *The Compleat Cladist: A Primer of Phylogenetic Procedures*.

60. Hennig, *Phylogenetic Systematics*.

61. Peter Andrews, "Evolution and Environment in the Hominoidea," *Nature* 360 (1992): 641–646.

62. Tim White, Gen Sowa, and Berhane Asfaw, "*Australopithecus ramidus*, a New Species of Early Hominid from Aramis, Ethiopia," *Nature* 375 (1995): 88.

SUGGESTED READINGS

Andrews, Peter. "A Revision of the Miocene Hominoidea from East Africa." *Bulletin of the British Museum of Natural History (Geology)* 30, no. 2 (1978): 85–224. The most recent and comprehensive revision of the early Miocene Hominoidea. Now substantially out of date in details of taxonomy, it remains a very useful reference for early Miocene hominoid anatomy and diversity.

Andrews, Peter. "Evolution and Environment in the Hominoidea." *Nature* 360 (1992): 641–646. A summary and synthesis by one of the leading authorities in Miocene hominoid studies. One of several papers presenting different views of the Miocene.

Begun, David R. "Relations among the Great Apes and Humans: New Interpretations Based on the Fossil Great Ape *Dryopithecus*." *Yearbook of Physical Anthropology* 37 (1994). A recent interpretation of the relations among Miocene and recent hominoids.

Harrison, Terry. "The Phylogenetic Relationships of the Early Catarrhine Primates: A Review of the Current Evidence." *Journal of Human Evolution* 16 (1987): 41–80. A comprehensive summary and synthesis of relations among early Miocene apes.

Kelley, Jay, and David Pilbeam. "The *Dryopithecines*: Taxonomy, Comparative Anatomy, and Phylogeny of Miocene Large Hominoids." In Daris R. Swindler and J. Erwin, eds. *Comparative Primate Biology, vol. 1: Systematics, Evolution, and Anatomy.* New York: Alan R. Liss, 1986, pp. 361–411. A recent survey of large Miocene hominoids, with particular attention focussed on *Sivapithecus*.

Walker, Alan, and Mark F. Teaford, "The Hunt for *Proconsul*." *Scientific American* 260 (1989): 76–82. A different interpretation of the relations of *Proconsul*, with interesting details of the behavior and biology of this fossil form.

CHIMPANZEE HUNTING BEHAVIOR
AND HUMAN EVOLUTION

CRAIG B. STANFORD

In a forest in Tanzania in East Africa, a group of a dozen chimpanzees is travelling along the forest floor, stopping occasionally to scan the trees overhead for ripe fruit. The group is composed of five adult males weighing nearly one hundred pounds each, plus several females and their offspring. They come upon a tree holding a group of red colobus monkeys; these are long-tailed leaf-eating monkeys weighing about twenty-five pounds each. This group has twenty-five members, about average for the species in this forest. The male chimpanzees scan the colobus group looking for immature animals or mothers carrying small babies. The colobus, meanwhile, have heard the pant-hoot calls of the chimpanzees approaching for the past several minutes and have gathered up their offspring and positioned themselves in order to defend against a possible attack.

The chimpanzees do indeed attack, the five males—Frodo, Goblin, Freud, Prof, and Wilkie—climbing the larger limbs of the tree. They meet the male colobus, who have descended to counterattack their potential predators. In spite of repeated lunges by the chimpanzees against the colobus group, they are turned back by the colobus' aggressive defense; at one point two male colobus even leap onto Frodo's back, trying to bite him as he runs along a tree limb, hurling them off. In the end, however, the chimpanzees prevail; Frodo scatters the male colobus and manages to pluck a newborn infant off of its mother's belly. Some of the chimpanzees continue hunting, while others gather around Frodo, begging with extended hands for scraps of meat from the baby colobus' tiny carcass. Frodo offers bits of meat to his allies and to females with whom he has a close relationship; rivals, however, are denied meat. Meanwhile, the other hunters capture the mother of the baby, who has strayed too close in her effort to rescue her now-consumed infant and has fallen from the tree to the forest floor. The mother is grabbed by a young chimpanzee, Pax, and flailed against the tree trunk until nearly dead. The alpha (dominant) male,

Wilkie, promptly steals the prey from Pax, however, and a number of females and juveniles crowd around him. An hour later, the last strands of colobus meat, bone, and skin are still being consumed amid occasional outbursts of aggression by individuals who have not received the meat they desired.

THE SIGNIFICANCE OF CHIMPANZEE HUNTING BEHAVIOR TO HUMAN EVOLUTIONARY RESEARCH

Two of the most important and intriguing questions in human evolution are when and why meat became an important part of the diet of our ancestors. Physical anthropologists and archaeologists try to answer these questions using a number of techniques. The presence of primitive stone tools in the fossil record tells us that 2.5 million years ago, early hominids were using stone implements to cut the flesh off the bones of large animals that they had either hunted or whose carcasses they had scavenged.[1] The pattern of obtaining and processing meat by more recent people has been studied by examining archaeological sites in Europe and elsewhere,[2] and also by studying the hunting and meat-eating behavior of modern foraging people, the so-called hunter-gatherers.[3]

Earlier than 2.5 million years ago, however, we know very little about the foods that the early hominids ate or the role that meat may have played in their diet. We know that the earliest upright-walking (bipedal) hominids, currently classified as *Australopithecines*, evolved in Africa about five million years ago, and that they shared a common ancestor with modern chimpanzees before that time. Modern people and chimpanzees share an estimated 98.5 percent of the DNA sequence, making them more closely related to each other than either is to any other animal species.[4] Therefore, understanding chimpanzee hunting behavior and ecology may tell us a great deal about the behavior and ecology of those earliest hominids. This is the approach I have taken in my field study of the hunting behavior of wild chimpanzees; I especially focus on their relationship with the animal that is their major prey, the red colobus monkey. I am trying to answer the following questions:

1. What are the social and ecological factors that predict when chimpanzees will hunt and whether they will be successful?
2. What is the effect of chimpanzee predation on the populations of their prey animals, such as the red colobus?
3. What are the likely similarities in meat-eating patterns between chimpanzees and the earliest hominids?

In the early 1960s, when Dr. Jane Goodall began her now-famous study of the chimpanzees of Gombe National Park, Tanzania, it was thought that chimpanzees were strictly vegetarian. In fact, when Goodall first reported this behavior, many people were skeptical or claimed that meat was not a natural part of the chimpanzee diet. Today, hunting by chimpanzees at Gombe has been well documented.[5] Hunting has also been observed at other sites in Africa where chimpanzees have been studied, such as Mahale Mountains National Park,[6] also in Tanzania, and Taï National Park in Ivory Coast in West Africa.[7] At Gombe, we now know that each year chimpanzees may kill and eat more than 150 small and medium-sized animals, such as monkeys, wild pigs, and small antelopes. Because of the complex fission-fusion nature of chimpanzee society, in which there are no stable groups, only temporary subgroupings called parties that congregate and separate throughout the day, the size and membership of hunting parties vary greatly, from a single chimpanzee to as many as thirty-five. The hunting abilities of the party members, as well as the number of hunters present, can thus influence when a party hunts as well as whether it will succeed in catching a colobus.

STUDYING CHIMPANZEE HUNTING BEHAVIOR

Studying the relationship between predators and prey of any two species is always difficult, because in order to observe hunts the researcher must accustom both the hunter and the prey to his or her presence. Because the chimpanzees of Gombe are thoroughly used to being followed throughout the day by human researchers, habituating the predators to my presence was not a problem; it has been a slower process, though, to accustom two colobus groups that inhabit the territory of the Gombe chimpanzees to human observers. In addition, chimpanzees do not usually hunt every day and sometimes two weeks will pass without any hunting. During each week in the field, I follow chimpanzee parties in the hope of seeing a hunt and also observe any of several colobus groups that may become the targets of hunts. While this may sound like a chancy way to observe a hunt, in practice it has worked very well. At least one party of chimpanzees at Gombe is followed daily by researchers; at the end of each day, the chimpanzees build leafy nests in trees where they will sleep for the night. The following morning they will often head off together, giving loud pant-hoot calls as they travel. These calls allow me to hike early in the morning to a high point in the valley above the chimpanzees' sleeping trees to listen for the direction in which they are moving. I can then walk to any colobus group that I know to be in the path taken by the chimpanzees in order to reach the colobus before the chimpanzees do. In this way I have been able to observe and record nearly one hundred encounters between chimpanzee foraging parties and colobus (from the perspective of the colobus prey) and watch the colobus' reaction to the approach of potential predators. Early morning, therefore, frequently finds me sitting atop a high point in Kakombe Valley (one of the main valleys used by the chimpanzees) called the peak. It was from this point that Jane Goodall made many of her important early observations of chimpanzee behavior many years ago, and it has served me well in my own research. It is also a beautiful vantage point for seeing the whole valley and the animals that inhabit it: chimpanzee, colobus and other monkeys, eagles soaring past, and sometimes a shy bushbuck antelope. As the chimpanzee parties around the valley awake at dawn and set off on their day of travel and feeding, they usually pant-hoot, and this tells me their direction of travel and the likelihood of their meeting a colobus group.

WHAT IS CHIMPANZEE PREDATORY BEHAVIOR?

After three decades of research on the hunting behavior of chimpanzees at Gombe and elsewhere, we already know a great deal about their predatory patterns. We know that, although chimpanzees have been recorded to eat more than twenty-five types of vertebrate animals,[8] the most important vertebrate prey species in their diet is the red colobus monkey. At Gombe, red colobus account for more than 80 percent of the prey items eaten. But Gombe chimpanzees do not randomly select the colobus they will kill; infant and juvenile colobus are caught in greater proportion than their availability[9]—75 percent of all colobus killed are immature. Chimpanzees are largely fruit eaters, and meat-eating comprises only about 3 percent of the time they spend eating overall. Adult and adolescent males do most of the hunting, making about 90 percent of the kills recorded at Gombe over the past decade. Females also hunt, though more often they receive a share of meat from the male who either captured the meat or stole it from the captor.

One of the main recent findings about hunting by Gombe chimpanzees is its seasonality.[10] Nearly 40 percent of the kills of colobus monkeys occur in the dry season months of August and September. At Gombe, it appears that this is a time of food shortage, since the chimpanzees' body weights decline.[11] Here, the killing is actually less strongly seasonal than in the Mahale Mountains, where 60 percent of kills occur in a two-month period in the early wet season. Why would chimpanzees hunt more often in some months than in others? This is an important question, because studies of early hominid diets have shown that meat-eating occurred most often in the dry season, at the same time that Gombe chimpanzees are eating most of their meat. And the amount of meat eaten, even though it composed a small percentage of the chimpanzee diet, is substantial. I estimate that in some years the forty-five chimpanzees of the main study community at Gombe kill and consume more than 1,500 pounds of prey animals of all species. This is far more than most previous estimates of the weight of live animals eaten by chimpanzees. A large proportion of this amount is eaten in the dry season months of August and September. In fact, during the peak dry season months, the estimated per capita meat intake is about sixty-five grams of meat per day for each adult chimpanzee. This approaches the meat intake by the members of some human foraging societies in the lean months of the year. Chimpanzee dietary strategies may thus approximate those of human hunter-gatherers to a greater degree than we had imagined.

Several other aspects of hunting by Gombe chimpanzees are noteworthy. First, although most successful hunts result in a kill of a single colobus monkey, in some hunts from two to seven colobus may be killed. The likelihood of such a multiple kill is tied directly to the number of hunters in the hunting party. Interestingly, the percentage of kills that are multiple kills rose markedly in the late 1980s and early 1990s, which in turn meant that many more colobus, overall, were being eaten in the late 1980s compared to five years earlier.[12] This is most likely due to changes in the age and sex composition of the chimpanzee community. The number of adult and adolescent male chimpanzees in the study community rose from five to twelve over the 1980s due to a large number of young males who were maturing and taking their places in hunting parties. One could therefore say that the fate of the Gombe red colobus monkeys is in the hands of the chimpanzee population; this is reflected in the colobus mortality rate in relation to the number of hunters available in a given era.

Although both male and female chimpanzees sometimes hunt by themselves, most hunts are social. In other species of hunting animals, cooperation among hunters may lead to greater success rates, thus promoting the evolution of cooperative behavior. Such cooperation has also been posited as important in our own evolution.[13] Whether or not chimpanzee hunters cooperate is a question that has been debated, and the degree of cooperative hunting may differ from one forest to another.[14] In the Taï forest in the Ivory Coast, Christophe Boesch has documented highly cooperative hunting behavior and meat-sharing behavior after a kill that rewards those chimpanzees who participated in the hunt.[15] The highly integrated action by Taï hunters has never been seen at Gombe. In both Gombe and Taï, however, there is a strong positive relationship between the number of hunters and the odds of a successful hunt.[16] This points out the difficulty of interpreting cooperative behavior; even though Gombe hunters do not seem to cooperate, the greater success rate when more hunters are present suggests that some cooperation is occurring. We are still looking for measures of cooperation that can distinguish true cooperation from hunts in which some chimpanzees hunt and others follow along hoping to capitalize on the efforts of others.

Throughout years of research, Jane Goodall noted that the Gombe chimpanzees displayed a tendency to go on "hunting crazes," during which they would hunt almost daily and kill large numbers of monkeys and other prey.[17] The explanations for such binges have always been unclear. My own research has focused on the causes for such spurts in hunting frequency, with unexpected results. The explanation for sudden changes in frequency seems to be related to whatever factors promote hunting itself; when such factors are present to a high degree or for an extended period of time, frequent hunting occurs. For example, the most intense hunting binge we have seen occurred in the dry season of 1990. From late June through early September, a period of sixty-eight days, the chimpanzees were observed killing seventy-one colobus monkeys in forty-seven hunts. It is important to note that this is the observed total, and the actual total of kills, which includes hunts at which no human observer was present, may be one-third greater. During this time the chimpanzees thus may have killed more than 10 percent of the entire colobus population within their hunting range.[18]

To try to solve the binge question my colleagues and I examined the enormous database of hunts recorded by field assistants over the past decade to see what social or environmental factors coincided with the hunting binges. Knowing that hunting was seasonal helped, in that I expected binges to occur mainly in the dry season, which was indeed the case. But other interesting correlations leapt out as well. Periods of intense hunting tended to be times when the size of chimpanzee foraging parties was very large; this corresponded to the direct relationship between party size and both hunting frequency and success rate. Additionally, hunting binges occurred especially when there were female chimpanzees with sexual swellings (the large pink anogenital swellings that females exhibit during their periods of sexual receptivity, or estrus) travelling with the hunting party. When one or more swollen females was present, the odds of a hunt occurring were substantially greater, independent of other factors. This co-occurrence of party size, presence of swollen females, and hunting frequency led me to ask the basic question, "Why do chimpanzees hunt?"

WHY DO CHIMPANZEES HUNT?

Among the great apes (the gorilla, orangutan, bonobo, and chimpanzee) and ourselves, only humans and chimpanzees hunt and eat meat on a frequent basis. Since neither humans nor chimpanzees are truly carnivorous—most traditional human societies eat a diet made up mostly of plant foods—we are considered omnivores. Therefore, the important decisions about what to eat and when to eat it should be based on the nutritional costs and benefits of obtaining that food compared to the essential nutrients that the food provides. However, as I discussed previously, there are social influences, such as party size and composition, that also seem to play an important role in mediating hunting behavior. Understanding when and why chimpanzees choose to undertake a hunt of colobus monkeys rather than simply continue to forage for fruits and leaves—even though the hunt involves risk of injury from colobus canine teeth and a substantial risk of failure to catch anything—is a major goal of my research.

In his study of Gombe chimpanzee predatory behavior in the 1960s, Geza Teleki considered hunting to have a strong social basis.[19] Some early researchers proposed that hunting by chimpanzees might be a form of social display, in which a male chimpanzee tries to show his prowess to other members of the community.[20] In the 1970s Richard Wrangham conducted the first systematic study of Gombe chimpanzee behavioral ecology and concluded that predation by chimpanzees was nutritionally based, but that some aspects of the behavior were not well explained by nutritional needs alone.[21] More recently, Toshisada Nishida and his colleagues in the Mahale Mountains chimpanzee research project reported that the alpha there, Ntilogi, used captured meat as a political tool to withhold from rivals and dole out to allies.[22] And William McGrew has shown that those female Gombe chimpanzees who receive generous shares of meat after a kill have more surviving offspring, indicating a reproductive benefit from hunting.[23]

My own preconception was that hunting must be nutritionally based. After all, meat from monkeys and other prey would be a package of protein, fat, and calories hard to equal in any plant food. I therefore examined the relationship between the odds of success and the amount of meat available with different numbers of hunters in relation to each hunter's expected payoff in meat obtained. That is, when is the time, energy, and risk (the costs) involved in hunting worth the potential benefits, and, therefore, when should a chimpanzee decide to join or not to join a hunting party? And how does it compare to the costs and benefits of foraging for plant foods? Because of the difficulty in learning the nutritional components of the many plant foods in the chimpanzees' diverse diet, these analyses are still underway. But the preliminary results are surprising. I expected that as the number of hunters increased, the amount of meat available for each hunter would also increase. This would explain the social nature of hunting by Gombe chimpanzees. If the amount of meat available per hunter declined with increasing hunting party size (because each hunter got smaller portions as party size increased), then it would be a better investment of time and energy to hunt alone rather than join a party. The hunting success rates of lone hunters is only about 30 percent, while that of parties with ten or more hunters is close to 100 percent. As it turned out, there is no relationship, either positive or negative, between the number of hunters and the amount of meat available per capita. This may be because even though the likelihood of success increases with more hunters in the party, the most frequently caught prey animal is a one kilogram baby colobus monkey. Whether shared among four hunters or fourteen, such a small package of meat does not provide anyone with much food.

CHIMPANZEES AND PREDATOR-PREY SYSTEMS

THE OCTOBER 7 MASSACRE

This hunting pattern and its potential effects on the colobus population are best illustrated by my observation of one of the largest colobus hunts observed in the thirty-four-year history of research at Gombe. On October 7,

1992, I located the twenty-five members of my main colobus study group feeding and socializing on a hillside in Kakombe Valley, known as Dung Hill. From 7:00 to 11:00 A.M. they moved slowly across the hill slope and into a ravine known as KK6. It was a quiet morning, and the colobus were relaxed as they munched on foliage and young fruits. But beginning about 9:00 A.M., the distant pant-hoots of one or more chimpanzee foraging parties could be heard coming from further down the valley. The male colobus gave occasional alarm calls, high-pitched bird-like calls that warn other group members of nearby danger, but the chimpanzees did not approach. Then, at about 11:00 A.M., the pant-hoots rang out in two directions at close range, coming from both north and south of the location of the colobus group and me. For several minutes these two chimpanzee parties called, then the calls converged and moved toward us. Clearly, two foraging parties had met and become one larger party that was headed in the colobus' direction. For several suspenseful minutes, the colobus and I waited to learn whether the chimpanzees were headed directly toward us.

Minutes later, the vanguard of the chimpanzee party arrived, a male named Beethoven and several of the adult females and their offspring. They were being followed that morning by two Tanzanian researchers, Msafiri Katoto and Bruno Herman. The colobus were wary and alarm calling, but such a small party was not a great risk to them. Then the main party arrived, with all twelve adult and adolescent males and many females and juveniles—thirty-three chimpanzees in all. The hunt began, as usual, with Frodo climbing a tall emergent tree in which some of the colobus group was clustered, and for the next twenty minutes the trees shook and the foliage crashed with the sounds of leaping and calling colobus and equally frenzied chimpanzee hunters. As the hunt progressed, I felt sure that the colobus would succeed in driving the chimpanzees away, but Frodo and the other males managed to scatter the male colobus, whereupon the rest of the group fled and became easy prey. Just in front of me a young colobus whom I had watched all morning as it fed on leaves and played with other juveniles attempted to flee the chimpanzees by leaping onto a branch that unfortunately held a male chimpanzee named Atlas. Atlas quickly grabbed the young colobus and dispatched it with a bite to the skull. Within seconds, an estrous female chimpanzee named Trezia ran up to Atlas and begged for meat. Atlas held the colobus carcass away from her; she then turned and presented her sexual swelling to him, they copulated, and only then did she receive a share of the meat. A few feet away, Beethoven had caught a young infant colobus and was engaging in identical behavior with the female chimpanzee Gremlin. The number of colobus killed, however, was difficult to know because after an hour some chimpanzees were still hunting while others who had captured colobus sat on the ground over a fifty-yard circle eating and sharing meat. My reaction to seeing my colobus being killed and eaten one by one before my eyes was initially one of excitement; I was in the unique position of observing a hunt and knowing both predators and prey as individuals. The excitement paled quickly, however, when Msafiri called out through the forest that there had been at least six colobus killed (the final tally turned out to be seven). Four hours later, the chimpanzees finally finished their feast of colobus meat and the ensuing rest and socializing period and departed the scene of the kill.

A hunt like this one does not occur often at Gombe; indeed, this was only the second kill of seven colobus observed in thirty-four years. But multiple kills of two or more colobus happen more frequently—twenty-one times in 1990 alone—illustrating the powerful influence chimpanzees may have as predators on the populations of prey animals within their hunting range. I estimate that from 1990 through 1993, the colobus kills made by the male chimpanzee Frodo alone have eliminated about 10 percent of the colobus monkeys in the home range of the Gombe chimpanzees.

EFFECTS OF CHIMPANZEE PREDATION ON THE COLOBUS POPULATION

As the previously described hunt illustrates, one chimpanzee hunting party can decimate a group of red colobus prey in a matter of minutes. What is the likely long-term effect of intensive chimpanzee predation on the colobus population? Using information on the size, age, and sex composition of red colobus groups, combined with knowledge of the hunting patterns of Gombe chimpanzees, it is possible to estimate the impact of predation on the colobus. Based on my monitoring of five colobus groups over the past four years, plus censusing of a number of other groups that occupy the eighteen square kilometers of the chimpanzees' hunting range, I estimate there are about 500 (± 10 percent) in the chimpanzees' range. I estimate that from approximately 75 to 175 colobus are killed by chimpanzees annually; I base this estimate on those kills that have been observed, plus the expected number of kills per day in which no human observer was following them in the forest. The annual mortality rate in the colobus population that is due to chimpanzee predation is thus between 15 and 35 percent, depending on the frequency of hunting that year.[24] While 15 percent mortality due to predation has been recorded for other species of mammals, it must be noted that this figure represents predation by chimpanzees only and does not include death at the hands of other predators (leopards and eagles exist at Gombe and eat monkeys) or mortality due to disease, infanticide, or other factors. And 35 percent mortality would mean, if it happened every year, that the red colobus population would almost certainly be in sharp decline. It appears, however, that the average mortality of colobus due to predation by chimpanzees over the past decade has been about 20 percent of the population killed by chimpanzees each year; this figure is comparable to what many other populations of prey animals sustain.[25]

To understand the impact of this mortality on the colobus population, it is important to consider certain aspects of the monkey population. First, female colobus appear to give birth about every two years, and births occur in every month of the year. Since chimpanzees prey mainly upon young colobus (under two years old), female colobus that lose a baby to chimpanzee hunters are able to begin cycling again soon afterward and to produce a new offspring as soon as seven months later. These two facts, lack of breeding seasonality and mortality of immatures rather than adults, may minimize the impact of predation on the colobus, in that a single infant lost is more quickly replaced than an older offspring or adult would be.

To learn whether chimpanzee predation has the potential to be a limiting factor in the size of the colobus population at Gombe, I compared the intensity of hunting by chimpanzees with the size of red colobus groups in each of the valleys of the chimpanzees' hunting range. The central valley of the chimpanzees' range (their so-called core area) is Kakombe Valley; the chimpanzees made about one-third of all their hunts there over the past decade. As one travels away from the center and toward the northern and southern borders of the chimpanzees' range, their use of the more peripheral valleys is much less frequent, and their frequency of hunting there is also less. Only about 3 percent of all hunts took place at the northern and southern edges of their range. I found that the size of red colobus groups also varied over the area of the chimpanzees' hunting range. In the core area, red colobus groups averaged only nineteen animals, little more than half the average of about thirty-four at the outer boundaries.[26] In other words, colobus groups are small where they are hunted frequently and larger where hunting is infrequent. Moreover, I found that this size difference was due largely to a difference between core area and peripheral groups in the percentage of the groups that was immature colobus. In the core area, only 17 percent of each group were infants and juveniles, while fully 40 percent of peripheral groups were immature. This is a direct demonstration of the power of predation to limit both group size and population size in a wild primate population. From now on, we must consider the possibility that in addition to their other interesting traits, chimpanzees may be among the most important predators on certain prey species in the African ecosystems where they live.

WHAT DOES CHIMPANZEE HUNTING BEHAVIOR SUGGEST ABOUT EARLY HOMINID EVOLUTION?

Did early hominids hunt and eat small and medium-sized animals in numbers as large as these? It is quite possible that they did. We know that colobus-like monkeys inhabited the woodlands and riverside gallery forest in which early hominids lived three to five million years ago. We also know that these earliest hominids were different from chimpanzees in two prominent anatomical features: They had much smaller canine teeth, and they had a lower body adapted for walking on the ground rather than swinging through trees. They almost certainly continued to use trees for nighttime shelter and for daytime fruit foraging, as do modern ground-living primates such as baboons. In spite of lacking the weaponry such as large canine teeth and tree-climbing adaptations that chimpanzees possess, early hominids probably ate a large number of small and medium-sized animals, including monkeys. Chimpanzees do not use their canine teeth to capture adult colobus; rather, they grab the prey and flail it to death on the ground or a tree limb. And once the prey is cornered in an isolated tree crown, group cooperation at driving the monkeys from one hunter to another would have been a quite efficient killing technique.

In addition to the availability of prey in the trees, there were of course small animals and the young of larger animals to catch opportunistically on the ground. Many researchers now believe that the carcasses of dead animals were an important source of meat for early hominids once they had stone tools to use for removing the flesh from the carcass.[27] Wild chimpanzees show little interest in dead animals as a food source, so scavenging may have evolved as an important mode of getting food when hominids began to make and use tools for getting at meat. Before this time, it seems likely that earlier hominids were hunting small mammals as chimpanzee do today, and that the role that hunting played in the early hominids' social lives was probably as complex and political as it is in the social lives of chimpanzees. When we ask when meat became an important part of the human diet, we therefore must look well before the evolutionary split between apes and humans in our own family tree

NOTES

1. Richard Potts, *Early Hominid Activities in Olduvai Gorge* (New York: Aldine de Gruyter, 1988).
2. Mary C. Stiner and Steven L. Kuhn, "Subsistence, Technology, and Adaptive Variation in Middle Paleolithic Italy," *American Anthropologist* 94 (1992): 306–339.
3. Hillard Kaplan and Kim R. Hill, "The Evolutionary Ecology of Food Acquisition," in Eric Alden Smith and Bruce Winterhalder, eds., *Evolutionary Ecology and Human Behavior* (New York: Aldine de Gruyter, 1992), pp. 167–202.
4. Maryann Ruvolo, Todd R. Disotell, Michael W. Allard, W. M. Brown, and R. L. Honeycutt, "Resolution of the African Hominoid Trichotomy by Use of a Mitochondrial Gene Sequence," *Proceedings of the National Academy of Science* 88 (1991): 1570–1574.
5. Jane Goodall, *The Chimpanzees of Gombe: Patterns of Behavior* (Cambridge, MA: Harvard University Press, 1986); Geza Teleki, *The Predatory Behavior of Wild Chimpanzees* (Lewisburg, PA: Bucknell University Press, 1973); Craig B. Stanford, Janette Wallis, Hilali Matama, and Jane Goodall, "Patterns of Predation by Chimpanzees on Red Colobus Monkeys in Gombe National Park, Tanzania, 1982–1991," *American Journal of Physical Anthropology* 94 (1994): 213–229.
6. Shigeo Uehara, Toshisda Nishida, Miya Hamai, Toshikazu Hasegawa, H. Hayaki, Michael Huffman, Kenji Kawanaka, S. Kobayashi, John Mitani, Y. Takahata, Hiro Takasaki, and T. Tsukahara, "Characteristics of Predation by the Chimpanzees in

the Mahale Mountains National Park, Tanzania," in Toshisada Nishida, William C. McGrew, Peter Marler, Martin Pickford, and Frans B. M. de Waal, eds., *Topics in Primatology, Volume 1: Human Origins* (Tokyo: University of Tokyo Press, 1992), pp. 143–158.

7. Christophe Boesch and Hedwige Boesch, "Hunting Behavior of Wild Chimpanzees in the Taï National Park," *American Journal of Physical Anthropology* 78 (1989): 547–573.

8. Richard W. Wrangham and Emily van Zinnicq Bergmann-Riss, "Rates of Predation on Mammals by Gombe Chimpanzees, 1972–1975," *Primates* 31 (1990): 157–170.

9. Goodall, *The Chimpanzees of Gombe: Patterns of Behavior.*

10. Stanford, Wallis, Matama, and Goodall, "Patterns of Predation by Chimpanzees on Red Colobus Monkeys in Gombe National Park, Tanzania, 1982–1991."

11. Richard W. Wrangham, *Behavioural Ecology of Chimpanzees in Gombe National Park, Tanzania* (Ph.D. diss., University of Cambridge, 1975).

12. Stanford, Wallis, Matama, and Goodall, "Patterns of Predation by Chimpanzees on Red Colobus Monkeys in Gombe National Park, Tanzania, 1982–1991."

13. Sherwood L. Washburn and Jane B. Lancaster, "The Evolution of Hunting," in Richard B. Lee and Irven DeVore, eds., *Man the Hunter* (Chicago: Aldine, 1968), pp. 293–303.

14. Curt Busse, "Do Chimpanzees Hunt Cooperatively?" *American Naturalist* 112 (1978): 767–770.

15. Christophe Boesch, "Hunting Strategies of Gombe and Taï Chimpanzees," in William C. McGrew, Frans B. M. de Waal, Richard W. Wrangham, and Paul Heltne, eds., *Chimpanzee Cultures* (Cambridge, MA: Harvard University Press, 1994), pp. 77–92.

16. Craig B. Stanford, Janette Wallis, Eslom Mpongo, and Jane Goodall, "Hunting Decisions in Wild Chimpanzees," *Animal Behaviour* 131 (1994): 1–20.

17. Goodall, *The Chimpanzees of Gombe: Patterns of Behavior.*

18. Stanford, Wallis, Matama, and Goodall, "Patterns of Predation by Chimpanzees on Red Colobus Monkeys in Gombe National Park, Tanzania, 1982–1991."

19. Teleki, *The Predatory Behavior of Wild Chimpanzees.*

20. Adrian Kortlandt, *New Perspectives on Ape and Human Evolution* (Amsterdam: Stichting Voor Psychobiologie, 1972).

21. Wrangham, *Behavioural Ecology of Chimpanzees in Gombe National Park, Tanzania.*

22. Toshisada Nishida, T. Hasegawa, H. Hayaki, Y. Takahata, and Shigeo Uehara, "Meat-Sharing as a Coalition Strategy by an Alpha Male Chimpanzee," in Toshisada Nishida, William C. McGrew, Peter Marler, and Martin Pickford, eds., *Topics in Primatology, vol. I* (Tokyo: University of Tokyo Press, 1992), pp. 159–174.

23. William C. McGrew, *Chimpanzee Material Culture* (Cambridge: Cambridge University Press, 1992).

24. Craig B. Stanford, "The Influence of Chimpanzee Predation on Group Size and Anti-Predator Behaviour in Red Colobus Monkeys," *Animal Behaviour* 49 (1995): 577–587.

25. Stanford, Wallis, Matama, and Goodall, "Patterns of Predation by Chimpanzees on Red Colobus Monkeys in Gombe National Park, Tanzania, 1982–1991."

26. Ibid.

27. Henry T. Bunn and Ellen M. Kroll, "Systematic Butchery by Plio/Pleistocene Hominids at Olduvai Gorge, Tanzania," *Current Anthropology* 27 (1986): 431–452.

SUGGESTED READINGS

de Waal, Frans. *Chimpanzee Politics*. Baltimore, MD: Johns Hopkins Press, 1982. A popular account of the political and social intrigue of a chimpanzee colony in the Arnhem Zoo in the Netherlands.

Goodall, Jane. *The Chimpanzees of Gombe: Patterns of Behavior*. Cambridge, MA: Harvard University Press, 1986. A scholarly compilation of Goodall's first twenty-five years of research on the Gombe chimpanzees. The most comprehensive book on chimpanzee behavior ever published.

Goodall, Jane. *Through a Window*. Boston: Houghton Mifflin Co., 1990. A nontechnical book summarizing some of the most exciting discoveries made by Goodall about wild chimpanzees, including warfare, cannibalism, and meat-eating.

Johannson, Donald. *Lucy: The Making of Mankind*. New York: Simon & Schuster, 1981. The story of the discovery of the most important early human fossil yet discovered, where it fits into the human lineage, and what its behavior was probably like.

McGrew, William C. *Chimpanzee Material Culture*. Cambridge: Cambridge University Press, 1992. A scholarly work on the manufacture and use of tools and other aspects of behavior in wild chimpanzees. The book makes valuable comparisons between the different wild chimpanzee populations that have been studied.

Teleki, Geza. *The Predatory Behavior of Wild Chimpanzees*. Lewisburg, PA: Bucknell University Press, 1973. The first study of hunting by wild chimpanzees, Teleki's book describes hunting and the chimpanzees of Gombe in the 1960s, some of whom are also mentioned in this chapter.

AUSTRALOPITHECUS AFARENSIS AND HUMAN EVOLUTION

SCOTT W. SIMPSON

The two-day drive from Addis Ababa, the capital of Ethiopia, to our field site near the Awash River had left me dusty and tired. The second day began well enough. Just after dawn we reached the western rim of the East African rift. The view from the edge of this massive rip in the earth is extraordinary. At the bottom, two thousand meters below, the barren badlands of the Afar depression stretch away into the haze.

It is difficult to work in the Afar depression. Because the sun always shines in the Ethiopian rift, it can get hot—very hot. Except for the sluggish Awash River, there are no permanent sources of water. We get our water from shallow wells dug in the dry river beds. Despite purification, the drinking water is usually cloudy. Unappealing, but in this treeless desert the tepid dun-colored water is refreshing. Despite these difficulties, we return to this part of the Ethiopian desert year after year because these arid deposits contain fossilized animal bones that provide direct evidence of terrestrial faunal evolution during the Pliocene (5.2 to 1.8 million years ago [mya]) and Pleistocene (1.8 mya to 10,000 ya) epochs. Entombed in the ancient clays, sands, and gravels of the Afar depression are the fossilized bones of innumerable animals. Many hours are spent each day walking across the sediments, examining the thousands of bones and teeth of extinct animals that litter the surface. The dusty landscape and glaring sunlight quickly cause a permanent squint and a bad attitude. After each long day of searching, every new fossil has to be examined and its location carefully recorded. Although most fossils are from long-extinct antelopes, elephants, pigs, monkeys, hippos, and crocodiles, the next one could be an early human ancestor. Finding an ancient hominid fossil produces immediate euphoria. The heat, frustration, bone-jarring rides, and sore feet are all instantly forgotten. Without delay, the sight of a possible human ancestor causes everyone to drop to the searingly hot ground and begin crawling around looking for more. Each little piece of fossilized bone is a rare and important link to the past—a clue that can help answer fundamental questions about our own biological evolution.

OUR FAMILY: APES, HOMINIDS, AND HUMANS

The living African apes, which include humans, chimpanzees, and gorillas, are part of a common evolutionary radiation that began in the Miocene (23.5 to 5.2 mya) epoch. Hominids are upright walking, or bipedal,[1] apes that include humans and our extinct relatives. Anatomically and behaviorally, humans (*Homo sapiens*), chimpanzees (*Pan troglodytes* and *Pan paniscus*), and gorillas (*Gorilla gorilla*) share many common features, such as the absence of an external tail, a conical trunk with shoulder joints that face sideways, absolutely and relatively massive brains allowing greater behavioral complexity and plasticity, prolonged periods of development (including gestation, infancy, adolescence), and single births that are infrequent. If we compare the biochemistry of the different ape species, the similarities among them are even more striking. Modern humans and common chimpanzees, our closest relatives, share approximately 98.5 percent of their nonrepeating DNA (DeoxyriboNucleic Acid).

Even a cursory examination reveals marked morphological differences between humans and the other African apes. Modern humans are large-brained, erect-walking, small-toothed, tool-using apes. Our hair is less pronounced (although no less dense) and we communicate via symbolically-based talking and gesturing. African apes have smaller brains and larger canine teeth, are well adapted to tree climbing, and are limited in distribution to the forests and woodlands of equatorial Africa. These differences raise some extremely interesting questions. First, when did the human lineage arise, and second, when and in what sequence did the unique specializations found in modern humans occur?

Researchers use biochemical and anatomical data to answer these questions. Biochemists can study and compare the chemical composition (especially DNA) of living species. Anatomists can examine and compare the shape, function, and development of anatomical structures (bones, teeth, muscles, etc.) in living and extinct animals. Using these two approaches, we can estimate the time when two species separated and reconstruct their evolutionary history.

Despite their morphological and behavioral differences, all modern apes (which include humans) are derived from a common ancestral species, or gene pool. In other words, a now extinct species existed from which the living African apes and humans both descended. Following the separation of these chimpanzee and human lineages, each species continued to evolve and adapt to its environment. Although many of the anatomical differences that distinguish these lineages (including bipedal walking and larger brains in humans) are products of natural selection, other genetic changes have accumulated that have no apparent anatomical counterpart. Such spontaneous changes are due to silent mutations in the DNA of both lineages. Biochemists can measure the chemical difference between species produced by such mutations. The closer the biochemical similarity between different lineages, the more recent their shared common ancestor. If we measure the degree of biochemical difference produced by mutations in the DNA between species and combine it with an estimate of the mutation rate, the time of the speciation event can be calculated. Current research suggests that hominids became a genetically distinct lineage separated from other African apes approximately five to eight mya.

Explaining why morphological changes occurred in the human lineage seems more interesting to me. Anatomical changes are not random. Bipedalism is not a historical accident. Large brains didn't just happen. These adaptations are the products of natural selection. This means that individuals who displayed brain enlargement or bipedal walking produced more offspring who survived to maturity than individuals who did not. Adaptations can allow individuals to obtain food more successfully, reduce risk from predation, gain and maintain reproductive opportunities, or somehow enhance the survivorship of their offspring. Ultimately, these anatomical changes are always an adaptive response resulting in the production of more babies that survive to adulthood.

FINDING OUR ANCESTORS: HOMINID PALEONTOLOGY IN AFRICA

PRIMITIVE HOMINIDS FROM SOUTH AFRICA

To understand changes in functional anatomy, we must learn in which order these anatomical modifications occurred and understand their ecological context. The only way paleoanthropologists can reconstruct the timing and sequence of morphological change in hominids is by analysis of the fossil record. The first primitive hominid fossil was reported by Raymond Dart in 1925.[2] A juvenile skull with associated endocast[3] was recovered from the Taung lime mine in South Africa. The Taung skull, now known to be over two million years old, allowed Dart to define a new primitive hominid genus and species named *Australopithecus africanus*.[4] Although the phylogenetic position of this small-brained, erect-walking hominid as a human relative was vigorously debated, fossil discoveries from the South African cave sites of Sterkfontein and Makapansgat during the next three decades vindicated Dart and proved the validity of the species *A. africanus*. Meanwhile, Robert Broom was discovering fossils of a different hominid species from the South African limestone cave sites of Swartkrans and Kromdraai. Unlike *A. africanus*, this new collection of fossils had larger molar and premolar teeth, smaller canines and incisors,[5] a flatter or less projecting face, and a longitudinal ridge of bone along the top of the skull known as a sagittal crest.[6] Clearly these fossils represented a species different from *A. africanus*. Although they were initially attributed to several different species, they are now included within a single taxon, *Australopithecus robustus* (although some anthropologists contend that these fossils should be named *Paranthropus robustus*). Whatever these extinct species are called, they existed during the late Pliocene and early Pleistocene in South Africa with *A. africanus* (2.8 to 2.2 mya), living earlier than and perhaps giving rise to *A. robustus* (1.8 to 1.0 mya). Anatomically, both species were small-brained (420cc to 550cc, which is slightly larger than the brain of a living chimpanzee or gorilla, but only about 40 percent the size of the brain of a modern human), and their molar and premolar teeth were unlike those of both modern humans and apes. For their body size, these species had very large postcanine teeth covered by thick enamel caps. Like the teeth of modern humans, the australopithecine canine teeth were small and very different from the large projecting canines of the other apes. Analysis of their fossilized pelves, lower limbs, and vertebrae demonstrate that both species walked upright on two legs, as do modern humans. Phylogenetically, *A. robustus* is our cousin. They apparently diverged from the lineage that includes modern humans sometime before two mya. Their unique and specialized cranial and dental anatomy makes them an unlikely human ancestor. This evolutionary experiment among hominids became extinct about one million years ago.[7]

THE HOMINIDS OF EAST AFRICA

In 1959 Mary and Louis Leakey discovered a remarkable hominid fossil from early Pleistocene lake margin deposits at Olduvai Gorge in Tanzania.[8] The cranium, known as OH 5 (Olduvai Hominid specimen #5) and dated to approximately 1.8 mya, is now attributed to the species *Australopithecus boisei* (or *Paranthropus boisei*). This specimen and others recovered from Olduvai Gorge, Peninj in Tanzania and around Lake Turkana in Kenya and Ethiopia are best described as extreme versions of the South African *A. robustus*. Similar to the southern species, *A. boisei* had a small brain, a sagittal crest, a flattened face, and large postcanine and small anterior teeth. However, the sagittal crest and molar teeth were larger than, and the canines and incisors were smaller than, those of their South African contemporaries. At approximately the same time (1.8 to 1.0 mya), the two large-toothed, flat-faced species lived thousands of miles apart yet shared many similar adaptations in their skulls and teeth.

In the early 1960s the Leakeys found other early Pleistocene hominid fossils at Olduvai Gorge that were unlike the large-toothed, crested *A. boisei*. Instead, these fossils had smaller molars and premolars and larger brains (greater than six hundred cc). Here was the first good evidence in East Africa of two very different hominid species living at the same place and time. But what was this other, more gracile hominid? Louis Leakey, along with South African anatomist Phillip Tobias and British anatomist John Napier, concluded that these fossils should be attributed to a new species, which they named *Homo habilis*, and which they suggested was ancestral to modern humans.[9] Here was the oldest evidence of the genus *Homo* and it coexisted with the larger-toothed robust australopithecines. Despite these differences, however, both were hominids, meaning they must have shared a unique common ancestor since their ancestral lineages separated from the African apes.

But what was the common stem hominid from which all subsequent hominids are derived? The only other possible candidate known was *A. africanus*. It had the advantage of being older than both of the East African lineages and it appeared to have a more generalized morphology from which both could arise. However, two problems prevented universal acceptance of *A. africanus* as the last common ancestor (LCA) of all subsequent hominids. First, paleoanthropologists were divided on the phyletic position of *A. africanus*. Some proposed that it was ancestral only to the genus *Homo*, whereas others contended that it was uniquely related to the robust australopithecines. Second, no older (>2.2 mya) fossil material had been recovered from East Africa that could unequivocally be assigned to *A. africanus*. Where was the East African hominid LCA?

HOMINID PALEONTOLOGY IN ETHIOPIA: OMO AND HADAR

One group that worked to resolve this problem was the Omo Research Expedition. This international cooperative effort, led by the American Clark Howell, Camille Arambourg and Yves Coppens of France, and Kenyan Richard Leakey, collected many hominid fossils from the four to one myo (million-year-old) sedimentary deposits along the Omo River in southern Ethiopia.[10] In deposits more recent than 2.5 million years of age, at least two hominid lineages were present, and these were a larger-brained *Homo* and a large-molared robust australopithecine. But in sediments older than 2.5 million years, only one type of hominid was identified. The older sediments (>2.5 mya) from the Usno and Shungura Formations at Omo yielded dozens of isolated hominid teeth but few other skeletal elements. Although these dental remains bore similarities to *Australopithecus africanus*, the unspecialized, primitive nature of these new fossils suggested to Howell and Coppens that the specimens may belong to a new species, perhaps ancestral to all later hominids.[11] Unfortunately, the fragmentary condition of the fossils prevented resolution of the problem.

In the late 1960s Maurice Taieb, a French geologist conducting research for his dissertation on the geologic history of the Awash River in the Ethiopian rift, mapped and surveyed a large basin in the north central portion of the country known as the Afar depression. This area, among the hottest and driest on earth, is a large (~two hundred thousand km^2 or ~seventy-eight thousand mi^2) triangular region where three rifting systems intersect. Three large land masses (East Africa, Africa, and Saudi Arabia) have been slowly moving away from one another for the last twenty or so million years, and the point from which they are diverging is the Afar triangle. It is a low area extending from 700 m above sea level to about 120 m below sea level. During his geological survey, Taieb noticed that in places the ground was extensively littered with fossils. Subsequently, he was introduced to Donald C. Johanson, who agreed to assist in a reconnaissance survey to evaluate the potential of the area for hominid fossils. In 1972 they explored an area along the Awash River known as Hadar. It was a hominid paleontologist's dream. There were expansive, fossiliferous deposits dated to the crucial period of 2.8 and 3.4 mya. The fossils were entombed in sands and clays deposited by the streams, rivers, and lakes present in the Ethiopian rift during the middle Pliocene.[12] This continuous deposition built a layer-cake of sediments, retaining a record of the plants and animals that lived and died along those wooded lake, swamp, and river margins.

Equally significant to our understanding of the fossils is their geologic context. The East African rift system is volcanically active. Fallout from the many volcanic eruptions becomes incorporated into the sediments. If the eruptions are large, they can form distinct layers in the sediments, known as tuffs. Such tuffs have a characteristic chemical "signature" and also contain unstable (radioactive) isotopes. The unique chemical composition of the tuffs allows geologists to match tuff layers from widely separated localities. Tuffs with the same elemental makeup must have been produced from the same eruption; therefore, the sediments surrounding them must be of similar age. If the crystals in the tuffs have not been too badly weathered, geochemists can estimate their age based on the geochemistry of isotope decay. Isotopes are elemental variants that can decay from an unstable state to a stable state at a known and constant rate. Therefore, the amount of the daughter product (the result of the decay process) depends on the age of the sample. The older the crystals, the greater the accumulation of the stable daughter isotopes. By measuring the ratio of parent to daughter elements, the age of the crystals can be calculated quite accurately.

HADAR, LAETOLI, AND THE DISCOVERY OF AUSTRALOPITHECUS AFARENSIS

Following the initial survey of the area, Johanson and Taieb, now joined by Yves Coppens and Jon Kalb, formed the IARE (International Afar Research Expedition) and initiated a long-term multidisciplinary research project focusing on the middle Pliocene deposits at Hadar. The group was very lucky. They soon discovered the oldest hominid species, *Australopithecus afarensis*. Hadar is a rich paleontological locality, and their collections of hominid fossils were extraordinary, forcing anthropologists to rethink early hominid evolution. Remarkable hominid fossils were found in each of the first three field seasons (1973–1975). In 1973 they found a hominid knee joint. Despite its great

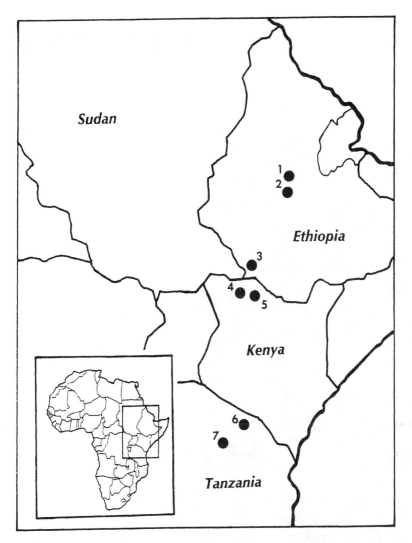

FIGURE 8-1 LOCATION OF SITES DISCUSSED IN TEXT

1 = Hadar; 2 = Middle Awash; 3 = Omo; 4 = East Rudolf; 5 = West Turkana; 6 = Olduvai Gorge; 7 = Laetoli

antiquity and extremely small size (smaller than that of a modern human), its bony anatomy clearly showed that it was fully adapted to bipedal walking.

During the 1974 field season at Hadar, Johanson and field assistant Tom Gray discovered what is one of the most extraordinary specimens ever found in hominid paleontology. We know the fossil as "Lucy" (named after the Beatles song "Lucy in the Sky with Diamonds"); more formally, it is known as specimen AL 288-1.[13] This number means that Lucy was the first fossil found at the 288th fossiliferous outcrop discovered in the Afar Locality (Hadar). Although other beautifully preserved hominid fossils were also found that year, the quality of Lucy overshadowed the rest. Most fossils are small, battered fragments of teeth and mandibles, with each fragment generally from a separate individual. In contrast, about 40 percent of Lucy's skeleton was found,

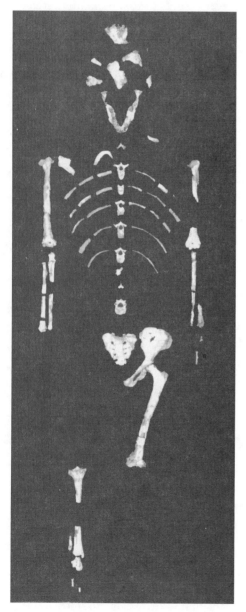

FIGURE 8-2   "LUCY" (AL 288-1)

Hadar, 1974. Cleveland Museum of Natural History.

including her left os coxa (hip bone); sacrum; left femur; portions of her lower leg and foot, including the three bones that comprise the ankle joint; some vertebral fragments; upper limb elements, including portions of the scapula, clavicle, right and left humeri, ulnae, and radii; and some hand bones. Although only a few parts of her cranium were recovered, the associated mandible (jaw bone) was nearly complete. Lucy is an important fossil because her completeness allows anthropologists to study the relationships between the size and shape of structures within a single individual. We can now estimate stature, study the functional anatomy of joints (hip, knee, ankle, shoulder, elbow, wrist), and calculate limb proportions from this 3.2 myo hominid.

In 1975 Hadar revealed its greatest treasure. Site 333, a thin clay deposit, contained over 130 hominid fossils representing at least 13 individuals. The collection includes the remains of very young to very old individuals, and it also spans a broad range of adult size from small (Lucy-sized) to large. Now we could study growth, development, and populational variation in this extinct species.

In all, the five field seasons at Hadar produced more than 250 hominid fossils representing dozens of different individuals sampling a period between 3.0 and 3.4 mya. The upright walking species at Hadar is characterized by a small brain volume (300 to 450cc), canine teeth larger than those of all other hominids but markedly smaller than those of any living ape, and a body mass between 25 and 55 kilograms (55 to 125 pounds). The Pliocene habitat at Hadar showed that these early human ancestors lived in a diverse environment that varied from open to closed woodlands near a permanent source of water.

But Hadar was not the only middle Pliocene site yielding hominid fossils. At the same time, Mary Leakey and colleagues were collecting hominid fossils from the 3.6 myo sediments at Laetoli in northern Tanzania. Laetoli was first surveyed in the mid-1930s by Mary and Louis Leakey and later collected by L. Kohl-Larsen. Although primitive hominid fossils were recovered during this preliminary work, they were either ignored or misidentified. Research began anew at Laetoli in the mid- through late-1970s, and approximately two dozen hominid specimens were recovered from sediments deposited in an arid upland savanna environment. The collection of primitive hominid fossils includes portions of a juvenile mandible (LH 2 [LH-Laetoli Hominid specimen #2]), an adult mandible (LH 4), and an incomplete and fragmentary juvenile skeleton (LH 21).[14]

Are the fossil collections of Laetoli and Hadar related? Fortunately, one of Mary Leakey's assistants at Laetoli was paleoanthropologist Tim White. Because of his intimate familiarity with the Laetoli hominids, when shown the Hadar fossils White recognized that the Laetoli and Hadar hominids, although separated by approximately 300,000 years and 1,500 kilometers (1,000 miles), represented the same species. Johanson, who earlier suggested that the Hadar material represented two species,[15] was soon convinced that both sites sampled a single hominid species. Following their analysis of the material from

Hadar and a comparison with other early hominid fossils, Johanson, White, and Coppens announced in 1978 that these fossils represented a new hominid species named *Australopithecus afarensis*.[16] Not only was *A. afarensis* the earliest hominid species yet discovered, but also they concluded that it was ancestral to all other hominid species, including the other australopithecines (*A. africanus*, *A. robustus*, and *A. boisei*) and the *Homo* lineage. This simple conclusion has immense taxonomic and phylogenetic implications that continue to provoke intense debate (summarized in note 7).

ANALYSIS AND INTERPRETATION

Taxonomy and phylogeny aside, what did these early hominids do? What information about the biology of this extinct species can the fossils from Hadar and Laetoli tell us? What did they eat? Can their reproductive and social behaviors be reconstructed? Although paleoanthropologists address these and other questions, we will focus on just two. First, do the fossil remains from Hadar and Laetoli represent only a single species? After all, at many other sites, multiple hominid taxa are present. Second, how did Lucy and her conspecifics walk?

MORPHOLOGICAL VARIATION: HOW MANY SPECIES AT HADAR?

Let's start with the number of species represented by the fossils from Hadar and Laetoli. Although Johanson and White concluded that these materials represent a single species, other researchers suggested that the amount of morphological variation found in this collection was too great for a single species and that the Hadar and Laetoli fossils sample two or more contemporaneous hominid species. How can we resolve this problem? First, we must learn why variation is a necessary prerequisite of evolution. Second, we have to be familiar with the factors that contribute to the amount of variation in living and fossil ape species.

Variety in form and behavior is a crucial element of evolution. We live with anatomical variation every day. How else do we distinguish among people? When I teach human anatomy to medical students, every group complains during dissection that the muscles, arteries, and nerves in their cadaver look different from the pictures and descriptions in anatomy texts. Why? Because no two humans are morphologically identical. We are all variations on a common theme. All humans have the same bones, muscles, nerves, organs, and so forth, but their size, shape, and relationships differ. Most variation is a natural consequence of sexually reproducing organisms. Without variation, evolution by natural selection could not occur. Because no two individuals are behaviorally or anatomically identical, not all individuals are equally adapted to their environment. Some will have a slight edge. This advantage allows them to produce more offspring who survive to maturity. What initially was a rare or uncommon anatomical advantage may, over time, become prevalent in a species. This is evolution by natural selection. Not all diversity, however, affects our fitness, and some variation may be selectively neutral. Other factors contribute to the amount of variation in a population—age composition of the sample, for instance. Obviously, you look different today than when you were a child or than you will in twenty years. A fossil collection sampling a diversity of ages will appear heterogeneous.

Sex differences in morphology (sexual dimorphism) are another source of variation. Male and female humans do not look the same. Although the sexes differ in their primary reproductive roles and this is reflected in our reproductive anatomy, sexual dimorphism generally describes those anatomical differences associated with gaining access to and retaining a mate. In African apes (including hominids), males are generally larger than females. Male gorillas can weigh twice as much (or more) than a female. Male gorillas also look different from females. As the males mature, the normally black hair on their backs becomes gray or silver colored. This does not occur in females. Males also have much larger canine teeth than do females, and develop sagittal crests. Chimpanzee males are approximately the same stature as females but they weigh about 15 percent more. Except for this difference in muscle mass and noticeably larger canine teeth, male and female chimps look pretty much the same. Humans are very sexually dimorphic. Human males are taller, weigh more, and have a different distribution of fat and hair than do females. From available fossil evidence it appears that australopithecine males also were larger than females, to a greater degree than modern humans. Therefore, when estimating size variation from fossils, researchers must consider age variation, sexual dimorphism, and natural variety as contributing factors to the morphological heterogeneity in *Australopithecus afarensis*.

As informative as one fossil can be, numerous anatomical specimens are necessary to understand the scope of normal biological variation. In paleontological studies the fossil evidence for extinct animals is usually fragmentary. It cannot provide a complete picture of the biology and behavior of the long dead animals. In historical studies we must begin with what can be observed directly and only then extrapolate to the unknown. Therefore, anthropologists must be familiar with anatomy and its variation in humans and African apes. Fortunately, Don Johanson served as curator of the Laboratory of Physical Anthropology at the Cleveland Museum of Natural History (CMNH) in Cleveland, Ohio, when he addressed the species question at Hadar. The CMNH houses the Hamann-Todd osteological collection, which contains over three thousand well-documented (age, sex, cause of death, race) human skeletons and the largest collection of chimpanzee and gorilla skeletons in the world. These extensive collections provide direct evidence of the normal range of variation in living species.

Johanson and White, with their extensive experience in human and ape musculoskeletal variation, were well aware of the amount of normal variation that could be found in temporally diverse anatomical collections. The *A. afarensis* fossils represent a population of individuals that spanned more than six hundred thousand years in an ecologically dynamic habitat. Considering the earlier discussion, it is not unexpected that the Hadar and Laetoli fossils, although belonging to a single species, were not morphologically homogeneous.[17]

The first time I saw the Hadar fossils at the Ethiopian National Museum in Addis Ababa, I was impressed by the great range of size and shape of the specimens. Lucy's femur is much smaller than the largest femur from Hadar. Is this too much variation for a single species? First impressions suggest it is, but scientists must always question their initial assessments. Lucy is the centerpiece of the collection. Because of her completeness, she figures prominently in any comparison. However, with a height of only 1.1 meters, she is one of the smallest hominids ever discovered. Therefore, any comparison involving Lucy must take her short stature into account. The large proximal femur (AL 333-3) is also well preserved and is among the largest individuals from Hadar. It is natural to pick up the best preserved fossils to make a comparison (i.e., Lucy and AL 333-3), while ignoring the other more fragmentary, banged-up fossils. Quite simply, our natural bias toward the nicest specimens from Hadar causes us to compare the extremes in size. Any comparison that involves the largest and smallest individuals will necessarily overestimate the degree of size variation in a species. However, when all of the proximal femora from Hadar are examined, a continuum of small to large is seen with the best preserved specimens at the extremes. Independent analyses estimating sexual dimorphism by Owen Lovejoy and his colleagues and Henry McHenry[18] concluded that skeletal sexual dimorphism at Hadar only slightly exceeded that seen in modern humans. The early australopithecines were more dimorphic than chimpanzees and humans but much less so than modern gorillas and orangutans.

HOW DID "LUCY" WALK?

Considerable debate surrounds the manner in which *A. afarensis* moved around. Quite simply, did they walk upright on two legs like modern humans or was their locomotor pattern unlike any living species? Fortunately, we can reconstruct with some accuracy the locomotor behavior of this extinct species from their fossilized bones. Some authors suggest that the collection of fossils attributed to *A. afarensis* may represent the missing locomotor link between modern African apes and humans. Randy Susman, Jack Stern, and Bill Jungers (all of the State University of New York at Stony Brook) proposed that Lucy was anatomically adapted to both arboreal quadrupedality and terrestrial bipedality.[19] They suggest that the bipedal locomotion of *A. afarensis* was not like modern humans; Lucy and her type walked about with bent hips and knees. Not only is this an energetically expensive and uncomfortable way to get around (try it for a couple of minutes), but also it is inconsistent with the available fossil evidence. Although *A. afarensis* looked like a chimpanzee with small canines above the neck, below the neck the locomotor anatomy had evolved away from the primitive quadrupedal condition toward human-like bipedal function.[20] This species may be phyletically intermediate between humans and the ape/human LCA, but, like modern humans, it was fully adapted to terrestrial bipedality.

How do chimpanzees move around? Modern apes are among the largest arboreal animals alive today. They spend much time climbing in the canopies of trees as they feed or escape from enemies. Clearly, climbing is a major component of their daily activities and this is reflected in their anatomy. Although male gorillas rarely climb trees, they do, nevertheless, maintain the essential climbing adaptation seen in smaller apes. As you can imagine, a fall from a tree by so large an animal has severe consequences. Because even one fall can kill a large animal, selection has favored those who minimize the risk of falling by enhancing their anatomical adaptations to climbing. They display multiple anatomical specializations for climbing, reaching, and grasping. While moving about on the ground, chimps and gorillas use a unique quadrupedal locomotor style, known as knuckle-walking. When knuckle-walking, chimps and gorillas support themselves by resting their weight on the backs of their fingers. In the wild, they only infrequently walk bipedally on the ground. Apes are capable of this behavior (watch a trained chimpanzee at the circus), but it is energetically expensive for them. They do not demonstrate any anatomical adaptations to this method of progression.

What are the anatomical specializations that allow these large mammals to climb about in the trees? If we focus on the pelvis and the lower limbs in apes, we can identify several major and important morphological adaptations to arboreality, including an elongated ilium (a part of the hip bone), a stiff, inflexible trunk, a medially directed ankle joint, a mobile and abducted great toe, a flexible mid-tarsal joint in the foot, and absence of a bicondylar angle of the knee. Together, these anatomical specializations allow a large-bodied primate to climb into the highest portions of the canopy and traverse along the canopy in adjacent trees.

Many different aspects of the musculoskeletal system must be altered to evolve a terrestrial biped from an arboreal quadruped. Owen Lovejoy of Kent State University in Ohio has devoted much time to documenting these changes.[21] Bipeds, unlike quadrupeds, must support themselves on a single leg at some point during each gait cycle. To accommodate this functional shift, the musculoskeletal anatomy of the lower limb and hip must change. The human pelvis has a much shorter and laterally directed ilium. This changes the functional relationship of the gluteal musculature (muscles acting across the hip joint) and alters their role from that of extensors or thigh straighteners (as seen in other primates and quadrupeds) to that of trunk supporters or thigh abductors. Similar modifications are seen in the pelves of Lucy and in *A. africanus*. As Lovejoy and his colleagues—Jim Ohman of Johns Hopkins University and Bruce Latimer of the Cleveland Museum of Natural History (CMNH)—have noted, evidence of this muscular shift can be identified not only in the shape and external morphology of the hip and thigh bones but also in the internal bony organization of the femoral neck. Bone is a dynamic tissue that remodels (adds or removes bone, which modifies its internal or external shape) according to the direction and magnitude of the mechanical forces acting on it. Because of differences in mode of locomotion and orientation of their locomotor muscles, the way in which humans and apes transmit forces across their hip joint differs. Consequently, their bony anatomy differs as well. The morphology of the internal bony structure and external surface topography in the proximal thigh bones of *A. afarensis* is similar to that of humans, thus suggesting that the extinct species walked bipedally like humans.

The knee of a striding biped is placed under the center of mass to support the body when walking. If you look at a standing person, you will notice that his or her hips are wider than his or her knees. Humans are knock-kneed. In contrast, the knee in quadrupeds is located directly beneath the hip joint. To verify this for yourself, notice that the thighs of a dog, cow, or gorilla, when seen from the front, are perpendicular to the ground. This angulation of the thigh in bipeds, known as the bicondylar angle, is a product of modifications in the distal end of the femur or thigh bone. Apes do not have this characteristic feature but, like all hominids, *A. afarensis* does.

The biped's foot is very different from that of a climbing ape. Bruce Latimer of the CMNH has carefully identified the many anatomical differences between apes and humans.[22] The ape foot is a grasping organ, more like our hands. In humans, the foot is best described as a propulsive lever. In apes, the big toe (hallux) is very mobile and abductable. This means that it diverges from the other toes and is not parallel to the remaining toes as in humans. Their hallux can be used for gripping and holding. To facilitate this grasping function, apes also maintain a greater amount of mobility between the ankle bones (mid-tarsal joint).

Humans propel themselves during bipedal walking by pushing against the ground. The foot, acting as a propulsive structure, is relatively rigid. This rigidity is maintained by the shapes of the tarsal (ankle) and metatarsal (foot) bones, ligaments, and muscles of the foot. When humans walk, they push off with the hallux. Apes, with the divergent, or thumb-like, position of their great toe, cannot transmit the propulsive force of walking in the same fashion as humans. Consequently, the bones of the big toe in humans, unlike those of chimpanzees but similar to those of *A. afarensis*, are large and robust. Therefore, the morphology of the bones of the foot is characteristic of and can be used to reconstruct the way animals walk. In each instance in which the function of the foot fossils from Hadar could be assessed, Latimer showed that *A. afarensis* used its foot as a propulsive lever, like humans, and not as a grasping structure like chimpanzees and gorillas.

Most quadrupedal animals use the hindlimb for propulsion or acceleration and the front limb for maneuvering and as a shock absorber. Bipeds must employ the hindlimb for all these functions. Not only must the hindlimb propel and support the body (as discussed earlier), but also the foot and leg must be adapted to absorb the repeated impacts of the foot striking the ground. Again, the anatomy reflects the function. Unlike apes, who have flat feet, humans have arched feet. Thus, not all of the sole of the foot contacts the ground during walking. This arch is maintained by both the shapes of the bones and the surrounding soft tissues. When humans walk, the arch deforms or straightens slightly. The deformations of the arches act like the shock absorbing springs in a car. They prevent the sudden jarring at impact that would ultimately lead to the deterioration of the joints and ligaments of the feet. That is why individuals with flat feet (less-developed or absent foot arches) were routinely rejected from military service. Flat-footed soldiers would soon develop painful and injured feet from the many long marches. In addition, humans and australopithecines, unlike other apes, have modified the shape and distribution of bone in their calcaneus (heel bones) to help dissipate the repeated shock of striking the ground during walking, thus preventing joint degeneration. Overall, the foot bones of *A. afarensis* show clearly that they had an arched foot, an adducted hallux, a less mobile midtarsal joint, and a human-like heel bone. The anatomy of the early hominid fossils demonstrates that *A. afarensis* walked bipedally.

But other data reinforce the anatomical conclusions. The site of Laetoli in Tanzania is famous for preserving a very rare and unusual fossil. Although an important series of fossilized bones was recovered there, the sediments include a 3.6-myo-volcanic tuff, which contains a series of footprint trails.[23] The ash from a volcanic eruption blanketed the savanna 3.6 million years ago, and many different animals walked, slithered, hopped, crawled, or ran across the ancient landscape that day and left their marks in the freshly deposited ash. The rain-moistened layer hardened and was soon covered by materials from another volcanic eruption, thus preserving the footprints. Unlike fossil bone collections that represent remains sampled over a very long period, these footprints represent a snapshot of just a few minutes of time. Significantly for anthropologists, three hominids, one larger and two smaller individuals, were walking across the savanna that day 3.6 mya. Interestingly, one of the smaller trails parallels the larger individual while the other small-footed individual carefully walked in the impressions left by the larger australopithecine. Does this represent a male and female walking side by side with their child following behind? Obviously, we can never know. But the evidence for a modern human-like foot morphology and striding bipedal gait is unequivocal.

The preserved skeletal anatomy of the hip, knee, ankle, and foot (and other aspects not discussed here, i.e., upper limb, hand, vertebral column) in *A. afarensis* demonstrates that it was undoubtedly a terrestrial biped. In the anatomical specializations associated with locomotion found in *A. afarensis*, every one shows an adaptive response to upright, bipedal walking. This assessment is reinforced when the footprints from Laetoli are considered. *A. afarensis*, like modern humans, was behaviorally and morphologically adapted to terrestrial bipedalism. This does not mean that they could not or did not use the trees as a source of food or safety, merely that they had become adapted to life on the ground. If *A. afarensis* climbed the trees, they climbed them like modern humans. Why? Because they exhibit no anatomical specializations for arboreality.

THE SEARCH CONTINUES

The search for *A. afarensis* continues throughout East Africa, especially in Ethiopia and Kenya. During the past twenty years Hadar and two other areas in Ethiopia, known as Fejej and the Middle Awash, have produced fossils of *A. afarensis*. Fejej (pronounced Fedj-edj) is a hot, desolate area east of the Omo site in the southern part of the country. The site was originally discovered in 1989 during the Paleoanthropological Inventory organized by the Ethiopian Ministry of Culture.[24] Subsequent survey of the area by John Fleagle (SUNY at Stony Brook) and his associates yielded hominid teeth dated to about four mya.[25] Future surveys at Fejej should produce more early hominids.

The Middle Awash area, initially studied by Jon Kalb and associates during the 1970s,[26] is an extensive series of fossiliferous sediments along the Awash River about fifty kilometers (thirty-five miles) upstream (or south) of Hadar. Like Hadar, these sediments sample woodland environments associated with streams, swamps, and lakes. The Middle Awash deposits have yielded a series of cranial and postcranial remains dated to 3.4 and 3.85 mya. The first Middle Awash early hominid remains were found in 1981 by Tim White (University of California at Berkeley) and his colleagues in the adjacent dry stream drainages of Maka and Belohdelie.[27] In 1990, when fieldwork resumed, White and his fossil hunters were successful again and more 3.4 myo hominid fossils were recovered from Maka.[28] The Maka fossils, which include a mostly complete lower jaw, other mandibular fragments, isolated teeth, a proximal femur, and a humerus, are morphologically similar to the Hadar and Laetoli finds yet are temporally intermediate. Berhane Asfaw, who described the 3.85 myo cranial remains from Belohdelie, concluded that they were very similar to the cranial fragments recovered from Hadar.[29] Therefore, the earliest appearance of *A. afarensis* can now be expanded by another two hundred thousand years. The Middle Awash finds serve to strengthen the links between the Hadar and Laetoli collections, extend the earliest appearance of *A. afarensis* in Ethiopia to 3.85 mya, and reinforce the idea that *A. afarensis* was a single, bipedal, widely distributed, sexually dimorphic species.[30]

Recent paleontological research at Hadar, led by Don Johanson and Bill Kimbel of the Institute of Human Origins (IHO), has continued to add more high quality fossils to the already extensive Hadar collections. Beside the usual assortment of teeth and mandibles (fifty-three new specimens discovered between 1990 and 1993) the IHO team has also recovered a partial arm and a virtually complete skull.[31] Previously, Hadar had not yielded a complete (or near complete) adult skull (cranium and mandible), but with the recovery of three myo AL 444-2 by Yoel Rak (an Israeli anatomist), that changed. This very large, presumably male, skull is a spectacular find. We can use the AL 444-2 skull to study the size and relationship between the face and the cranial vault, giving us insight into such factors as brain size and the chewing muscles in this early hominid species. Future research at Hadar and other African sites will continue to refine our understanding of the evolution, ecology, anatomy, and behavior of this early hominid species.

In tandem with the increasing number of *A. afarensis* fossils being recovered, researchers are asking new questions, reanalyzing existing data, and using improved analytic approaches, including increasingly sophisticated biomechanical studies, computerized tomography imaging, and scanning electron microscopic studies, to examine the fossils. In addition, new techniques

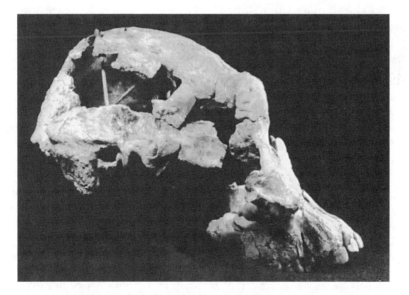

FIGURE 8-3   AL 444-2
Hadar, 1992. Institute of Human Origins. (*Donald C. Johanson, Ph.D.*)

of aerial and satellite survey allow researchers to locate and prospect new fossiliferous areas.[32] Also, the many recent advances in geochronology give us a better understanding of the ages of the fossils we find. These new data and independent studies of previously recovered fossils and their context reinforce earlier assessments that *A. afarensis* was a single, upright-walking species that arose about four mya and lived in slightly to heavily wooded areas throughout Ethiopia, Kenya, and Tanzania for at least one million years. But so many other questions remain. What did they eat? How long did they live? What were the size and makeup of their social groups? Did they habitually make or use tools? Are bipedal locomotion and canine reduction linked together as part of an adaptive complex or did they arise independently? To date, the earliest australopithecines have been recovered only from sediments in the East African rift. Were they confined to this area or did they live outside this ecological zone? Why and when did *A. afarensis* become extinct? Did this lineage continue as the South African australopithecines, or the East African australopithecines, or as the *Homo* lineage that includes us? Clearly *A. afarensis* is an early hominid but is it the earliest hominid? Recently recovered fossils from the Aramis site in the Middle Awash suggest otherwise. With the announcement in 1994 of a new and older type of hominid, *Ardipithecus ramidus*, we have pushed back even farther the origins of our lineage to 4.4 mya and beyond.[33] Now we must search for more evidence of this newest early hominid. Unfortunately, deposits older than four mya are uncommon and only infrequently contain hominid fossils. But we will continue searching the Ethiopian badlands for our ancient relatives. Many long days of walking across the multicolored sediments still stand between us and the earliest hominids. With the hot sun and cloudy water, looking for our early ancestors isn't easy, but we, like many others, are anxious to continue. In East Africa, our past is lying at our feet. We just have to look.

NOTES

1. Hominids are bipeds, meaning they walk on two feet (*bi* = two; *ped* = foot). All other primates are quadrupeds (*quad* = four) or use all four limbs during locomotion.

2. Raymond A. Dart, "*Australopithecus africanus*: The Man-Ape of South Africa," *Nature* 115 (1925): 195–199.

3. An endocast forms when sediments accumulate and harden within an empty braincase. This fossil retains the shape, size, and markings of the inside of the skull, allowing measurement of brain size and description of brain anatomy.

4. Dart named the newly described hominid from South Africa *Australopithecus africanus*, which means "southern ape of Africa" (*Austral* = south; *pithecus* = ape; *africanus* = African).

5. Many mammals, including all apes and monkeys, have four types of teeth. From front to back they are the incisors, canines (cuspids or unicuspids), premolars (bi-cuspids), and molars. Each tooth type has a characteristic shape and function.

6. The sagittal crest is a ridge of bone running from the front to the back of the skull and is formed by the enlargement of the chewing muscles (Temporalis muscle). This is commonly found in male gorillas, orangutans, and robust australop-ithecines.

7. Fred E. Grine, "Australopithecine Taxonomy and Phylogeny: Historical Back-ground and Recent Interpretations," in Russell L. Ciochon and John G. Fleagle, eds., *The Human Evolutionary Sourcebook* (Englewood Cliffs, NJ: Prentice Hall, 1993), pp. 198–210; Fred E. Grine, ed., *Evolutionary History of the "Robust" Australopithecines* (New York: Aldine de Gruyter, 1988).

8. Louis S. B. Leakey, "A New Fossil Skull from Olduvai," *Nature* 184 (1959): 967–970.

9. Louis S. B. Leakey, Phillip V. Tobias, and John R. Napier, "A New Species of the Genus *Homo* from Olduvai Gorge," *Nature* 202 (1964): 7–9. *Homo habilis* means "handy man."

10. Yves Coppens, F. Clark Howell, Glynn Ll. Isaac, and Richard E. F. Leakey, eds., *Earliest Man and Environments in the Lake Rudolf Basin* (Chicago: University of Chica-go Press, 1976).

11. F. Clark Howell and Yves Coppens, "An Overview of Hominidae from the Omo Succession, Ethiopia," in Yves Coppens, F. Clark Howell, Glynn Ll. Isaac, and Richard E. F. Leakey, eds., *Earliest Man and Environments in the Lake Rudolf Basin* (Chicago: University of Chicago Press, 1976), pp. 522–532.

12. Donald C. Johanson, Maurice Taieb, and Yves Coppens, "Pliocene Hominids from the Hadar Formation, Ethiopia (1973–1977): Stratigraphic, Chronologic, and Paleoenvironmental Contexts, with Notes on Hominid Morphology and Sys-tematics," *American Journal of Physical Anthropology* 57 (1982): 373–402.

13. Donald C. Johanson, C. Owen Lovejoy, William H. Kimbel, Tim D. White, Steven C. Ward, Michael E. Bush, Bruce Latimer, and Yves Coppens, "Morphology of the Partial Hominid Skeleton (AL 288-1) from the Hadar Formation, Ethiopia," *Amer-ican Journal of Physical Anthropology* 57 (1982): 403–452; Donald C. Johanson and Maitland Edey, *Lucy: The Beginnings of Humankind* (New York: Warner Books, 1981).

14. Tim D. White, "Additional Fossil Hominids from Laetoli, Tanzania: 1976–1979 Specimens," *American Journal of Physical Anthropology* 53 (1980): 487–504.

15. Donald C. Johanson and Maurice Taieb, "Plio-Pleistocene Hominid Discoveries in Hadar, Ethiopia," *Nature* 260 (1976): 293–297.

16. Donald C. Johanson, Tim D. White, and Yves Coppens, "A New Species of the Genus *Australopithecus* (Primates: Hominidae) from the Pliocene of Eastern Africa," *Kirtlandia* 28 (1978): 1–14.

17. William H. Kimbel and Tim D. White, "Variation, Sexual Dimorphism, and the Taxonomy of *Australopithecus*," in Fred E. Grine, ed., *Evolutionary History of the "Ro-bust" Australopithecines* (New York: Aldine de Gruyter, 1988), pp. 175–192.

18. C. Owen Lovejoy, Kevin F. Kern, Scott W. Simpson, and Richard S. Meindl, "A New Method for Estimation of Skeletal Dimorphism in Fossil Samples with an Application to *Australopithecus afarensis*," in G. Giacobini, ed., *Hominidae: Proceed-ings of the 2nd Congress of Human Paleontology* (Milan, Italy: Jaca Books, 1989), pp. 103–108; Henry M. McHenry, "Body Size and Proportions in Early Hominids," *American Journal of Physical Anthropology* 87 (1992): 407–431; Henry M. McHenry,

"Early Hominid Postcrania: Phylogeny and Function," in R. S. Corruccini and R. L. Ciochon, eds., *Integrative Paths to the Past: Paleoanthropological Advance in Honor of F. Clark Howell* (Englewood Cliffs, NJ: Prentice Hall, 1994), pp. 251–268.

19. Jack T. Stern and Randall L. Susman, "The Locomotor Anatomy of *Australopithecus afarensis*," *American Journal of Physical Anthropology* 60 (1983): 279–317; Randall L. Susman, Jack T. Stern, and William L. Jungers, "Arboreality and Bipedality in the Hadar Hominids," *Folia Primatologica* 43 (1984): 113–156.

20. C. Owen Lovejoy, "Evolution of Human Walking," *Scientific American* 256 (1988): 118–125.

21. Ibid.; C. Owen Lovejoy, "The Gait of Australopithecines," *Yearbook of Physical Anthropology* 17 (1974): 147–161; C. Owen Lovejoy, "A Biomechanical View of the Locomotor Diversity of Early Hominids," in Clifford Jolly, ed., *Early Hominids of Africa* (New York: St. Martin's, 1978), pp. 403–429.

22. Bruce Latimer, James C. Ohman, and C. Owen Lovejoy, "Talocrural Joint in African Hominoids: Implications for *Australopithecus afarensis*," *American Journal of Physical Anthropology* 74 (1987): 155–175; Bruce Latimer and C. Owen Lovejoy, "The Calcaneus of *Australopithecus afarensis* and Its Implications for the Evolution of Bipedality," *American Journal of Physical Anthropology* 78 (1989): 369–386; Bruce Latimer, "Locomotor Adaptations in *Australopithecus afarensis*: The Issue of Arboreality," in Yves Coppens and Brigitte Senut, eds., *Origine(s) de la Bipedie chez les Hominides* (Paris: Editions du CNRS, 1991), pp. 169–176.

23. Tim D. White and Gen Suwa, "Hominid Footprints at Laetoli: Facts and Interpretations," *American Journal of Physical Anthropology* 72 (1987): 485–514.

24. Berhane Asfaw, Yonas Beyene, Sileshi Semaw, Gen Suwa, Tim White, and Giday WoldeGabriel, "Fejej: A New Paleoanthropological Research Area in Ethiopia," *Journal of Human Evolution* 21 (1991): 137–143.

25. John G. Fleagle, D. T. Rasmussen, S. Yirga, T. M. Bown, and Fred E. Grine, "New Hominid Fossils from Fejej, Southern Ethiopia," *Journal of Human Evolution* 21 (1991): 145–152.

26. Jon Kalb, Clifford Jolly, Assefa Mebrate, Sileshi Tebedge, Charles Smart, Elizabeth B. Oswald, Douglas Cramer, Paul Whitehead, Craig B. Wood, Glenn C. Conroy, Tsrha Adefris, Louise Sperling, and B. Kana, "Fossil Mammals and Artefacts from the Middle Awash Valley, Ethiopia," *Nature* 298 (1982): 25–29; Jon E. Kalb, Elizabeth B. Oswald, Assefa Mebrate, Sileshi Tebedge, and Clifford Jolly, "Stratigraphy of the Awash Group, Middle Awash Valley, Afar, Ethiopia," *Newsletter of Stratigraphy* 11 (1982): 95–127.

27. Tim D. White, "Pliocene Hominids from the Middle Awash, Ethiopia," *Courier Forschungininstitut Senckenberg* 69 (1984): 57–68.

28. Tim D. White, Gen Suwa, William K. Hart, Robert C. Walters, Giday WoldeGabriel, Jean deHeinzelein, J. Desmond Clark, Berhane Asfaw, and Elisabeth Vrba, "New Discoveries of *Australopithecus* at Maka in Ethiopia," *Nature* 366 (1993): 261–264; Henry Gee, "Why We Still Love Lucy," *Nature* 366 (1993): 207.

29. Berhane Asfaw, "The Belohdelie Frontal: New Evidence of Early Hominid Cranial Morphology from the Afar of Ethiopia," *Journal of Human Evolution* 16 (1987): 611–624.

30. Leslie C. Aiello, "Variable but Singular," *Nature* 368 (1994): 399–400.

31. William H. Kimbel, Donald C. Johanson, and Yoel Rak, "The First Skull and Other New Discoveries of *Australopithecus afarensis* at Hadar, Ethiopia," *Nature* 368 (1994): 449–451.

32. Berhane Asfaw, Cynthia Ebinger, David Harding, Tim D. White, and Giday Wolde-Gabriel, "Space Based Imagery in Paleoanthropological Research: An Ethiopian Example," *National Geographic Research* 6 (1990): 418–434.
33. Tim D. White, Gen Suwa, and Berhane Asfaw, "*Australopithecus ramidus*, a New Species of Early Hominid from Aramis, Ethiopia," *Nature* 371 (1994): 306–312; Giday WoldeGabriel, Tim D. White, Gen Suwa, Paul Renne, Jean deHeinzelin, William K. Hart, and Grant Heiken, "Ecological and Temporal Placement of Early Pliocene Hominids at Aramis, Ethiopia," *Nature* 371 (1994): 330–333; Tim D. White, Gen Suwa, and Berhane Asfaw, "*Australopithecus ramidus*, a New Species of Early Hominid from Aramis, Ethiopia: Corrigendum," *Nature* 375 (1995): 88.

SUGGESTED READINGS

Aiello, Leslie C., and M. Christopher Dean. *An Introduction to Human Evolutionary Anatomy.* Academic Press: London, 1990. A summary textbook presenting comparative and functional analyses of human, ape, and fossil hominid anatomy.

Ciochon, Russell L., and John G. Fleagle. *The Human Evolution Sourcebook.* Englewood Cliffs, NJ: Prentice Hall, 1993. An extensive collection of readings covering many different aspects of human evolution during the past four million years.

Johanson, Donald C., and Maitland Edey. *Lucy: The Beginnings of Humankind.* New York: Warner Books, 1981. An entertaining first-hand account of the discovery, analysis, and announcement of *Australopithecus afarensis.*

Lovejoy, C. Owen. "Evolution of Human Walking." *Scientific American* 256 (1988): 118–125. A clearly written analysis of hominid locomotion focusing on *Australopithecus afarensis.*

White, Tim D., Donald C. Johanson, and William H. Kimbel. "*Australopithecus africanus*: Its Phyletic Position Reconsidered." *South African Journal of Science* 77 (1981): 445–470. A formal and thorough analysis of the phyletic relationships of the australopithecines, especially *Australopithecus afarensis.*

White, Tim D., Gen Suwa, William K. Hart, Robert C. Walters, Giday WoldeGabriel, Jean de Heinzelein, J. Desmond Clark, Berhane Asfaw, and Elisabeth Vrba. "New Discoveries of *Australopithecus* at Maka in Ethiopia." *Nature* 366 (1993): 261–264. The announcement and preliminary description of some newly discovered *Australopithecus afarensis* fossils from the Middle Awash region.

"Robust" Australopithecines, Our Family Tree, and Homoplasy

Henry M. McHenry

Darwin never predicted the existence of the "robust" australopithecines.[1] In his 1872 book *The Descent of Man* he foretold the discovery of fossils linking the evolutionary lineages of apes and people in Africa.[2] He speculated that bipedal walking probably evolved before brain expansion, and fossil evidence for that sequence was eventually discovered. But he did not set the stage for what a school boy would hammer out of the rocks at a site called Kromdraai in South Africa in 1938. That discovery was so unexpected that even after more than half a century and the discovery of hundreds of similar fossils, the robust australopithecines remain a mystery.

The mystery stems from the fact that they are so unlike anything living today. They walked erect on hindlimbs remodeled from the common pattern seen in other primates to the unique configuration typical of only the human family. They had relatively larger brains than did apes or earlier humans. But they had what an experienced portrait artist would call bizarre faces, with no foreheads, ridiculously flat cheeks, and enormous mouths. They had quite small canine teeth but huge molars. General consensus has them on a side branch of the human evolutionary tree, as implied by the original name given to them, "Paranthropus." They are often portrayed as our herbivorous cousins who made no tools and who became extinct at least a million years ago. But now there are new clues to the mystery that are bringing some surprises.

DISCOVERY

The school boy at Kromdraai gave his fossil to the foreman of a nearby mine, who sold it to Robert Broom on a Wednesday in June, 1938. Broom was one of the most colorful heroes in the drama of human origins research. He was a physician by training but his real love was paleontology. He was particularly well known for his work with the mammal-like reptiles from the Karoo of South Africa. He was an early defender of Raymond Dart's claim that *Australopithecus africanus* had human affinities, and in 1936 he discovered more of these human-like fossils. By this time he had written several books, including *The Coming of Man: Was It Accident or Design?* When he bought the Kromdraai fossil he was seventy-one years old, but still full of youthful vigor and mischief. His mischievousness included playing tricks on the press: He once advised a young apprentice to "publish only part of what you know, so when critics harp you can devastate them with new information." It is said that he always wore a stiff collar and tie on the off chance that photographers would show up. Sometimes when he found important fossils he would cover them up again, invite the press out to the site for a routine interview, and "discover" the fossils before their eyes (and cameras). One story tells of an assistant who grew tired of these antics and painted a museum catalogue number on one of these "rediscovered" fossils, which somewhat reduced the spontaneity of Broom's feigned astonishment at the moment of discovery.

It is interesting to look up Broom's original announcements of discoveries.[3] He did not waste time. A new find would appear in the British science journal *Nature* very soon after its discovery. Accompanying the announcement would be Broom's remarkable sketches, which captured the essential details of the fragmentary and distorted fossils. Broom would distill the essential importance of a discovery without paying much attention to previous scientific literature. Often he sent casts of fossils to various other scientists. Most of these scientists did not realize the significance of the Kromdraai hominid. But Broom, who was one of the wild men of Africa along with Raymond Dart and Louis Leakey, did.

The strangeness of the Kromdraai hominid haunted the writers of human evolution for years. From the point of view of comparative anatomy at the time, it had a mix of human and ape characteristics. It was an ape by the fact that its brain was so small (502 cc by recent measures, although Broom gave various estimates that were higher). It was gorilla-like in that it had a crest of bone on the top of the skull for the attachment of powerful chewing muscles. If one measured humanness by brain size (as Broom did), this was an ape. But why did it have so many human attributes? Between 1938 and 1947 Broom had the chance to reflect on what he had found. He considered the advice of various sympathetic colleagues, particularly Franz Weidenreich. Ultimately he kept to his original opinion that it belonged to the human family. In the textbooks of the time, the Kromdraai hominid and its kin were still considered of the human lineage.

Close to his eightieth birthday in 1948, Broom and his young assistant John Robinson began excavations at Swartkrans. Swartkrans proved to be the most important site for understanding the robust australopithecines.[4] Their method of excavation was speeded by the liberal use of TNT. The results were spectacular in fossil hominids but, inevitably, problematic to those who came later to determine geological age. What they found were Kromdraai-like fossils different enough to warrant separate species names according to some (Broom, How-ell, Grine), but most paleontologists refer them to *Australopithecus robustus*. The richness of Swartkrans was astounding. Whole skulls, complete denti-tions, and a few bits of the rest of the skeleton came to light. Among the skele-tal remains were remains of a hip. The hip of these robust australopithecines appeared to have the fundamental reorganization for bipedalism that char-acterized other early hominids. Unfortunately, the site was owned by a min-ing company that took over when the paleontologists uncovered commercially valuable minerals. The mess left by the miners took decades to sort out. For-tunately, a highly competent and persistent geologist, C. K. Brain (who be-came director of the Transvaal Museum), sorted out the jumble left by the miners and by Broom's rapid excavations so that Swartkrans is now one of the best understood early hominid sites.

Broom worked quickly in the last decades of his life. He did not worry too much about convention. Nor did Louis Leakey, a contemporary of Broom's who also made great strides in hominid discovery. Leakey was a Kenyan by birth, steeped in Kikuyu tradition and language and formally educated in the British system, complete with a Ph.D. from Cambridge University. With his wife Mary he began working at Olduvai Gorge in Tanzania in the mid-1930s. The site yielded much ancient fauna and archaic stone tools, but unlike the spectacularly hominid-rich sites of South Africa (especially Swartkrans), it contained almost no hominid fossils. There were many hominid tools there, however, and Mary became the foremost authority on the earliest material culture of our ancestors. The big event happened in 1959 with Mary's dis-covery of Olduvai Hominid 5.

O.H. 5 was discovered in 1959 and proved to have its closest affinities with the robust australopithecines of South Africa.[5] But it was quite different in many respects. Most conspicuously it had enormous cheek teeth that were way above the size seen in even the largest specimen of the robust australo-pithecines of South Africa. Leakey gave it the name *Zinjanthropus boisei*, but that name was changed to *Australopithecus boisei* by Phillip Tobias, who wrote the definitive monograph on the specimen. Hundreds of additional speci-mens of *A. boisei* are now known thanks to the efforts of a host of skillful col-lectors at various sites in Tanzania, Kenya, and Ethiopia.

A third species of robust australopithecine, *A. aethiopicus*, is earlier and more primitive than *A. boisei*. A few jaws and teeth have been discovered since the late 1960s. In 1985 a complete skull of *A. aethiopicus* came to light from west of Lake Turkana in Kenya in beds as old as 2.5 million years.[6]

SPECIES OF "ROBUST" AUSTRALOPITHECINE

We will never know precisely what happened in history even if we have writ-ten records because those records will be one author's version of events. But we do have the paleontological record of mammals in the past and the geochronology. We are blessed with thousands of specimens from East and South Africa and we can begin to understand what these near-humans were like. Let us turn to look at the three species of "robust" australopithecine: *A. robustus*, *A. boisei*, and *A. aethiopicus*.

Australopithecus robustus is known only from two cave sites in South Africa: Kromdraai and Swartkrans. Neither site can be dated with precision but the associated fossil animals fit with animals between 1.8 and 1.0 million years ago. The habitat in which they lived was a dry and open grassland. Their skulls and teeth are designed for heavy chewing. The cheek teeth are quite large, especially relative to the size of their bodies. The roots of these teeth are fit into heavily built jaws. The chewing muscles were apparently very large, as can be seen by the attachment areas on their robust cheek bones and sagittal crest. The face is buttressed against the chewing forces as well.

Heavy chewing left such a conspicuous mark on the skulls and teeth of *A. robustus* that it is easy to overlook features that are *Homo*-like and unlike *Australopithecus*. The face is more tucked under the braincase, for example. The brain is larger. The base of the skull is more flexed. The jaw joint is deeper. The thumb is relatively longer and its tip is broad and flat like later *Homo* and unlike earlier *Australopithecus*.

Although the term *robustus* implies a large and powerfully built body, newly discovered skeletal parts show that *A. robustus* ranged in body weight from quite small (perhaps as little as 62 pounds) to only moderately heavy (120 pounds) compared to modern humans. The average female may have been about seventy pounds and the average male about eighty-eight pounds. The fossil material is too fragmentary to make precise estimates of stature, but the available evidence suggests the female stood at about three feet seven inches and the male stood at about four feet four inches. The small size of the body implies that the relative size of the brain was larger than may be apparent from its absolute size. In fact, its relative brain size is very close to that seen in the earliest species of *Homo*.

In the last years of his life Broom was assisted by John Robinson. Upon Broom's death in 1951, Robinson took on the task of excavation and fossil description. He developed what came to be known as the dietary hypothesis. According to this theory there were fundamentally two kinds of hominids in the Plio-Pleistocene. One was the "robust" australopithecine (which he called *Paranthropus*) that was specialized for herbivory, and the other was the "gracile" australopithecine (*A. africanus*, which he later referred to as *Homo africanus*) that was an omnivore/carnivore. By this theory the former became extinct while the latter evolved into *H. erectus*. The specialization for herbivory in *A. robustus* includes the suite of traits listed earlier as adaptations for heavy chewing.

Like most generalizations about human evolution, Robinson's dietary hypothesis was controversial, but it stood as a useful model for several decades. Detailed analyses of the tooth surface using the scanning electron microscope appeared to confirm that the diet of *A. robustus* consisted primarily of plants, particularly small and hard objects like seeds, nuts, and tubers, while early *Homo* was more omnivorous. But as new fossil hominid species were discovered in East Africa and new analyses were done on the old fossils, the usefulness of the model diminished. Now there is a new understanding of how similar the two South African species—*A. africanus* and *A. robustus*—are when compared to other early hominid species. They share a suite of traits that are absent in earlier species of *Australopithecus*, including expanded cheek teeth and faces remodeled to withstand forces generated from heavy chewing. There is also new evidence that *A. robustus* was not a strict vegetarian.

The possibility that *A. robustus* was omnivorous is suggested by the distribution of plants and animals and their availability for consumption by creatures such as this large primate. Omnivory is also suggested by studies of the stable carbon isotopes and strontium-calcium ratios in their teeth and bones. Simply put, they have the chemical signal associated with animals whose diet is omnivorous and not specialized herbivory. In fact, there is some direct evidence of animal butchering associated with the cave deposits containing *A. robustus*. Distinctive cut marks made by stone tools occur on animal bones in Member 3 of Swartkrans as well as evidence of controlled use of fire. *A. robustus* is the only hominid recovered from this layer of the cave, but *Homo* was around earlier (in Member 1 and 2) and may have been in the area during Member 3 times and simply escaped preservation.

Australopithecus boisei is known from East African deposits from northern Tanzania to southern Ethiopia. It spans the time between approximately 2.2 and 1.3 million years ago. It is distinguished by its huge chewing apparatus. The architecture of the skull and teeth of this species is dominated by the stresses of heavy chewing. The molar teeth are enormous, even relative to the size seen in *A. robustus*. The premolars have expanded so much that they take on the look of molars. The jaw is massively thick and deep. The attachment areas for the muscles that move the jaw are powerfully built, including a strong sagittal crest on top of the skull and thick cheek bones. The cheek bones are pulled forward so that the sides of the face project ahead of the root of the nose. The skull and jaw are arranged to maximize biting force at the level of the cheek teeth.

Like its cousin to the south, *A. boisei* shares many features with *Homo* that are not seen in earlier species of *Australopithecus*. The face tends to be tucked in under the braincase more, although this is variable. The base of the skull is strongly flexed. The jaw joint is deep. The brain is expanded with an average size of 488 cc compared to the 384 cc of *A. afarensis*. The variation in size of the jaws and faces is considerable, which suggests that sexual dimorphism in size was greater than that in recent *Homo*.

Until recently, it was assumed that *A. boisei* had a large body to match its huge teeth, but no postcranial bones were directly associated with the crania or teeth of this species. This created a problem because the deposits that contained diagnostic craniodental fossils of *A. boisei* also contained early *Homo* fossils. The isolated pieces of postcrania could not be sorted by species with any confidence because no one knew what the skeleton of *A. boisei* should look like. Fortunately, a fragmentary skeleton has come to light that is associated with an identifiable piece of *A. boisei* jaw. There are also bits of isolated postcrania at one site that contains only *A. boisei* craniodental material, so it is likely that all of it is *A. boisei*. From these comes the surprising fact that *A. boisei*, like *A. robustus*, had a relatively petite body, with females weighing approximately seventy pounds and standing at approximately four feet one inch. Males may have weighed approximately 108 pounds and stood at four feet six inches.

These small body weight estimates imply that the relative brain size of *A. boisei* was larger than that of *A. afarensis*. They also show just how relatively enormous the cheek teeth were: One estimate is that the area of these teeth was at least 2.5 times larger than expected from that seen in modern great apes or humans.

Tools and other archaeological indications of hominid activity in East African sites are relatively abundant throughout the time span of *A. boisei*. Authorship of these cultural relics is usually attributed to species of *Homo*, however, because *Homo* was present during this time, and after the extinction of *A. boisei* the tools continue.

Australopithecus aethiopicus is the least well known of the "robust" australopithecines. The name *aethiopicus* comes from the 1967 discovery of a 2.6-million-year-old jaw from Omo. The Omo sediments have yielded a substantial number of these "robust" australopithecines. Careful study of the lower premolars shows that *A. boisei* can be identified by many distinctive features in teeth dated from between 2.2 and 1.8 million years. There also are isolated teeth dated from between 2.7 and 2.2 million years ago that are "robust" australopithecine but not *A. boisei*. These may be referred to *A. aethiopicus*. Such tenuous attribution erodes confidence in the reality of this species; but whatever it is, we do have one great jewel, the Black Skull (KNM-WT 17000).

The Black Skull is nearly complete except for the crown of its teeth. It lay in sediments known to be 2.5 million years old until Alan Walker (a member of the team led by Louis and Mary Leakey's middle son, Richard) picked it up in 1985. A glance at its face brings quick recognition followed by doubt. It has many superficial resemblances to *A. boisei*. There are wide cheeks with a deeply set root of the nose made even deeper by the forward projection of the cheeks. The huge cheek teeth are there and also the sagittal crest. But look further.

Behind the superficial resemblances to *A. boisei* lie some real surprises: The sagittal crest peaks way back on the skull, not forward as in *A. boisei*; the muzzle protrudes way forward; the skull base is unflexed; the jaw joint is shallow. The brain case housed almost one hundred cc less brain than did that of *A. boisei*. All of these are traits of the early and primitive species, *A. afarensis*, of "Lucy" fame.

HOMOPLASY AND THE "ROBUST" AUSTRALOPITHECINES

One of the most interesting aspects of the "robust" australopithecines is what they reveal about homoplasy. Homoplasy is the independent appearance of similar structures in two or more lines of descent. The term *independent* is the key here. It applies to resemblances between organisms that are not attributable to inheritance from a shared ancestor. Homoplastic resemblance comes about because lineages often change through time in similar ways. In Darwin's words, "... animals belonging to two most distinct lines of descent may readily become adapted to similar conditions, and thus assume a close external resemblance."[7] He went on to warn, "... but such resemblances will not reveal—will rather tend to conceal their blood-relationship to their proper line of descent." The fin-like limbs of whales and fishes, he observed, resembled each other not because of common descent but as adaptations for swimming. The resemblance is due to convergent or parallel evolution, not to inheritance from a common ancestor. The wings of birds, bats, and butterflies are due to homoplasy. The opposable big toes of lemurs, monkeys, and apes, on the other hand, are due to inheritance from an ancestor who also had this trait.

The idea is simple, but subtleties can obscure the distinction between resemblances due to homoplasy and those due to common inheritance. In the sixth edition of *On the Origin of Species* Darwin pointed out one reason for the obscuration. Closely related organisms, he observed, "... have inherited so much in common in their constitution that they are apt to vary under similar exciting causes in a similar manner; and this would obviously aid in the acquirement through natural selection of parts or organs strikingly like each other, independently of their direct inheritance from a common progenitor."[8]

Among species of fossil hominids, some resemblances are due to homoplasy and some are inherited from a shared ancestor. Homoplastic resemblances occur when species are so closely related that they evolve similarities in parallel as they adapt to the same environments. Homoplasy obscures attempts to find phylogenetic relationships. An excellent example of this obscuration is the problem of interpreting the Black Skull (KNM-WT 17000).

When Alan Walker found the Black Skull there was little doubt that it belonged to the "robust" australopithecines. It shared with *A. robustus* and *A. boisei* a suite of traits related to heavy chewing, including huge cheek teeth, massive jaws, and a heavily buttressed skull to withstand the chewing forces. These resemblances imply close phylogenetic affinity among these hominids *if* these traits are due to descent from a shared ancestor. However, most authors agree that the "robust" australopithecines form a branch of our family tree that is quite separate from the lineage leading to *Homo*. The black skull and other "robust" hominids from between 2.7 and 2.3 million years ago form the base of this branch as the species *A. aethiopicus*. The species from South Africa, *A. robustus* (1.8–1.0 million years ago), and from East Africa, *A. boisei* (2.2–1.3 million years ago), are the terminal parts of the "robust" branch. Relative to other contemporary hominid species, they form one branch, or, more precisely, they are monophyletic. They share a similar complex of features related to heavy chewing. Their faces, cranial vaults, jaws, and teeth are strikingly similar in many specific ways. Presumably they inherited these similarities from a common ancestor, making these resemblances homologous.

But the view that the robust australopithecines are quite separate from the *Homo* line presents a problem. If the "robusts" are monophyletic with *A. aethiopicus* at the base, and *A. robustus* and *A. boisei* arise out of this common stem, then why do these two later species resemble early *Homo* in so many ways? Early *Homo* and the later "robust" species share numerous traits that are not present in *A. aethiopicus*. These resemblances include brain expansion, flexion of the cranial base, reduction of prognathism, deepening of the jaw joint (TMJ), and a host of other features. In fact, in many ways *A. robustus* and *A. boisei* resemble early *Homo* more than any of these resembles *A. africanus* (the 2.4- to 3-million-year-old South African "gracile" australopithecine). Perhaps these resemblances are due to homoplasy. On the other hand, perhaps the resemblances between *A. aethiopicus* and the later "robust" australopithecines are due to homoplasy and the "robust" species are not monophyletic.

It is a difficult paradox to resolve. Some of these resemblances are concealing the true "… blood-relationships to their proper lines of descent," to use Darwin's words. Clearly, some procedure needs to be applied to partial out homoplasy in a way that makes assumptions and biases clearly visible. Many procedures are available, but those developed by Willi Hennig have evolved into an approach that has been effectively applied to this problem.[9] Although there are many extreme views that have developed out of Hennig's system, some fundamental features of what is commonly referred to as cladistic, or phylogenetic, analysis have proved to be very useful.

CLADISTIC ANALYSIS

One useful feature of cladistic analysis is that when it is properly applied, assumptions and biases are clearly revealed. At each step one has to expose one's thinking to critical analysis. This exposure safeguards against the corrupting desire to advocate a fixed position.

There are many ways to proceed in a cladistic analysis, but it is helpful to follow a few basic steps. First, traits and species must be defined clearly. This step exposes a weak flank for critics to attack but ensures that the practitioner has some depth of defense. Paleospecies are hard to define, of course, and traits must be selected with special care. Care means that the traits are selected without the bias of a preconceived desire to advocate a fixed position. Care must also be given to the functional meaning of the trait. A paradox arises here because the interpreter of the functional meaning of a feature may have a bias about how the overall scheme of phylogenetic relationships ought to be.

A second step involves following the sequence of changes in the trait in the species under study without regard to preconceived notions about the direction. Brain size in human evolution increases through time and there is no problem with bias in that. The chewing surface area of cheek-teeth is medium in the earliest species of hominid (*A. afarensis*), large in one of the next oldest species (*A. africanus*), huge in the "robust" australopithecines that came after *A. africanus*, and medium again in the earliest *Homo*. This second step disregards time and preconception. The sequence of changes in cheek-tooth size places *A. afarensis* and the earliest *Homo* together.

The beauty of this formal procedure is that the practitioner is exposed at every step to corrections kindly provided by colleagues. A third step, exposing even greater vulnerability, consists of arranging the species according to where they fall—from most primitive to most derived. There are formal procedures for such ordering. Time provides an imperfect clue; usually the most primitive is the earliest, but not always. A check is provided by comparing the expression of the trait in closely related species that are not part of the analysis (outgroups that for hominid studies consist of nonhominid members of the ape and human superfamily, *Hominoidea*). A variety of other methods exist for finding the direction of change for each trait, but usually time and outgroup tell a consistent tale.

At this point one has a trait list with the expression of each trait in a list of species and a direction of change for each trait. From this one can derive a branching tree of relationships (cladogram) for each trait. The procedure further exposes the practitioner to scrutiny by doubting colleagues, although drawing a cladogram is quite lock-step. One simply takes each trait individually, joins the two most derived species by two intersecting lines, connects the next most derived species, and so on. The simple diagram for each trait is meaningful. When the two lines join from the two most derived species, the resulting mutual line means that these species are united by descent from a common ancestor (the joined line) who also expressed the trait. It is so simple, but so easily missed.

The final step is to compile all the cladograms for all the traits and look for patterns. Usually there are many different cladograms. Brain size and cheek-tooth area in hominid species are two quite distinct patterns. Here again the cladist exposes the weaknesses and strengths of the analysis for all to judge. The most common way to resolve this conflict between cladograms is to choose the one that requires the least amount of homoplasy and is the most consistent with the data (i.e., the most parsimonious).

OTHER SPECIES OF EARLY HOMINID

There are many ways to divide the hominid bone pile into genera and species. In what follows, early hominids are divided into six species of *Australopithecus*. Early *Homo* is treated as a single species in this analysis. The three "robust" australopithecines, *A. robustus*, *A. boisei*, and *A. aethiopicus* have already been described. The remaining species are as follows:

Australopithecus ramidus is the earliest well-defined species of hominid, and it is best known from deposits in Ethiopia dated to 4.4 million years ago. Overall, it is quite ape-like, but it does share a few unique features with later hominids, such as a broader, less projecting canine, a shorter cranial base, and some details of the elbow. It had thinner molar enamel than did later hominids, perhaps implying a diet more similar to that of African apes. Its habitat was closed woodland. Unfortunately, as of yet there are no hindlimb fossils to ascertain its locomotion.

Australopithecus afarensis is the next oldest (3.9–2.8 million years old). It is difficult to appreciate fully because it has such a wonderful mixture of ape-like and human-like qualities. Its skull is close to what one might expect in the common ancestor of apes and people, with an ape-sized brain (384 cc of endocranial volume, roughly the same as that of a chimp and not at all like that of a modern human, which averages about 1350 cc), big muzzle, flat cranial base, flat jaw-joint, and sagittal crest that is highest in the back. Its teeth bridge the gap between ape and people, with large central and small lateral upper incisors (ape-like), reduced upper canine (human-like) but still large with shear facets formed against the lower premolar (ape-like), variable lower first premolar, with some individuals having only one strong cusp (ape-like), and others having some development of a tongue-sided (metaconid) cusp (between modern ape and human), and parallel or convergent tooth rows (ape-like). Their cheek teeth were quite large relative to their body weight. Below the head (postcranially), *A. afarensis* is mostly human-like in having a hip, thigh, knee, ankle, and foot adapted to bipedality. But superimposed on this human-like body are many traits reminiscent of the common ancestor, such as somewhat elongated and curved fingers and toes, a relatively short thigh, and backwardly facing pelvic blades. Sexual dimorphism in body size is higher than in modern humans, but not as high as in *Gorilla* or *Pongo*. Males weighed approximately one hundred pounds and females weighed approximately sixty-five pounds. They lived in a mixed habitat, with some in well-watered woodland conditions and others in more open environments.

Relative to *A. afarensis* and *A. aethiopicus*, *Australopithecus africanus* has more *Homo*-like craniodental features. It is known only in South Africa and its age is only approximately established (three to two million years ago). Its vault is higher and more rounded than that of the earlier species, its face is less prognatic, and its jaw-joint is deeper. The lower first premolars are bicuspid. Cranial capacity is larger (442 cc). Although the skeleton below the head is much like that of *A. afarensis*, the hand bones are more *Homo*-like. Body size resembles that of *A. afarensis*, although sexual dimorphism appears to be slightly reduced, with males weighing approximately ninety pounds and females weighing approximately sixty-seven pounds. The cheek-teeth are larger than those of *A. afarensis*.

There is evidence that there may be two species represented among specimens attributed to *Homo habilis*, although some authors make a strong case for just one. For the purposes of this study, it is appropriate to regard specimens from 2.4 to 1.6 million years ago that have been referred to as *Homo* as a single unit. Variability is high, but some consistent differences from *Australopithecus* are apparent. Brain-size is higher (597 cc average), vaults are more rounded and higher, and cheek-teeth are smaller. Body size for males may have been approximately 144 pounds, and females may have weighed approximately 70 pounds.

TRAITS AND STATES

The next step in cladistic analysis is selecting traits and their expressions in each species. Randall Skelton's and my study uses seventy-seven variable morphological traits and their expression in all of these species (except *A. ramidus*) and in an outgroup (extant great apes).[10] The traits include twenty-two features of the face, palate, and zygomatic arch; twenty-five dental traits; seven mandible traits; ten features of the basicranium; and thirteen features of the cranial vault. These can be grouped into five functional complexes, including heavy chewing, front teeth, bending of the base of the skull, muzzle protrusion, and encephalization. We provide a further description and discussion of these traits and their functional meaning.

MORPHOCLINES AND CLADOGRAMS

The direction of evolutionary transformation for each trait (i.e., the polarity) flows from primitive to derived. The outgroup (i.e., great apes) determines the primitive pole unambiguously for all of the craniodental traits in this study. For example, brain size is 343 cc in *Pan paniscus* (outgroup), 384 cc in *A. afarensis*, 399 cc in *A. aethiopicus*, 420 cc in *A. africanus*, 488 cc in *A. boisei*, 502 cc in *A. robustus*, and 597 cc in early *Homo*. This sequence is the polarized morphocline. It implies that early *Homo* and *A. robustus* are the most highly derived for this trait and can be joined as sister taxa relative to all other species. Their joint line connects next to *A. boisei* to form a group of three species who are derived relative to all other species. The process continues until all groups are connected into a cladogram, as shown in Figure 9-1.

The simplicity and straightforwardness of this procedure allows for conflicting evidence. For example, unlike endocranial volume, cheek-tooth area goes from 227 mm^2 in the outgroup to 460 mm^2 in *A. afarensis* to 479 mm^2 in early *Homo* to 516 mm^2 in *A. africanus* to 588 mm^2 in *A. robustus* to 688 mm^2 in *A. aethiopicus* to 799 mm^2 in *A. boisei*. This results in the cladogram displayed in Figure 9-2. It is incompatible with the cladogram in Figure 9-1. To choose the one that most likely reflects the true evolutionary relationships, one must use the principle of parsimony.

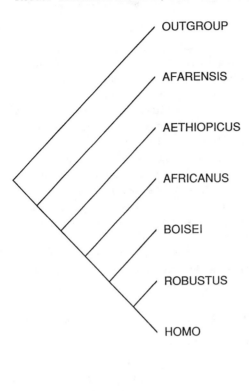

FIGURE 9-1   CLADOGRAM IMPLIED BY THE POLARIZED MORPHOCLINE BASED ON ENDOCRANIAL VOLUME

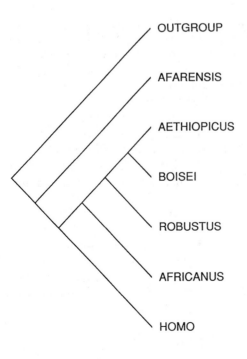

FIGURE 9-2   CLADOGRAM IMPLIED BY THE POLARIZED MORPHOCLINE BASED ON CHEEK–TOOTH AREA

PARSIMONY

The theory of parsimony is the subject of much discussion, but fundamentally it is quite straightforward. To deal with the conflicting evidence revealed by incompatible cladograms, parsimony assumes that the true phylogeny resulted from the fewest evolutionary steps. There are various measures of parsimony. The most commonly used measure is the consistency index, which is simply the minimum number of steps possible divided by the actual number of steps. If no homoplasy were present, then the consistency index would equal one.

The most parsimonious cladogram that can be constructed out of the seventy-seven traits described by Skelton and me is the one shown in Figure 9-3. The two most derived taxa are *A. robustus* and *A. boisei*, whose stem joins *Homo* in forming the next most derived group relative to the other species. The *A. robustus/boisei/Homo* clade then joins *A. africanus* and that stem next joins *A. aethiopicus*. *A. afarensis* forms a sister clade to all other hominids. The consistency index is 0.722 when all 77 traits are used. This is also the most parsimonious cladogram when traits are grouped into anatomical regions or functional complexes.

OUR FAMILY PHYLOGENY

Figure 9-4 displays the phylogenetic tree implied by the most parsimonious cladogram. *A. ramidus* was not included in the analysis but its position is unequivocally at the root of the entire tree as the most primitive of all hominid species. These results imply that there was a large amount of parallel evolution in our family tree. The most conspicuous case of parallel evolution involves heavy chewing in *A. aethiopicus*, *A. robustus*, and *A. boisei*. This phylogeny implies that the specific resemblances between *A. aethiopicus* and the later "robust" australopithecines are due not to descent from a common ancestor who had these traits but to independent acquisition. This is a very surprising result. The Black Skull looks so much like *A. boisei* that its discoverers and original describers attribute it to that species and not to *A. aethiopicus*. For example, both have extreme forward projection of the cheek bone, huge cheek teeth, enormous lower jaw robusticity, a heart-shaped foramen magnum (the hole for the spinal cord), and similarity in how the vault bones articulate above the ear.

But all of these traits except for the heart-shaped foramen magnum are related to the functional complex of heavy chewing. The huge cheek-teeth and robust mandibles of both species are obviously part of masticatory heavy chewing. The forward projection of the cheek bones brings the masseter muscles into a position of maximum power. The encroachment by the root of the cheek bones obscures the expression of the pillars of the face. Even the way the vault bones fit together above the ear is related to the function of the forces generated by the chewing muscles.

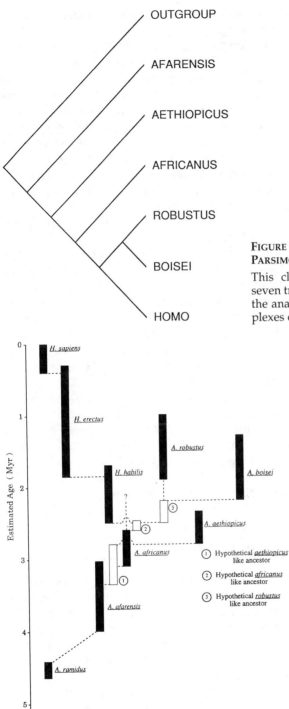

OUTGROUP

AFARENSIS

AETHIOPICUS

AFRICANUS

ROBUSTUS

BOISEI

HOMO

FIGURE 9-3 THE MOST PARSIMONIOUS CLADOGRAM

This cladogram uses all seventy-seven traits or summary scores from the analyses of five functional complexes or seven anatomical regions.

H. sapiens

H. erectus

A. robustus

H. habilis

A. boisei

Estimated Age (Myr)

?

③

②

A. aethiopicus

A. africanus

① Hypothetical *aethiopicus* like ancestor

② Hypothetical *africanus* like ancestor

③ Hypothetical *robustus* like ancestor

A. afarensis

A. ramidus

FIGURE 9-4   PHYLOGENY IMPLIED BY THE MOST PARSIMONIOUS CLADOGRAM

Three hypothetical ancestors are predicted. The horizontal axis is calibrated to the cheek–tooth area.

Theoretically, it is understandable how such detailed similarity could be due to parallel evolution. This is an example of what Darwin referred to: These species are closely related and share "… so much in common in their constitution" that similar selective forces produce similar morphologies. The selective forces in this case are related to a feeding adaptation that is associated with a specialized ecological niche. As Ernst Mayr points out, "Most adaptations for special niches are far less revealing taxonomically than they are conspicuous.… Occupation of a special food niche and the correlated adaptations have a particularly low taxonomic value."[11] In fact, many of the same traits characteristic of *A. aethiopicus* and the other "robust" australopithecines reappear in distantly related species adapted to heavy chewing. Expansion of the cheek-teeth, shortening of the muzzle, and anterior migration of the attachment areas of the chewing muscles are seen in other primates whose diet requires heavy chewing (e.g., *Hadropithecus*, *Theropithecus*, probably *Gigantopithecus*, and *Ekmowechashala*).

Although the most parsimonious cladogram implies this phylogeny, other cladograms are possible but less probable. A cladogram linking *A. aethiopicus* to *A. boisei* and *A. robustus* as one branch and *A. africanus*/early *Homo* as another requires more evolutionary steps because the later "robusts" resemble early *Homo* in so many features. These features include many aspects of bending of the base of the skull, loss of a muzzle, changes in the front teeth, and encephalization. The skeleton below the head, although not included in this analysis, supports the view that at least *A. robustus* and early *Homo* are monophyletic relative to other species of early hominid.

Whatever the true phylogeny is—and there can be only one—the fact remains that homoplasy is commonplace. There is just no avoiding it: Some resemblances appeared independently, not because of evolution from a common ancestor who possessed the same features. Either adaptations for heavy chewing evolved twice, or bending of the base of the skull, loss of a muzzle, reduction in the front teeth, and encephalization evolved more than once. Darwin's astute observations apply to our own family tree.

GENERAL LESSONS

One general lesson from this approach to hominid evolutionary biology is how to deal with ambiguity. As the King of Siam said in Rodgers and Hammerstein's *The King and I*, "What was so was so; what was not was not," but now "some things nearly so, others nearly not." It's a common experience. Perhaps it is uncommon to have such a clear example of ambiguity as is provided by the hominid fossil record. Either heavy chewing resulted in the independent evolution of *A. aethiopicus* and *A. robustus*/*boisei* or other forces shaped *A. boisei*, *A. robustus*, and early *Homo* to resemble each other in encephalization, bending of the base of the skull, loss of a muzzle, and reduction in the front teeth.

From this point of view it is not particularly useful to advocate a fixed position. One needs to make the best of our tiny sample of life in the past, to remain open to new discoveries and ideas, and to enjoy the pleasure of learning and changing.

NOTES

1. The phrase "robust" australopithecines refers to early hominids that have specializations for heavy chewing. Various taxonomic names are associated with these fossils, including *Paranthropus robustus* (from the South African site of Kromdraai), *Paranthropus crassidens* (from Swartkrans of South Africa), *Zinjanthropus boisei* of Olduvai, and *Paraustralopithecus aethiopicus* from Member C of the Shunguru Formation of Omo. They are very similar to one another in features related to heavy chewing and many authors prefer to recognize their similarity by designating them as a separate genus, *Paranthropus*.
2. Charles Darwin, *The Descent of Man and Selection in Relation to Sex* (London: D. Appleton and Co., 1872).
3. Robert Broom, "The Pleistocene Anthropoid Apes of South Africa," *Nature* 142 (1938): 377–379.
4. Robert Broom, "Another New Type of Fossil Ape-man," *Nature* 163 (1949): 57.
5. Louis B. Leakey, "A New Fossil Skull from Olduvai," *Nature* 184 (1959): 491–493.
6. Alan Walker, Richard E. Leakey, John M. Harris, and Frank H. Brown, "2.5 Myr. *Australopithecus boisei* from West of Lake Turkana, Kenya," *Nature* 322 (1986): 517–522.
7. Charles Darwin, *On the Origin of Species by Means of Natural Selection* (London: John Murray, 1859), p. 427.
8. Charles Darwin, *The Origin of Species*, 6th ed. (New York: Random House, 1872), p. 328.
9. Willi Hennig, *Phylogenetic Systematics* (Urbana: University of Illinois Press, 1966).
10. Randall R. Skelton and Henry M. McHenry, "Evolutionary Relationships among Early Hominids," *Journal of Human Evolution* 23 (1992): 309–349.
11. Ernest Mayr, *Principles of Systematic Zoology* (New York: McGraw-Hill, 1969), p. 125.

SUGGESTED READINGS

Grine, Fredrick, ed. *The Evolutionary History of the "Robust" Australopithecines*. New York: Aldine de Gruyter, 1988. Thorough but technical discussions of all aspects of these creatures.

Jones, Steven, Robert Martin, and David Pilbeam, eds. *The Cambridge Encyclopedia of Human Evolution*. Cambridge: Cambridge University Press, 1992. A beautifully written and authoritative work on all aspects of human evolution.

Klein, Richard C. *The Human Career*. Chicago: University of Chicago Press, 1989. A starting point for information about hominid species, sites, archaeology, and more.

Ridley, Marc. *Evolution*. Boston: Blackwell Scientific Publications, 1993. A very readable account of our current understanding of evolutionary processes.

Tattersall, Ian, Eric Delson, and John Van Couvering. *Encyclopedia of Human Evolution and Prehistory*. New York: Garland Publishing, 1988. Includes articles on early hominid species and has nice illustrations.

THE NATURAL HISTORY
AND EVOLUTIONARY FATE
OF HOMO ERECTUS

ANDREW KRAMER

Although scientists who study human evolution are popularly perceived as constantly being involved in rancorous debates, these paleoanthropologists would unanimously agree that we *have* evolved from more primitive predecessors. *Homo erectus,* a hominid species that flourished for over one million years in Africa and Asia, is generally regarded as humanity's immediate ancestor. However, there is still plenty of controversy surrounding the question of how (and even if) *Homo erectus* evolved into *Homo sapiens.*

In this chapter I present the remarkable story of the discoveries of and the ideas surrounding the original *Homo erectus* fossils. This leads into a discussion of how these early interpretations have influenced the present-day debates concerning the evolution of *Homo erectus.* Finally, I detail my own perspectives and contributions to the resolutions of these questions, and I conclude with some suggestions for future research.

<hr>

DUBOIS'S APE-MAN[1]

In the late 1800s the famous German naturalist Ernst Haeckel posited that a form of prehuman that bridged the evolutionary gap between apes and humans existed sometime in the distant past. Haeckel was even bold enough to name this hypothetical creature "*Pithecanthropus alalus*," literally, "speechless ape-man." This idea fired the popular imagination and was the original source of the term *missing link,* a phrase coined by an American journalist at the time. In the early 1880s a young Dutch physician named Eugène Dubois, an anatomy assistant under Haeckel at the University of Jena, fell under the thrall of his mentor's evolutionism. In fact, Haeckel's ideas captivated Dubois so completely that he gave up his promising medical career to devote himself full time to searching for the missing link!

Although Dubois's chances amounted to what was in all likelihood a million-to-one shot, he defied the odds and, amazingly enough, actually discovered what he had set out to find. Dubois decided to search for his fossils in what is today the island country of Indonesia, in southeast Asia. His decision was based on a combination of theoretical and pragmatic considerations. First, Haeckel thought that the gibbon was the closest living relative to humans, not the African apes as Darwin had proposed (correctly, it turned out). Therefore, because gibbons occupy the forests of mainland and island southeast Asia, Dubois logically concluded that the common ancestor of these apes and humans may have lived in this same region. The young Dutchman's decision to direct his energies to the area's islands, not to the mainland, was purely practical: What is today known as the Republic of Indonesia was the Dutch East Indies then.

Dubois enlisted in the Dutch colonial army as a health officer and arrived on the island of Sumatra in 1887. His paleontological research was eventually supported by the colonial government because much of the geological information he recovered was of economic value, such as sites that could produce potentially profitable mines. By 1890 Dubois had himself transferred to Java, and two years later he made the discovery that would rock the anthropological world. In September of 1891, near the village of Trinil along the banks of the Solo River, his team of convict excavators uncovered a long and low skull cap with protruding, ape-like brow ridges. The following August, only forty feet from the original find, a humanlike femur (thigh bone) was discovered that belonged, Dubois believed, to the same individual as the skull. Dubois published his interpretations of these finds in 1894 and concluded that because the skull was intermediate in size between apes and humans he had truly found the missing link. Honoring Haeckel, and acknowledging the upright, bipedal gait suggested by the femur, Dubois named the fossil *"Pithecanthropus erectus"* ("upright ape-man").[2]

Upon his return to Europe in 1895, Dubois was plunged into the maelstrom of scientific controversy swirling around his finds. Although there were those who agreed with his missing link interpretation, including (not surprisingly) Haeckel, there were others, led by the renowned German pathologist and anthropologist Rudolf Virchow, who dismissed Dubois's fossils as nothing more than an extinct, giant gibbon. The acrimony of these exchanges may have been more than Dubois could take, for he became less and less involved in the public debates over the following years. Legend has it that he ultimately signaled his complete withdrawal by burying the fossils beneath the floorboards of his dining room and leaving them there unstudied for the next twenty years! Although Dubois's final thoughts concerning the status of *"Pithecanthropus"* currently remain a contentious topic,[3] it is acknowledged by all that his discoveries set the stage for those that followed during the succeeding decades.

SPECIES, SPECIES, AND MORE SPECIES

Beginning in the 1920s and continuing through the 1930s, fossils found in China demonstrated that Dubois's find was not unique. The remains of ancient hominids that were remarkably similar to *"Pithecanthropus"* of southeast Asia were recovered in a cave now known as Zhoukoudian, approximately thirty miles from Beijing. Davidson Black, an anatomist at the Peking Union Medical School, placed those specimens into a new genus and species, *"Sinanthropus pekinensis"* ("Chinese man of Peking"). Black created the new name in 1927 on the basis of a single molar tooth, and although the skulls that were found later in the same cave were much like *"Pithecanthropus,"* there was no effort at the time to consolidate the Javan and Chinese fossils into the same genus, much less the same species (see Figure 10-1).

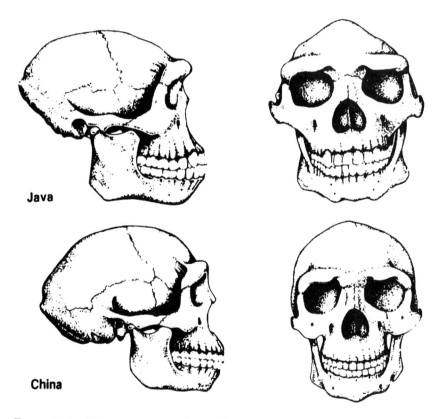

FIGURE 10-1   "PITHECANTHROPUS" FROM JAVA AND "SINANTHROPUS" FROM CHINA

Today both are considered to be representatives of *Homo erectus*. Note how they share relatively large brain cases that are long and low, projecting brow ridges, jutting lower faces, and the lack of a chin.

This lack of consolidation reflected the "splitting" mentality that was pervasive throughout paleoanthropology until the 1960s. Almost every new hominid fossil that was discovered, despite its resemblance to the Javan and Chinese forms, was given at least a new species, and often a new genus, name reflecting less the realities of biology and more the egos of the discoverers and namers. This trend is well illustrated by the treatment of the fossils discovered in Africa during the middle decades of the twentieth century. The genus names proposed for these specimens, such as *"Telanthropus," "Atlanthropus,"* and *"Tchadanthropus,"* were biologically meaningless labels that served only to clutter the taxonomic landscape.[4]

The lone voice in the wilderness during this "age of splitters" belonged to the famed German paleoanthropologist Franz Weidenreich. A refugee from Hitler's holocaust, Weidenreich published minutely detailed monographs describing and interpreting the finds from Zhoukoudian. He also reproduced extremely accurate casts and molds of these fossils. The scientific world owes a debt of everlasting gratitude to Weidenreich for these scholarly activities because the original Chinese fossils were mysteriously lost during World War II. In 1940 Weidenreich was the first to suggest that the proliferation of names given to the Javan and Chinese fossils was hindering the understanding of human evolution:[5]

> Those terms which are generally used to designate different human types involve the idea that each one represents a more or less divergent genus without generic connections. In order to avoid this incorrect interpretation, the time has come ... to eliminate all those names which may lead to some misunderstanding in this regard.[6]

Weidenreich observed that *"Pithecanthropus"* and *"Sinanthropus"* were not different enough from modern humans (*Homo sapiens*) to be placed into separate genera, and they were not different enough from one another to be considered separate species. Therefore, Weidenreich concluded that both could be accommodated by the name *Homo erectus*, recognizing that the Javan and Peking hominids belonged to the same early species of humanity, and their differences were no greater than those seen between modern humans living in southeast Asia and China today. Weidenreich truly was a visionary. He was decades ahead of his time in his recognition of the ubiquity of normal, intraspecific (within species) variation among fossil hominids and its importance in any reconstruction of human evolution.

Weidenreich's perspective became increasingly popular in anthropology over the following decades. Particularly persuasive arguments that *Homo erectus* was the appropriate taxonomic assignment for the Chinese and Javan fossil hominids were made by the American evolutionary biologist Ernst Mayr in 1950, and by the British paleoanthropologist W. E. LeGros Clark in 1955.[7] The 1960s and 1970s signalled the ascendancy of the "lumpers," who, unlike the "splitters" of the first half of the century, tried to bring paleoanthropology into line with the rest of modern biology. These researchers were much less inclined to name new fossil hominid genera and species and believed that *Homo erectus* could accommodate the variation present not only in the Javan and Chinese forms but also in similar fossils discovered later in Africa. Most anthropologists at this time viewed *Homo erectus* as humanity's immediate predecessor, a fossil species occupying an intermediate position on the unbroken evolutionary continuum between modern humans and the earliest African hominids, the australopithecines.

These ideas held sway throughout the 1970s and 1980s, as exemplified by the writings of such scholars as F. Clark Howell and William Howells, and continue to be championed today by Philip Rightmire.[8] However, in the mid-1980s an alternative viewpoint was presented concerning the taxonomic and evolutionary affinities of *Homo erectus*. Researchers such as Peter Andrews, Chris Stringer, and Bernard Wood suggested that the differences between the Asian and African forms of *Homo erectus* were significant enough to separate them into different species.[9] The Asian fossils would remain in *Homo erectus* while the African hominids would be placed into a new species, alternately called *Homo ergaster*,[10] or *Homo leakeyi*.[11] These paleoanthropologists employed cladistics, an analytical approach that determines evolutionary relationships based on the presence or absence of certain traits shared between groups of fossils. Their analyses isolated what they perceived to be unique features shared by the Javan and Chinese fossils that were absent not only in the East African representatives of *Homo erectus*, but also in modern humans. They concluded that Asian *Homo erectus* went extinct and that the African form was the sole ancestor of modern humans.

WAS HOMO ERECTUS A DEAD END?

Is this "neo-splitting" position justified? Was Asian *Homo erectus* simply a doomed twig on the bush of human evolution, leaving no descendants among modern people? Or is it more likely that these archaic hominids were an integral part of the human evolutionary tree that significantly contributed to the origins of modern Asians? Before the latter two questions can be addressed, the first must be resolved, because the "resplitting" of *Homo erectus* bears directly on the issue of this fossil species' influence upon the evolution of modern *Homo sapiens*.

After the first wave of publications claiming that *Homo erectus* in Africa was a different species from its Chinese and Indonesian cousins, other scientists turned a critical eye on the features that were supposedly unique to the Asian hominids. For example, Günter Bräuer and Emma Mbua studied African and Asian *Homo erectus*, and later hominids from these continents and from Europe as well. They demonstrated that the characteristics supposedly unique to Asia were not confined to Asian *Homo erectus*, but were also present in varying frequencies in the fossils from both Africa and Europe.[12]

I became interested in the problem of "lumping" versus "splitting" for a variety of reasons. As a graduate student at the University of Michigan I was trained by professors who were decidedly "lumpers." These scholars emphasized the importance of factors that could produce significant variation within species, such as sexual dimorphism (size and shape differences between adult males and females) and polytypism (geographic variation). My professors argued reasonably that these intraspecific factors had to be eliminated first as potential sources of variation in fossil samples before the presence of multiple species could be claimed. During the latter half of my graduate studies and the beginning of my professional career, from the mid-1980s through the early 1990s, it seemed to me that paleoanthropology was slipping "back to the future"—more and more publications were trumpeting the reality of new species that were split from other well-established taxa. I decided to investigate whether or not this trend was warranted with respect to the splitting of African from Asian *Homo erectus*. However, unlike other researchers, I chose to examine this question quantitatively by comparing skull measurements instead of the osteological (bony) features that were being argued over by the cladists.

My research compared *Homo erectus* with a sample of modern humans (made up of over 2,500 individual skeletons from all over the world) and another sample composed of various fossils representing 2 to 3 different hominid species (called the mixed hominid sample).[13] The modern human sample was chosen because it exemplified the nature and degree of variation to be expected in a single but geographically variable hominid species. The mixed hominid sample was used to depict the variation present in a sample composed of multiple fossil hominid species. If my comparisons showed that *Homo erectus* was most similar in its magnitude and pattern of variation to the mixed hominids, then this would support the cladists' conclusion that *Homo erectus* included more than one species. However, if *Homo erectus* proved to be no more variable than modern humans, then this would support the "lumpers'" position that it was a single species.

The results of these comparisons would be quite important to the reconstruction of later human evolution. If there were multiple species of *Homo erectus*, this would support a very "bushy" view of human evolution, with many origins and extinctions of regionally isolated hominid species. This perspective would indicate that modern humans probably arose relatively late in the Pleistocene epoch from a geographically restricted area, such as Sub-Saharan Africa. In this scenario, the descendants of east African *Homo erectus* (*Homo ergaster*) were the sole ancestors of modern humanity. In contrast, if the results indicated that *Homo erectus* was indeed a single species, this would support a human evolutionary "tree," whose "trunk" was composed of *Homo erectus*, gradually growing into *Homo sapiens* around the world.

Most people think that science is objective. This objectivity may sometimes be illusory, however. People bring biases and preconceived notions to everything they do, and scientists are no different. It is important to acknowledge these biases whenever possible. As one can easily tell by the foregoing discussion, I was predisposed to reconfirming that *Homo erectus* was a single species. But I did take precautions in my study not to make this a foregone conclusion. For example, the *Homo erectus* sample that I used was chronologically as broad as possible, dating from 1.8 million to less than 500,000 years old. Because of their great time-depth, these fossils were potentially much more variable than the modern humans, who were sampled from a single point in geological time. This comparison, then, predisposed my study to conclude that *Homo erectus* was significantly different from *Homo sapiens* and therefore was composed of more than one species. In effect, I bent over backwards to prevent my conclusions from being predetermined by my biases.

In my analyses I used eight skull measurements that were common to all three samples (*Homo erectus*, the mixed hominid group, and the modern humans). I examined each of the variables individually and in combination, but the results of these preliminary investigations were not sufficient to resolve the *Homo erectus* species problem. Whether or not the fossils attributed to *Homo erectus* belonged to one or more species was ultimately a statistical question: What is the probability that the variation present in a fossil sample (such as *Homo erectus*) could be found in a sample taken from a single species (such as *Homo sapiens*)?

To answer this question I used a randomization procedure that is ideal for solving problems such as these. This procedure uses a computer to generate many random samples of a particular reference species (in this case, modern humans). The variation in these samples is then compared to that present in a fossil sample (in this case, *Homo erectus*) to determine whether or not the variation in the fossils is greater than the variation in equivalently-sized samples randomly drawn from a known single species, such as *Homo sapiens*. If the variation in the fossil sample exceeds the variation in 95 percent or more of the randomized modern human samples, then it is likely that the fossil sample is composed of two or more species. On the other hand, if a significant percentage (defined as greater than 5 percent) of the randomized modern human samples are more variable than the fossils, this provides evidence that the fossil sample represents a single species.

Let me illustrate this technique with the following example (see Figure 10-2). One of the eight measurements that I recorded was the greatest width of the brain case, formally known as *maximum cranial breadth* and abbreviated as XCB. This measurement could be taken on all 8 of the fossils in the mixed hominid sample, on 16 of 19 *Homo erectus* skulls, and on all 2,533 of the modern humans. How variable XCB was in the two fossil samples was determined by calculating the coefficient of variation, known more simply as the CV. To begin with, was the CV for XCB in the mixed hominid fossil sample greater than expected for a single species, such as modern *Homo sapiens*? This was answered as follows: First, eight skulls were randomly drawn by the computer from the modern human sample and their CV for XCB was calculated. Only eight

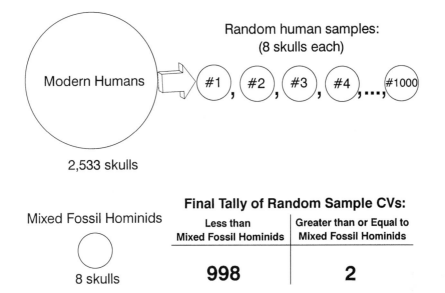

FIGURE 10-2

The randomization procedure randomly draws, with replacement, one thousand eight-skull samples from the modern human sample and determines the coefficient of variation (CV) for maximum cranial length (XCB) for each sample. The CV for XCB in the eight mixed hominid skulls is then compared to the one thousand CVs of the one thousand random modern human samples. Because 99.8 percent of the modern human CVs are smaller than the mixed hominid fossil CV, it is likely that this fossil sample includes at least two species.

human skulls were taken because that was the number of fossil specimens present in the mixed hominid sample. After the CV was calculated, the eight skulls were returned to the human pool and the computer randomly drew eight more and calculated this new sample's CV. The computer repeated this process one thousand times, generating one thousand CVs for one thousand different eight-skull samples. Finally, the CV for XCB in the mixed hominid sample was compared to the modern human CVs generated by randomization. The extremely high CV of the mixed hominid sample exceeded 99.8 percent (998 of the 1,000) of the randomized modern human CVs, a result confirming the presence of multiple species in the mixed hominid sample.

In contrast, the randomization procedure told a different story regarding variation in *Homo erectus* (see Figure 10-3 on page 148). This time the computer drew one thousand samples of sixteen skulls each from the modern human pool—sixteen skulls each because the *Homo erectus* sample included sixteen individual fossil specimens. When the CVs of the randomized samples were compared to the *Homo erectus* CV it was revealed that most (81 percent) of the randomized modern human CVs for XCB were greater than

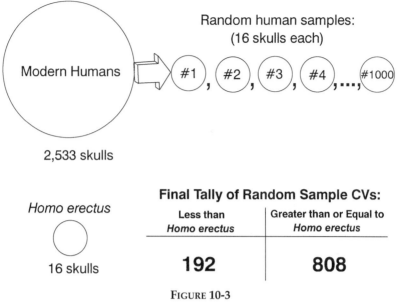

FIGURE 10-3

The randomization procedure randomly draws, with replacement, one thousand sixteen-skull samples from the modern human sample and determines the coefficient of variation (CV) for maximum cranial length (XCB) for each sample. The CV for XCB in the sixteen *Homo erectus* skulls is then compared to the one thousand CVs of the one thousand random modern human samples. Because 81 percent of the modern human CVs are larger than the *Homo erectus* CV, it is likely that the *Homo erectus* sample includes only one species.

or equal to the relatively low *Homo erectus* CV for XCB. This result strongly supports the retention of *Homo erectus* as a single species because variation in these fossils is usually exceeded by the variation present in samples drawn from the known single species, modern *Homo sapiens*. The other results from my study corroborate this conclusion.

The fact that the *Homo erectus* sample, whose members were separated from each other by thousands of miles and by over one million years, was generally less variable than randomly drawn modern human samples directly counters the claims of the "neo-splitters." Those who think that African *Homo ergaster* is a species distinct from Asian *Homo erectus* would expect that the reproductive isolation necessary to produce two species would result in the development of significant differences between the two forms. Instead, I showed that African and Asian *Homo erectus* shared a level and pattern of variation most similar to modern humans, and that their differences could be best explained by polytypism: geographic variation within a species. Thus, this evidence suggests that *Homo erectus* was like us, a far-flung species that developed regionally distinct forms that were never reproductively isolated enough from each other to evolve into separate species.

The larger question remains: What became of *Homo erectus*? Did this species gradually transform into modern humans around the world, or did only one geographically constrained population of *Homo erectus* provide humanity's ancestry while the rest were doomed to extinction?

HOMO ERECTUS AND THE ORIGINS OF MODERN HUMANS

The debate about modern human origins has been raging in paleoanthropology for the last decade. In its most basic form, the controversy can be stated as two polar opposites: replacement versus multiregionalism. The replacement view, supported by Stringer, Andrews, and their colleagues, states that modern humans evolved relatively recently (one hundred thousand to two hundred thousand years ago) in Sub-Saharan Africa and subsequently spread around the Old World, replacing all of the indigenous, archaic human populations that they encountered.[14] In contrast, multiregionalism, espoused by Milford Wolpoff, Alan Thorne, David Frayer, and their co-workers, contends that archaic hominids from throughout the Old World (not just in Africa) contributed to the evolution of their local modern successors.[15] Both of these hypotheses produce very different predictions concerning the evolutionary fate of Asian *Homo erectus*: Replacement suggests that the Javan and Chinese hominids had nothing to do with the origins of modern humans in those regions while multiregionalists maintain that these fossil hominids are part of an unbroken genetic continuum linking Asia's ancient past to its present.

I decided to test these predictions with data I collected during my dissertation research. The fossils I studied are a group of hominid mandibles (lower jaws) from the site of Sangiran in central Java that date to approximately one million years ago. Initially I was intrigued by these jaws because of their variability: Some were as huge as the biggest australopithecine mandibles while others were quite a bit smaller, as is typical for *Homo erectus*. My studies of the anatomy and measurements of these fossils led me to conclude that they all represented *Homo erectus* and that their great size variation could be best explained by sexual dimorphism.[16] Later I realized that the morphology of these mandibles could provide some important additional information bearing on the origins of modern humans.

The Sangiran mandibles are among the oldest *Homo erectus* fossils found outside of Africa and as such provide an excellent test case of the polarized predictions generated by the replacement and multiregional models. I compared the Javan jaws to samples of modern human mandibles from Kenya and Australia to explicitly test the following expectations.[17] According to the replacement hypothesis, the two modern human samples should display much more in common with one another, when compared to the fossils, because the Kenyans and Australians presumably share a relatively recent

African ancestor that had nothing to do with one million year old Javan *Homo erectus*. In contrast, multiregionalism suggests that the Sangiran hominids' ancestry to modern humans in the region, such as Australian Aborigines, would be reflected in the number of features shared between the Sangiran and Australian jaws that are not found in the mandibles of modern Kenyans.

Most previous studies of modern Asian origins have generally presented varying lists of morphological features to promote either the replacement or the multiregionalism models. For example, Wolpoff and his colleagues support the multiregional position by noting numerous skull features that are shared between Middle Pleistocene (≈two hundred thousand to five hundred thousand years ago) Javan hominids and recent Australians that are absent in early modern humans from Africa.[18] Critics of this interpretation contend that these morphological similarities are due either to cultural practices of cranial deformation or parallelism (independent evolution of the same features by ancient Javans and recent Australians).[19]

Little has been done to actually quantify these similarities and differences, particularly with respect to the earliest *Homo erectus* specimens from Java. Therefore, I used a statistical test to determine which of the two predictions would be borne out by the data. If the statistics showed that the modern humans from Kenya and Australia shared more features in common when compared to the fossils, this would support the replacement model. If the Sangiran and Australian jaws were demonstrably more similar to each other than either were to the Kenyans, then multiregionalism was a more likely explanation. Fisher's Exact Test of Independence is an analytical tool that can be used to answer these types of questions.

Fisher's test determines whether trait frequencies between two samples are significantly different (i.e., whether the differences are unlikely to have occurred by chance). For example, suppose that "Feature A" is present in all (100 percent) of the fossil jaws, in 90 percent of the Australian mandibles, but in only 20 percent of the Kenyans. Fisher's Exact Test of Independence would show that the frequency of "Feature A" is statistically indistinguishable when the Sangiran and modern Australian mandibles are compared, but that the frequencies are significantly different when the Australians are compared to the Kenyans. This was the predominant finding in my study. Of the sixteen mandibular features analyzed by Fisher's test, thirteen displayed insignificant differences in the Sangiran and modern Australian comparisons. In contrast, nine of sixteen trait frequencies were statistically different in the comparisons between modern Australians and Kenyans.

If the replacement model is closer to the historical truth, then the similarities between the ancient Javans and modern Australians could not be simply explained by an ancestral-descendant relationship. A more tortuous explanation involves the independent evolution of these similarities twice:

once in the *Homo erectus* fossils and a second time among the modern Australians. Although the small size of the fossil sample tempered my conclusions with caution, my results clearly provide more support for the multiregional hypothesis—namely, that early *Homo erectus* from Java did contribute to the evolution of modern Australian Aborigines.

WHERE DO WE GO FROM HERE?

The evidence discussed in this chapter establishes that *Homo erectus* was a single, hominid species that evolved into *Homo sapiens* throughout the Old World over the past million years. Ironically, the very fact that modern *Homo sapiens* is the product of this gradual transformation has spurred calls for the "sinking" of *Homo erectus*! Wolpoff, Thorne, Jan Jelinek, and Zhang Yinyun have recently published a paper arguing that because there is no obvious morphological gap in the direct evolution of *Homo erectus* into *Homo sapiens* the former species should be formally "sunk" into the latter.[20] The authors maintain that *Homo erectus* could only be retained as a separate species if the fossil record indicates that the origin of *Homo sapiens* was the result of a branching speciation event, whereby the ancestral species (i.e., *Homo erectus*) ceased to exist by dividing and producing two descendant species. I agree with Wolpoff and his colleagues who do not see any evidence of such branching evolution in modern human origins. *Homo sapiens* appears to have a much greater time-depth and much more morphological variability than traditional views would assume.

Is this interpretation justified? Given the evolutionary species concept that Wolpoff et al. employ in conjunction with the evidence from the fossil record, their logic is unassailable.[21] But does their argument illuminate or obfuscate evolutionary relationships in labeling both big-browed, smaller-brained ancient hominids and high-browed, bigger-brained modern humans as *Homo sapiens*? This point will be debated for years to come. Most scholars would agree, however, that the label is not important in and of itself. The reconstruction of evolutionary patterns and relationships should remain our primary focus.

To that end I hope that future research on *Homo erectus* will concentrate on the regional patterns of evolutionary change leading to the emergence of *Homo sapiens*. Was the tempo of this evolution gradual throughout or was there a period of acceleration that could be used to mark the transition, thereby rendering the boundary between these two species less arbitrary? Although questions such as these may be answered by applying new quantitative methods to old data, the age old battle cry of paleoanthropology will certainly continue to ring out across our ancestral homelands: more fossils, more fossils!

NOTES

1. Much of the information in this section comes from C. Loring Brace, "Tales of the Phylogenetic Woods: The Evolution and Significance of Evolutionary Trees," *American Journal of Physical Anthropology* 56 (1981): 411; C. Loring Brace, *The Stages of Human Evolution*, 4th ed. (Englewood Cliffs, NJ: Prentice Hall, 1991); F. Clark Howell, "Thoughts on Eugene Dubois and the 'Pithecanthropus' Saga," *Courier Forschungsinstitut Senckenberg* 171 (1994): 11.

2. Eugène Dubois, *Pithecanthropus Erectus: Eine Menschenähnliche Uebergangsform Aus Java* (Batavia: Landersdruckerei, 1894).

3. Compare, for example, Brace, "Tales of the Phylogenetic Woods," with Stephen J. Gould, "Men of the Thirty-Third Division," *Natural History* (April 1990): 12.

4. The following are the references for original works in which these genera were named: *"Sinanthropus"*—Davidson Black, "On a Lower Molar Hominid Tooth from Chou-kou-tien Deposit," *Palaeontologica Sinica Series D7* (1927): 1; *"Telanthropus"*—Robert Broom and John T. Robinson, "New Type of Fossil Man," *Nature* 164 (1949): 322; *"Atlanthropus"*—Camille Arambourg, "L'hominien fossile de Ternifine (Algérie)," *Comptes Rendus de l'Academie des Sciences (Paris)* 239 (1954): 893; *"Tchadanthropus"*—Yves Coppens, "L'hominien du Tchad," *Comptes Rendus de l'Academie des Sciences (Paris)* 260D (1965): 2869.

5. Franz Weidenreich, "Some Problems Dealing with Ancient Man," *American Anthropologist* 42 (1940): 375.

6. Ibid., p. 383.

7. Ernst Mayr, "Taxonomic Categories in Fossil Hominids," *Cold Spring Harbor Symposium on Quantitative Biology* 15 (1950): 109; W. E. LeGros Clark, *The Fossil Evidence for Human Evolution* (Chicago: University of Chicago Press, 1955).

8. F. Clark Howell, "Hominidae," in Vincent J. Maglio and H. B. S. Cooke, eds., *Evolution of African Mammals* (Cambridge, MA: Harvard University Press, 1978), pp. 154–248; William W. Howells, *"Homo erectus*—Who, When, and Where: A Survey," *Yearbook of Physical Anthropology* 23 (1980): 1; G. Philip Rightmire, *The Evolution of Homo erectus: Comparative Anatomical Studies of an Extinct Human Species* (New York: Cambridge University Press, 1990).

9. Peter Andrews, "An Alternative Interpretation of the Characters Used to Define *Homo erectus,"* *Courier Forschungsinstitut Senckenberg* 69 (1984): 167; Christopher B. Stringer, "The Definition of *Homo erectus* and the Existence of the Species in Africa and Europe," *Courier Forschungsinstitut Senckenberg* 69 (1984): 131; Bernard A. Wood, "The Origin of *Homo erectus,"* *Courier Forschungsinstitut Senckenberg* 69 (1984): 99.

10. Originally named by Colin P. Groves and V. Mazak, "An Approach to the Taxonomy of the Hominidae: Gracile Villafranchian Hominids of Africa," *Casopis pro Mineralogii a Geologii* 20 (1975): 225.

11. Originally named by G. Heberer, "Über einen neuen archanthropinen Typus aus der Oldoway-Schlucht," *Zeitschrift für Morphologie und Anthropologie* 53 (1963): 171.

12. Günter Bräuer and Emma Mbua, *"Homo erectus* Features Used in Cladistics and Their Variability in Asian and African Hominids," *Journal of Human Evolution* 22 (1992): 79.

13. Andrew Kramer, "Human Taxonomic Diversity in the Pleistocene: Does *Homo erectus* Represent Multiple Hominid Species?" *American Journal of Physical Anthropology* 91 (1993): 161.

14. Christopher B. Stringer, "The Emergence of Modern Humans," *Scientific American* 263 (1990): 98; Christopher B. Stringer and Peter Andrews, "Genetic and Fossil Evidence for the Origin of Modern Humans," *Science* 239 (1988): 1263.

15. Alan G. Thorne and Milford H. Wolpoff, "The Multiregional Evolution of Humans," *Scientific American* 266 (1992): 76; David W. Frayer, "Testing Theories and Hypotheses about Modern Human Origins," in Peter N. Peregrine, Carol R. Ember, and Melvin Ember, eds., *Physical Anthropology: Original Readings in Method and Practice* (Upper Saddle River, NJ: Prentice Hall, 2002).

16. Andrew Kramer, "A Critical Analysis of Claims for the Existence of Southeast Asian Australopithecines," *Journal of Human Evolution* 26 (1994): 3; Andrew Kramer and Lyle W. Konigsberg, "The Phyletic Position of Sangiran 6 as Determined by Multivariate Analyses," *Courier Forschungsinstitut Senckenberg* 171 (1994): 105.

17. Andrew Kramer, "Modern Human Origins in Australasia: Replacement or Evolution?" *American Journal of Physical Anthropology* 86 (1991): 455.

18. Milford H. Wolpoff, Wu Xinzhi, and Alan G. Thorne, "Modern *Homo sapiens* Origins: A General Theory of Hominid Evolution Involving the Fossil Evidence from East Asia," in Fred H. Smith and Frank Spencer, eds., *The Origins of Modern Humans: A World Survey of the Fossil Evidence* (New York: Alan R. Liss, 1984), pp. 411–483; Milford H. Wolpoff, "Multiregional Evolution: The Fossil Alternative to Eden," in Paul Mellars and Chris Stringer, eds., *The Human Revolution: Behavioural and Biological Perspectives on the Origins of Modern Humans* (Edinburgh: Edinburgh University Press, 1989), pp. 62–108; Milford H. Wolpoff, "Theories of Modern Human Origins," in Günter Bräuer and Fred H. Smith, eds., *Continuity or Replacement: Controversies in* Homo sapiens *Evolution* (Rotterdam: Balkema, 1992), pp. 25–63.

19. Erik Delson, "One Source Not Many," *Nature* 332 (1988): 206; Stringer and Andrews, "Genetic and Fossil Evidence for the Origin of Modern Humans," p. 1267; Christopher B. Stringer, "Replacement, Continuity, and the Origin of *Homo sapiens*," in Günter Bräuer and Fred H. Smith, eds., *Continuity or Replacement: Controversies in* Homo sapiens *Evolution* (Rotterdam: Balkema, 1992), pp. 9–24.

20. Milford H. Wolpoff, Alan G. Thorne, Jan Jelinek, and Zhang Yinyun, "The Case for Sinking *Homo erectus*: 100 Years of Pithecanthropus Is Enough!" *Courier Forschungsinstitut Senckenberg* 171 (1994): 341.

21. An "evolutionary species" can span a considerable amount of geological time and is formally defined as a single lineage of ancestor-descendant populations that maintains its identity from other such lineages and has its own evolutionary tendencies and historical fate. In contrast, the traditional "biological species" has no time depth and is defined as a group of actually or potentially interbreeding individuals who are reproductively isolated from other such groups.

SUGGESTED READINGS

Howells, William W. "*Homo erectus*—Who, When, and Where: A Survey." *Yearbook of Physical Anthropology* 23 (1980): 1–23. State of the art in 1980 on the distribution, taxonomy, and evolution of *Homo erectus*; today a bit dated.

Rightmire, G. Philip. *The Evolution of* Homo erectus: *Comparative Anatomical Studies of an Extinct Human Species*. New York: Cambridge University Press, 1990. State of the art today in book length, by the acknowledged leading expert on the subject.

_____. "*Homo erectus*: Ancestor or Evolutionary Side-branch?" *Evolutionary Anthropology* 1 (1992): 43–49. State of the art today in easily digestible article length.

Wu, Rukang, and Lin Shenglong. "Peking Man." *Scientific American* 248 (1983): 86–94. A fascinating and lively look at the excavations and interpretations of the most famous Chinese *Homo erectus* site.

Neandertal Growth: Examining Developmental Adaptations in Earlier Homo Sapiens

Nancy Minugh-Purvis

Modern humans are characterized by certain patterns of growth and maturation, including a lengthy childhood dependency period and a rapidly growing, slowly maturing large brain. When did these patterns, so crucial to making us human, evolve? Are they found in all hominids, or are they unique to our subspecies, *Homo sapiens sapiens*? To answer these questions we need to identify the appearance of clearly *human* biological and behavioral patterns in the prehistoric record, a task that may be approached from several perspectives, one of which is growth and development.

Traditionally, paleoanthropologists (scientists who study human evolution) have almost exclusively focused on the skeletal remains of adults in studying the fossil record. Increasingly, however, they are concerning themselves with the remains of children as well. There are numerous reasons for this shift, but perhaps the most important is the realization that immature individuals offer us the best source of information concerning the growth and development (ontogeny) of earlier hominids. These processes are fundamental to an organism's biological adaptation, or ability to survive in its environment, and may provide crucial insights for understanding patterns of biological and behavioral change through time.

As paleoanthropologists struggle to identify the events leading up to the emergence of modern humans, they must, of necessity, focus on the archaic populations who immediately preceded our appearance. Perhaps the best known of these ancient peoples are the Neandertals, earlier members of *Homo sapiens*, whose remains have been unearthed in Europe and western and central Asia (see Figure 11-1 on page 156).

Most people have heard the term *Neandertals*, even if only from colloquial speech or the popular press. These ancient people, who once inhabited Ice-Age Europe and surrounding areas, have come to be popularly known as the archetypical cave dwellers of our past. In part, the popular image of

FIGURE 11-1   NEANDERTAL GEOGRAPHIC RANGE

Although Neandertals were primarily Europeans, several sites containing their skeletal remains have been found in West Asia. The most eastern Neandertal site is Teshik-Tash, located in the central Asian republic of Uzbekistan.

Neandertals, which assigns them a subhuman status, is attributable to the interesting mixture of features such as a huge brain housed in a fairly flat skull with a low forehead and a large barrel-chested thorax at the center of a generally short, extremely muscular body. These and many other differences from modern humans contribute to what many regard as the rather unusual appearance of Neandertals. But should we consider evidence such as the relatively recent appearance of symbolic art in the prehistoric record indicative of significant qualitative differences in levels of cognitive ability between the earliest *Homo sapiens sapiens* and their Neandertal predecessors in the European fossil record? We can address this last issue by studying growth and development, because our elaborate capacity for symbolic behavior is possible primarily through two biological adaptations: a long growth period, which provides an opportunity for extended learning, and an extremely large, sophisticated brain, which experiences an extended period of rapid growth unique among primates. Specifically, we need to look closely at Neandertal craniofacial growth and compare it to *Homo sapiens sapiens*. Only then will we be able to gauge the importance of learned behavior to Neandertals and know whether or not Neandertals emphasized learning as part of a human adaptive strategy in much the same way we do.

Most Neandertals date to a geologic time period known as the Upper Pleistocene, which lasted from 128,000 to 10,000 years ago. However, none lived later than 32,500 years ago; later portions of the human paleontological record contain only modern humans, *Homo sapiens sapiens*. Yet despite their eventual disappearance, Neandertals should be regarded as a highly successful people who survived life in Europe for over one hundred thousand years, during a time of severe climatic change as glacial sheets retreated and advanced over much of their geographic range. How did Neandertals come to be the massive, powerful people they were? How should we interpret the significance of their huge brains, low skulls, massive browridges, and full, puffy cheeks above chinless jaws? Were these distinctive features due purely to genetic differences from ourselves, or were they, in part, features whose development was influenced by certain behavioral patterns affecting Neandertals during their growth period? How helpless were Neandertal infants at birth? How long did they take to grow to reproductive maturity? Were they highly dependent for years upon adults, thus giving them ample opportunity to observe and learn sophisticated, recognizably human behaviors? These, and many other questions, can be addressed through an examination of Neandertal growth and development.

To examine Neandertal growth we must study the skeletal remains of their children, which have been recovered from the hominid fossil record over the years. However, the examination of the fossil remains of children is a difficult undertaking for many reasons, including the fact that their relatively delicate bones do not preserve as well as those of adults. They can be damaged by gnawing scavengers prior to fossilization, and by physical forces during interment or excavation. Fortunately, however, we have many excellent bones and teeth of Neandertal children available due to the fact that Neandertals were among the first hominids to intentionally bury their dead. Owing to these ancient mortuary practices, the Neandertal fossil record is rich in skeletal remains of all developmental ages, including newborn infants and even one or two probable fetuses. In total, approximately one hundred Neandertal children have been discovered. Many of these fossils are highly fragmentary and incomplete, as one would expect, but others are remarkably well-preserved and provide captivating glimpses of Neandertal lives. They are known from skulls, teeth, and limb bones, with a very few specimens preserving major portions of all areas of the skeleton. Unfortunately, brains do not fossilize, so we cannot directly examine neural maturation in Neandertals. What we can do, however, is examine the growth of their braincase, the bony part of the skull that houses the brain during life. By molding the inside of the braincase we can obtain a crude replica, called an endocranial cast, of what the external surface of the brain and its overlying membranous coverings, or meninges, looked like. Considered together, this evidence provides us with many interesting possibilities for better understanding these ancient people.

STUDYING GROWTH FROM THE FOSSIL RECORD

Reconstruction of any aspect of life from paleontological evidence is largely dependent upon two major sources of information. The first, of course, is the fossil record itself. Because neither soft tissues nor behaviors fossilize, we are left only with whatever calcified tissue structures (bones and teeth) survive many thousands of years in the ground. A second important source of information comes from living species known to be closely related to the fossil animals being studied. Thus, when examining any question in human evolution, including growth and development, it is important to keep in mind that despite our elaborate cultural systems and adaptations, humans are first of all mammals. As mammals, we share numerous biological and behavioral attributes with other members of that group, including the nourishing of young with milk produced by the mammary glands of the female parent and an emphasis on learned rather than innate behavior. Also, humans are primates—the group of mammals that also includes monkeys and apes. Among the mammals higher primates are unusual in that they experience relatively prolonged periods of growth and development, and many possess relatively large brains. In addition, higher primates usually live in social groups.

Because humans are mammals and primates, we share a long evolutionary history with these groups, and many human biological and behavioral adaptations are simply variations on common mammalian and primate patterns. Although the shapes of our skeletons differ, the tissues that make them up are nearly identical; thus we can understand the biological properties of the bone of any given fossil if we know it was a mammal. For this reason, it is important and useful to examine Neandertal growth and development by starting within the context of mammalian growth in general.

MAMMALIAN GROWTH AND MATURATION

Unlike the infants of reptiles and lower vertebrates, infants of mammalian species are often born helpless. They change from helpless, dependent creatures into adults, themselves capable of reproducing, through the processes of growth and maturation.

Growth, in the pure sense, refers to increases in size. Growth may be studied in several ways, but one of two approaches is most commonly utilized when attempting to understand typical growth patterns in a population. The first is by way of longitudinal growth studies. Such studies involve the documentation of growth in a series of individuals over part or all of their growth period. However, such studies are often difficult because they take many years to complete. Moreover, because we have no living fossil children, we cannot use the longitudinal approach to investigate the growth of any archaic hominids. Thus, studies of growth in our ancestors must rely upon the cross-sectional approach. Cross-sectional growth studies sample data from individuals of various ages in a given population, then look at changes from one age group to another to create an artificial composite growth curve. Logistically, they are far simpler to conduct than longitudinal studies of the living, so most growth studies are cross-sectional by design. For obvious reasons, in attempting to reconstruct growth and development from the remains of deceased children we need to use a type of cross-sectional approach as we trace the changes in size and shape from infancy to adolescence. In looking at growth in the paleontological record specifically, the scarcity of specimens necessitates that fossils from a wide geographic range and dating to fairly long spans of time must often be lumped together in order to delineate growth patterns.

Maturation, on the other hand, refers to the transformation of an infant into an individual who functions—behaviorally and biologically—as an adult. Maturation describes the rate of growth and development, and many maturational indicators in mammals, such as eruption of specific teeth, are so precisely timed that they are quite closely correlated to an animal's chronological age.

Following birth, mammals reach adulthood after passing through three well-defined stages of growth and development: infancy, childhood, and adolescence. Mammalian growth stages follow a very definite timetable. This is clearly illustrated by the differences between mammalian and reptilian bone growth. Throughout a reptile's lifetime, bones simply grow as body size increases. In fact they can (and in some reptiles do) continue to grow until some environmental factor, such as a limit in the food supply, restricts the animal's growth. In contrast, mammalian bones are very finite in their growth, which occurs following a very specific schedule of maturation through a process called epiphyseal union.

Before it becomes bone, a human—or any mammalian—embryo's skeleton is largely cartilage. Early in development, however, the bones begin to calcify as centers of ossification appear in the limb bones and elsewhere. As the fetus matures and grows, these centers gradually spread out toward the edges of the bone. The mineralization begins from a single main center *in utero*, but later, in infancy and childhood, additional centers appear at the ends of the bones. Between these centers of mineralization are growth zones, where increases in bone length occur, permitting the young mammal, or child, to grow in body length or height. Eventually, growth ceases and the mineralized parts fuse. However, fusion between these parts occurs at different times depending upon their location in the skeleton. This schedule is the same for all members of a mammalian species: The bones making up the human knee, for example, all mature at approximately fourteen to seventeen years of age. In other words, mammalian skeletons, including human skeletons, follow very set, predictable maturational schedules. About the time all have fused, the mammal has reached its adult size.

The patterns by which teeth develop and mature further illustrate the differences between reptilian and mammalian growth. Reptiles have teeth that erupt continuously as the jaws grow and are simply replaced as they wear out and are shed. However, because reptilian teeth do not occlude, that is, they do not come together in a precise, interlocking pattern when the jaws close, this pattern of continuous dental replacement does not adversely affect the way reptiles use their teeth. In contrast, mammals have only two sets of teeth during their lifetime—a milk, or deciduous set, and an adult, or permanent set. Mammalian teeth occlude, or come together when the jaws are closed, in a consistent pattern that permits chewing and grinding. Because these two sets of teeth last a mammal its entire lifetime, it is important that teeth erupt into the jaws in a precise, organized manner that does not disrupt occlusal function.

In general, mammalian teeth grow in three stages. First, the crowns develop within the bony jaws. Second, the teeth "erupt," or emerge, through the bone and the soft tissue of the gum. And third, after the tooth is in place in the mouth and functional, the roots (or root) finish growing until the tooth is securely anchored within the bony jaw. Each tooth develops and erupts at a specific time during the growing mammal's life, and all the members of a mammalian species follow the same schedule of dental maturation.

In modern humans the milk teeth are already developing within the jaws at the time of birth, and the full set of twenty milk teeth is usually in place by two and one-half years of age. At approximately five or six years of age, the adult teeth, some of which have been forming within the bone of the jaws since infancy, begin to appear as the first permanent molars erupt. Also around this time, beginning at the front of the mouth, the baby teeth begin to fall out and are replaced by their permanent counterparts. The adult dentition is not fully mature until the completion of root growth in the third molars, or wisdom teeth, an event usually occurring in the late teens or early twenties in *Homo sapiens sapiens* today.

Because teeth develop and mature according to a fairly regular schedule, they are extremely valuable in the analysis of skeletal remains. Depending upon which teeth are present in a child's skull, it is possible to determine, fairly precisely, a specimen's age at death. In other words, by looking at the state of dental maturation, one can tell how old that child was when he or she died, just as one can determine age at death by looking at the degree of fusion in the bones of an immature skeleton. Both methods, of course, are of major importance in our ability to determine the developmental ages of immature hominid fossils.

Mammalian growth and maturation are closely linked to mammalian behavior. Mammals are intelligent animals; in marked contrast to lower vertebrates, in which innate or preprogrammed patterns of behavior play a major role in how an animal will survive, mammals rely heavily upon learned behavior in successfully adapting to their environment. This pattern is possible because mammals not only grow in stages but also their growth period is very slow and prolonged prior to becoming independent adults. It is during this extended time, while the young mammal is growing up, that it is exposed to the spectrum of behaviors necessary for its survival as an adult. This period of dependency is a crucial part of a mammal's adaptation, for it provides the opportunity for extensive, intensive observation of adult behavior. In short, it sets the ideal stage for learning.

Among the higher primates and humans, a youngster must learn what behavior is acceptable in order to get along successfully with other members of its social group. A youngster must also acquire a repertoire of learned behaviors to deal with its environment, and learn how to utilize these behaviors successfully. Such learned standards of appropriate behavior are the group's culture. Because it is learned, not inherited, cultural behavior can only be passed on through traditions, not through genes. However, the biological bases for this sort of learned behavior—namely, a prolonged period of dependency and a large, complex brain—are themselves genetically inherited. Thus, we are able to examine biological structures preserved in the fossil record to gain an understanding of the potential for learning among earlier members of the genus *Homo*.

Humans are unique among mammals in one outstanding feature: the size of their brains relative to their body weight.[1] Moreover, the highly specialized human brain is unique because, although large at birth, it still weighs only 25 percent of its future adult size. In other words, 75 percent, or three fourths, of human brain growth occurs after birth, a greater proportion than the postnatal brain growth seen even in such close relatives as chimpanzees.[2] The modern human brain is unique among primates in yet another way: Before birth, late in the fetal period, it grows extremely rapidly, at a rate 20 to 60 percent greater than the growth rate of brains of other higher primates, including our closest living relative, the chimpanzee. Thus, humans have evolved a unique adaptive strategy for brain growth among primates, one that involves considerably rapid growth of the brain both before and after birth. Yet, because this rapid growth of the human brain begins before birth, human babies must be born in an extremely helpless state in order for the large-brained infant to pass successfully through the mother's birth canal. This helpless, or altricial, state at birth explains, in part, why humans experience the most extended period of dependency of all primates.

At birth, a newborn human baby has a head that is 25 percent of its total body length. Over the next eighteen years that baby is transformed until, as an adult, its head makes up only 12 percent of its entire body length. Although our heads are fairly large at birth, the brain continues to grow very rapidly during the first few years of life, reaching 80 percent of its adult size by age six (see Figure 11-2 on page 162). Of course, the brain and surrounding skull vault are not the only areas growing early in life. Even before birth, tooth germs are developing within the bony jaws. As these germs enlarge, the

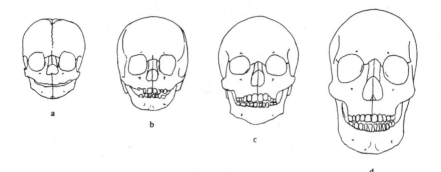

FIGURE 11-2 CHANGES IN CRANIOFACIAL PROPORTIONS
THROUGH GROWTH AND DEVELOPMENT

Humans are born with a relatively large braincase and small face. Through childhood, as the face grows, these proportions change until growth ceases at maturity: (a)
infant; (b) child; (c) early adolescent; (d) adult.

surrounding jaws must also grow to keep pace with them. By the time weaning begins, the muscles, bones, and teeth making up the biting and chewing
apparatus are well in place and functioning. Thus, while growth of the skull
vault or neurocranium is intimately related to the development of the brain,
facial growth is largely related to the nasal and oral complexes, which function in respiration and digestion. The fact that the braincase and face grow at
different rates, as their different functions dictate, is quite obvious as the growing child is followed from infancy to adulthood (see Figure 11-2). Early on, the
braincase is far larger than the face—approximately eight times larger. However, by adulthood considerable facial growth has occurred, so that the adult
braincase is usually only twice the size of the face.

EXAMINING GROWTH IN THE NEANDERTAL FOSSIL RECORD

NEANDERTAL BIRTH AND NEONATES

Were Neandertal infants born in as helpless a condition as we ourselves are?
This is an important question, for if they were not, perhaps Neandertals did
not require as lengthy a period of infant dependency as we do. This could,
in turn, imply that Neandertals may have been characterized by simpler
systems of learned behavior and should perhaps be considered as less than
fully "human."

Two sources of information in the paleoanthropological record lend themselves to the study of Neandertal birth and early infancy: adult remains of the
pelvis—the region of the skeleton including the bony birth canal—and the
skeletal remains of Neandertal infants themselves.

Although fewer than six specimens have been recovered, we do know that the adult Neandertal pelvis was somewhat different than that of modern humans. Portions of their pelves (plural for pelvis) were quite wide—even in males. This apparent width was, in part, a result of the very elongated Neandertal pubis. In modern humans, only the adult female pubis is typically elongated, a secondary sexual characteristic that increases maternal pelvic diameter after puberty, thus enhancing the chances for successful childbirth.

Erik Trinkaus of the University of New Mexico once suggested that the wide Neandertal pelvis might indicate that these hominids gave birth to extremely large infants—so large they might have been born following twelve months rather than the modern human nine-month gestation period.[3] Because nine months is an unusually short gestation period for a species our size, Trinkaus reasoned that perhaps a shift to our current, short gestation period, resulting in the birth of an extremely helpless infant, became possible only after the appearance of increasingly sophisticated behaviors in the earliest modern humans.[4] Karen Rosenberg of the University of Delaware also originally interpreted the wide Neandertal pelvis as designed to accommodate large babies, but emphasized that this proportioning could be attributed to the fact that Neandertal mothers had heavy body builds and so probably gave birth to large infants.[5] However, since the discovery of a large male Neandertal with an essentially complete pelvis at Kebara, Israel, Yoel Rak and Baruch Arensburg of Tel-Aviv University have convincingly argued that the elongated Neandertal pubis probably reflects an adaptation for meeting specific postural or ambulatory—rather than obstetric—requirements in these hominids.[6] Unfortunately, its precise functional significance is not yet understood. As Rosenberg has pointed out, the nature of pelvic sexual dimorphism in Neandertals remains essentially unknown.[7]

Fortunately, we need not rely exclusively on the pelvic remains of Neandertal adults to learn about birth and infancy in these hominids. The few available neonates known from the Neandertal fossil record shed some light on this subject. The site of La Ferrassie in southern France has yielded the remains of six children, including the fragmentary skeletons of two infants and another baby that appears to have been a fetus. They are believed, by some investigators, to have belonged to the same population or even a single family. Jean-Louis Heim, the French paleoanthropologist who has studied the La Ferrassie children, has found interesting differences between these fetal and newborn Neandertals and what one would usually see in modern human babies of comparable age, including greater thickness of some skull bones and stronger markings where muscles once attached to their limb bones.[8] The few fragmentary pieces of infant braincase from La Ferrassie suggest that Neandertal neonatal crania may have been thicker than those of modern humans so that head molding, such as that experienced by modern infants during vaginal delivery, may have been impossible or more limited in Neandertal babies. Theoretically, this could have necessitated a wider bony birth canal.[9]

However, remains of a partial newborn Neandertal's cranial vault from L'Hortus, France, suggest a somewhat different scenario. The dimensions of this newborn indicate that Neandertal babies had heads of the same size, with cranial vault bones of the same thickness, as modern newborns.[10] Moreover, the size of the large fontanelle, or soft spot on the baby's head, suggests that this little Neandertal was born at a stage of neurocranial development similar to that of a modern human baby.[11] In my own studies I have found that the individual bones of the Neandertal skull are proportioned slightly differently than in modern humans from infancy.[12] In particular, the shorter Neandertal mid-vault segment, or parietal bone, may have permitted a Neandertal baby's head to pass through its mother's pelvis without the drastic head molding common in modern humans. Overall, the evidence from infant remains suggests that Neandertal birth was probably quite similar to our own.[13]

NEANDERTAL CHILDHOOD AND ADOLESCENCE

In infancy, the Neandertal skull looked in many ways very much like that of a modern human child. As in modern humans, the braincase was disproportionately large during this very young developmental period, dominating the facial skeleton in size. The youngest well-preserved Neandertal child's skull on record is from the site of Pech de l'Azé, one of many Neandertal sites located in the Dordogne region of southwest France. Judging from its dental development (all of the milk teeth are erupted and their roots are complete) this child was about two and one-half years old when it died. Interestingly, the Pech de l'Azé toddler had not yet developed many of the exaggerated, rugged features typical of adult Neandertals. The same is true of another fairly complete Neandertal child's skull from Subalyuk, Hungary. Similar findings from other, less well-preserved Neandertal infants also show a large, smooth, globular cranial vault to house a large, growing brain and have the same gracile, or delicate, appearance, clearly establishing this as a typical pattern in very young Neandertals.

However, slightly older Neandertal juveniles are a different story, and their remains indicate that, following infancy, some marked growth changes occurred. Few of these changes are evident in the braincase, but the facial region shows dramatic growth in size and shape. In a four-and-one-half-year-old from the site of Engis, Belgium, the development of the browridges was clearly well underway at the time the child died (see Figure 11-3). In a seven-and-one-half-year-old from La Quina, another site in the French Dordogne, it is apparent that not only had the face-braincase proportions changed, but also the development of several adult facial features was well underway by midchildhood. For example, in the midfacial region the very flat maxillary, or cheek, area typical of adult Neandertals was clearly already established on either side of the very large nasal opening. Marked browridges had started to develop above the eye sockets, or orbits. In the lower jaw, or mandible, of

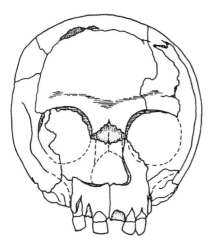

FIGURE 11-3   NEANDERTAL CHILD
This reconstruction of a Neandertal child excavated from a cave at Engis, Belgium in 1829 shows the prominent browridges present even in a youngster of four or five years of age. The lower jaw was not recovered.

Neandertal children this age, a very familiar feature—the chin—is missing. This characteristic is usually present in modern humans by childhood, but seldom develops in Neandertals—even in the most robust, muscular adult males. The absence of the chin in Neandertals and other earlier hominids is not fully understood, but one commonly cited theory explains that the front of the mandible has become much more delicately built over time, except for the chin, which is the only remnant of the strong, robust lower jaws of our predecessors. Perhaps future investigations of lower jaw growth and development in Neandertals and modern humans will clarify exactly what function the chin serves and why it appeared when it did in our evolutionary history.

We know early adolescence in Neandertals primarily from bits and pieces recovered from the fossil record and from one of the most beautiful, complete Neandertal skulls ever discovered: the early adolescent from Teshik-Tash, Uzbekistan. Although only approximately ten and one-half to eleven years old when it died, Teshik-Tash shows a striking resemblance to adult Neandertals. The braincase is long and low, the browridges are distinct, and an occipital bun, a projecting area at the back of the skull, is clearly present and much more accentuated than in younger Neandertal children. The Teshik-Tash face also closely resembles an adult Neandertal in its large nasal and "swollen" cheek regions. We know of late adolescence from a sixteen-year-old Neandertal from the site of Le Moustier, France, whose skull was essentially mature and indistinguishable from that of an adult, except perhaps not quite as rugged.

Thus, we have an entire series of fairly complete specimens, in addition to dozens of more fragmentary remains that document, stage by stage from infancy to adulthood, the progression of Neandertal craniofacial growth.

DEVELOPMENTAL DIFFERENCES BETWEEN
THE NEANDERTAL AND EARLY MODERN HUMAN PHYSIQUE

If we want to understand the differences between Neandertal and modern human growth more precisely, we need to extend our study of Neandertal growth to the earliest *Homo sapiens sapiens* who followed the Neandertals most immediately in time. Most of the early *Homo sapiens sapiens* children known from the Upper Pleistocene fossil record are quite incomplete and fragmentary but still contribute to our knowledge of how these ancient people grew. We can examine differences in growth by comparing Neandertals and early *Homo sapiens sapiens* of comparable developmental ages (as determined by their dental development).

We find that most growth of the frontal part of the Neandertal skull, excluding the massive browridges, which should really be considered part of the face rather than the braincase, occurred slightly earlier in life in Neandertals than in modern humans. Similarly, growth in the front of the skull occurred earlier in ancient than in modern *Homo sapiens sapiens*.[14] However, in Neandertals and early *Homo sapiens sapiens*, growth at the rear of the skull continued much longer than it does in modern humans—in fact, a noted increase occurred quite late in their growing years, during adolescence.[15] These results tell us that the Neandertal braincase, and therefore the Neandertal brain, did not grow exactly like that of modern humans. It also indicates that the earliest so-called modern Europeans who followed the Neandertals in time grew slightly differently than do modern humans. These differences are subtle, but they are consistently seen in the fossils.

The Neandertal face is remarkably distinctive and has attracted perhaps more attention than any other single morphological complex in all of paleoanthropological research. Two major theories have been advanced in attempting to explain the unique combination of features characterizing the Neandertal face. One of these is biomechanical and is based on evidence that Neandertals used their teeth for gripping things, so their jaws and supporting muscles were exercised far more vigorously than our own.[16] Another popular theory used to explain the uniqueness of the Neandertal face is climatic and is based on the possibility that Neandertal faces were specialized adaptations to the cold, dry periglacial environment of Upper Pleistocene Europe.[17]

In examining the growth of the facial skeleton we need to keep in mind that the face is very underdeveloped at birth relative to the braincase; in infancy, therefore, few differences are apparent between the Neandertal and the modern human face. However, by early childhood the large Neandertal facial dimensions begin to emerge. Interestingly, it is at just this time that we begin to find some evidence of specializations appearing in the chewing apparatus, a finding that supports, in part, the theory that the form of the Neandertal face was perhaps due to tremendous masticatory stress. One such feature, a strong bony projection where the powerful temporalis muscle attaches to the lower jaw, tips backward in Neandertals. This indicates considerable use of that part of the temporalis muscle important for pulling the jaw backward against resistance, suggesting use of the teeth for gripping and pulling objects (see Figure 11-4). The telltale backward orientation of this bony projection often develops for a brief period of time in modern children, but quickly disappears. In Neandertals, however, it appeared in midchildhood and became increasingly more accentuated through life, apparently a developmental response to the use of their teeth as tools.[18] By adolescence, the Neandertal face was clearly more massive than that of both modern humans and early *Homo sapiens sapiens*, and had taken on its distinctive long, projecting appearance.

Aspects of limb growth in Neandertals are not nearly as well-studied as are the bones of the skull and the teeth. This is in part due to the preservation problems with immature individuals. In the case of the limb bones, the growing end of the bone is connected to the main shaft of the bone by a zone of cartilage. Because cartilage is a soft tissue, it decomposes after death, leaving the two small end portions of a growing bone detached from the main shaft. These

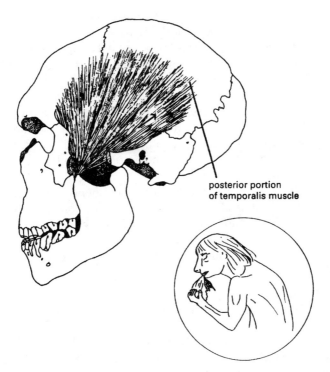

posterior portion
of temporalis muscle

FIGURE 11-4   USING THE TEETH AS TOOLS

The backward orientation of the bony projection by which the temporalis muscle attaches to the lower jaw, combined with the heavy wear found on Neandertal front teeth, suggests that these people often used their teeth to hold and steady hides, tendons, and other materials against resistance while working on them.

are easily destroyed, and when they are lost so too is valuable information regarding the total length of the immature limb bone, which is used to estimate total body height or its relative degree of maturity (what is called the skeletal age). Also lost is information on the size of the joint articular surfaces, often important for reconstructing the relative strength of an individual joint, which may assist in understanding behavior.

Despite these problems, we know that certain specialized, distinctively Neandertal limb features appeared early in growth and development. For example, we mentioned earlier that a part of the pelvis called the pubis is peculiarly elongated in Neandertals and was once considered a possible adaptation to permit Neandertal mothers to give birth to very large-brained infants. However, Robert Tompkins and Erik Trinkaus have demonstrated that in the ten-year-old La Ferrassie child this feature is elongated just as much as in Neandertal adults.[19] This further supports the notion, mentioned earlier, that the elongated pubis formed a part of the postural/locomotor complex of these hominids, rather than providing a widened pelvic aperture in Neandertal females for easier parturition.

Nearly every researcher who has examined the limb bones of Neandertal children has noted the evidence for unusually great muscularity—even in infants. This is visible from the large markings left by muscles and ligaments where they once attached to the bones during life. In addition, Chris Ruff, Alan Walker, and Erik Trinkaus have found that the thickness of limb bone shafts in Neandertal children is greater than that of comparably aged modern juveniles.[20] The presence of these clues, even in the very young, suggests a possible genetic component to the tremendous strength and muscularity of Neandertals, although possible differences in their activity levels may also explain these differences from the limb bones of modern humans, even as infants and children.

However, it should be noted that heftier does not necessarily mean healthier, as Mary Ursula Brennan has found. Her studies of bone density in the limb skeletons of Neandertal babies and young children, compared with the earliest modern Europeans, indicate that young Neandertals were far more stressed by disease and/or poor nutrition than were early *Homo sapiens sapiens*.[21]

MATURATION

On the basis of his detailed study of the Neandertal children from La Ferrassie, Jean-Louis Heim concluded that these people matured more rapidly than modern humans.[22] He is not the only investigator to have reached this conclusion. Christopher Dean and his colleagues Christopher Stringer and Timothy Bromage have also suggested that Neandertals perhaps grew more rapidly than we do.[23] If correct, this would mean that Neandertals would have experienced a shorter period of infant dependency and learning than we did, suggesting that learned behavior was not as important to Neandertals. This in turn would imply that they were not fully human in their adaptations. That is a staggering suggestion for, if correct, it means that hominids who lived as recently as 32,500 years ago, who had brains as large and larger than ours, and who intentionally buried their dead, were not capable of learning and thinking as we do. Of course, this may not have been the case; not all investigators have reached the same conclusions about Neandertal growth and development.

Michelle Lampl, Alan Mann, and Janet Monge have found that dental enamel development in Neandertals was similar to that of living Europeans but different from that of modern *Homo sapiens sapiens* from the Middle East.[24] Might this be due to a genetic trait and indicative of regional continuity between Neandertals and modern European populations? Or, given the known sensitivity of dental enamel to environmental stress,[25] could it simply result from the fact that populations inhabiting Europe experience greater systemic stress related to climatic seasonality than do humans living in warmer, more equatorial regions? At present, we simply do not know.

Ralph Holloway, a paleoneurologist at Columbia University, has examined a number of Neandertal endocranial casts, but can find no evidence of any difference between Neandertal brains and the brains of modern humans. Not even in areas of the brain devoted to language and higher integrative functions is Holloway able to find any substantive differences between Neandertals and modern humans—except for a possible expansion of the posterior part of the brain in the region of the visual cortex;[26] however, this is the region of the bony braincase that grows the longest in both Neandertals and the earliest *Homo sapiens sapiens*.[27]

What possible behavioral significance a larger visual cortex might have had is unknown. But overall, the overwhelming similarities between the brains of Neandertals and the earliest European *Homo sapiens sapiens* are perhaps most important. Brains are the most metabolically expensive of organs to grow, operate, and maintain. Thus, it seems reasonable to assume that the modern human pattern of extended, rapid brain growth would not have evolved had it not proven to be a highly adaptive feature of our biology. Clearly, despite a few subtle differences, the Neandertal brain grew in a manner strikingly similar to that of the modern human brain, and provided Neandertals with the time and equipment necessary to learn the cultural behavior of their social groups.

OTHER REASONS FOR STUDYING NEANDERTAL GROWTH

Many other reasons exist for studying Neandertal growth and development. One is the importance of being able to correctly interpret the morphology, or form, of the fossil remains of juveniles. Children cannot be studied using adult standards. As we have seen, the shapes of some bones, such as the skull, change through the course of growth and development. The bony pelvis undergoes shape changes in modern human females at puberty. If we do not understand the sequence of changes characterizing the immature skeleton through the course of growth and development, many fossil remains will not be available for interpretation or, perhaps worse, will be misinterpreted.

Much of the research on Neandertal growth by Anne-Marie Tillier[28] of the University of Bordeaux and by myself[29] has concentrated on just this sort of problem: attempting to understand the sequence of development in the shape-related changes accompanying growth. Without this sort of knowledge it is difficult, and sometimes impossible, to know whether a subadult fossil is a Neandertal, an early modern human, or a member of some other taxonomic group. One past example of this difficulty was the unnecessary division of the Krapina Neandertal fossils into two groups by the eminent Croatian paleontologist Gorjanovic-Kramberger. Gorjanovic, noting that some of the Krapina upper jaws were shorter than others, suggested that both Neandertals and modern humans were present at the site.[30] As it turned out, however, those Krapina faces with lower facial heights were all juveniles, and today we realize that, just as in modern humans, Neandertal faces grew gradually in height through the course of a child's maturation.[31] Thus, Gorjanovic's lower maxillas were simply the incompletely grown Neandertal children in his sample. Another example is provided by the Tangier maxilla, a fragment of a child's upper jaw from the Upper Pleistocene of Morocco, which for years had been regarded as possible evidence of a Neandertal presence in North Africa. However, recent reanalysis of the Tangier fossil, in comparison with Neandertal and modern children, now suggests that it was probably not a Neandertal and thus cannot be used as evidence of Neandertals in that part of the world.[32] It is hoped that our ability to analyze Neandertal growth will help avoid such errors in the future.

CONCLUSIONS

We must continue to study how Neandertals grew if we are to appreciate fully the biological and behavioral adaptations of these fascinating people. While we often focus on the many intriguing and unique aspects of Neandertal form, we should not lose sight of the evidence that suggests that, despite their unusual appearance and what many archaeologists regard as a less than innovative cultural repertoire, Neandertals possessed large brains that grew much like those of the early modern Europeans who followed them in time. In this and in many areas of their growth and maturation, Neandertals were quite similar to modern humans. Clearly, this indicates a tremendous reliance on learned behavior, and perhaps the more important tasks now confronting paleoanthropologists include dissecting out, together with archaeologists, specific patterns of Neandertal learned behavior from the prehistoric record.

NOTES

1. Robert D. Martin, "Evolution of the Brain in Early Hominids," *Ossa* 14 (1989): 49–62.
2. Paul H. Harvey, Robert D. Martin, and Clutton-Brock, "Life Histories in Comparative Perspective," in Barbara B. Smuts, Dorothy L. Cheney, Robert M. Seyfarth, Richard W. Wrangham, and Thomas Struhsaker, eds., *Primate Societies* (Chicago: University of Chicago Press, 1986), pp. 181–196.
3. Erik Trinkaus, "Neandertal Pubis Morphology and Gestation Length," *Current Anthropology* 25 (1984): 509–514.
4. Ibid., p. 512.
5. Karen R. Rosenberg, "The Functional Significance of Neandertal Pubic Length," *Current Anthropology* 29 (1988): 595–617; Karen R. Rosenberg, "The Evolution of Modern Human Childbirth," *Yearbook of Physical Anthropology* 35 (1992): 89–124.
6. Yoel Rak and Baruch Arensburg, "Kebara 2 Neanderthal Pelvis: First Look at a Complete Inlet," *American Journal of Physical Anthropology* 73 (1987): 227–231.
7. Karen R. Rosenberg, "Reconstructing Birth from the Fossil Record," paper presented at the *63rd Annual Meeting of the American Association of Physical Anthropologists*, Denver, March 31, 1994.
8. Jean-Louis Heim, *Les Enfants Néandertaliens de La Ferrassie* (Paris: Masson, 1982).
9. Nancy Minugh-Purvis, *Patterns of Craniofacial Growth and Development in Upper Pleistocene Hominids* (Ann Arbor: University Microfilms, 1988).
10. Marie-Antoinette de Lumley, "Anténéanderthaliens et Néanderthaliens du bassin méditerranéen occidental européen," *Études Quaternaires, Mémoire no. 2* (Marseille: Université de Provence, 1973).
11. Ibid.
12. Nancy Minugh-Purvis, "Metric Aspects of Ontogenetic Patterning in Upper Pleistocene Hominids: I. Neurocranium," submitted to the *American Journal of Physical Anthropology* (nd).
13. Nancy Minugh-Purvis, "The Neurocranial Evidence for Neandertal Birth: A Model for the Recent Evolution of Modern Human Parturition," paper presented at the *22nd Annual Meeting of the Canadian Association for Physical Anthropology*, Windsor, Ontario, October 27, 1994.
14. Minugh-Purvis, "Metric Aspects of Ontogenetic Patterning in Upper Pleistocene Hominids."
15. Ibid; Erik Trinkaus and Marjorie LeMay, "Occipital Bunning among Later Pleistocene Hominids," *American Journal of Physical Anthropology* 57 (1982): 27–35.
16. Milford H. Wolpoff, *Paleoanthropology* (New York: Knopf, 1980); Fred H. Smith, "A Behavioral Interpretation of Changes in Craniofacial Morphology across the Archaic/Modern *Homo sapiens* Transition," in Erik Trinkaus, ed., *The Mousterian Legacy* (Oxford: British Archaeological Reports S164, 1983), pp. 141–163; Erik Trinkaus, "The Neandertal Face: Evolutionary and Functional Perspectives on a Recent Hominid Face," *Journal of Human Evolution* 16 (1987): 429–443; Fred H. Smith and Steven P. Paquette, "The Adaptive Basis of Neandertal Facial Form, with Some Thoughts on the Nature of Modern Human Origins," in Erik Trinkaus, ed., *The Emergence of Modern Humans: Biocultural Adaptations in the Later Pleistocene* (New York: Cambridge University Press, 1989), pp. 181–210.
17. Carleton S. Coon, *The Origin of Races* (New York: Knopf, 1962).

18. Nancy Minugh-Purvis and Julia Lewandowski, "Functional Anatomy, Ontogeny, and Behavioral Implications of Coronoid Process Morphology in Upper Pleistocene Hominines," poster presented at the *61st Annual Meeting of the American Association of Physical Anthropologists*, Las Vegas, Nevada, April 4, 1992.

19. Robert H. Tompkins and Erik Trinkaus, "La Ferrassie 6 and the Development of Neandertal Pubic Morphology," *American Journal of Physical Anthropology* 73 (1987): 233–239.

20. Christopher B. Ruff, Alan C. Walker, and Erik Trinkaus, "Postcranial Robusticity in Homo. III. Ontogeny," *American Journal of Physical Anthropology* 93 (1994): 35–54.

21. Mary Ursula Brennan, "Nonspecific Indicators of Stress in the Upper Paleolithic," paper presented at the *86th Annual Meeting of the American Anthropological Association*, Chicago, November 20, 1987.

22. Heim, *Les Enfants Néanderthaliens de La Ferrassie*.

23. M. C. Dean, Christopher B. Stringer, and Timothy G. Bromage, "Age at Death of the Neanderthal Child from Devil's Tower (Gibraltar) and the Implications for Studies of General Growth and Development in Neanderthals," *American Journal of Physical Anthropology* 70 (1986): 301–309.

24. Michelle Lampl, Alan E. Mann, and Janet M. Monge, "Population Variation in the Microstructure of Human Dental Enamel," paper presented at the *62nd Annual Meeting of the American Association of Physical Anthropologists*, Toronto, April 16, 1993.

25. Mark F. Skinner and Alan H. Goodman, "Anthropological Uses of Developmental Defects of Enamel," in S. R. Saunders and A. Katzenberg, eds., *Skeletal Biology of Past Peoples: Advances in Research Methods* (New York: Wiley-Liss, 1992), pp. 157–178.

26. Ralph L. Holloway, "The Poor Brain of *Homo sapiens neaderthalensis*: See What You Please ...," in Eric Delson, ed., *Ancestors: The Hard Evidence* (New York: Liss, 1985), pp. 319–324.

27. Trinkaus and LeMay, "Occipital Bunning among Later Pleistocene Hominids"; Minugh-Purvis, "Metric Aspects of Ontogenetic Patterning in Upper Pleistocene hominids."

28. Anne-Marie Tillier, "Evolution de la région symphysaire chez les Homo sapiens juvéniles du Paléolithique moyen: Pech de l'Azé, Roc de Marsal et La Chaise 13," *C.R. Acad. Sciences (Paris)* 293 (1981): 725–727; Anne-Marie Tillier, "Les enfants Néanderthaliens de Devil's Tower (Gibraltar)," *Zeitschrift für Morphologie und Anthropologie* 73 (1982): 125–148; Anne-Marie Tillier, "Le crâne de l'enfant d'Engis 2: Un example de distribution de caractères juvéniles, primitifs et néanderthaliens," *Bulletin de la Société Royale Belge d'Anthropologie et de Préhistoire* 94 (1983): 51–75; Anne-Marie Tillier, "L'enfant Homo 11 de Qafzeh (Israël) et son apport à la compréhension des modalités de la croissance des squelettes moustériens," *Paléorient* 10 (1984): 263–271; Anne-Marie Tillier, "The Origins of Modern Humans in Southwest Asia: Ontogenetic Aspects," in Takeru Akazawa, Kenichi Aoki, and Taswku Kimura, eds., *The Evolution and Dispersal of Modern Humans in Asia* (Tokyo: Hokusen-Sha, 1992), pp. 15–28.

29. Nancy Minugh-Purvis, "A Comparison of Ontogenetic Patterning and Morphological Variation in the Mandibular Symphysis of *Homo sapiens neanderthalensis* and *Homo sapiens sapiens*," paper presented at the *17th Annual Meeting of the Canadian Association of Physical Anthropology*, Vancouver, British Columbia, November

2, 1989; Nancy Minugh-Purvis, "Ontogenetic Variation in the Mid-Face of Upper Pleistocene *Homo sapiens*," paper presented at the *60th Annual Meeting of the American Association of Physical Anthropologists*, Miami, Florida, April 6, 1990; Nancy Minugh-Purvis and Jakov Radovcic, "Krapina A: Neandertal or Not?" paper presented at the *61st Annual Meeting of the American Association of Physical Anthropologists*, Milwaukee, Wisconsin, April 1991; Nancy Minugh-Purvis, "Reexamination of the Immature Hominid Maxilla from Tangier, Morocco," *American Journal of Physical Anthropology* 92 (1993): 449–461.

30. Dragutin Gorjanovic-Kramberger, *Der diluviale Mensch von Krapina in Kroatien* (Wiesbaden: Kreidels, 1906).

31. Nancy Minugh-Purvis, "Interpreting Immature Craniofacial Morphology at Krapina: Problems and Possibilities," paper presented at the *XII International Congress of Anthropological and Ethnological Sciences*, Zagreb, Croatia (Yugoslavia), July 1988.

32. Minugh-Purvis, "Reexamination of the Immature Hominid Maxilla from Tangier, Morocco."

SUGGESTED READINGS

Trinkaus, Erik, and Pat Shipman. *The Neandertals: Changing the Image of Mankind*. New York: Alfred A. Knopf, 1992. An engaging review of the history of human evolutionary studies, with a focus on Neandertals.

Stringer, Chris, and Clive Gamble. *In Search of the Neanderthals*. New York: Thames and Hudson, 1993. An interesting examination of Neandertal biology and behavior.

Wolpoff, Milford H. *Paleoanthropology*, 2nd ed. New York: McGraw Hill, 1995. The state-of-the-art examination of the fossil evidence for human evolution.

TESTING THEORIES AND HYPOTHESES ABOUT MODERN HUMAN ORIGINS

DAVID W. FRAYER

The study of human evolution has always had a reputation for being a contentious subject. There is a long history of debates about the general course of human evolution, the details of the evolutionary process, the authenticity of the fossils, the reliability of their dates, and even the relevance of the fossils themselves for answering evolutionary questions. In some respects paleoanthropology is no more acrimonious than research on crickets or about black holes, but the academic battles in paleoanthropology are more often reported in the popular literature, making it seem like there is constant bickering about ideas and theories. In another respect, the "bone wars," as one journalist called them,[1] often persist because there is incomplete information due to a spotty and fragmentary fossil record. Even if paleoanthropologists wanted to reach an agreement on some issues, the incompleteness of the fossil record often allows it to be read in multiple ways and these inevitably lead to controversy. Still another source of troubles is the inability to frame hypotheses in ways that allow unambiguous testing and refutation. This is important since the primary mechanism for resolving scientific disagreements is through rejecting hypotheses on the basis of available data. Unlike some ongoing debates in paleoanthropology, however, the development of specific, testable hypotheses combined with an adequate fossil record has recently allowed the resolution of two contradictory theories about modern human origins.

Paleoanthropology has had a decades-long debate about the emergence of modern humans in the Old World. This debate has involved two different models. One model is that modern humans in each area are descended from the long line of fossils who preceded them in the area, which is evidenced by anatomical continuity within regions across time. Combining aspects of local selection, migration and gene exchange, and the effect of genetic isolating mechanisms, this theory is called multiregional evolution.[2] The other theory, previously labeled the Noah's Ark model,[3] contends that modern humans originated in one place, then spread throughout the Old World, displacing all the original inhabitants.[4] It is important to recognize that this spread of modern humanity was not the first wave of people out of Africa; both sides of the debate agree that the earliest humans left Africa about one million years ago. But, as its name implies, the Noah's Ark model argues for another, much more recent wave in which resident populations were displaced by new immigrants. It was not until the late 1980s that the debate over the two contradictory models really heated up. The heat was generated not by paleoanthropologists or by new fossil discoveries, but by molecular geneticists who claimed they had answered once and for all the question of modern human origins. Their resolution had nothing to do with the fossil record, but with patterns of variation in DNA. The hypotheses and predictions about the fossil record proposed by the new genetics-based theory were so fundamentally at odds with the multiregional model that it became possible to test unambiguously the two models of human origins.

The genetic solutions for the timing and appearance of modern humans appeared in two separate publications in the prestigious journal *Nature*. The first article by Wainscoat et al.[5] reviewed geographic variation in a genetic system known as the ß-globin gene cluster. This set of genetic loci is supposedly non-functional, a crucial consideration since evolutionary forces (such as natural selection) can have major confounding effects in reconstructing ancestor-descendant relationships and in calculating the rate at which they diverged. Wainscoat and his colleagues studied eight geographic groups (represented by samples from Africa, Britain, Cyprus, India, Italy, Melanesia, Polynesia, and Thailand) and argued that "all non-African populations share a limited number of common haplotypes (a set of closely linked genetic loci) whereas Africans have predominantly a different haplotype not found in other populations."[6] According to their interpretation of the patterns of genetic variation in the samples, Wainscoat et al. speculated that (1) there was a small founding population for all living humans, (2) the population that gave rise to all living humans derived from Africa, and (3) the replacement occurred relatively recently (~100,000 years ago). The article by Wainscoat et al. coincided with the release of the box office hit "Out of Africa," and within a short time their interpretation was dubbed the "Out of Africa" theory.[7] Even though a few geneticists expressed doubts about the conclusions,[8] the scientific implications of the article were in tune with the Noah's Ark model and some paleontologists felt this particular version of human origins was strengthened, if not finally confirmed.

Before the article had time to really settle in, it was eclipsed by a much more influential publication by the geneticists Rebecca Cann, Mark Stoneking, and Allan Wilson. This article, which also appeared in *Nature*, bolstered the Noah's Ark model and boldly proclaimed that humans could trace their origins to "one woman ... who lived about two hundred thousand years ago, probably in Africa."[9] Besides asserting a recent African origin of all living humans, the argument traced the ancestor to a single female, dubbed "Eve" by Wilson. While the ß-globin gene cluster results created only a minor puff in human paleontology, the Eve hypothesis hit the field like a cyclone, setting the stage for an often rancorous debate about recent human origins. The conclusions of the genetic argument and the ensuing debate between the "Eveists" and the "multiregionalists" have been widely reported in the popular media, with articles on modern human origins appearing as cover stories in *Newsweek*, *U.S. News and World Report*, *Time*, a *Nova* documentary, and numerous popular science and newspaper accounts on the Eve theory. There is also a book[10] aimed at the popular audience that focuses on the debate and I recommend it to readers of this article. Like no other issue in human paleontology, this debate was recounted in the popular literature, so that by the early 1990s many people outside anthropology had heard about the Eve debate.

Besides the scientific implications, a few researchers suggested there were social consequences stemming from the recent origin of modern humans. With the publication of the ß-globin gene cluster results, the narrow variation in this gene complex suggested to some that the human species went through a population crisis and that "[hu]mankind was an endangered species during an important part of its evolution."[11] With the publication of the molecular genetics results, Stephen Jay Gould (one of the leading evolutionary scientists and popularizers of modern biology) pondered in a lead article in *Newsweek*: "it makes us realize that all human beings, despite differences in external appearance, are really members of a single entity that's had a recent origin in one place. There is a kind of biological brotherhood that's much more profound than we ever realized."[12] Gould neglected to note that the Eve model involved a total replacement of one group of humans by another *without* admixture. The Eve theory did not allow interbreeding between the resident and invading groups, which means that the descendants of the original wave of settlers across the Old World would have been fully replaced by the invaders. As Milford Wolpoff once noted, this theory might be better named the "Cain" theory in that "[t]his rendering of modern population dispersals is a story of 'making war, not love,' and if true its implications are not pleasant."[13] Thus, in addition to claiming to solve the riddle of human origins, the Eve theory purportedly told us something about modern human nature, drawing all of us closer together due to our recent common genesis, however unpleasant the implications of the population replacement. Whatever the case, an important consequence of the Eve theory was that it led to very specific predictions about patterns of past variation and these could not be confused with the predictions of the multiregional model. Consequently, with the strictures imposed by the genetic analyses it was possible to test the Old World fossil record against the predictions of the two competing models.

The Essentials of the Debate

While argument over the Noah's Ark and multiregional models preceded the genetics results, several things triggered the relevance and intensity of the debate after 1987. Most important were the implications drawn from the molecular genetics. These data were viewed as sophisticated, technical information that could give an independent, unbiased assessment of what to expect in the fossil record. Some molecular geneticists were quick to point out that their data were qualitatively superior to the fossil record, and there was a certain amount of hubris among some molecular geneticists who felt the genetic data provided "objective information," while interpretations in the fossil record were riddled with subjective assessments.[14]

Another factor in the debate was the publication of new dates for sites in Western Asia and South Africa where some paleoanthropologists argued the earliest modern *Homo sapiens* fossils were found. Supporters of the Noah's Ark model often looked to the Near East for the origin of modern Europeans at two sites (Skhul and Qafzeh) in the Mount Carmel area of northern Israel. Some even called these fossils "proto-Cro-Magnoids" stressing their unique links to the early Upper Paleolithic populations of Europe and their distinctiveness from European and Near Eastern Neanderthals. Initially, it was thought these two sites were dated around thirty thousand to forty thousand years ago, which made the replacement coincide with the last evidence of Neanderthals in Europe. However, at about the same time the molecular estimates for the origin of modern humans were being published, new electron spin resonance and thermoluminescence dates were appearing for Skhul and Qafzeh.[15] These more than doubled their estimated antiquity and greatly affected the debate, in that there was now a long temporal overlap of so-called "modern" and archaic human forms. For some, due to the contemporaneity of Near Eastern Neanderthals and the so-called "proto-Cro-Magnoids," this meant that two different species of humans lived side by side for a very long time, then eventually the archaic forms were totally replaced by the "modern" Near Eastern forms. For others, the dates of the Skhul and Qafzeh samples were questioned as was the "modernity" of the sample. In addition, a series of anatomical descriptions and new dates were published for fossil human material from the South African sites Border Cave and Klasies River Mouth.[16] For some, fossil material from these two sites was also considered anatomically modern and the dates indicated an antiquity of about one hundred thousand years.

These factors set the stage for a debate on the origins of modern humans. While it's doubtful that any of the participants anticipated an imminent resolution, in 1993 the Eve theory was refuted. To understand the debate and appreciate how it was resolved, it is necessary to review the crucial aspects of the two competing theories and contrast their nonoverlapping predictions about the fossil record.

The Eve theory was based on patterns of variation in mitochondrial DNA (mtDNA) among individuals representing different geographic areas. Mitochondrial DNA is a special type of DNA found outside the nucleus and is associated with energy metabolism in the mitochondria. Several important biological principles about mtDNA made it an attractive tool for attempting to unravel evolutionary relationships.[17]

The complete genetic makeup of mtDNA is relatively short (compared to nuclear DNA) and was fully sequenced so it was possible to make loci by loci comparisons, looking for links among different individuals. This information was used to reconstruct geographic relationships.

Mitochondrial DNA is only inherited through the maternal line (there is no paternal contribution in humans), so in effect it is cloned from one generation to the next. This is significant since during gamete production nuclear DNA is recombined, mixing maternal and paternal genes. Thus, tracing genetic similarities through generations in nuclear DNA is complicated by the "pollution" of the father's genes, while in mtDNA the maternal generations pass along basically unaltered genetic sequences, except for occasional mutations. This characteristic of mtDNA greatly facilitated its use in reconstructing evolutionary phylogenies.

Mutations accumulate more rapidly in mtDNA (compared to nuclear DNA) and this accumulation is presumed to occur at a constant rate, estimated at a 2 to 4 percent change per million years. This rate, coupled with the patterns of geographic variation, led to the estimate of a two-hundred-thousand-year-old "mother of us all."

Finally, it was assumed that no selection operated on mtDNA and that mutations were neutral, causing no change in an individual's fertility or survivorship. This is important since the rate of incorporation of new mutations can be affected by natural selection. The operation of natural selection on mtDNA would markedly (and fatally) affect the regularity of the molecular clock's ticking, reducing the two-hundred-thousand-year-old estimate to a guess.

Using these assumptions, Cann, Stoneking, and Wilson[18] studied the mtDNA variation drawn from 147 individuals and through a statistical program known as PAUP (Phylogenetic Analysis Using Parsimony) reconstructed human phylogeny. Based on their statistical analysis, they rooted the phylogenetic tree in Africa, due to the finding that both "primary branches lead exclusively to African mtDNAs." Also, since there was a very narrow range of variation in non-African mtDNA, they argued there was no input of ancient, non-African mtDNA in the formation of the modern sample. This meant that the African replacement was complete and did not involve hybridization between the African invaders and the resident, native populations they replaced.

The multiregional evolution model, formulated by Alan Thorne, Xinshi Wu, and Milford Wolpoff,[19] is also based on patterns of worldwide variation. Instead of proposing a major disjunction across the Old World fossil populations, these paleoanthropologists argued that humans were descended from their forerunners in the region, not uniquely from an immigrating group. In many respects this model was an updated version of ideas first developed by Franz Weidenreich in his "polycentric theory."[20] Weidenreich's model was constructed after a long career of studying human fossils from Europe and Asia. His initial work in human paleontology was a reconstruction of an early Neanderthal skull from Ehringsdorf in Germany. He later was involved in the discovery and description of the important middle Pleistocene Chinese human remains from Zhoukoudian, and was well acquainted with the fossil material from Indonesia and with morphological variation in recent populations across Eurasia to Australia. Based on his familiarity with this material, Weidenreich saw regional patterning in certain morphological features. For example, he noted the high incidence of shovel-shaped incisors in fossil and living Asian populations. From these observations, he proposed that human evolution proceeded in each region of the world as an unbroken evolutionary stream and that the living inhabitants of each region exhibited morphological features that could be traced back into the distant fossil record of each region. Rather than a single place for the origin of modern humans, Weidenreich argued for separate geographic centers. In these places populations developed their own morphological features, leading to the inter-regional differences typical of populations today. However, the evolutionary changes did not occur in total isolation; gene exchange and migrations always occurred and all human populations remained members of the same species worldwide.

Multiregional evolution combined Weidenreich's perspective with an updated accounting of the fossils, especially those from North Asia, Indonesia, and Australia. It also incorporated the concept of "center and edge." This was an idea proposed by Alan Thorne,[21] who argued that patterns of variation relate to the geographic position of human populations. For example, those populations near the center of the species' range exchange genes with groups on all sides and maintain high levels of population variation. Those that are more peripheralized (1) take on unique features because they lack the magnitude of gene exchange typical of populations at the center and (2) are more likely to experience genetic drift (random changes) because of their relative isolation. This concept can be used to account for the morphological differences, say, between Europeans and aboriginal Australians. In a geographic sense, both regions are marginal or peripheral areas and at least in prehistoric times both were isolated at opposite ends from the center of the geographic range of *Homo sapiens*. Because of this isolation, genetic drift (or random factors) would increase variation between the native European and Australian populations. In addition, distinctive patterns of natural selection would operate to differentiate the populations since, given the ecological, climatological, and cultural differences between the two regions, human biology would respond in different ways to meet the specific fitness requirements. Consequently, Europeans and Australians have a constellation of features that differentiate them and that can be used to trace their evolution within their own region. Despite these differences, however, there was sufficient gene flow across the whole human range to maintain species integrity. In short, multiregional evolution proposes that geographic regions have chronologically deep human lineages in which unique features develop over time. These unique features serve to unite the fossil and extant humans in an evolving sequence that can be differentiated from other evolving sequences in other regions.

From these brief sketches of the Eve and multiregional theories, it should be apparent that they have contradictory predictions about the mode of origin for modern *Homo sapiens*. The Eve model requires complete replacement outside of Africa and a major break in the evolutionary sequence within a region. Thus, if the Eve theory is correct, the fossil record should reflect clear evidence of an Old World-wide replacement in the late Pleistocene. Following the assumptions of the Eve model, the replacers would have originated in Africa about two hundred thousand years ago, so the earliest modern populations everywhere should resemble the earliest modern populations from Africa, if indeed such fossils exist. Moreover, the replacing fossils would not be expected to resemble the resident populations, since the interpretation of the mtDNA data by the Eveists does not allow for mixing of the invading (Eve) and resident (original) populations.[22] Just the opposite, the multiregional theory hypothesizes the persistence of ancient traits through time since this model assumes that the ancestors of a particular region contribute to the formation of the descendants. Thus, the multiregional view predicts that the fossil record will not show an abrupt appearance of new (modern) human populations, but that ancient morphological features typical of the region will persist in the later populations.

THE FOSSIL TEST

Using these unambiguous, nonoverlapping predictions about ancient and recent patterns of geographic variation, it is possible to test the two models. This was the topic of a recent article by myself and four colleagues: Geoffrey Pope, Fred Smith, Alan Thorne, and Milford Wolpoff.[23] In our approach we followed the Popperian view of science, that hypotheses cannot be proven correct, but only refuted. We tested the basic predictions outlined above against the fossil record. It is not possible here to go through all the evidence we reviewed for Africa, Europe, Western Asia, North Asia, and Australasia, but for the full account, consult our detailed article in *American Anthropologist*. By now it should be obvious that since the Eve theory requires total replacement everywhere throughout the Old World, finding evidence for continuity of anatomical traits from ancient to modern populations *even in one region outside Africa* is sufficient evidence to refute the Eve hypothesis.

We started our review with an examination of the fossil record of Australasia (Southeast Asia and Australia), which has an extensive prehistoric sequence spanning probably more than seven hundred thousand years. Figure 12-1 (on page 182) shows four skulls, all of which are probably males. The skull (Sangiran 17) on the bottom is the most complete Middle Pleistocene skull from Java. Some of its distinctive features include a low flat frontal, large browridges that are continuous from side to side and project anteriorly, a well-developed torus (bony ridge) at the back of the skull, an extensive nuchal plane (the area below the torus where numerous muscles at the back of the neck attach to the skull), thick cranial bones, and a large face marked by massive zygomatics (cheek bones) and large teeth. The skull in the left middle (Willandra Lakes 50) is the oldest known human skull from Australia, probably about sixty thousand years old. Its cranial features clearly resemble Sangiran 17. The forehead is low and flat, the brows are massive, the posterior projection of the skull has a well-demarcated nuchal plane, and the bones of the vault are extremely thick. While there is no face, it is hard to imagine anything but a massive one associated with WLH 50. The top skull is Kow Swamp 1 from the late Pleistocene of Australia. Kow Swamp 1 shows all the regional features found in the earlier two skulls (for example, it has a very flat frontal), but is clearly more modern in features such as skull height and reduction of the brows. Three skulls do not show all the anatomical variation in the Australasian sequence, but they do demonstrate the basic pattern for change within the region, linking morphological patterns across time in Australasia.

The other skull is Border Cave 1, a specimen from South Africa identified by the Eve supporters as a representative of the early modern populations that left Africa and replaced all other groups.[24] It does not take a specialist in human paleontology to recognize the fundamental anatomical differences separating Border Cave 1 from the three Australasian skulls. If the Eve replacement theory is correct, we would expect Border Cave 1 to differ from one of the oldest specimens from Australasia (Sangiran 17), because the Border Cave 1 fossil is much more recent. We might also expect Border Cave 1 and WLH 50 to differ substantially, since some might argue that WLH 50 predates the total replacement in Australia. However, since Kow Swamp 1 could only be descended from the Eve group, there should be some resemblance between it and Border Cave 1. But, Kow Swamp 1 continues the morphological pattern found in the earlier skulls from the region. It does not particularly resemble Border Cave 1 and, since descendants resemble their ancestors, Border Cave 1 is a poor candidate as the precursor of native Australians. While these Australasian skulls represent only a portion of the entire variation of the region, the pattern they show typifies the general evolutionary relationships over time. It is clear from Figure 12-1 that the skulls on the top, left, and bottom form the more likely evolutionary sequence. To insert populations resembling the Border Cave

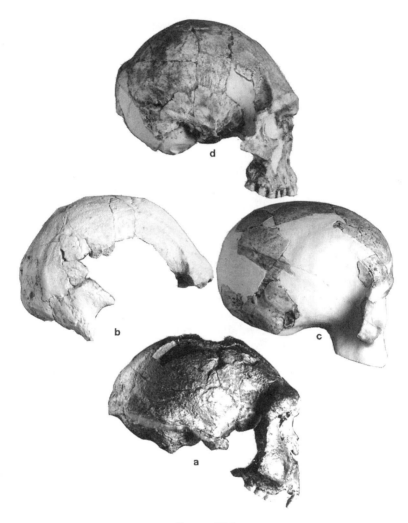

FIGURE 12-1

skull with a completely different morphology requires that the descendant populations take on the exact same constellation of features that uniquely typify the populations they totally replaced. Our analysis concluded that there is no major break in the Australasian sequence that would provide evidence for the sudden appearance of modern *Homo sapiens* invading from Africa. Rather, regionally restricted features persist over time; if the African Eves did invade and replace all the resident groups in Australasia, they left no trace of their features in the populations they would have founded. Thus, although the fossil evidence does not prove multiregional continuity, it directly contradicts the Eve predictions.

This problem of similarity between ancient and modern populations in Australasia did not go unnoticed by some Eve supporters. To interpret these observations in a way compatible with the Eve theory, Stringer and Andrews reached for an explanation which is unacceptable to most anthropologists: "Perhaps, Australia was a special case where local differentiation, cultural practices, or pathologies led in some cases to apparent evolutionary reversals."[25] Such an unfortunate conclusion is, perhaps, not surprising since an earlier definition of modern *Homo sapiens* by Stringer[26] defined modern humans on the basis of European features and, when applied to native Australians, about one-third of these modern people[27] were excluded from the category of *Homo sapiens*! Yet, rather than recognize the anatomical connections over time which unequivocally refuted the Eve hypothesis, Stringer and Andrews relegated native Australians to evolutionary throwbacks. In addition to the perpetuation of this deplorable stereotype about native groups and their lifeways, there is no biological reason to suspect that "local differentiation, cultural practices, or pathologies" would produce a convergence of identical traits which, according to the Eve hypothesis, were lost due to a total population replacement by an invading group. Stop for a moment to consider the evolutionary trail that would have to be hypothesized in the Australasian sequence to make it consistent with the Eve theory.

1. There is an initial colonization of the Southeast Asian archipelago by around one million years ago.
2. Human groups migrate over sea to Australia, perhaps by sixty thousand to eighty thousand years ago. These earliest Australian fossils bear little resemblance to the fossil African Eves, but strongly resemble the earlier fossils from the same region.
3. A replacement of all the region's original inhabitants occurs either before the colonization of Australia or after it. The African immigrants (who have left no currently known fossils in Australasia) with their geographically distinct features do not interbreed with the resident populations. Moreover, they are able to swamp and totally re-place the native groups (even though there is not a shred of archaeological evidence for the introduction of a new technology associated with the earliest modern Australians). Note here that even the European immigration to Australia with its accrued benefits of the Industrial Revolution and the intent and action to eliminate the native peoples did not succeed in completely replacing the native Australians.
4. Finally, in recent times, modern native Australians carry specific anatomical features that plainly link them to past populations of the region. These identical features evolve a second time, transforming the African Eve morphology back to the basic pattern typical of populations before the invasion. Visually this convoluted sequence can be traced by following the sequence a-c-d up the right side of Figure 12-1. If this sequence represents reality, it is important to note that there are no skulls found in

middle- to late-Pleistocene times in Australasia that even remotely resemble the morphology typical of the African Eve Border Cave 1 individual. Consequently, besides having to construct some questionable
and objectionable explanations for the links between the past and present variation, the Eve model requires an immigrant population (with
origins in Africa), for which no biological or archaeological evidence
exists. On the other hand, if one follows the a-b-d sequence in Figure 12-
1, there is no necessity for speculating about a total population replacement or about the reappearance of anatomical features in the
immigrating groups. Rather, native Australians could be seen as developing out of long-term change of the region's inhabitants, along with
gene flow from other areas.

Clearly, in Australasia the basic predictions of the Eve theory are violat-
ed. These effectively refute the Eve hypothesis, since the Eve theory requires
a complete, total replacement in all populations across the Old World. Even
so, it is reasonable to ask if Australia is the exception to a general pattern with
substantial evidence for replacement elsewhere around the Old World. Or, do
other areas also show the persistence of ancient traits in late Pleistocene and
recent populations? As my colleagues and I have argued,[28] evolutionary sequences throughout the Old World provide undeniable evidence for some degree of continuity from ancient to modern populations. If one examines the
fossil record for East Asia, there is overwhelming evidence for the persistence
of specific cranial, facial, and dental features through time. One example will
suffice. Table 12-1 reviews data for the incidence of shovelling in maxillary
incisors for large samples of modern Chinese, Europeans, and African-Amer-
icans. Shovel-shaped incisors are defined by the existence of ridges along the
margins of the central and lateral incisors in the upper jaw. According to some
recent research,[29] there are details of incisor shovelling that are unique in East
Asians compared to those of European or African descent. But, even ignoring
these trait distinctions, there are unmistakable differences in frequency that
distinguish the three groups. As is clear from the table, shovelled incisors exist
in high frequencies in Chinese populations: 90 percent of the Chinese sample
has marked shovelling (semi-shovel + shovel-shaped), while these categories
reach less than 15 percent in European and African-American samples. This
is not a new observation, since this trait is often used as an important feature
in modern forensic cases to identify suspects of Asian descent. Indeed, this
regional trait is found in the initial founding populations of China, where the
earliest human teeth show distinct shovelling of the upper incisors. As in the
Australasian case, it is important to recognize that modern patterns of anatomical variation extend into the deep past, and traits typical of ancient populations persist through time. In addition to incisor shovelling there is a
constellation of features that appear early and are unique to East Asia.[30] Most
of these would have had to evolve a second time if the Eve theory were correct—and that is hard to believe.

TABLE 12-1   INCIDENCE OF SHOVELLING (PERCENTAGES)
IN CHINESE, EUROPEAN, AND AFRICAN-AMERICAN SAMPLES

	SAMPLE SIZE	NO SHOVEL	TRACE	SEMI-SHOVEL	SHOVEL-SHAPED	TOTAL
Chinese[a]	651	8.3	1.4	23.2	67.1	100.0
Europeans[a]	1000	62.5	28.5	7.4	1.6	100.0
African-Americans[a]	807	51.0	35.0	9.9	4.1	100.0

[a]From Hrdlicka.[31] Represents an average for males and females and for central and lateral incisors.

Even in Europe where the traditional view has held that Neanderthals were totally replaced by invasions of "modern" *Homo sapiens*, there is considerable evidence for the persistence of anatomical features through time.[32] These unique European features link the Neanderthal and Upper Paleolithic samples and run completely contrary to the Eve predictions, unless in yet another area, unique features would have evolved again in a replacing population that wiped out all the original inhabitants who possessed exactly the same features. It is difficult to accept repeated evolution of the same trait in one area, but a model that requires this type of origin for important sets of traits in every geographic area across the Old World is beyond the range of scientific possibility.

THE AFRICAN EVIDENCE OF MODERN HOMO SAPIENS

The persistence of traits across long stretches of time is not the only prediction of the Eve hypothesis that is refuted by the fossil record. There is also no evidence for the early appearance of a modern *Homo sapiens* population in Africa. Remember that this is a fundamental prediction of the Eve hypothesis, since it is argued that the sole source of mtDNA in living people today is derived from an African population that differentiated around two hundred thousand years ago. It is reasonable to ask then if there is evidence for the appearance of a modern population in Africa. It might be that such a population has not yet been found in the fossil record. But this is not an acceptable premise, since we are required to work with the fossil record as we know it. Otherwise, if we relied on the unfound and unknown, anything would be possible. Hypotheses cannot be refuted on the basis of discoveries that have yet to be made! If so, there would be no scientific basis for any theory of human evolution. Some workers have identified fossils from Klasies River Mouth and Border Cave (South Africa) as the ancestors of us all. Much of the Border Cave material will always be without provenience due to the excavation procedures; for example, the most complete skull (Border Cave 1) was discovered when a farmer was digging for bat guano in the cave sediments. Beyond this, there are severe problems in accepting the rather fragmentary specimens from these sites as representing a modern population.[33] For example, three of the four mandibles from Klasies River Mouth Cave lack a chin, a feature that everywhere in the world is considered a mark of modernity. Moreover, even if the dates of Klasies are correct (eighty thousand to one hundred thousand years), an equally well-developed chin is found in the Tabun B mandible from Israel, which may be older by as much as fifty thousand years. There are numerous other features of the so-called "anatomically modern" *Homo sapiens* specimens from Africa which belie a modern classification.[34] While it may be true that some modern traits occur in a few specimens from South Africa, the same can be found in other areas in the world.[35] The fact is that there are a series of archaic features also present, and these disqualify the material as constituting a modern population.

THE GENETIC REFUTATION

From our analysis of the fossil record, we were able to reject the most basic predictions of the Eve theory,[36] which represents a clear refutation of the Eve hypothesis. But as it turns out, the Eve hypothesis is also rejected by the very genetic data on which it was based. This refutation comes from a detailed analysis by Alan Templeton,[37] an expert in phylogenetic analysis and creator of some of the statistical procedures used in the analyses of the mtDNA which culminated in the Eve theory. In his analysis of the original mtDNA data (which were provided by Stoneking), Templeton demonstrated that (1) the "geographic location of the common ancestor is ambiguous," (2) the date of the ancient Eve is "extremely ambiguous but is likely to be considerably more than two hundred thousand years ago," (3) the patterning in phylogenetic trees of mtDNA variation is a consequence "of a few recent population expansions of limited geographic range" along with some "geneflow throughout the entire time period tracing back to the common mitochondrial ancestor," and (4) mtDNA and nuclear DNA provide no evidence for a "single source population for all genetic variation."[38] Templeton's results are consistent with other analyses,[39] which taken together demonstrate that the genetic underpinnings of the Eve theory are shaky at best. In fact, instead of being an objective, accurate rendering of the course of human evolution, many unsupportable presumptions about the molecular data were made that directly affect the reliability of the conclusions based on the molecular data.

CONCLUSION

Coupled with the evidence from paleoanthropology, the undoing of the Eve theory of human origins is now total. The genetic basis on which it rested has collapsed and the fossil record, which represents the real remains of individuals who existed in the past, unambiguously contradict each of the basic predictions of the Eve theory. The ultimate measure of progress in science is the ability to refute hypotheses and then move on and attempt to refute others. The death of the Eve theory does not prove that the theory of multiregional evolution is necessarily correct. But, as Templeton concluded in his review of the mtDNA evidence, "all humans represent a single long-term evolutionary lineage with regional subdivision and always have throughout the entire period marked by mtDNA." This is multiregional evolution and this theory should now be the focus for refutation.

NOTES

1. J. E. Ferrell, "Bone Wars," *Image, The San Francisco Examiner*, August 23, 1987, pp. 14–35.
2. Milford H. Wolpoff, Wu Xinshi, and Alan G. Thorne, "Modern *Homo sapiens* Origins: A General Theory of Hominid Evolution Involving the Fossil Evidence from East Asia," in Fred H. Smith and Frank Spencer, eds., *The Origins of Modern Humans: A World Survey of the Fossil Evidence* (New York: Alan R. Liss, 1984), pp. 411–483; Milford H. Wolpoff and Alan G. Thorne, "The Case against Eve," *New Scientist* 22, no. 1774 (1991): 33–37; Alan G. Thorne and Milford H. Wolpoff, "The Multiregional Evolution of Humans," *Scientific American* 266, no. 4 (1992): 76–83.
3. William W. Howells, "Explaining Modern Man: Evolutionists versus Migrationists," *Journal of Human Evolution* 5 (1991): 477–496.
4. William W. Howells, *Getting Here* (Washington, D.C.: Compass, 1993).
5. J. S. Wainscoat, A. V. S. Hill, A. L. Boyce, J. Flint, M. Hernandez, S. L. Thein, J. M. Old, J. R. Lynch, A. G. Faust, D. J. Weatherall, and J. B. Clegg, "Evolutionary Relationships of Human Populations from an Analysis of Nuclear DNA Polymorphisms," *Nature* 319 (1986): 491–493.
6. Ibid.
7. Eugene Giles and Stanley H. Ambrose, "Are We All Out of Africa?" *Nature* 322 (1986): 21–22.
8. Ibid.
9. Rebecca L. Cann, Mark Stoneking, and Allan C. Wilson, "Mitochondrial DNA and Human Evolution," *Nature* 325 (1987): 31–36.
10. Michael H. Brown, *The Search for Eve* (New York: Harper and Row, 1990).
11. J. S. Jones and S. Rouhani, "How Small Was the Bottleneck?" *Nature* 319 (1986): 449–450.
12. John Tierney, Lynda Wright, and Karen Springen, "The Search for Adam and Eve," *Newsweek* (January 11, 1988): 46–52.
13. Brown, *The Search for Eve*, p. 229.
14. Allan C. Wilson and Rebecca L. Cann, "The Recent African Genesis of Humans," *Scientific American* 266 (1992): 68–73.
15. H. P. Schwarcz, R. Grün, B. Vandermeersch, O. Bar Yosef, H. Valladas, and E. Tchernov, "ESR Dates for the Hominid Burial Site of Qafzeh," *Journal of Human Evolution* 17 (1988): 733–737; C. B. Stringer, R. Grün, H.P. Schwarcz, and P. Goldberg,

"ESR Dates for the Homonid Burial Site of Es Skhul in Israel," *Nature* 338 (1989): 756–758.

16. G. P. Rightmire and H. J. Deacon, "Comparative Studies of Late Pleistocene Human Remains from Klasies River Mouth," *Journal of Human Evolution* 20 (1991): 131–156.

17. Cann, Stoneking, and Wilson, "Mitochondrial DNA and Human Evolution," pp. 31–32.

18. Ibid.

19. Wolpoff, Wu, and Thorne, "Modern *Homo sapiens* Origins: A General Theory of Hominid Evolution Involving the Fossil Evidence from East Asia."

20. Franz Weidenreich, "The Skull of *Sinanthropus pekinensis:* A Comparative Study of a Primitive Hominid Skull," *Palaeontologia Sinica* n.s. D, no. 10 (1943).

21. Alan G. Thorne and Milford H. Wolpoff, "Regional Continuity in Australasian Pleistocene Hominid Evolution," *American Journal of Physical Anthropology* 55 (1981): 337–349.

22. Chris Stringer and Peter Andrews, "Genetics and the Fossil Evidence for the Origin of Modern Humans," *Science* 239 (1988): 1263–1268.

23. David W. Frayer, Milford H. Wolpoff, Alan G. Thorne, Fred H. Smith, and Geoffrey G. Pope, "Theories of Modern Human Origins: The Paleontological Test," *American Anthropologist* 95 (1993): 14–50.

24. Chris Stringer, "The Emergence of Modern Humans," *Scientific American* 263 (1990): 98–104.

25. Stringer and Andrews, "Genetics and the Fossil Evidence for the Origin of Modern Humans," p. 1267.

26. Michael H. Day and Chris B. Stringer, "A Reconsideration of the Omo Kibish Remains and the *erectus-sapiens* Transition," in Henri deLumley, ed., *L'Homo erectus et la Place de l'Homme de Tautavel Parmi les Hominidés Fossiles,* vol. 2 (Nice: Louis-Jean Scientific and Literary Publications, 1982), pp. 814–816.

27. Milford H. Wolpoff, "Describing Anatomically Modern *Homo sapiens*: A Distinction without a Definable Difference," *Anthropos* (Brno) 23 (1986): 41–54.

28. Frayer, Wolpoff, Thorne, Smith, and Pope, "Theories of Modern Human Origins: The Paleontological Test."

29. Tracy L. Crummett, "A New Handle on the Shovel," *American Journal of Physical Anthropology,* supplement 12 (1991): 64.

30. Geoffrey G. Pope, "The Craniofacial Evidence for the Emergence of Modern Humans in China," *Yearbook of Physical Anthropology* 35 (1992): 243–298; Wolpoff, Wu, and Thorne, "Modern *Homo sapiens* Origins: A General Theory of Hominid Evolution Involving the Fossil Evidence from East Asia," pp. 424–436.

31. Ales Hrdlicka, "Shovel-Shaped Teeth," *American Journal of Physical Anthropology* 3 (1920): 429–465.

32. Frayer, Wolpoff, Thorne, Smith, and Pope, "Theories of Modern Human Origins: The Paleontological Test"; Milford H. Wolpoff, "The Place of the Neandertals in Human Evolution," in E. Trinkaus, ed., *The Emergence of Modern Humans. Biocultural Adaptations in the Later Pleistocene* (Cambridge: Cambridge University Press, 1989), pp. 97–141; Fred H. Smith, "The Neandertals: Evolutionary Dead Ends or Ancestors of Modern People?" *Journal of Anthropological Research* 47 (1991): 219–238; David W. Frayer, "Evolution at the European Edge: Neanderthal and Upper Paleolithic Relationships," *Préhistoire Européene* 2 (1992): 9–69.

33. Rachel Caspari and Milford H. Wolpoff, "The Morphological Affinities of the

Klasies River Mouth Skeletal Remains," *American Journal of Physical Anthropology* 81 (1990): 203; Fred H. Smith, "Models and Realities in Modern Human Origins: The African Fossil Evidence," *Philosophical Transactions of the Royal Society of London, series B* 337 (1992): 243–250.

34. Smith, "Models and Realities"; Frayer, Wolpoff, Thorne, Smith, and Pope, "Theories of Modern Human Origins: The Paleontological Test."
35. Frayer, Wolpoff, Thorne, Smith, and Pope, "Theories of Modern Human Origins: The Paleontological Test."
36. Ibid.
37. Alan R. Templeton, "The 'Eve' Hypotheses: A Genetic Critique and Reanalysis," *American Anthropologist* 95 (1992): 51–72.
38. Ibid.
39. P. Darlu and P. Tassy, "Roots (A Comment of the Evolution of Human Mitochondrial DNA and the Origins of Modern Humans)," *Human Evolution* 2 (1987): 407–412; Laurent Excoffier and André Langaney, "Origin and Differentiation of Human Mitochondrial DNA," *American Journal of Human Genetics* 44 (1989): 73–85; David R. Maddison, "African Origin of Human Mitochondrial DNA Re-examined," *Systematic Zoology* 40 (1991): 355–363.

SUGGESTED READINGS

Brown, Michael H. *The Search for Eve.* New York: Harper and Row, 1990. A detailed account of the genesis and debate about the Eve theory before its resolution in 1993. The book also gives a feel for the personalities involved in the debate with sketches and interviews of some of the main scientific participants.

Lewin, Roger. "The Mitochondrial Route to Human Origins." *Mosaic* 22 (1991): 46–55. A concise review of the basic premises of the Eve and multiregional views by one of the world's premier science writers.

Stringer, Chris, and Peter Andrews. "Genetics and the Fossil Evidence for the Origin of Modern Humans." *Science* 239 (1988): 1263–1268. The first attempt by the "Eveists" to integrate evidence from mtDNA and the fossil record. The article ended with the statement that "paleoanthropologists who ignore the increasing wealth of genetic data on human population relationships will do so at their peril"—an ironic statement given the recent evidence for the misinterpretations of the molecular data.

Thorne, Alan G., and Milford H. Wolpoff. "The Multiregional Evolution of Humans." *Scientific American* 266 (1992): 76–83. A detailed, popular statement about the multiregional model from two prominent paleoanthropologists.

Wilson, Alan C., and Rebecca L. Cann. "The Recent African Genesis of Humans." *Scientific American* 266 (1992): 68–73. A detailed, popular statement about the Eve model from two of the originators of the molecular basis for Eve.

Wolpoff, Milford H., James N. Spuhler, Fred H. Smith, Jakov Radovcic, Geoffrey G. Pope, David W. Frayer, Robert Eckhardt, and Geoff Clark. "Modern Human Origins." *Science* 241 (1988): 772–773. A succinct, one-page response to the Stringer and Andrews article on modern human origins in *Science*. This was the opening round in the scientific debate about modern human origins.

Natural Variation
in Human Fecundity

Peter T. Ellison

Thomas Malthus has a secure place in the history of ideas. He sowed the
seeds of the modern theory of evolution by natural selection in the minds
of Charles Darwin and Alfred Wallace while at the same time helping to lay
the foundations of the modern fields of demography, ecology, and political
economics. Yet the same ideas that proved so inspiring also carried with them
certain unrecognized, or at least unchallenged, assumptions which became
firmly embedded in the way most scholars thought about human reproduction for the next two hundred years. Malthus's great contribution was the understanding that population growth tends to be exponential, that the number
of people added to a population in a unit of time is a function of the number
of people already in the population. At the same time he knew that population growth was the net result of two demographic processes: birth and death.
Realizing that exponential growth cannot continue indefinitely, or even for
very long, without outstripping necessary resources, he reasoned that some
change in demographic dynamics must eventually limit the growth of any
population. At this point he introduced a great dichotomy into Western
thought, a dichotomy that has persisted to the present day, though current
research is now calling it into question.

The dichotomy was embodied in the assertion that "natural" checks to
population growth would occur through increases in mortality rates (e.g.,
via plagues, pestilence, famine, and war), while decreases in fertility would
have to be the result of "moral restraint," or the action of social forces (e.g.,
marriage rules, religious prescriptions, sexual taboos, and individual absti-
nence). No evidence was required for this assertion; the superprolific nature
of socially unrestrained human fertility was considered to be self-evident
and without significant variation—certainly without any relationship to population size or resource abundance that might constitute a natural check on
population growth.[1]

The Malthusian assumption that significant variation in human fertility is socially, not biologically, determined has persisted to the present day, and not without reason. Certainly the dramatic decline in fertility rates that has occurred in conjunction with the rise of modern industrial economies in the West and that is occurring with increasing frequency throughout the developing world is a consequence of changing social forces molding individual reproductive behavior. Physiology has little, if anything, to do with it. Our hope for stabilizing the world population within the next century similarly lies clearly within the domain of moral restraint. Yet the degree of social control of human fertility that we currently experience is a relatively recent phenomenon, and the unquestioning acceptance of Malthus's assumption may have blinded us to an understanding of the ways in which human fecundity (the biological *capacity* to bear offspring, as opposed to fertility, or the *fact* of having borne children) may also be subject to natural variation. Such natural variation in fecundity may have been an important part of our ecology in the distant and not so distant past, and may continue to influence patterns of fertility in the developing world today.

LOUIS HENRY AND THE IDEA OF VARIATION IN NATURAL FERTILITY

The first challenge to the Malthusian assumption came from the pen of French demographer Louis Henry in the middle of the twentieth century.[2] At that time considerable effort was focused on understanding the social causes of variation in human fertility in order to better "engineer" a rapid transition to lower fertility levels in the developing world. In a particularly influential article Kingsley Davis and Judith Blake identified two major determinants of fertility variation that were clearly within the social domain: marriage patterns (including ages at marriage, percent of women ever married, and rates of widowhood, divorce, and remarriage) and contraceptive use.[3] Henry was interested in something else, however—the phenomenon he termed "natural fertility," or fertility that showed no evidence of conscious efforts to limit family size. He could recognize such a fertility pattern in a population empirically when the probability of a woman having an additional child was largely independent of the number of children already born, also called *parity*. In such natural fertility populations the probability of having yet another child declines steadily with increasing parity, but without any abrupt drop. In contrast, Henry introduced the term "controlled fertility" to describe populations in which the probability of having another child drops precipitously after a target family size is reached. Henry collected data on populations that displayed the natural fertility pattern, considering only the fertility of married women, and made two quite surprising observations.

First, there was a great deal of variation in the level of fertility that such populations displayed. The Malthusian assumption predicted that unrestrained human fertility would be high and relatively invariant near the maximum physiologically attainable. Yet Henry's populations varied in the number of children born to premenopausal women by nearly 100 percent from lowest to highest, a range that has only been increased by subsequent research. This variation was not a consequence of differences in marriage rates, since the comparison was only of married women. Nor was it a consequence of conscious family limitation, since fertility in all the populations was only weakly dependent on parity. Henry reasoned that the difference must lie in factors determining the average length of the time interval separating successive births. After considering and rejecting various possibilities, Henry suggested that variation in the effectiveness of lactation as a natural suppressor of ovulation might underlie the observed variation in levels of natural fertility between populations. He also explicitly noted that such a mechanism would be inherently physiological.

Henry's second observation was that the age pattern of female fertility was remarkably constant across different natural fertility populations, despite differences in the overall level of fertility. Fertility rates tended to rise until the mid-twenties and then to fall, slowly at first, more rapidly after age forty, until further offspring production ceased in all populations around age fifty. Not only did all populations show the same general parabolic rise and fall with age, the rate of change with age was proportionally very similar in all populations. This constant age pattern also seemed to Henry suggestive of physiological rather than sociological variation, though the mechanisms were more obscure.

Henry was careful not to confuse his definition of natural fertility with fecundity. It is quite possible, according to his definition, for couples in a natural fertility population to consciously manipulate their fertility, or even to use modern contraception, as long as they do so only to control the timing of their births, and not the number. Yet he clearly felt that the study of natural fertility was a first approach to the empirical study of variation in human fecundity. Far from closing the book, Henry's work opened a new and exciting chapter in our study of our own reproduction, underscoring human fertility as an area where biology and behavior are supremely interactive, and undermining the Malthusian dichotomy that had begun to constrict rather than aid our understanding.

LACTATION, FECUNDITY, AND THE "CHOREOGRAPHY" OF BREASTFEEDING

The question of the natural variability of human fertility has become a subject of interest to individuals from a broad array of disciplines, including demographers, sociologists, physicians, public health analysts, physiologists, and anthropologists. The interaction of social and biological perspectives in a field that was formerly considered a purely sociological domain has generated both excitement and controversy. Henry's two basic observations about natural fertility patterns continue to motivate current research even as new ideas are developed. Three decades of research have confirmed the fact that variation in the level of fertility between populations that do not practice parity-specific birth control is substantial, greater than the variation between populations that do practice family size limitation. It also remains true that variation in the level of fertility among natural fertility populations is a consequence of variation in inter-birth intervals, not in ages at first or last birth. The remarkable consistency in the age pattern of natural fertility, despite differences in level of fertility, has also been confirmed. The phenomena themselves are not in question, but their causes are. The search for these causes has focused more on the regulation of female reproductive capacity than on male, since female fertility is the primary limiting factor in human reproduction.

Henry suggested that the primary factor regulating birth interval lengths in natural fertility populations might be found by understanding the way breastfeeding delays the resumption of ovulation. It was already clear that women who never nurse their offspring, because of infant mortality or the use of bottles or wet-nurses, resume menstruation much earlier than women who nurse their offspring for any length of time. But among women who do breastfeed, the variation in timing of the resumption of cyclic ovarian function, as evidenced by the return of menstruation, is immense and not easily comprehensible. Some nursing women, Henry noted, resume menstruating right away, some only after a considerable time but before they wean their children, and others only after weaning. Since the practice of breastfeeding is prevalent in most natural fertility populations, Henry suggested that we would go a long way toward understanding natural variation in interbirth intervals if we could understand why women fell into one or another of these categories.[4]

A breakthrough in unraveling this problem came from studies of the physiology of lactation. The hormone prolactin, which bears major responsibility for the maintenance of milk production in a lactating woman, was shown to respond episodically to each nursing event. Each time the baby begins nursing at its mother's breast, prolactin levels rise dramatically in the mother's blood. As soon as the baby stops nursing, prolactin levels begin a slower, exponential decline.[5] Physiologically, this mechanism helps to regulate milk "supply" according to "demand": The frequency of the signal promoting milk production depends on the actual pattern of feeding. As the baby becomes less dependent on its mother's milk, the production of milk will taper off. However, because it was suspected that prolactin might also act to inhibit ovarian function, the same mechanism might work to regulate the return of female fecundity. The key variable, if this hypothesis were true, would not be the fact of breastfeeding, or even the total amount of time spent nursing in a day, but the *frequency* of nursing. Short episodes of nursing spread throughout the day at frequent intervals would result in higher average levels of prolactin than a few long, widely-separated episodes, such as the half-hour sessions at four hour intervals often recommended by American doctors of Dr. Benjamin Spock's generation.

Field studies of natural fertility populations began to confirm this hypothesis. Belgian workers in Zaire found that prolactin levels remained higher in women who reported nursing more frequently than in women who reported nursing less frequently throughout the first postpartum year, and that the less frequent nursers were more likely to resume menstruation in that time.[6] Anthropologists Melvin Konner and Carol Worthman reported that !Kung San hunter-gatherers of Botswana continued to nurse their children at very high frequency for two to four years after birth, and that levels of ovarian steroid hormones indicative of ovarian function were more strongly correlated with nursing frequency than with infant's age.[7] Evidence appeared to support the idea that the solution to Henry's problem lay in the temporal patterning of nursing behavior, the choreography of this most intimate relationship between mother and child.

The choreography of breastfeeding shows clearly the close relationship of social and biological influences regulating human fertility. The mechanisms linking the frequency of suckling to the suppression of the mother's reproductive system are strictly physiological, the result of millions of years of evolution shaping this peculiarly mammalian pattern of maternal investment in offspring. The factors affecting the frequency of suckling itself, however, are largely social, and reflect the multiple constraints and demands that human mothers face. Anthropologist Catherine Panter-Brick has argued compellingly, on the basis of her studies of the Tamang of highland Nepal, that breastfeeding choreography is often structured more by opportunity than by demand. In the case of the Tamang, opportunity may be constrained by the mother's necessary participation in subsistence activities, such as transplanting rice, that separate her from her children for long stretches of time.[8] Sara Nerlove reached a similar conclusion in a cross-cultural study of eighty-three societies, finding that supplemental foods are introduced into infants' diets at earlier ages in societies where women are heavily involved in subsistence work.[9] Social attitudes and conventions about the "right" way to raise children, the availability of appropriate supplemental foods and alternative caretakers, competing demands on the mother's time and energy, and the advice of "experts" and friends can all influence the breastfeeding behavior of individual women and the typical patterns in individual societies. All of these social and environmental factors, acting through the agency of nursing frequency, could contribute to the variation in interbirth intervals observed among natural fertility populations. Indeed, data collected from a broad array of populations throughout the world indicate a strong correlation between the average duration of breastfeeding in a population and the average interbirth interval.[10]

Yet as compelling as this relationship between breastfeeding and interbirth intervals may be, it cannot be the whole story. Certain aspects of the relationship have been questioned in recent years. For example, it no longer seems that prolactin is directly involved in the suppression of ovarian function. Nor has the frequency of nursing always been found to correlate strongly with the duration of amenorrhea (absence of menstruation) either between individuals within a given population or between populations. Part of the answer to Henry's original question—why do some nursing women resume menstruation early and others late?—seems to involve variation in the temporal choreography of breastfeeding, but part of the answer may lie elsewhere, perhaps in the physical condition of the mother herself.[11]

AGE AND FEMALE FECUNDITY

One important aspect of maternal condition is age. Declining fertility with advancing age, such as Henry described for natural fertility populations, has long been ascribed to a declining frequency of intercourse in older couples, and research on sexual behavior in Western societies has appeared to support this hypothesis. The increase in natural fertility with age among married women under twenty cannot be explained by the same mechanism, and is often either ignored or attributed to "adolescent sterility," a period of physiological sub-fecundity following the onset of menstruation characterized by irregular menstrual cycling. Recent re-evaluations of the data on declining frequency of intercourse with advancing age, however, challenge the idea that this mechanism alone can account for observed patterns of natural fertility decline.[12] Furthermore, even if declining frequency of intercourse were shown to be responsible for the age-related decline in natural fertility, we would still need to explain why age patterns of intercourse should be so consistent between different populations.

Once again, a possible answer to this question has come from the study of reproductive physiology. Until recently, the fact that menstrual patterns show little variation with age between the very earliest and very latest years of a woman's reproductive career was taken as evidence that her underlying pattern of fecundity was also quite constant. This notion crumbled when contrary evidence was presented from the realm of infertility research. Success in establishing pregnancies in women undergoing artificial insemination with donor semen (because their husbands had been found to be unable to produce viable sperm) has been shown to be strongly affected by a woman's age, with rates that begin to decline as early as age thirty.[13] Subsequent studies provided evidence of similar age dependency in success rates of *in vitro* fertilization, ovulation induction, and ovum donation.[14] The popular press quickly picked up on these reports and spread the notion of a "biological clock" within each woman determining her fecundity. The poignancy of this issue for women who might have delayed childbearing in order to pursue careers has been widely recognized and has given rise to numerous editorials in both newspapers and medical journals.

Investigating the causes of age-related declines in female fecundity requires sophisticated methods for monitoring a woman's reproductive system. Many of these methods are highly invasive, uncomfortable, expensive, and difficult to perform outside of a hospital or clinical setting. One method that can shed some light on the issue and that avoids many of these drawbacks is the monitoring of ovarian steroid hormone levels in samples of saliva. Saliva samples can be collected easily and painlessly, can be collected by women themselves at home on a regular basis, and can be collected even under remote field conditions. The steroid hormones that can be measured in saliva provide important information on aspects of a woman's reproductive system that are crucial to her fecundity, including the maturation of the egg, the release of the egg at mid-cycle, the preparation of the uterus for the possible implantation of an embryo, and the support for the early stages of pregnancy if it occurs. For these reasons my colleagues and I have relied heavily on this method for more than a decade in our own studies of variation in female fecundity.[15]

Using salivary steroid measurements, we have been able to show that female ovarian function varies significantly with age, even in women who are menstruating regularly. Hormonal indices of ovarian function in regularly menstruating Boston women increase steadily with age until the mid-twenties, a decade or more after the onset of menstruation, and begin to decline by the early thirties, more than a decade in advance of menopause. This parabolic trajectory roughly parallels the trajectory of natural fertility observed by Henry, as well as the trajectory of declining female fecundity uncovered in infertility research.[16]

When the same methods are used to investigate age patterns of ovarian function in quite different populations, such as the Lese of Zaire's Ituri Forest and the Tamang of Nepal, the results are strongly reminiscent of Henry's original observations. The Lese are slash-and-burn horticulturalists who grow subsistence crops of cassava, dry rice, maize, and peanuts, supplemented with meat from wild game, much of which is acquired in trade with Efe pygmies.[17] The Tamang are agro-pastoralists who grow wet rice, maize, millet, wheat, and barley, and tend mixed flocks of buffalo, oxen, cows, sheep, and goats at different elevations on the slopes of the Himalayas.[18] Women in Zaire and Nepal show parabolic patterns of age variation in ovarian function virtually parallel to each other and to the patterns in Boston, but the average levels of ovarian function at any age differ significantly between the three populations. Salivary progesterone levels in Boston, for example, average 100 to 150 pmol/L higher than those in Zaire at all ages, while levels in Zaire are 50 to 70 pmol/L higher than those in Nepal. The overall picture of age-patterns of ovarian function that are similar in shape but different in level is very reminiscent of Henry's original observation of a consistent age pattern to natural fertility, despite differences in level between populations.[19]

The factors contributing to age variation in female fecundity are likely to be multiple, but the age pattern of ovarian function, at least, appears to be a common feature of human reproductive biology, similar even in populations widely separated by geography, culture, and ecology. Unlike the variation in female fecundity associated with lactation, the variation in fecundity associated with age appears to be mediated by biology alone, providing a foundation on which other sources of variation, both social and biological, are elaborated. Some evidence suggests, for example, that lactational suppression of ovarian function may last longer in older women, even when their pattern of nursing is the same as that of younger women.[20] Interactions of this kind between different variables affecting natural fertility, such as age and lactation, constitute an important domain of future research.

Energetics and Female Fecundity

Along with age, nutritional status is also a potentially important aspect of maternal condition that might affect fecundity. Reproduction requires a substantial investment of metabolic energy on a woman's part, and natural selection may have molded her reproductive physiology to be sensitive to her potential for successfully making that investment. Rose Frisch and her colleagues first drew attention to this possibility by noting that girls are unlikely to begin menstruating and that adult women often stop menstruating if they are excessively lean.[21] Women athletes, especially those engaged in endurance sports, have also been found to be amenorrheic more often than the general population.[22]

Once again, the ability to monitor ovarian function directly, rather than relying on indirect evidence such as the occurrence or regularity of menstruation, has provided additional insight into the relationship of energetic stress and female fecundity. Hormonal indices of ovarian function have been observed to decline in American and German women who voluntarily lose only moderate amounts of weight by dieting, even when their weights remain in the normal range for their heights.[23] Similarly, women who jog for recreation have been found to have lower ovarian steroid levels than otherwise comparable but inactive women, even though their weights are well within the normal range.[24] In all these cases, menstrual patterns remain unchanged.

It is tempting to extrapolate from these results on exercise and dieting, athletes and anorexics, to the sorts of energetic stresses that women in traditional societies face, or that women might have faced regularly throughout our evolutionary past. Some have suggested, for example, that the long distances that hunter-gatherer women may travel in foraging for food could constitute an energetic stress similar to that faced by track and field athletes.[25] Hypotheses based on analogy alone are unsatisfactory, however. Evidence to support the idea that energetic stresses which arise from subsistence ecology, rather than from self-imposed regimes of exercise or diet, could affect ovarian function had to come from field studies of human populations.

Several such studies have now confirmed the fact that energy balance, the net of energy intake and energy expenditure, does affect ovarian function in a variety of populations. The Lese of Zaire show seasonal changes in ovarian function that parallel seasonal weight losses caused by regular food shortages. Conceptions are also less frequent during these periods of suppressed ovarian function.[26] Among the Tamang of Nepal, some women lose weight during the hard agricultural work of the monsoon season while others do not. Those who lose weight show lower indices of ovarian function than those who maintain or gain weight.[27] The Turkana of northern Kenya have also been studied in this regard by Michael Little, Paul Leslie, and their colleagues. The Turkana traditionally have relied on pastoral nomadism for their subsistence, maintaining herds of cattle in the arid regions of Kenya's northwestern plateau. In recent years some Turkana have turned to a settled, agricultural lifestyle. Settled Turkana have higher body weights for their heights and other indicators of lower energetic stress than nomadic Turkana. They also have hormonal patterns indicative of higher levels of ovarian function.[28]

Interactions of nutritional status, energetic stress, and lactational suppression of ovarian function have also been reported. Peter Lunn, of the Dunn Nutrition Unit of the Medical Research Council of the UK, and colleagues have studied the effect of nutritional supplements on the reproductive biology of women living by traditional agriculture in the Gambia. Baseline data revealed that the Gambian women were both chronically and seasonally undernourished. Caloric intake was below recommended levels even in the best of times, while seasonal food shortages resulted in regular periods of weight loss. Women in the study received substantial nutritional supplements during pregnancy and lactation, increasing their daily caloric intake by a quarter to a third. Birth weights were slightly increased, maternal weights and weight gains largely unaffected, and milk production unaltered by the supplements. However, average prolactin levels declined more quickly, menses resumed sooner, and birth intervals were shorter when women received the supplements than when they did not.[29]

Like the age pattern of ovarian function, the responsiveness of ovarian function to energetic stress seems to be a general feature of human reproductive biology. A decline in hormonal indices of female fecundity can be observed under conditions of relative energetic stress in a wide range of populations differing dramatically in culture, ecology, and geography. The responses evoked by unavoidable ecological conditions are directly comparable to those evoked by voluntary behaviors. The responses are so consistent, and so graded in degree, that they are unlikely to be pathological. That is, the response of ovarian function to energetic stresses does not seem to indicate a system failing or breaking down with abrupt loss of function, but rather a system undergoing progressive adjustments to varying conditions. This responsiveness seems rather to be a beneficial aspect of the healthy functioning of the female reproductive system as will be discussed later.

ECOLOGY AND MALE REPRODUCTION

As noted earlier, most efforts to better understand natural variation in human fertility have focused on females, for the simple reason that the capacity of females to bear offspring is ultimately limiting on the fertility of any population. Yet it seems reasonable to ask whether male reproductive biology shows any of the same patterns of natural variation as described for females, or any unique patterns that might contribute to natural variation in human fertility.

Male testicular function shows evidence of progressive decreases with age, though studies differ as to the age at which this decline is first apparent. Certainly there is no evidence of an abrupt cessation of male testicular function in mid-life comparable to female menopause.[30] At least one study, among the Gainj of Papua New Guinea, a remote group of subsistence horticulturalists, indicates an earlier average onset of male reproductive senescence than normally observed in Western populations.[31] It is not clear, however, whether this represents an atypical and possibly pathological variation, or whether male reproductive aging is generally more variable than female.

Males in several traditional societies, including the !Kung San of Botswana and Namibia, the Lese of Zaire, and the Turkana of Kenya, have been found to have lower levels of the testicular steroid testosterone than males in the United States and Europe, but the reasons for this difference are unclear.[32] Extreme energetic stress, such as the starvation produced by dramatic famines or conditions of war, clearly decreases testicular function in males and can totally disrupt sperm production. But Lese males in Zaire and Tamang males in Nepal do not show an acute testicular responsiveness to energetic stress comparable to the ovarian response of females.[33] Chronic energetic stress, however, might still be responsible for chronic differences in testicular function between populations.

High environmental temperatures have also been suggested as having an adverse affect on sperm production in some populations. Seasonal variations in temperature have been associated with seasonal variations in the quantity and quality of sperm produced by men who work outside in hot climates, such as in New Orleans and San Antonio. Observations of comparable variations in the sperm production of men working in air-conditioned situations, however, have cast doubt on temperature as the important factor.[34]

Interpretation of the evidence for variation in male reproductive function is complicated further by the lack of a clear relationship between those indicators that can be measured and male fecundity. For example, levels of hormones such as testosterone are at best only weakly correlated with sperm production. Sperm production in turn may be only weakly correlated with the ability to impregnate a fecund woman, as long as sperm counts are above some relatively low threshold.[35] In general, although there is evidence that male testicular function may vary, there is little evidence for consistent patterns of natural variation that might contribute to patterns of natural variation in fertility among human populations.

THE ECOLOGY OF HUMAN REPRODUCTION

Contrary to Malthus's assumption, the results of current research, both in the clinic and in the field, indicate that many aspects of human fecundity show evidence of significant natural variability. Female ovarian function in particular appears to vary in response to age, lactation, and other energetic stresses. Rather than simply setting a biological maximum for the production of offspring with actual fertility being shaped by social constraints, natural variation in human fecundity appears to provide the foundation upon which the social regulation of fertility is elaborated. Many important features of achieved fertility patterns are the product of sociological and individual psychological factors, but others reflect variation in the underlying patterns of biological fecundity.

The patterns of variation that have been described for female ovarian function do not appear to be pathological. Rather they appear to represent calibrated responses of the organism to its environmental context. It is likely that these responses have been shaped by the action of natural selection in ways that benefit the lifetime reproductive success of the individual organism. For instance, young women characteristically have continuing energetic requirements for their own growth and maturation and greater potential for future reproduction than do older women. Hence natural selection may have molded female physiology to favor relatively more investment in continued growth and survival in young women, and more investment in reproduction in mature women. After a certain point, however, the probable success of new reproductive attempts begins to decline with age, either as a consequence of maternal condition or the quality of the eggs remaining in the ovary. Natural selection may have resulted in declining female fecundity in later reproductive ages as a result.

The reproductive response to varying energetic conditions may also be adaptive. An adult woman in a natural fertility population can be thought of as alternating between two states: "metabolizing for one" when she is neither pregnant nor lactating, and "metabolizing for two" when she is pregnant or lactating. Pregnancy and lactation increase a woman's energy requirements by a third to a half, and there is compelling evidence that under certain conditions women will divert energy from their own metabolic needs to meet those of gestation and milk production.[36] The ability to meet these energetic demands must have been the focus of intense natural selection during human evolution. Modulating fecundity in response to energetic stress probably represents one way in which the organism has been shaped to try to optimize its reproductive efforts. When energy is scarce and limiting, reducing fecundity increases the proportion of time a woman spends metabolizing for one relative to that spent metabolizing for two, thus helping her to maintain long term energy balance. When energy is abundant, increasing fecundity reduces the same ratio. If a woman's physical condition is very poor her fecundity may drop to zero until she recovers to a point where a successful energetic investment in reproduction again becomes possible.

Understanding the underlying patterns of human fecundity helps us to make sense out of observed patterns of natural variation in human fertility, such as the consistency of the age pattern of fertility in natural fertility populations, the wide variation in fertility levels among populations with high rates of marriage and low usage of effective contraception, and patterns of seasonal reproduction in subsistence agricultural populations. The same insights shed light on the reproductive physiology of individuals in Western populations. Declining female fecundity with age after the mid-thirties is not an anomaly; menstrual irregularity in female athletes is not pathological; in some cases, simply gaining weight increases the probability of conception in women under treatment for infertility.[37] Broadening our view of the human condition and shedding unexamined assumptions about our biological heritage are keys to expanding our understanding of ourselves.

NOTES

1. Thomas Malthus, *An Essay on the Principle of Population* (New York: Penguin Books, 1970).
2. Louis Henry, "Some Data on Natural Fertility," *Eugenics Quarterly* 8 (1961): 81–91.
3. Kingsley Davis and Judith Blake, "Social Structure and Fertility: An Analytical Framework," *Economic Development and Culture Change* 4 (1956): 211–235.
4. Henry, "Some Data on Natural Fertility," p. 91.
5. John E. Tyson, "Neuroendocrine Control of Lactational Infertility," *Journal of Biosocial Science, Supplement* 4 (1977): 23–40.
6. P. Delvoye, M. Demaegd, J. Delogne-Desnoek, and C. Robyn, "The Influence of the Frequency of Nursing and of Previous Lactation Experience on Serum Prolactin in Lactating Mothers," *Journal of Biosocial Science* 9 (1977): 447–451.
7. Melvin Konner and Carol Worthman, "Nursing Frequency, Gonadal Function, and Birth Spacing among !Kung Hunter-Gatherers," *Science* 207 (1980): 788–791.
8. Catherine Panter-Brick, "Lactation, Birth Spacing, and Maternal Work-Loads among Two Castes in Rural Nepal," *Journal of Biosocial Science* 23 (1991): 137–154.
9. Sara B. Nerlove, "Women's Workload and Infant Feeding Practices: A Relationship with Demographic Implications," *Ethnology* 13 (1974): 207–214.
10. N. Goldman, C. E. Westoff, and L. E. Paul, "Variations in Natural Fertility: The Effect of Lactation and Other Determinants," *Population Studies* 41 (1987): 127–146.
11. Peter T. Ellison, "Breastfeeding and Fertility," in Katherine A. Dettwyler and Patricia Stuart-Macadam, eds., *Breastfeeding: Biocultural Perspectives* (New York: Aldine de Gruyter, 1995).
12. M. Weinstein, J. Wood, M. A. Stoto, and D. D. Greenfield, "Components of Age-Specific Fecundability," *Population Studies* 44 (1990): 447–467.
13. Federation CECOS, D. Schwartz, and M. J. Mayaux, "Female Fecundity as a Function of Age," *New England Journal of Medicine* 306 (1982): 404–406.

14. See review in Peter T. Ellison, "Advances in Human Reproductive Ecology," *Annual Review of Anthropology* 23 (1994): 255–275.

15. Peter T. Ellison, "Human Salivary Steroids: Methodological Considerations and Applications in Physical Anthropology," *Yearbook of Physical Anthropology* 31 (1988): 115–142; Peter T. Ellison, "Measurements of Salivary Progesterone," *Annals of the New York Academy of Sciences* 694 (1993): 161–176; Peter T. Ellison, "Salivary Steroids and Natural Variation in Human Ovarian Function," *Annals of the New York Academy of Sciences* 709 (1994): 287–298.

16. Susan F. Lipson and Peter T. Ellison, "Normative Study of Age Variation in Salivary Progesterone Profiles," *Journal of Biosocial Science* 24 (1992): 233–244; Mary T. O'Rourke and Peter T. Ellison, "Salivary Estradiol Levels Decrease with Age in Healthy, Regularly-Cycling Women," *Endocrine Journal* 1 (1993): 487–494.

17. Robert C. Bailey and Irven DeVore, "Research on the Efe and Lese Populations of the Ituri Forest, Zaire," *American Journal of Physical Anthropology* 78 (1989): 459–471.

18. Panter-Brick, "Lactation, Birth Spacing, and Maternal Work-Loads among Two Castes in Rural Nepal."

19. Peter T. Ellison, Catherine Panter-Brick, Susan F. Lipson, and Mary T. O'Rourke, "The Ecological Context of Human Ovarian Function," *Human Reproduction* 8 (1993): 2248–2258.

20. N. Goldman et al., "Variations in Natural Fertility."

21. Rose E. Frisch and Janet W. McArthur, "Menstrual Cycles: Fatness as a Determinant of Minimum Weight for Height Necessary for Their Maintenance and Onset," *Science* 185 (1974): 949–951.

22. C. B. Feicht, T. S. Johnson, B. J. Martin, K. E. Sparkes, and W. W. Wagner, Jr., "Secondary Amenorrhoea in Athletes," *Lancet* 2 (1978): 1145–1146.

23. Catherine Lager and Peter T. Ellison, "Effect of Moderate Weight Loss on Ovarian Function Assessed by Salivary Progesterone Measurements," *American Journal of Human Biology* 2 (1990): 303–312; K. M. Pirke, U. Schweiger, W. Lemmel, J. C. Krieg, and M. Berger, "The Influence of Dieting on the Menstrual Cycle of Healthy Young Women," *Journal of Clinical Endocrinology and Metabolism* 60 (1985): 1174–1179.

24. Peter T. Ellison and Catherine Lager, "Exercise-Induced Menstrual Disorders," *New England Journal of Medicine* 313 (1985): 825–826; Peter T. Ellison and Catherine Lager, "Moderate Recreational Running is Associated with Lowered Salivary Progesterone Profiles in Women," *American Journal of Obstetrics and Gynecology* 154 (1986): 1000–1003.

25. Gillian R. Bentley, "Hunter-Gatherer Energetics and Fertility: A Reassessment of the !Kung San," *Human Ecology* 13 (1985): 79–109.

26. Robert C. Bailey, Mark R. Jenike, Peter T. Ellison, Gillian R. Bentley, Alisa M. Harrigan, and Nadine R. Peacock, "The Ecology of Birth Seasonality among Agriculturalists in Central Africa," *Journal of Biosocial Science* 24 (1992): 393–412.

27. Catherine Panter-Brick, Deborah S. Lotstein, and Peter T. Ellison, "Seasonality of Reproductive Function and Weight Loss in Rural Nepali Women," *Human Reproduction* 8 (1993): 684–690.

28. Paul W. Leslie, Kenneth L. Campbell, and Michael A. Little, "Reproductive Function in Nomadic and Settled Women of Turkana, Kenya," *Annals of the New York Academy of Sciences* 709 (1994): 218–220.

29. P. G. Lunn, S. Austin, A. M. Prentice, and R. G. Whitehead, "The Effect of Improved Nutrition on Plasma Prolactin Concentrations and Postpartum Infertility in Lactating Gambian Women," *American Journal of Clinical Nutrition* 39 (1984): 227–235.

30. A. Gray, H. A. Feldman, J. B. McKinlay, and C. Longcope, "Age, Disease, and Changing Hormone Levels in Middle-Aged Men: Results of the Massachusetts Male Aging Study," *Journal of Clinical Endocrinology and Metabolism* 73 (1991): 1016–1025.

31. Kenneth L. Campbell, "Blood, Urine, Saliva and Dip-Sticks: Experiences in Africa, New Guinea, and Boston," *Annals of the New York Academy of Sciences* 709 (1994): 312–330.

32. Benjamin C. Campbell and Paul W. Leslie, "Male Reproductive Ecology," *Yearbook of Physical Anthropology* 38 (1995): 1–26.

33. Peter T. Ellison, Susan F. Lipson, and Mark Meredith, "Salivary Testosterone Levels in Males from the Ituri Forest, Zaire," *American Journal of Human Biology* 1 (1989): 21–24; Gillian R. Bentley, Alisa M. Harrigan, Benjamin C. Campbell, and Peter T. Ellison, "Seasonal Effects on Salivary Testosterone Levels among Lese Males of the Ituri Forest, Zaòre," *American Journal of Human Biology* 5 (1993): 711–717; Catherine Panter-Brick, Deborah Lotstein, Sara Sukalich, and Peter T. Ellison, unpublished data.

34. Richard J. Levine, "Male Factors Contributing to the Seasonality of Human Reproduction," *Annals of the New York Academy of Sciences* 709 (1994): 29–54.

35. Emmet J. Lamb and Sean Bennett, "Epidemiologic Studies of Male Factors in Infertility," *Annals of the New York Academy of Sciences* 709 (1994): 165–178.

36. A. M. Prentice and R. G. Whitehead, "The Energetics of Human Reproduction," *Symposia of the Zoological Society of London* 57 (1987): 275–304.

37. G. W. Bates, S. R. Bates, and N. S. Whitworth, "Reproductive Failure in Women Who Practice Weight Control," *Fertility and Sterility* 37 (1982): 373–378; G. W. Bates, "Body Weight Control Practice as a Cause of Infertility," *Clinical Obstetrics and Gynecology* 28 (1985): 632–644.

SUGGESTED READINGS

The following are useful collections of conference papers combining physiological and demographic perspectives on human fertility:

Campbell, Kenneth L., and James W. Wood, eds. *Human Reproductive Ecology: Interactions of Environment, Fertility, and Behavior. Annals of the New York Academy of Sciences*, vol. 709 (1994)

Dunbar, Robin I., ed. *Human Reproductive Decisions: Biological and Social Perspectives.* London: Macmillan, 1994.

The following are slightly more detailed reviews of the topics covered in this chapter:

Ellison, Peter T. "Human Ovarian Function and Human Ecology: New Hypotheses." *American Anthropologist* 92 (1990): 933–952

Ellison, Peter T. "Reproductive Ecology and Human Fertility." In C. G. N. Mascie-Taylor and G. W. Lasker, eds. *Applications of Biological Anthropology to Human Affairs.* Cambridge, UK: Cambridge University Press, 1991.

Ellison, Peter T. "Advances in Human Reproductive Ecology." *Annual Review of Anthropology* 23 (1994): 255–275.

WHAT ACCOUNTS FOR POPULATION VARIATION IN HEIGHT?

J. PATRICK GRAY AND LINDA D. WOLFE

A glance at a map of adult stature around the world gives the impression of a chaotic pattern that will withstand any attempt at explanation. Most surprising is how frequently populations with extremely different heights are found near one another. For example, the tallest Amerindian population in South America, the Ona, (m=174.3 cm [68.6"], f=159.3 cm [62.7"]) shared the extreme southern tip of the continent with one of the shortest, the Yahgan (m=158.3 cm [62.3"], f=148.3 cm [58.4"]).[1] In northern Europe the Lapps (m=157.2 [61.9"], f=144.6 [56.9"]) live near Norwegians (m=174.4 cm [68.7"], f=162.7 cm [64.0"]), while in Africa the Tutsi (m=176.5 cm [69.5"]) and the Twa (m=153.0 cm [60.2"]) both live in Rwanda. The tallest (Nuer, m=184.9 cm [72.8"]) and shortest (Efe, m=144.0 cm [56.7"], f=135.0 [53.1"]) people in the world live in Africa about one thousand miles apart.

We became interested in the distribution of adult stature while investigating if different marriage systems explained cross-cultural differences in the ratio of male to female height (they did not).[2] In our review of the literature we encountered a puzzle. Most introductory texts in anthropology discuss two widely accepted explanations of the distribution of stature: the thermoregulatory and the nutritional. A third explanation, the stress hypothesis, is rarely mentioned, although it appeared to us to have strong empirical support. We decided to explore the stress hypothesis to see if it warranted more serious attention. Our goal was to use a large cross-cultural sample to compare the relative power of the three explanations.

Our basic premise is that since each explanation claims to apply to all human populations, each requires cross-cultural testing. This methodology treats entire societies as single data points and uses ethnographies as sources for coding data on variables. Cross-cultural research involves an inescapable trade-off between quality of data and breadth of coverage. On the one hand, coding a variable such as nutritional quality from comments in ethnographies that do not focus on nutrition is obviously a poor substitute for actual measures of food consumption. On the other hand, if we restrict our studies to the few cases with high quality data on nutrition we exclude the vast majority of societies and our results may not generalize to the full range of human lifestyles. The results of cross-cultural tests must be interpreted with the method's weaknesses in mind and with an eye toward continually improving the quality of the data used in tests.

The explanations reviewed in this chapter assume that natural selection and/or a form of heredity-environment interaction is responsible for the distribution of human height around the world. However, historical accidents do play a role in the patterns we observe. An important source of such accidents is non-directional evolutionary forces such as Founder's Effect, which occurs when migrants to a new area are not genetically representative of the larger population from whence they came. As humans migrated from place to place, it is possible that unusually tall or short individuals founded some populations. The limited genetic potential in such groups might restrict their ability to respond to the climatic or nutritional conditions of their new environment. While Founder's Effect may have some influence on the distribution of human height we do not analyze it further because it is not amenable to holocultural testing. We believe that natural selection and/or the interaction between heredity and environment—the effects of which are amenable to testing—can explain most of the variation of adult stature around the world.

The remainder of the chapter consists of six sections. We first review the basic human growth pattern. The next section discusses the thermoregulatory hypothesis and evaluates its empirical support, focusing on holocultural tests. The next two sections review the nutritional and stress hypotheses. The fifth section summarizes our new holocultural tests and the chapter ends with a brief conclusion.

GROWTH AND ADULT STATURE

Adult stature results from the complex interplay between genetic inheritance and the environments encountered during growth. Analysis of population variation in adult stature requires knowledge of how genetic and environmental factors influence the patterning of growth in different populations. We briefly describe the basic pattern of human growth and discuss several factors creating differences in the course and outcome of this pattern.[3]

An individual's genetic makeup (the genotype) ultimately affects every aspect of his or her biology and behavior. Differences in stature between individuals may be correlated with differences in their genotypes, independent of any differences in their environments. Imagine that we could subject two individuals to the same environments from conception to when both reached their maximum height. Any differences in the height they attained (or when they achieved it) would be attributable to differences in the genes relevant to growth. A study of Efe pygmy and Lese Bantu children of the African Ituri rain forest approximates this thought experiment. The 142.0 cm (55.9″) average stature of adult Efe males is 16.6 cm (6.5″) lower than Lese males. Bailey[4] measured children from each group at birth and recorded height at six-month intervals up to the age of five. Efe children are born lighter and shorter than Lese children and the gap in stature widens to age five. The Lese are not better nourished than the Efe, suggesting that genetic differences between the groups explain the differing growth patterns.

Evidence for a genetic component to stature includes: (1) the high correlation between the height of parents and offspring when both generations experience similar environments; (2) the higher correlation of adult stature for monozygotic (from the same ova) twins than for dizygotic twins (from different ova); and (3) the different growth patterns and heights of peoples of different genetic backgrounds living in the same climatic and nutritional environments. Because many genes influence stature and because environment strongly affects height, geneticists do not yet have a clear picture of how genes control stature. Malnutrition, chronic childhood stress, or disease may cause a person's adult stature to be much lower than his or her genetic potential would permit, a situation complicating the analysis of the genetic control of height.

Although the outcomes vary widely, populations exhibit the same pattern of childhood growth. Well-nourished children in the United States grow rapidly in the first year of life, often increasing 50 percent in length and 200 percent in weight. The rate at which the infant gains length (the growth velocity) decreases rapidly in the first year, reaching a plateau at about three years of age. Growth velocity remains steady until a rapid growth spurt associated with puberty, although there is evidence of a moderate growth spurt at seven to eight years. Females start their adolescent spurt roughly two years earlier than males and exhibit a less intense episode of growth. Velocity declines rapidly after the adolescent spurt, with females attaining adult stature at about eighteen and males at about twenty-one.

Poor nutrition or disease may impact adult stature by affecting the amount of growth in a stage and by altering the timing of stages. For example, in some populations malnourished children exhibit lower stature at every age than their adequately nourished cohorts. They may continue to grow for several years after better fed children have stopped, although they may never be as tall their advantaged contemporaries. The timing of disease or malnourishment may also affect the patterning of growth. Acute shortages of food or serious diseases may depress growth briefly, but once the situation improves the children may have a rapid period of "catch-up" growth that brings them up to the stature they would have achieved if they had not experienced the event.

A review of the endocrinology of growth is beyond the scope of this paper, but research on growth hormones clearly has implications for explaining cross-cultural variations in stature.[5] Work with several populations of "pygmies" reveals that there are different hormonal pathways to small stature. The Efe of Africa produce as much growth hormone (GH) as non-pygmy populations, but their hormone receptors are less responsive. Both the Efe and the Aeta of the Philippines produce lower levels of insulin-like growth factor 1 (IGF 1) and growth-hormone-binding proteins (GH-BP) than other populations, while the Mountain Ok of New Guinea produce "normal" levels of both GH and IGF 1 but low levels of GH-BP.

Such work suggests that differences in the patterning of growth hormone release, in the amount of hormones produced or in the responsiveness of receptors to the hormones, might explain some population variation in adult stature. We do not yet know what roles genes and environment play in the creation of such differences. We do know that environmental factors such as nutrition, exercise, and physical or emotional stress affect the amount of growth hormones an individual produces. Cross-cultural research on growth hormones has just started, but such research clearly is relevant to each theory we review. The finding that greatest secretion of growth hormone occurs during deep sleep suggests a new hypothesis: that the sleeping arrangements of societies may influence population variation in stature. In a British sample, children sharing a bed were 1.3 cm (0.5 inches) shorter than those who slept alone, perhaps because of more frequent disruption of deep sleep.[6] Although anthropologists have documented a wide range of sleeping arrangements, coded data are not available for a cross-cultural test of the hypothesis that sleeping arrangements affect growth.

We omit much that is known about human growth from this review and recommend that the interested reader consult the suggested readings at the end of the chapter. We turn now to the thermoregulatory explanation of population differences in human stature.

STATURE AND CLIMATE

Two ecogeographic rules applicable to warm-blooded animals explain population differences in stature as adaptations to different climates. Bergmann's rule is that populations in the colder regions of a species' range will be larger than those in the warmer regions. The ratio of body weight (W) to surface area (SA) and the need to maintain core body temperature within a narrow range explain this distribution. The surface area is the amount of skin through which heat can be lost. Heat loss through radiation is reduced when the W/SA ratio is high, while a decrease in the ratio permits more rapid dissipation of body heat.[7] Allen's rule predicts that populations in colder environments will exhibit shorter appendages than their cohorts in warmer climates. This rule suggests, for example, that legs might be shorter in colder climates, resulting in reduced stature (unless trunk length increased). The combination of Bergmann's and Allen's rules suggests that two body shapes could be adaptations to cold climates because they produce similar W/SA ratios: tall with moderate weight or short with greater weight. The assumption behind the thermoregulatory hypothesis is that body shape was directly selected for and is, therefore, under strong genetic control.

Humidity must also be considered when analyzing the relationship between climate and body shape. Sweating does not dissipate heat effectively in hot climates with high humidity[8] and thus increased surface area does not aid in thermoregulation in these conditions. This suggests that hot climates may also exhibit two adaptive body shapes: shorter with moderate weight in humid regions, and taller with less weight in dry areas.

Early studies noted that the distribution of human stature seemed to fit the predictions of Bergmann's and Allen's rules, but provided no statistical tests of the relationship. Newman[9] observed that the shortest Amerindian groups were near the equator and that stature increased with distance from the equator. Eskimo populations reversed the trend, but in conformity with Allen's rule their shorter stature is due to their relatively short legs.

A definitive test of the thermoregulation hypothesis requires data on surface area, stature, limb lengths, muscle mass, fat distribution, and so on. Unfortunately, such data are rare for the societies found in most cross-cultural samples. Therefore we view the tests we discuss as suggestive rather than conclusive.

Two cross-cultural studies tested aspects of the thermoregulatory explanation of human body size. Marjorie Whiting[10] found that societies located between 20 and 60 degrees away from the equator were more likely to be classified as "tall" than were societies located within 20 or beyond 60 degrees away. This curvilinear relationship between stature and latitude is expected, given the combined operation of Bergmann's and Allen's rules. Ruff[11] tested a cylindrical thermoregulatory model that a constant surface area/mass (SA/M) ratio is maintained with varying heights if the breadth of the body stays constant. He divided his sample into four regional/climate categories (tropical sub-Saharan Africa, subtropical southeast Asia, temperate Europe, and Arctic/subarctic north Asia) and compared stature and maximum pelvis width (bi-iliac breadth) within and between these categories. Within categories there was much variation in stature but little variation in bi-iliac breadth, suggesting that as populations within a climatic region become taller they become relatively more linear. In contrast, bi-iliac breadth varied greatly between categories, with wider bodies being found in colder climates. Ruff's study demonstrates that tests of thermoregulatory models analyzing just climate and stature will find only weak correlations because other components of body shape are not considered.

Table 14-1, generated from the HOMPLOT anthropometric data base,[12] displays sex-averaged weights, heights, and the weight/surface area ratio for a cross-cultural sample grouped in five climatic zones.

Groups in temperate and cold climates are characterized by a higher average weight than those in hot climates. Temperate, wet-cold, and dry-heat groups exhibit greater average stature than wet-heat and dry-cold groups. As predicted by thermoregulatory considerations, the temperate and cold groups have higher W/SA ratios than the groups in hot climates. The hot climate groups have very similar W/SA ratios, indicating that the increased stature of the dry-heat groups is not matched by a similar increase in weight.

Explanations of human body shape with Allen's and Bergmann's rules have drawn three forms of criticism. First, laboratory studies that subject different body shapes to heat or cold stress have found only moderate differences in coping with thermal stress. Although these studies are limited by small samples and by the fact that experimenters cannot subject participants to extreme thermal stress, they cast doubt on the importance of thermoregulation as a selective force on human stature.

A second criticism is that, except for one study correlating "extra" weight relative to stature with fatal heart attacks in American soldiers during intense desert training, there is no evidence linking body shape, thermal stress, and differential reproduction or mortality in any human group. Critics of the thermoregulation hypothesis suggest that such evidence is not likely because human interaction with the environment is mediated through cultural practices assuring that most people rarely experience extreme thermal stress. Most societies schedule work and travel to avoid thermal extremes. In hot climates, for example, heavy work in the early morning or late afternoon and rest during the early afternoon lessens heat stress. Many anthropological studies of housing and clothing show how these actions moderate thermal stress, thereby lessening selective pressure for particular body shapes.

A final criticism of the thermoregulatory hypothesis is that nutrition better explains the worldwide distribution of stature. The key point separating

TABLE 14-1   CLIMATE, SEX-COMBINED STATURE, WEIGHT, AND WEIGHT/SURFACE AREA RATIO IN THE HOMPLOT SAMPLE

CLIMATE	STATURE (CM)		WEIGHT (KG)		W/SA
	N	MEAN	N	MEAN	
Dry-hot	27	160.0 [63.0"]	24	52.7 [116.2 lb]	3.44
Wet-hot	103	155.6 [61.2"]	92	50.6 [111.6 lb]	3.42
Temperate	28	158.6 [62.4"]	25	56.9 [125.4 lb]	3.61
Wet-cold	9	158.1 [62.2"]	5	60.2 [132.7 lb]	3.74
Dry-cold	23	155.8 [61.3"]	14	59.8 [131.8 lb]	3.76>

the two hypotheses is whether body shape is at least partially a genetic adaptation to thermal stress (in which case genetic differences for body shape will manifest themselves in groups with equal nutrition) or mainly the result of differences in nutrition. If people in colder climates eat more calories than people in warmer climates, or if they have better access to nutrients necessary for growth, their greater stature might result from these dietary factors and have nothing to do with selection for efficient thermoregulation. We discuss the nutritional hypothesis in the next section.

STATURE AND NUTRITION

There is no doubt that nutrition is the major environmental influence on adult height. Evidence for diet's effect on stature comes from studies of different socioeconomic classes within single countries and from analyses of growth patterns in two or three societies with different diets; there are few systematic cross-cultural studies. We discuss three lines of research that indicate nutrition's affect on growth: (1) studies of chronic malnourishment; (2) studies of acute food shortages; and (3) studies of diet composition.

Chronically malnourished people subsist for long periods on inadequate diets. Most studies show that chronically malnourished children are lighter and shorter than their better nourished fellows. For example, a study of lower-income families in the United States found that while the composition of the diet was not correlated with level of income, families with less money consumed fewer total calories, and that children consuming fewer calories were shorter and lighter than children who ate more. Many other investigations have documented class differences in food consumption and growth around the world.[13]

Chronic malnourishment can alter both growth velocity and growth duration. As noted previously, increased duration of growth may not allow the chronically malnourished to achieve the same height as better nourished individuals. Chronic malnourishment may also affect growth by making people more vulnerable to disease or parasites. The finding that children in Bangladesh treated for roundworm gained an extra 1.2 cm (0.5") in height over untreated children in the year after treatment illustrates the negative impact of parasites on growth.

David Seckler[14] argues that the shorter stature of adults who were subjected to childhood chronic malnutrition results from an adjustment process that maintains vital physiological functioning by lowering growth rate. The energy derived from limited food is used to maintain brain growth, for example, rather than to increase stature. This "small but healthy" hypothesis also suggests that shorter adults are better able to cope with periods of food shortages. Seckler's hypothesis is controversial and has not been tested with cross-cultural data.

Studies of episodic acute malnourishment's effect on adult stature in otherwise adequately nourished populations are inconclusive. For example, sons born to Dutch women pregnant during the famine of 1944–1945 were shorter at birth than average, but when measured at age 19 they were as tall as same-age males born in areas of the Netherlands not subject to the famine. In contrast, German males born between 1943 and 1946 did not achieve the stature of males born outside this period, leading Dahlmann and Petersen[15] to argue that acute malnourishment before four years of age results in reduced adult height. Acute malnourishment may also affect growth if it occurs during the adolescent growth spurt. This may explain why the cohorts who were adolescents during the World Wars exhibited the only decreases in the stature of male French conscripts between 1880 and 1960.

It is difficult to separate the effect that the quantity of food has on growth from the influence of the quality of the diet. People with little to eat rarely have high quality diets. Most research on diet and stature has focused on protein. Several studies show a positive correlation between consumption of milk and stature. Takahashi[16] attributes the 5.3 cm (2.1″) increase in the height of Japanese boys between 1960 and 1975 to increased popularity of milk. His comparison of pastoralists and agriculturalists in East Africa and Central Asia shows that pastoralists, assumed to have more access to milk, are taller. Intervention studies comparing the growth of children given extra milk to that of controls also confirm milk's positive effect on stature.

Three cross-cultural studies test the associations between quality of diet and stature. Marjorie Whiting[17] found that both levels of calorie intake and the percentage of protein in the diet were positively correlated with stature in a sample of sixty-nine societies. Landauer and John Whiting[18] failed to replicate these results in the sample used to test the physical stress hypothesis. A review indicates that M. Whiting's significant results are due to her use of chi-square tests on dichotomized data. Finally, Gunders and J. Whiting[19] found an association between the presence of milking herds and increased adult male stature.

Acute Stress in Infancy and Stature

A third explanation of cross-cultural differences in stature predicts taller adults in societies that subject infants to acute physical stress before the age of two than in societies that do not engage in such practices. Two classes of stress have been identified: physical stress and maternal separation stress. Physical stressors hypothesized to increase stature include piercing (of the ears, nose, or lips), scarification (by cutting or burning), vaccination, and circumcision. Practices that separate infants from mothers are also seen as stressors that lead to greater height. These include a delay in nursing after birth, having another woman nurse the infant before the mother, ritual holding by individuals other than the mother or midwives, use of cribs during the day, and transporting infants in carrying devices that prevent skin contact.

Research on infant stress and adult stature was stimulated by the discovery that rats handled or given electrical shocks during the first two weeks of life exhibited increased growth and were larger as adults than their undisturbed siblings. The stressed subjects also behaved differently as adults, exhibiting less reactivity to novel situations than did controls. The mechanisms by which such brief periods of stress lead to accelerated growth are not understood at present, although, as noted earlier, stress can increase production of growth hormones.

The first cross-cultural test of the stress hypothesis[20] found that the societies that physically stressed infants before two years of age (the average age of weaning in nonindustrial societies) had an average adult male stature of 167.0 cm (65.7"), compared to an average of 160.1 cm (63.0") for those not stressing infants. Differences of this magnitude were replicated in several studies by Landauer and J. Whiting. Control analyses indicate that physical stress influences adult male stature independently of genetics, diet, and climate.

Cross-cultural tests also established that societies not practicing mother-infant separation exhibit average adult male stature of 162.3 cm (63.9"), while those that do average 166.5 cm (65.6"). Separation stress has an influence independent of genetics, climate, or diet. While separation stress and physical stress tend to be found in the same societies, the practices have independent impacts on adult male stature. Societies that practice both types of stress do not exhibit taller adult males than societies that practice only one form of stress, however.

Both types of stress accelerate female growth. Adult females are taller in societies that practice maternal separation or physical stress or both (155.7 cm [61.3"] versus 145.5 cm [57.3"] for societies with no stress). There is some weak evidence that females in societies practicing either form of stress experience menarche earlier than females in societies that do not stress infants.

In the most sophisticated cross-cultural test of the stress hypothesis, a multiple regression analysis shows that both stress and the presence of milking herds are positively correlated with adult male stature, while rainfall is negatively associated with height. The authors suggest that the presence of milking herds in Africa and Eurasia and their absence in Oceania and the Americas might explain regional differences in stature. Stress was the most important variable in the regression, explaining almost twice as much of the variance in stature as the next most important variable, rainfall.

A sample of children born to Yemenite immigrants to Israel provides evidence about the effect of maternal separation on growth. Children born in hospitals that separated infants from mothers except during feedings weighed more at one, two, and three years of age than children born at home, who remained with the mother constantly. Unfortunately, stature at the three ages is not reported, and we do not know if the two groups differed in adult stature. Two longitudinal growth studies in the United States showed that height at age 18 for both sexes (adjusted for parental height) was about 1.4 cm (0.56 inches) greater in children who had at least one vaccination before the age of 2 than in children who received no vaccinations in their first 2 years. The difference is statistically significant, and the authors suggest that its small magnitude (compared to the differences found in the cross-cultural studies) might indicate that many children who were not vaccinated in their first two years were born in hospitals and therefore experienced maternal separation stress. Children vaccinated at different ages did not differ in either death rate or history of illness during childhood.

A study that randomly assigned children in a Kenyan community to be vaccinated for smallpox before or after two years of age provides impressive support for the physical stress hypothesis. Measurements three years later showed that the early vaccination group grew more rapidly than the late vaccination group. The early group was above normative values for several traits, including sitting and standing height, while the later group was below normative values for each trait. The random assignment of subjects and the homogeneity of the climate, diet, and genetics of the sample mark this study as one of the few times a test of an anthropological hypothesis has approached the stereotypical image of a "scientific experiment." This makes the fact that no further data on the sample have been published especially unfortunate.

NEW CROSS-CULTURAL RESEARCH ON ADULT STATURE

Our sample contains 132 societies with data on stature and stress. We used this sample to replicate the results of Whiting and his colleagues and to conduct new control analyses for climate, region, and nutrition. Published codes were used in control analyses and therefore sample sizes differ for each test.[21]

Table 14-2 (on page 214) presents our test of the stress hypothesis. Analysis of variance (ANOVA) shows that in this sample separation practices are associated with increased stature for both sexes, while physical stress has an influence independent of separation rituals only for male height. We draw three conclusions from these results. First, unlike Whiting's 1965 results, our sample provides no evidence that physical stress relates to variation in female stature. Second, physical stress may affect male stature in a threshold manner, such that either type of stress will increase male height, but both types do not produce taller males than one type alone. Third, our sample provides evidence that separation stress is strongly associated with increased stature in both sexes.

TABLE 14-2 STRESS AND STATURE (CM)

STRESS		MALE STATURE		
SEPARATION	PHYSICAL	N	MEAN	SD
Absent	Absent	56	162.2 [63.8"]	5.57 [2.2"]
Absent	Present	27	165.3 [65.1"]	4.80 [1.9"]
Present	Absent	15	167.3 [65.9"]	3.80 [1.5"]
Present	Present	15	168.3 [66.2"]	5.11 [2.0"]
STRESS		FEMALE STATURE		
SEPARATION	PHYSICAL	N	MEAN	SD
Absent	Absent	39	150.7 [59.3"]	5.71 [2.2"]
Absent	Present	17	153.1 [60.3"]	5.00 [2.0"]
Present	Absent	13	155.9 [61.3"]	3.70 [1.5"]
Present	Present	6	1155.4 [61.2"]	3.64 [1.4"]

We conducted control analyses for both sexes, but discuss results only for males because sample sizes for females were often small. We created a dichotomized variable, contrasting societies that practiced neither physical nor separation stress with societies that engaged in either or both forms of stress. The purpose of the control analyses is to see if the relationship between stress and stature disappears when we introduce other variables into the model.

CONTROL FOR GEOGRAPHIC REGION

We found significant regional differences in male stature and stress practices. African and Amerindian societies are most likely to subject infants to physical stress, while separation stress showed no regional differences. ANOVA indicates that stress influences adult male height independent of region.

CONTROL FOR NUTRITION

We use cross-cultural codes for three variables in this control analysis: (1) protein availability; (2) presence of milking herds; and (3) risk of famine. None of these variables is associated with stress practices and each is correlated with male stature. Taller males are found in societies with milking herds, with higher protein availability, and under *increased* risk of famine. A multiple regression indicates that presence of milking herds is the best predictor of male stature, followed by stress and famine. Protein availability dropped out of the multiple regression.

The finding that males are taller in societies at higher risk of famine requires further study. The average diets of these societies might be superior to the diets of societies at low risk of famine. Famines may also be correlated with other nutritional variables that will be revealed only with better measures of dietary quality. It is likely that in societies at risk of famine the stature of cohorts that experience a famine during a critical period for growth will be lower than cohorts who did not.

CONTROL FOR CLIMATE

Societies stressing infants are not randomly distributed among climatic zones. Societies in dry-heat and temperate zones are more likely to stress infants than societies in wet-heat or wet-cold regions. Male stature also differs between climatic zones, with societies in dry-heat and temperate zones exhibiting taller adults. Climatic zone and stress independently affect male stature, with stress being the stronger predictor.

CONTROL FOR CHILD-REARING PRACTICES

Our analyses support the hypothesis that episodes of acute stress early in life are associated with increased adult stature and that this association is independent of nutritional, climatic, and genetic differences between societies. Confidence in the stress hypothesis would increase if we could show that societies that practice early infant stress (hereafter, *stress societies*) do not treat children differently than those societies that do not stress infants (hereafter, *nonstress societies*). If, for example, stress societies treat children either more harshly or more warmly throughout childhood than nonstress societies, it would not be possible to tell if difference in stature between the two types of societies results from stress practices or from differences in general child-rearing practices.

We found no systematic differences between stress and nonstress societies on several ratings of infant indulgence and affection. However, stress societies tend to place more emphasis on inculcating "toughness" (aggression, competition, and fortitude) in children than nonstress societies. Also, fathers were less likely to be in regular proximity to infants in stress societies. Emphasis on toughness and low father-infant proximity are both correlated with taller adult males. Stress remains associated with adult stature after controlling for either of these variables, however.

COMBINING THE CONTROL VARIABLES

Only twenty-nine cases in our sample had data for all of the variables discussed above, preventing us from testing a model containing all the control variables. We used a step-regression technique to predict male stature with six variables (milking herds, stress, climatic zone, socialization of toughness, and geographic region) and found that only region, climatic zone, and stress explain significant portions of the variation in male stature. A model that added father-infant proximity to the original six variables provided the same result, as did the model that added risk of famine to the original six variables.

Our results suggest that early childhood stress plays a role in explaining the patterning of adult male stature around the world. Limitations of our sample and methodology make such support less than perfect, but our research does point to new directions of inquiry into this problem. The most vital task is to increase sample sizes so that intra-regional tests using several predictors of stature are possible. This is important because several of our control variables are correlated with geographic region. A second goal is to discover if stress and nonstress societies treat children differently in ways that might influence growth. A replication of the association between father-infant proximity and adult stature is also necessary.

CONCLUSION

Our review of three explanations of population differences in stature finds some support for each at the level of bivariate analysis. Multivariate tests suggest that the stress hypothesis deserves consideration when explaining the distribution of human stature. However, the tests are weak due to imprecise measures of the independent variables (especially nutrition). Better tests of the validity and relative strength of three hypotheses require better coded data and large samples.

ACKNOWLEDGMENTS

Part of the research reported in this paper was supported by NSF grant BNS-8918815, awarded to J. Patrick Gray. Gray conducted some of the research as a member of the 1991 National Science Foundation-supported Summer Institute in Comparative Anthropological Research.

NOTES

1. The symbol "m =" stands for "mean male height" and "f =" for "mean female height." Reports from the small-scale societies traditionally studied by anthropologists often contain only measurements of males. When females were measured, the samples were usually much smaller than those of males.
2. Linda D. Wolfe and J. Patrick Gray, "A Cross-Cultural Investigation into the Sexual Dimorphism of Stature," in R. Hall, ed., *Sexual Dimorphism in Homo Sapiens: A Question of Size* (New York: Praeger, 1982), pp. 197–230.

3. Recommended references for human growth are Barry Bogin, *Patterns of Human Growth* (Cambridge: Cambridge University Press, 1988); Phyllis B. Eveleth and James M. Tanner, *Worldwide Variations in Human Growth,* 2nd ed. (Cambridge: Cambridge University Press, 1990).

4. R. C. Bailey, "The Comparative Growth of Efe Pygmies and African Farmers from Birth to Age 5 Years," *Annals of Human Biology* 18 (1991): 113–120.

5. For a review of growth hormones see Brian T. Shea, "Developmental Perspective on Size Change and Allometry in Evolution," *Evolutionary Anthropology* 1 (1992): 125–134.

6. C. G. Nicholas Mascie-Taylor, "Biosocial Influences on Stature: A Review," *Journal of Biosocial Science* 23 (1991): 123.

7. Some authors reverse the ratio and analyze surface area/weight. Bergmann's rule predicts the SA/W ratio to be high in warm climates and low in cold climates. Most cross-cultural studies of thermoregulation hypotheses estimate the surface area of the body using the following equation:

$$SA \ (\text{cm}^2) = \text{weight}^{0.425} \ (\text{kg}) \ \text{x height}^{0.725} \ (\text{cm}) \ \text{x } 71.84$$

Baker questioned the validity of applying this formula to populations other than white Europeans: see Paul T. Baker, "Climate, Culture, and Evolution," *Human Biology* 32 (1960): 8.

8. Sources for the thermoregulation hypothesis include Donald M. Austin and Michael W. Lansing, "Body Size and Heat Tolerance: A Computer Simulation," *Human Biology* 58 (1986): 153–169; A. Roberto Frisancho, *Human Adaptation: A Functional Interpretation* (Ann Arbor, MI: University of Michigan Press, 1981); Russell W. Newman, "Human Adaptation to Heat," in Albert Damon, ed., *Physiological Anthropology* (London: Oxford University Press, 1975), pp. 80–92; A.T. Steegmann, Jr., "Human Adaptation to Cold," in Albert Damon, ed., *Physiological Anthropology* (London: Oxford University Press, 1975), pp. 130–166.

9. Marshall T. Newman, "The Application of Ecological Rules to the Racial Anthropology of the Aboriginal New World," *American Anthropologist* 55 (1953): 311–327.

10. Marjorie Grant Whiting, "A Cross-Cultural Nutrition Survey of 118 Societies Representing the Major Cultural and Geographical Areas of the World" (Ph.D. diss., Harvard University, 1958), pp. 116–140.

11. Christopher B. Ruff, "Climate and Body Shape in Hominid Evolution," *Journal of Human Evolution* 21 (1991): 81–105.

12. Kenneth L. Beals, Stephen M. Dodd, and Courtland L. Smith, "HOMPLOT: Anthropometric Data Bases," *World Cultures* 3, no. 3 (1987).

13. Sources for nutrition and stature include Bogin, pp. 126–134; Eveleth and Tanner, pp. 194–203; and Jean Hiernaux, *Man in the Heat, High Altitude, and Society* (Springfield, IL: Charles C. Thomas, 1982), pp. 49–52.

14. David Seckler, "Small but Healthy? Some Basic Problems in the Concept of Malnutrition," in P. V. Sukhatme, ed., *Newer Concepts in Nutrition and Their Implications for Policy* (Pune: Maharashtra Association for the Cultivation of Science, 1982), pp. 139–148. A series of papers evaluating Seckler's hypothesis appears in *Human Organization* 48 (1989): pp. 11–52.

15. N. Dahlmann and K. Peterson, "Influences of Environmental Conditions during Infancy and Final Body Stature," *Pediatric Research* 11 (1977): 165–188.

16. Eiji Takahashi, "Geographic Distribution of Human Stature and Environmental Factors—An Ecologic Study," *Journal of the Anthropological Society-Nippon* 79 (1971):

259–286; Eiji Takahashi, "Secular Trend in Milk Consumption and Growth in Japan," *Human Biology* 56 (1984): 427–437.

17. M. G. Whiting, "A Cross-Cultural Nutrition Survey," pp. 117–134.
18. Thomas K. Landauer and John W. M. Whiting, "Infantile Stimulation and Adult Stature of Human Males," *American Anthropologist* 66 (1964): 1007–1028.
19. S. Gunders and J. W. M. Whiting, "Mother-Infant Separation and Physical Growth," *Ethnology* 7 (1968): 196–206.
20. References for studies of the stress hypothesis are in Thomas K. Landauer and John W. M. Whiting, "Correlates and Consequences of Stress in Infancy," in R. Munroe, R. Munroe, and B. Whiting, eds., *Handbook of Cross-Cultural Human Development* (New York: Garland STMP Press, 1981), pp. 355–375.
21. Details of methods, data sources, and results are in J. Patrick Gray, "Infant Stress and Adult Stature: Additional Tests."

SUGGESTED READINGS

Bogin, Barry. *Patterns of Human Growth*. Cambridge: Cambridge University Press, 1988. An excellent introduction to studies of human growth.

Ember, Carol R., Marc Howard Ross, Michael L. Burton, and Candice Bradley. "Problems of Measurement in Cross-Cultural Research Using Secondary Data." *Behavior Science Research* 25 (1991): 187–216. A good discussion of measurement in cross-cultural studies. This special issue of *Behavior Science Research* contains many useful articles on this type of research.

Eveleth, Phyllis B., and James M. Tanner. *Worldwide Variations in Human Growth*. 2nd ed. Cambridge: Cambridge University Press, 1990. A comprehensive review of growth studies conducted around the world.

Hiernaux, Jean. *Man in the Heat, High Altitude, and Society*. Springfield, IL: Charles C. Thomas, 1982. A short discussion of human responses to heat and altitude.

Landauer, Thomas K., and John W. M. Whiting. "Correlates and Consequences of Stress in Infancy." In R. Munroe, R. Munroe, and B. Whiting, eds. *Handbook of Cross-Cultural Human Development*. New York: Garland STMP Press, 1981, pp. 355–375. A complete review of the development and empirical support for the stress hypothesis.

Weiner, Herbert. *Perturbing the Organism: The Biology of Stressful Experience*. Chicago: University of Chicago Press, 1992. A review of the effects of both acute and chronic stress throughout the life cycle.

Growth and Development of Turkana Pastoralists

Michael A. Little

Nomadic Turkana Pastoralists and Their Environment

My first visit to the southern part of Kenya's Turkana District left an indelible impression of heat, dryness, and brittle sharpness. Termite mounds that rise abruptly from the bare earth, broad stony fields derived from volcanic rocks, sandy plains with patchy grass and scrub vegetation, and scattered acacia trees and thorn bush characterize much of this semiarid savanna land. A part of East Africa's rift valley system, the topography of the region is rugged with hills and mountains rising from the valley floor. This area has at least ten hours of bright sunlight per day, with temperatures moving above 90°F (35°C at midday), and reflected radiation from sand and rocks intensifying the heat. With such limited shade from sparse vegetation, I found myself always aware of the location of shadows and having an almost panicky sense of sunlight-avoidance because of the solar intensity. This is an environment of water impoverishment. Annual rainfall averages about 10 inches per year (250 mm/yr), but the rains tend to be concentrated within only a few months in a typical monsoon pattern. Seasonal drought occurs each year, while more serious droughts may appear once or twice each decade. The valley plains show a dramatic transformation during the rainy season when vegetation displays a rapid flush of flowers, grasses, shrubs, and leaves. Yet this seldom lasts for more than a few months, after which plants die off and the landscape reverts to tans and browns. Despite my initial impression of an arid-lands vegetation, there is considerable biodiversity within this ecosystem. There are sandy and volcanic plains grasses and shrubs, riverine woodlands, and wetter highland areas, all of which contribute to an ecosystem diversity that the Turkana people exploit quite effectively. To an outsider such as myself, this is an inhospitable environment; to the Turkana people, it is a difficult but manageable place that is their home.

My first meeting with a Turkana family at their settlement was somewhat tense, as with all new experiences, but also because the Turkana are a tall and imposing people whose men have a reputation throughout Kenya of being fierce warriors. The women, with their long leather skirts and aprons, seem to glide gracefully when they walk, and they are known for their independence and assertiveness. What struck me most about that first meeting, however, was my distinct sense of cheerfulness in these people, an attribute that seemed at odds with their harsh environment and the difficulty of their lives. Added to the sounds of children playing, adults talking, and livestock vocalizing were the sounds of people's laughter. In more than a decade of research following that initial meeting, my original impression has only been strengthened, while at the same time my respect for these people and the ways that they manage their own lives has grown enormously.

The people with whom we have lived and worked are members of a tribal subsection of the Turkana called the Ngisonyoka. (There are nineteen different tribal subsections in Turkana District.) The Ngisonyoka Turkana live in polygynous family units that include a herd owner, his wives and children, and other family members. These families may travel with other family units of friends or kin where the size of the unit will vary from ten to thirty or more individuals. The family settlements are highly mobile and settlement sites are moved up to fifteen times per year.[1] Their nomadic movement is designed to seek green forage for the five livestock species that they herd: dromedary camels, zebu cattle, fat-tailed sheep, goats, and donkeys.[2] Food provided by the livestock includes milk, blood, and meat—all animals are milked, blood from nonlactating animals is eaten (either raw, cooked, or mixed with other foods), and only small livestock are slaughtered for meat (except for infrequent ritual slaughter of large livestock). Maizemeal, sugar, and tea are traded for, and some wild foods are collected or hunted. In general, however, milk is the primary staple food and constitutes about 60 percent of the dietary intake.[3]

In addition to the nomadic Turkana, there are settled Turkana who live in villages along the Kerio and Turkwel Rivers where irrigation cultivation is practiced. Some of these sites include Kaputir and Nakwamoru along the Turkwel River and Lokori and Morulem along the Kerio River. The Nakwamoru site has the longest tradition of cultivation, which dates back to the early part of this century. The other irrigation sites are more recent and date to the 1960s or 1970s. The settled Turkana who live and work at these sites have few or no livestock and depend upon cultivation for their primary subsistence. We have conducted a number of studies of these sedentary people to compare with the nomads because of their differences in diet, activity, and lifestyle. Whereas the nomadic Turkana from the southern Turkana District are largely from the Ngisonyoka tribal subsection, Nakwamoru Turkana are from the Ngiketak subsection, and many of the people from Morulem are members of the Ngibelei subsection. Figure 15-1 is a map of the southern Turkana region with some place names for identification.

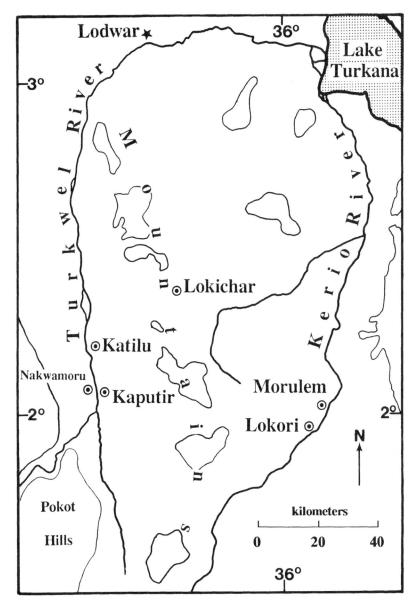

FIGURE 15-1

Map of the southern Turkana area showing some of the settlements where growth and other studies were conducted. This is the home territory of the Ngisonyoka Turkana.

Studies of growth and development of nomadic and settled Turkana constitute one component of a major research project that involved many scientists from anthropology, ecology, medicine, and range science. Before discussing the Turkana research, a few comments should be offered on the topic of human growth to place it in the proper anthropological context.

HUMAN GROWTH AS A PROCESS

Growth is a universal property of life. For humans, growth processes have special significance when compared with other mammalian or even primate species. First, learning and behavior—particularly social behavior—are extraordinarily important and unique aspects of human growth. Second, achievement of full maturation in size and reproductive capacity may take up to a third of an individual's lifetime. Finally, there is quite remarkable variation within our species in just how growth proceeds. This variation can be observed *within* groups with similar characteristics (populations), and substantial variation can be seen *among* groups or populations as well. Keeping in mind that adults are the product of many years' growth, the variations we see among adults are best understood by studying their formative growth processes. Such growth processes are regulated by complex interrelationships between heredity and environment through time.

Growth and development studies in anthropology are important to our understanding of what might be called "the human condition." These studies have a tradition that dates back to the early work of Franz Boas, a founder of American anthropology. One of Boas' commitments was to dispel the myth of "racial purity" by demonstrating that individuals' growth experiences could modify what were known in the early 1900s as "physical types." He did this in his classic study of European migrants.[4] In this work, he demonstrated that children from eastern and southern Europe who were raised in the United States had differently shaped heads and were larger in body size than their European counterparts. Children, then, were highly modifiable according to the environments within which they were raised. Boas also studied the considerable variation in growth "tempos," or rates, and was interested in the timing of the onset and termination of adolescence in American youths.[5]

Many anthropologists continue this tradition of research on human growth. The common thread that connects the research is an appreciation of how developmental, biobehavioral, and environmental processes can contribute to human variation. Current research ranges from the establishment of growth standards for healthy children to comparative studies of child growth in the Third World to investigations of the effects of lead and other toxic substances on child development.[6] Contemporary research is often based on the well-documented assumption that growth is highly flexible and dependent on continuing adaptation to a changing environment. This concept of adaptation in growth studies is an important one and will be discussed further.

STAGES OF GROWTH

Although growth, from conception to death, is really a continuous process, it is convenient to identify several stages of growth to characterize the process. Prenatal or intrauterine growth has three phases (zygote, embryo, and fetus) and infancy is usually identified as the first year after birth. Both prenatal and infant periods are identified by rapid growth in size. Growth in size slows down a bit during childhood, but cognitive and learning growth during this period are truly remarkable. Growth in size accelerates again during adolescence, where girls are universally two years earlier than boys in the onset and termination of adolescent growth. Adolescence is really defined by this event of accelerated growth. Sexual maturation also occurs during the period of rapid adolescent growth. During adulthood, changes in length (height) are minor, but changes in weight and shape often occur. Senescence, or old age, is characterized by some loss in height, but other changes, such as general disorganization of structures and declines in function, are substantial. Death is the final event, which occurs on average (life expectancy at birth) between seventy and seventy-five years of age for Western populations. The maximum life span for humans appears to be somewhat less than 120 years of age.

GROWTH AND ADAPTATION

The ability to respond to changes in the environment with adjustments in body function and form is identified as the process of adaptation. In the same way that growth is a universal property of life, so is adaptation. Relatively rapid adjustments to the environment are made in such systems as temperature regulation, immune responses, and cognitive decision-making. These are referred to as *short-term adaptations* and contribute to general survival and well-being. *Genetic adaptations* are the result of natural selection as an evolutionary process. *Developmental adaptations* are those adjustments that are made during growth periods, particularly growth up to adulthood.[7] For example, growth during infancy or childhood may be slowed or actually stopped because of inadequate food or some illness. The internal drive to grow, which is under the control of the genes and the hormones, is halted while the body conserves its resources. If health is restored, then a pattern of accelerated or "catch-up" growth may restore the increments of size lost during the period of ill health or poor nutrition.[8] Some environmental conditions produce irreversible effects, such as stunted (short) growth as the result of prolonged disease or malnutrition.

Finally, what might be said about the optimal conditions for growth? These are difficult to define, but some might be listed: adequate but not excessive food (energy and nutrients) to meet nutritional needs; relative freedom from a heavy disease burden, but with an opportunity to develop natural immune responses; adequate physical activity (exercise); an emotionally nurturing family and community environment; and an ability to satisfy curiosity and expression. In the history of our species, those who have enjoyed an optimal environment for growth are probably in a small minority. Hence, our adaptability to considerably less than optimal conditions has contributed to our very survival as a species.

THE TURKANA RESEARCH

In the early 1980s, my colleagues and I began a research project to study pastoral Turkana nomads of northwest Kenya.[9] We chose to study the Turkana for a number of reasons: (1) Although much research had been conducted on pastoralists within a sociocultural framework, little was known about their health, human biology, and ecology; (2) planned (economic development) and unplanned changes were occurring to move pastoral nomads away from this pattern of subsistence, so there was some urgency to such studies; and (3) since the Turkana savanna environment is highly variable and fluctuating, long-term studies were needed to understand how they were able to deal with these conditions. We designed the project as a multidisciplinary one, in that investigators from several different realms of science were to collaborate to understand this population and its environment. The broad project objectives were three-fold and were designed to understand and explain: (1) how the Turkana are able to extract resources and survive in an arid and stressful environment by nomadic pastoral subsistence; (2) how these extractive techniques modify the dry savanna ecosystem; and (3) what the effects are of the environment and Turkana cultural practices on the adaptability and health of the people. The first objective focused on sociocultural anthropology; the second objective was pursued through rangelands ecology; and the third objective was in the realm of biological anthropology. The project was called the "South Turkana Ecosystem Project" and continued for about a decade as a multidisciplinary program. A second decade of research continues today in a number of areas of anthropology and we still work with some of the same families with whom we worked in 1980. Ongoing studies include the ecology of reproduction, maternal and child health, female and male fertility, violence within Turkana society, and population demography. What is described here is the research on growth of infants, children, and adolescents—a single, but important, component of the project.

HEALTH AND ADAPTABILITY STUDIES OF TURKANA NOMADS

In order to characterize the health and adaptability of the Turkana, my colleagues, our students, and I initiated a series of studies that included the following categories: (1) diet and nutrition; (2) growth and development; (3) reproduction; (4) adult size and body composition; (5) physical activity; and (6) disease. Studies within each category served to define the biological status of the people. For example, the Turkana diet, high in milk products, provides an abundance of protein (up to four times the daily requirement), yet energy in the form of calories is quite limited.[10] We discovered that reproduction was a complex issue. Whereas fertility is relatively high so also is infant mortality, and births tend to be highly seasonal, reflecting some environmental limits placed on fertility.[11] Adults are generally tall (comparable to U.S. adults), although their body weight is quite light.[12] Hence, physiques of Turkana are tall and very linear, with relatively small muscle sizes and minimal body fat. The limited energy input from food is expended in the moderate and occasionally vigorous activities of herding and tending livestock and managing the household settlement. As might be expected from the moderate to high levels of day-to-day activity, levels of physical fitness are good.[13]

Disease has been studied only to a modest degree.[14] It appears that parasites are not a serious problem for the nomads, yet certain endemic diseases, such as malaria, produce considerable sickness and occasional mortality. There may also be some impairment of the immune system in children, linked to the diet, that leaves them susceptible to infection.[15] Among adults, cardiovascular disease appears to be in low prevalence and blood pressure values are among the lowest ever observed.[16]

The six categories of studies of Turkana health and adaptability that we performed are all highly interrelated. For example, the size and body composition (energy reserves) of the mother, her reproductive status (previous number of births, or "parity"), and her levels of physical activity and diet during pregnancy will all influence the prenatal growth of the developing fetus.

Moreover, in the newborn and growing infant, disease, diet, and maternal care (dependent, in turn, on maternal health) are crucial factors in the health and well-being of this infant. Adequate breastfeeding, which is contingent on good maternal health and nutritional status, not only provides the best diet for the infant, but also provides protection from infection (passive immunity from breast milk) and strengthened emotional bonds through close physical contact with the mother. Anything that interrupts this process, such as pregnancy, jeopardizes the health and normal growth of the infant.

As the child grows older, her or his dependence on the mother (and her healthy status) decreases. Rather, the dependence of the child shifts to the overall well-being of the family unit and availability of family resources.

GROWTH OF TURKANA CHILDREN

Our research to date includes anthropometric measurements of size and body composition of more than 1,500 Turkana men, women, and children. These data were collected between 1980 and 1994, and most are what are known as "cross-sectional data." Cross-sectional data include different individuals at different ages who are treated as if they were changing through time. Some measurements of the same individuals were repeated to provide what are known as "longitudinal data." From this limited longitudinal data it was possible to compute some rates of growth for individuals at different ages. Longitudinal data are more desirable but, because they require multiple visits to the same individuals over many years, are very difficult and time-consuming to collect.

Our earliest research concentrated on simple description of growth in children at different ages and of adult status.[17] Later research dealt with comparative studies of nomadic and settled Turkana, special problems of nutritional influences, maternal health and breastfeeding effects, and influences of pregnancy rates on maternal health.[18]

One of the problems we are currently exploring is the influence of seasonality in food availability and seasonal hunger on growth rates in children as well as seasonal influences on fertility in adults. In fact, a broad hypothesis that has influenced the overall design of the Turkana research concerns the influences of a fluctuating environment on the health and behavior of the people. For example, we hypothesized that seasonal and longer-term fluctuations in rainfall have led to corresponding fluctuations in resources that have affected nutritional status, health, growth patterns, reproductive performance, and a host of other variables. To date, we have been able to demonstrate a number of relationships between periodic environmental variation and health variables.[19]

The material that follows deals with fundamental growth characteristics and effects of the environment (social and natural) on growth. I then present a preliminary model of the relationships between environment and patterns of growth.

INFANCY, CHILDHOOD, AND ADOLESCENCE

Infants from many African populations tend to show what is known as growth faltering at about six months of age.[20] In these cases, infants at birth are within the normal ranges of length and weight for Western (U.S. and European) infants, up to six months, after which they begin to fall behind. This pattern seems to hold even for infants from well-off families. Some infants from impoverished populations will be small from birth. There are several hypotheses that have been proposed to explain this phenomenon: (1) breastfeeding is ended (weaning) at about six months and the nutritional quality and quantity of the food declines; (2) breastfeeding is ended or supplementation begins, which increases the rate of infection because of poor sanitation; (3) this pattern is a more natural one for African populations or human populations in general, and it is the Western infants who show unusual weight and height gains after six months of age, perhaps due to forced feeding; or (4) any combination of these may be operating.

Turkana infants show a pattern that is similar to that of other Africans but with a significant difference. This pattern is illustrated from birth to twenty-four months of age for both nomadic and settled Turkana in Figure 15-2.

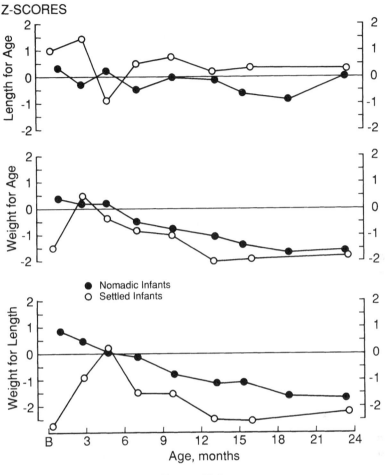

FIGURE 15-2

Z-scores (standard deviation units) for length, weight, and weight/length ratio of nomadic and settled Turkana infants from birth to twenty-four months of age. The zero lines are averages for U.S. infants. Positive Z-scores indicate that Turkana infants are larger than U.S. infants, while negative Z-scores indicate that Turkana are smaller.

Here, Z-scores, which are standard deviation units from the mean or average, are used to represent the distances in size of the Turkana babies from U.S. babies. The zero lines represent U.S. values. Although there are some differences between the nomads and the settled, both tend to maintain length at the Western level, but show declines in weight after six months of age in the typical African pattern. Nomad-settled differences in weight for length may be a function of the better nomad diet and a supplementation of butter fat in nomadic infants (the settled infants have limited access to milk products).

Heights and weights of nomadic Turkana from one year of age to adulthood are shown in Figure 15-3. Comparisons are made with U.S. fiftieth (average) and fifth (95 percent or greater) percentiles. There are several interesting things about these Turkana growth curves. First, growth in height is below U.S. values throughout childhood, adolescence, and early adulthood up to about twenty-three or twenty-four years of age, at which time Turkana catch up to U.S. young adults. This is an extraordinarily late maturation in size, but it simply reflects a prolonged but steady growth into the early twenties. Full maturation in height for U.S. girls is about sixteen years of age and for U.S. boys is about eighteen years. We cannot be absolutely sure, but this prolonged growth is probably the result of limited calories or energy in the normal nomadic diet and a conservation of energy needed for growth. The tall stature is probably "driven" by the high protein intake from milk. A second interesting observation is in the very low body weights of both boys and girls at or below the fifth percentile. This extreme linearity or thinness of physique is

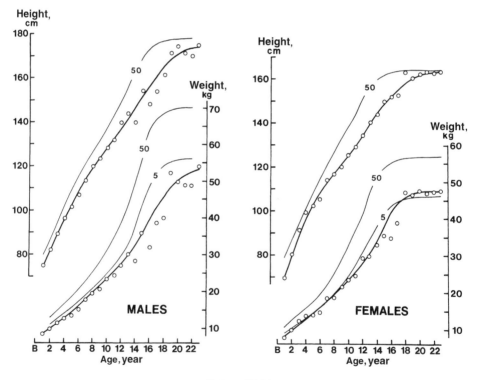

FIGURE 15-3

Growth curves for Turkana nomadic infants, children, and adolescents. Height and weight of Turkana are indicated by open circles and fitted dark lines. The lighter lines are fiftieth (average) and fifth percentiles for U.S. youths.

characteristic of East African pastoralists and is probably produced by a combination of limited food energy intake and a genetic tendency toward linearity.[21] Finally, girls seem slightly better off than boys after age sixteen years since body weights are above the fifth percentile for girls but well below the fifth percentile for boys. This may mean that young women of marriageable age are better nourished than young men due to differences in food access (women are responsible for milking the animals).

BODY COMPOSITION IN CHILDREN AND ADULTS

With height close to U.S. averages and weight hovering around the fifth U.S. percentile, body mass index (BMI = weight/height²), which is a measure of robusticity, is low indeed for Turkana at all ages. High BMI values indicate considerable body fat or muscle mass or both. The high BMI values of most Americans result from obesity and substantial body fat content, as well as substantial muscle mass resulting, in part, from a high-protein diet.

Although too much body fat is not healthy, some body fat is very important because it is a form of energy storage. One measure of body fat in humans is the skinfold, taken with constant-tension calipers. This measure takes a fold of skin at a specific site on the body and determines the thickness of the fold of skin and underlying subcutaneous (fat or adipose) tissue. Figure 15-4 (on page 230) presents the age changes in several skinfolds for girls and women throughout their lifespan. The Turkana pattern, which shows high body fat in infants, low body fat in children between ages five and ten years, and then a gradual increase up to and including adolescence, is similar to that seen in Americans. However, for Americans, the skinfold values would be considerably higher (perhaps as much as twenty millimeters higher). In American women into their thirties and forties, skinfolds and body fat increase. In contrast, Turkana women show a depletion of body fat that appears to be a function of the energy demands of pregnancy and breastfeeding, since an average Turkana woman will have seven live births during her reproductive lifetime.[22] This example illustrates one set of relationships between growth, body composition, availability of dietary energy, and the demands of reproduction in the Turkana.

SEASONAL AND LONGER-RANGE VARIATION

There is evidence for considerable seasonality in food availability and diet, adult body weight, disease, fertility, and infant growth in Ngisonyoka Turkana.[23] Season of birth appears to have little influence on growth of infants, but both Ngisonyoka and settled Morulem infants showed variations in size and fat content according to the season of measurement.[24] During the wet season, infant skinfolds are significantly larger than during the dry season, when livestock milk production is low. Nearly all Turkana infants less

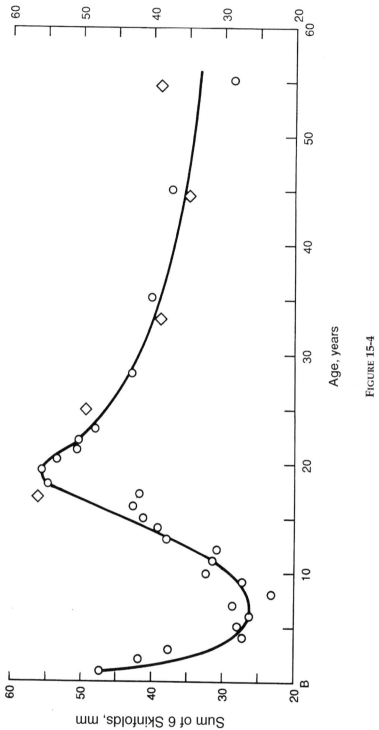

FIGURE 15-4

Age changes in body fat composition of nomadic Turkana girls and women as represented by the sum of six skinfold measurements. Body fat composition shows two peaks: the first in infancy and the second in late adolescence.

than two years of age are still being breastfed, so maternal nutritional status may influence the nutritional status of their infants. However, infant diets are supplemented with livestock milk products beginning shortly after birth, so livestock milk productivity probably plays a role in infant growth, as well.

Drought can have devastating effects on the health of children in a number of ways. First, food production from livestock falls off and herds may be depleted when animals die. This has both short-term and long-term economic consequences for the nomadic Turkana. Second, intertribal and intratribal raiding intensifies during drought because of the increased competition for resources. In southern Turkana, bandits, called "Ngingoroko," raid their own Turkana people and steal livestock. More serious raiding occurs when neighboring Pokot tribesmen with automatic weapons attack large clusters of Turkana settlements and steal thousands of livestock. These raids can impoverish herd owners, who then have no means of feeding their families. Third, when family herding units tend to cluster in larger population units for protection against Pokot raids, conditions are ripe for epidemics of infectious diseases. In July 1994, both settled and nomadic Turkana were suffering from hepatitis and other infections that almost certainly have an impact on child growth.

An example of long-term differences in infant growth in length for several groups taken on four separate occasions is shown in Figure 15-5 (on page 232). There is quite remarkable variation. The two groups of very small infants measured in July and August 1985 came at the end of an eighteen-month drought in which there was virtually no rainfall between October 1983 and March 1985. The group of infants measured in 1979 also coincided with a drought, whereas the groups measured in 1989 and 1990 had been raised during relatively good rainfall.

A SCHEMATIC MODEL FOR GROWTH IN TURKANA

There is always more research that can be done to test hypotheses further and verify relationships. However, it is possible, with the information at hand, to generate a model or conceptual framework to describe some of the relationships concerning health and growth of Turkana children. Such a model can also be used to identify areas in need of further exploration. The model is presented in Figure 15-6 (on page 233).

There are three independent variable categories: maternal health, herd owner's economic status, and environmental conditions. Maternal health, in our studies, was defined according to body size, body composition, and health and reproductive history. The importance of maternal health during pregnancy and the postnatal period of breastfeeding is clear, since the mother is the direct source of the fetus's or infant's nutrition, support, and care. Parity, or the number of births that the mother has had, is inversely related to body

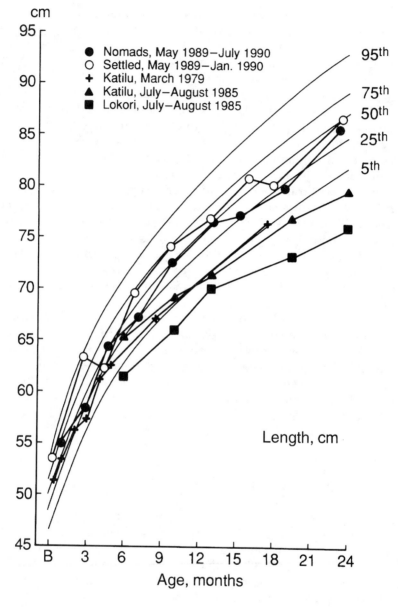

FIGURE 15-5

Growth in length of several different groups of Turkana infants. They illustrate the variations in size that can be attributed to differences in environmental conditions affecting growth patterns.

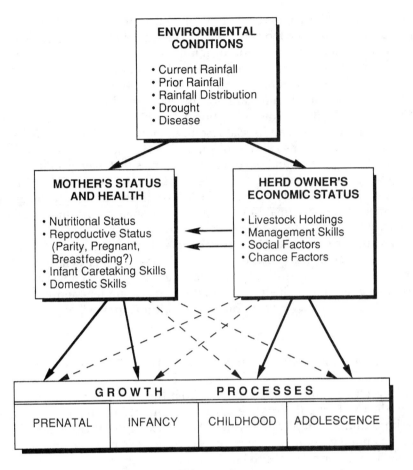

FIGURE 15-6

A schematic diagram to represent some of the influences on growth of Turkana from the prenatal period through adolescence. The solid-line arrows indicate a relatively stronger relationship than the dashed-line arrows.

fat stores (see Figure 15-4 on page 230), so birth order is an important variable, as well. Accordingly, maternal health has the most profound influence on the prenatal and infancy periods, and important but somewhat less influence during childhood and adolescence.

The herd owner's influence on the health and growth status of his children is certainly important at all ages because of his skills at generating and managing household resources, but his influence on his children is likely to increase as they become older and less dependent on maternal care. The model might have been expanded by adding another variable category—the family—to express the interactive processes of herd owner, wives, and other children.

For example, children, particularly young ones, are given high priority for milk distribution when food is scarce. The allocation of scarce food resources, particularly milk, is a function of family sharing, ownership of animals (women may inherit and own animals), and herd owner decisions on allocation. Environmental conditions can profoundly affect the herd owner's ability to produce food and care for his family. However, most of the environmental influences are a function of his ability to manipulate and manage the environmental and social resources that are available to him at any given time. Mothers also play a role in the management of resources, particularly when they own and have access to animals that may be milked.

Finally, there are certainly examples of direct environmental influence on infants, children, and adolescents in the form of infection, parasites, accidents, and other forms of trauma. However, the model suggests that much of the influence on the growing child operates through the family unit.

The picture given here of pastoral nomads and the growth of their children is one in which social, ecological, and human biological factors all play a role in growth processes. Although this presents a very complex picture indeed, such a view is likely to promote a greater understanding of these processes than unitary biomedical or sociocultural approaches.

IMPLICATIONS AND CONTRIBUTIONS OF THESE GROWTH STUDIES

There are two levels of contribution from the Turkana research on child growth. The first concerns the understanding of Turkana children, their health, and their adaptability within the context of the Turkana population, culture, and environment. We have learned, for example, that despite their living in an environment with limited resources, Turkana children will grow to heights that are comparable to United States values, but that the process takes five or more years longer. This suggests that the controls governing growth are sufficiently flexible to allow the same target sizes to be achieved by different pathways. We have learned, also, that individual Turkana children do not achieve this adult size by uniform growth, but probably by an irregular pathway resulting from environmental fluctuations in resources available throughout their infancy, childhood, and adolescence. And finally, these patterns of growth result from a variety of influences that arise from the environment, the family unit, health of the mother, status of the father, and a host of other factors.

The second level of contribution of the Turkana growth studies is within the realm of general knowledge and theory of child growth and development. Although not discussed at length here, we know that heredity plays an important role in growth processes. However, we know from studies as early as those of Boas (1912) that the environmental influences on growth are profound indeed. If the environment plays such a central role in human growth, then we can learn most by exploring the maximum range of environments to which humans are exposed. This suggests that we should go well beyond the study of children only from Western societies, and we should explore the patterns of growth of peoples vastly different from ourselves. This provides a richer base of information on child growth variation, and, again, emphasizes the value of comparative approaches in anthropology to the nature of scientific inquiry.

NOTES

1. J. Terrence McCabe, "Drought and Recovery: Livestock Dynamics among the Ngisonyoka Turkana of Kenya," *Human Ecology* 15 (1987): 371–389.
2. Neville Dyson-Hudson and Rada Dyson-Hudson, "The Structure of East African Herds and the Future of East African Herders," *Development and Change* 13 (1982): 213–238; Rada Dyson-Hudson, "Understanding East African Pastoralism: An Ecosystems Approach," in R. Berleant-Schiller and E. Shanklin, eds., *The Keeping of Animals: Adaptation and Social Relations in Livestock-Producing Communities* (Totowa, NJ: Allanheld and Osmun, 1983), pp. 1–10.
3. Kathleen A. Galvin, "Nutritional Ecology of Pastoralists in Dry Tropical Africa," *American Journal of Human Biology* 4 (1992): 209–221. The history of the paranilotic Turkana nomads has been well documented by John Lamphear, *The Scattering Time: Turkana Responses to Colonial Rule* (Oxford: Clarendon Press, 1992). The Turkana, who are closely related to the Jie and Karimojong tribes of the Sudan and Uganda, moved into the area of Turkana District, Kenya, between 150 and 200 years ago.
4. Franz Boas, *Changes in the Bodily Form of Descendants of Immigrants* (New York: Columbia University Press, 1912).
5. Franz Boas, "The Growth of Children," *Science* 5 (1897): 570–573; Franz Boas, "Studies in Growth," *Human Biology* 4 (1932): 307–350. A detailed description of Franz Boas's contributions to growth studies can be found in James M. Tanner, *A History of the Study of Human Growth* (Cambridge: Cambridge University Press, 1981).
6. Noel Cameron, "Human Growth, Nutrition, and Health Status in Sub-Saharan Africa," *Yearbook of Physical Anthropology* 34 (1991): 211–250; A. Roberto Frisancho, *Anthropometric Standards for the Assessment of Growth and Nutritional Status* (Ann Arbor: University of Michigan Press, 1990); Lawrence M. Schell, "Effects of Pollutants on Human Prenatal and Postnatal Growth: Noise, Lead, Polychlorobiphenyl Compounds, and Toxic Wastes," *Yearbook of Physical Anthropology* 34 (1991): 157–210.
7. A. Roberto Frisancho, *Human Adaptation and Accommodation* (Ann Arbor: University of Michigan Press, 1993).
8. James M. Tanner, "Growth as a Target-Seeking Function: Catch-Up and Catch-Down Growth in Man," in Frank Falkner and James M. Tanner, eds., *Human Growth*, vol. 1, 2nd ed. (New York: Plenum Press, 1986), pp. 167–180.
9. Neville Dyson-Hudson, a social anthropologist who has worked for many years on pastoral populations in East Africa, was the intellectual formulator of the South Turkana Ecosystem Project in the mid-1970s. He inspired me, a biological anthropologist, and two rangelands ecologists from the Natural Resource Ecology Laboratory at Colorado State University, James E. Ellis and David M. Swift, to become

involved in the project. Shortly after, Rada Dyson-Hudson, an anthropologist and ecologist, Peg H. Fry, an anthropologist and demographer, Paul W. Leslie, a biological anthropologist and demographer, and Michael B. Coughenour, a savanna ecologist, became active research participants in the project. Our Kenyan colleagues, Geoffrey M. O. Maloiy, a veterinary physiologist, and Mutuma Mugambi, a cardiologist, were participants from the very beginning. More than a dozen students in anthropology and ecology did Ph.D. dissertations on Turkana research.

10. Kathleen Galvin, *Food Procurement, Diet, Activities, and Nutrition of Ngisonyoka Turkana Pastoralists in an Ecological and Social Context* (Ph.D. diss., State University of New York, 1985).

11. Jean M. Brainard, *Health and Development in a Rural Kenyan Community* (New York: Peter Lang Publishing, 1990); Paul W. Leslie, Peggy H. Fry, Kathleen Galvin, and J. Terrence McCabe, "Biological, Behavioral, and Ecological Influences on Fertility in Turkana," in E. E. Whitehead, C. F. Hutchinson, B. N. Timmermann, and R. C. Varady, eds., *Arid Lands Today and Tomorrow: Proceedings of an International Research and Development Conference* (Boulder: Westview Press, 1988), pp. 705–712; Paul W. Leslie and Peggy H. Fry, "Extreme Seasonality of Births among Nomadic Turkana Pastoralists," *American Journal of Physical Anthropology* 79 (1989): 103–115.

12. Michael A. Little and Brooke R. Johnson, Jr., "Grip Strength, Muscle Fatigue, and Body Composition in Nomadic Turkana Pastoralists," *American Journal of Physical Anthropology* 69 (1986): 335–344.

13. Linda Curran-Everett, *Age, Sex, and Seasonal Differences in the Work Capacity of Nomadic Ngisonyoka Turkana Pastoralists* (Ph.D. diss., State University of New York, 1990).

14. Karen Shelley, *Medicines for Misfortune: Diagnosis and Health Care among Southern Turkana Pastoralists of Kenya* (Ph.D. diss., University of North Carolina, 1985).

15. Bettina Shell-Duncan, "Cell-Mediated Immunocompetence among Nomadic Turkana Children," *American Journal of Human Biology* 5 (1993): 225–235.

16. Mutuma Mugambi and Michael A. Little, "Blood Pressure in Nomadic Turkana Pastoralists," *East African Medical Journal* 60 (1983): 863–869.

17. Michael A. Little, Kathleen Galvin, and Mutuma Mugambi, "Cross-Sectional Growth of Nomadic Turkana Pastoralists," *Human Biology* 55 (1983): 811–830; Michael A. Little and Brooke R. Johnson, Jr., "Mixed Longitudinal Growth of Turkana Pastoralists," *Human Biology* 59 (1987): 695–707.

18. Jean M. Brainard, "Nutritional Status and Morbidity on an Irrigation Project in Turkana District, Kenya," *American Journal of Human Biology* 2 (1989): 153–163; Sandra J. Gray, "Comparison of Effects of Breast-Feeding Practices on Birth-Spacing in Three Societies: Nomadic Turkana, Gainj, and Quechua," *Journal of Biosocial Science* 26 (1994): 69–90; Sandra J. Gray, "Correlates of Dietary Intake of Lactating Women in South Turkana," *American Journal of Human Biology* 6 (1994): 369–383; Michael A. Little and Sandra J. Gray, "Growth of Young Nomadic and Settled Turkana Children," *Medical Anthropology Quarterly* 4 (1990): 296–314; Michael A. Little, Kathleen Galvin, and Paul W. Leslie, "Health and Energy Requirements of Nomadic Turkana Pastoralists," in Igor de Garine and G. Ainsworth Harrison, eds., *Coping with Uncertainty in Food Supply* (Oxford: Oxford University Press, 1988), pp. 288–315; Michael A. Little, Paul W. Leslie, and Kenneth L. Campbell, "Energy Reserves and Parity of Nomadic and Settled Turkana Women," *American Journal of Human Biology* 4 (1992): 729–738.

19. Sandra J. Gray, *Infant Care and Feeding among Nomadic Turkana Pastoralists: Implications for Child Survival and Fertility* (Ph.D. diss., State University of New York, 1992); Michael A. Little, Sandra J. Gray, and Paul W. Leslie, "Growth of Nomadic and Settled Turkana Infants of Northwest Kenya," *American Journal of Physical Anthropology* 92 (1993): 273–289.
20. Phyllis B. Eveleth and James M. Tanner, *Worldwide Variation in Human Growth*, 2nd ed. (Cambridge: Cambridge University Press, 1990).
21. Michael A. Little, "Designs for Human Biology Research among Savanna Pastoralists," in David R. Harris, ed., *Human Ecology in Savanna Environments* (London: Academic Press, 1980), pp. 479–503; Michael A. Little, "Human Biology of African Pastoralists," *Yearbook of Physical Anthropology* 32 (1989): 215–247; Michael A. Little, "Adaptability of African Pastoralists," in Stanley J. Ulijaszek and Rebecca Huss-Ashmore, eds., *Human Adaptability: Past, Present, and Future* (Oxford: Oxford University Press, 1997).
22. Little, Leslie, and Campbell, "Energy Reserves and Parity of Nomadic and Settled Turkana Women," pp. 729–738.
23. Galvin, "Nutritional Ecology of Pastoralists in Dry Tropical Africa," pp. 209–221; Kathleen Galvin and Michael A. Little, "Seasonal Patterns of Body Size and Composition among Pastoral Nomads from Northwestern Kenya," *American Journal of Physical Anthropology* 72 (1987): 200; Kathleen Galvin and Samuel K. Waweru, "Variation in the Energy and Protein Content of Milk Consumed by Nomadic Pastoralists of North-west Kenya," in A. A. J. Jansen, H. T. Horelli, and V. J. Quinn, eds., *Food and Nutrition in Kenya: A Historical Review* (Nairobi: UNICEF and University of Nairobi, 1987), pp. 129–138; Leslie and Fry, "Extreme Seasonality of Births among Nomadic Turkana Pastoralists," pp. 103–115; Little, "Human Biology of African Pastoralists," pp. 215–247; Little, Gray, and Leslie, "Growth of Nomadic and Settled Turkana Infants of Northwest Kenya," pp. 273–289; Shelley, "Medicines for Misfortune: Diagnosis and Health Care among Southern Turkana Pastoralists of Kenya."
24. Little, Gray, and Leslie, "Growth of Nomadic and Settled Turkana Infants of Northwest Kenya," pp. 273–289.

SUGGESTED READINGS

Bogin, Barry. *Patterns of Human Growth*. Cambridge: Cambridge University Press, 1988. As an introduction to studies of human growth, Bogin's book presents basic materials from anthropological and evolutionary perspectives. Also, the author draws examples from his considerable research experience with Guatemalan children.

Cameron, Noel. "Human Growth, Nutrition, and Health Status in Sub-Saharan Africa." *Yearbook of Physical Anthropology* 34 (1991): 211–250. This paper provides a review of growth studies of African children from a number of areas. South African and other populations, including the Kenyan Turkana, are compared according to a number of environmental and lifestyle differences.

Coughenour, Michael B., James E. Ellis, David M. Swift, D. Layne Coppock, Kathleen Galvin, J. Terrence McCabe, and T. C. Hart. "Energy Extraction and Use in a Nomadic Pastoral Population." *Science* 230 (1985): 619–625. In this paper, Coughenour and his colleagues argue persuasively that the Turkana do not degrade their environment. The paper is a good example of the value of collaboration between ecologists and anthropologists and reviews the South Turkana Ecosystem Project results up to 1985.

Dyson-Hudson, Rada, and Neville Dyson-Hudson. "Nomadic Pastoralism." *Annual Review of Anthropology* 9 (1980): 15–61. Rada and Neville Dyson-Hudson, anthropologists with extensive field experience with Ugandan Karimojong and Turkana, provide a comprehensive review of nomadic pastoralists in a sociocultural perspective.

Gulliver, Philip H. *The Family Herds*. London: Routledge and Kegan Paul, 1955. This is the earliest comprehensive monograph on the Turkana. Up until recently, Gulliver's papers and monographs were the principal source of knowledge in social anthropology on the Turkana.

Little, Michael A. "Human Biology of African Pastoralists." *Yearbook of Physical Anthropology* 32 (1989): 215–247. This review is useful in placing the Turkana within the context of other African pastoral populations. The emphasis in the paper is on health, nutrition, growth, activity, and reproduction in these populations.

THE CONCEPT OF RACE
IN PHYSICAL ANTHROPOLOGY

C. LORING BRACE

"RACE" AS A SOCIAL CONSTRUCT

The reader of an essay such as this will normally expect it to start with an acceptable anthropological definition of what "race" is considered to be. For many it will come as something of a surprise, then, to hear that "race" is whatever people think it should be, but that it has no basic biological reality. Since "race" holds such a prominent place in life in America and has done so since before the country gained its independence over two centuries ago, the reader can be forgiven for thinking that the statement that "race" does not exist amounts to a bit of academic double-talk or verbal sleight-of-hand. The practicing physician will query rhetorically, "What do you mean, race does not exist? I see it in my clinic every day!" One can be forgiven for being suspicious that the denial of the reality of "race" is just another manifestation of postmodern relativism where reality is defined as whatever people choose to believe and has no objective identity.

Actually, what is thought of as "race" is in fact a manifestation of cultural relativism, and each group will perceive it in a different way. In Hitler's Germany, Jews and Gypsies were perceived as distinct "races," while the English have often thought of the Irish and the French as racially distinct. Americans, on the other hand, use the term to apply to what they perceive as larger groupings such as Africans or Asians and assume somewhat simplistically that a single label can encompass the spectrum found in each continent. Europeans would agree that these qualify as "races," but they then go on to make finer discriminations under that term.

In saying that "race" does not exist as a biological category, I am not saying that human biological differences do not exist. These do, and can be productively studied, but only after the concept of "race" is rejected as a starting point. I shall return to that point later on. At the moment, it should be noted that the concept is relatively recent and basically did not exist prior to the

Renaissance. It is of some interest to reflect that neither the concept nor any word that could be used to designate it is present in the Judaeo-Christian Bible. One could say that, of course, the Biblical accounts describe a relatively restricted portion of the Middle East, although the scope covered actually ranges all the way from the Mediterranean up the Nile to Ethiopia.

There is no trace of a "race" concept in the extensive accounts in Egyptian hieroglyphics even though sub-Saharan Africans are represented in the accompanying illustrations. The "Father of History," Herodotus (ca. 484–420 B.C.), described his travels all the way from the Black Sea north of Greece southwards and up the Nile to Nubia, but never used a term that could be construed as "race" even though some of the translations insert that word where the original Greek used *anthropoi* or sometimes *ethnea*, "people."[1] The medieval Venetian traveler, Marco Polo (1254–1324) went all the way from Italy to China by way of the "Silk Road," and came back via Southeast Asia and the Indian peninsula. However, when he wrote about his travels and the people he encountered, he never used anything that could correspond to the concept of "race."[2] The same thing was true for the even more widely traveled medieval Arabic geographer, Ibn Battuta (1304–1377), who not only duplicated Marco Polo's west-to-east span but added a perspective that ran from the Atlantic coast of Europe southwards across the Sahara to Timbuktu in sub-Saharan Africa.[3]

The big change in the perception of how people differ from place to place came in the Renaissance. Prior to that time, travelers such as Herodotus, Marco Polo, and Ibn Battuta got from one place to another over land on foot or on horseback, one day at a time, and what they saw was the gradation of one population into the next without any discernible break. That means of seeing the world changed dramatically in the Renaissance because of the development of ocean-going ships that could set off from the shores of one continent and arrive at those of another without seeing anything in between. As a result, the sailors and their passengers perceived a world in which the people at the port of embarkation and the port of arrival appeared categorically different.

The marine technology and navigational skills that made such long-distance voyaging possible accompanied the emergence of the Renaissance in Europe and made possible the feats of Christopher Columbus, Vasco da Gama, and others. It also meant that European perceptions of other people were of categorical distinctions instead of the borderless gradations that were seen by Herodotus and his medieval successors. The modern phenomena of the jet plane and the television camera have simply reinforced the view that the world is inhabited by categorically distinct people. If this categorical picture of human differences was a construct that emerged from the circumstances of Renaissance Europe, it was still largely a vicarious view since it did not arise from the direct perceptions of the majority of the populace but rather from the second-hand reports of those who had actually been the travelers.

All that changed as a result of European colonization of other parts of the globe, in particular the western hemisphere. Colonization involved the actual movement of people from one relatively small segment of the world, western Europe, to other places such as the southern tip of Africa, Australia, and particularly to the western hemisphere. The western Europeans were then installed immediately adjacent to the indigenous populations whom they perceived as being categorically distinct.

The western hemisphere was particularly important in the construction of this categorical view of human differences because the Europeans had come from a relatively restricted region at the northwestern edge of the Old World. As it happened, the Native Americans with whom they came in contact had also come from a relatively restricted area but at the northeastern edge of the Old World, although no one knew this at the time of first contact. As near as we can tell, the movement of northeast Asians into the New World does not go back much more than 15,000 years, and that is not a long enough stretch of time for significant biological differentiation to have taken place. There is no gradation in skin pigment among the Native Americans from the Arctic to the equator—unlike virtually all of the continuously occupied parts of the Old World. European immigrants, wherever they went in the western hemisphere, perceived the indigenous people as being categorically distinct from them in essentially the same sort of way.[4]

Subsequently, the European-derived population imported slaves by the thousands from a relatively restricted section of West Africa. The western hemisphere, then, presents a picture of people from three separate portions of the Old World, artificially brought together, and left to contemplate the meaning of their perceived distinctions. As such, it is the worst possible model to use in an effort to make sense out of the normal circumstances of human biological variation. At the same time, the issue of the meaning of those differences had an immediacy that was true for no other large segment of the world. Such has become the unwitting power that America has upon the way the world thinks about things that the concept of "race" that was reified by the circumstances of the settling of the western hemisphere is now being accepted as a matter of course in many parts of the world—China for example—where it had not previously existed.

THE BIOLOGICAL NATURE OF HUMAN VARIATION

Curiously enough it is the biological part of anthropology that has been slow to accept the implications of the previous section.[5] Actually, the realization that human populations grade into each other without break and that "race" is a completely arbitrary appellation was articulated before the outbreak of World War II,[6] and this was the basis for the approach taken by the late Ashley Montagu in his most significant contribution, *Man's Most Dangerous Myth: The Fallacy of Race*.[7] This was an important first step in showing that the concept of "race" has no biological basis, but there was one more development that was necessary before that realization could be nailed down. This was the development and application of the concept of "cline," defined as "a gradation in measurable characters."[8]

Ironically, although that idea was proposed by Julian Huxley—one of the two who influenced Ashley Montagu to realize that the concept of "race" was biologically indefensible—Huxley never fully realized why the treatment of clines provided the final demonstration of the nonexistence of that category. This was because he lacked the information demonstrating that clines are distributed without any relationship to each other in a species without reproductive boundaries. In the decade after Ashley Montagu's book was published, studies in field biology involving deer mice, leopard frogs, butterflies, red-eyed towhees, the American marten, and others showed that the traits under separate genetic control within each species had distributions that were completely unrelated to each other. Early in the 1950s, this led to the demonstration that the category of *subspecies* simply could not be used for forms that were reproductively continuous over large areas.[9]

Within another decade, it was realized that, since *Homo sapiens* also is a continuously distributed species without reproductive barriers between adjacent groups, the same logic should apply to the nature of human variation. This led one biological anthropologist, Frank Livingstone, to declare that "There are no races, there are only clines."[10] He had come to this understanding by noting that the distribution of hemoglobin S, the cause of sickle-cell anemia when present in the homozygous (SS) condition, is related to the distribution of a particular kind of malaria. When present in the heterozygous condition (AS), it conveys an ability to survive that particular form of malaria.[11] The distribution of the gene for hemoglobin S, however, is completely unrelated to the distribution of skin color, and if one tries to combine the manifestations of both in a single region, one can make biological sense of neither one. Add a third trait to the picture with a distribution unrelated to the others, and the pattern made by the intersection of those genetically separate traits becomes completely senseless. Adding further traits simply erases all indications of any pattern whatsoever. The only way to understand the biological meaning of the distribution of those traits is to treat the distribution of each one separately and compare it to the distribution of the selective force to which it represents a response.[12]

SKIN COLOR

At this point, it will be instructive to look at the distributions of a few human traits that are inherited in straight-forward fashion and for which there is enough information to build up a world-wide picture. Actually I am going to restrict the portrayal to distributions in the Old World since the western hemisphere has not been inhabited long enough for many adaptive traits such as tooth size and skin color to have developed much in the way of differential gradients. The first such trait to be considered is skin color since it is so closely linked in the minds of the public with what is assumed to be "race." Skin color is produced by the pigment melanin, which blocks the penetration of the most damaging part of the ultraviolet component of sunlight. In high doses, ultraviolet rays with wave lengths between 280 and 320 millimicrons (UV-B) can penetrate to the lower levels of the epidermis and can contribute to the development of skin cancer. There is obvious survival value to the presence of melanin in the skin of the inhabitants of the tropics.[13]

The significance of maintaining epidermal melanin away from the tropics is of less evident importance, and it is not surprising to find that skin pigment tends to decrease in proportion to the distance of a given population from the equator. The reason for increased skin pigmentation in the tropics is clear enough, but why it should reduce to the north and the south is not agreed upon. One theory has it that the reduction allows enough UV penetration so that Vitamin D can be synthesized. Heavy pigmentation could lead to Vitamin D deficiency and rickets during growth in areas such as the north where the annual UV dosage is far less than in the tropics. Others have noted that enough Vitamin D is synthesized and stored for further use during the summer no matter what the amount of skin pigment so that there is no particular advantage to depigmentation in the north. Another theory suggests that when selection for skin pigment is relaxed, as it is in the north where the chances of UV-induced cancer are small no matter how little pigment there is in the skin, the accumulation of chance mutations affecting pigment production will result in an eventual failure to produce a full tropical amount of epidermal melanin.[14] The distribution of human skin pigment in the Old World is shown in Figure 16-1 (on page 244).[15]

As can be seen, there is a general association of skin color differences with latitude, but it is far from perfect. The maximum pigmentation occurs among tropical populations who have long been resident at the latitudes where they are now found. The greatest amount of depigmentation occurs where people have resided farthest away from the tropics for the longest period of time. The slightly lesser amount of depigmentation of people in the north temperate portions of Eastern Asia may be because they have not been resident at that latitude for quite so long as their counterparts at the northwestern edges of human habitation. Certainly the lack of fully tropical amounts of pigmentation of people in the tropics at the southeastern edge of the continental Old World—Southeast Asia—is because the current inhabitants have only come south from temperate latitudes within the past few thousand years.[16]

I have already mentioned that there is no pigment cline in the New World, so it is apparent that the 15,000 years or so that the western hemisphere has been occupied is not enough time for a pigment gradient to have developed in place. In Australia there actually is a north-south pigment cline with the darkest skin occurring in the tropical north. That gradient, however, is nowhere near so marked as the gradient from the Equator in Africa to the southern tip of the continent, and it is apparent that the 60,000 years that

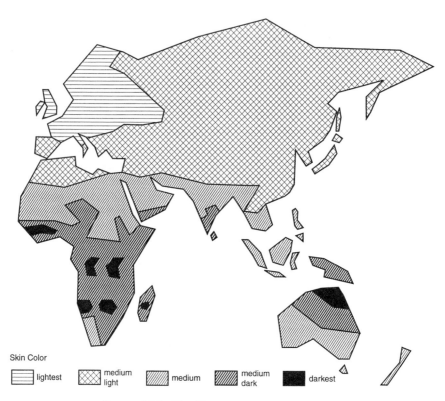

Skin Color

▦ lightest	▨ medium light	▨ medium	▨ medium dark	■ darkest

**FIGURE 16-1   THE DISTRIBUTION OF VARIATION
IN INTENSITY OF HUMAN SKIN COLOR IN THE OLD WORLD**

Australia has been occupied is long enough to have produced the beginnings of a north-south pigment cline, but nowhere near long enough to have produced the kind of differences that you get ranging north from the African tropics to Spain, a latitude change comparable to the tropics to southern Australia. The time needed to have produced a spectrum such as that from West Africa to Spain would have required nearly 200,000 years, which is more than three times as long as Australia has been occupied.[17]

TOOTH SIZE

If we are keenly sensitive to differences in human skin pigment, we are less so to differences in the size of the human dentition. Yes, we are aware that Africans tend to have larger teeth than Europeans, but it is not the uppermost impression in our minds when we compare the physical appearance of people from both places. If it has taken nearly 200,000 years to produce the differences in skin color that we see in the world today, the modern condition represented by the teeth we have has taken over 100,000 years to produce. No one has teeth as large as the common human ancestor had 130,000 years ago, but the reductions that have taken place during the past 100,000 years have proceeded faster in some places than in others. Throughout most of the two million years of the Pleistocene, our ancestors ate things as they found them, namely raw. When teeth wore out, that was it and life came to an end as it does today for aged elephants whose last teeth have worn to useless stumps. Now, of course, we cook things to mush or puree them in machines that reduce things to drinkable consistency. In the past, however, teeth had to last a life-time, and they had to have enough durability to reduce the toughest of un-cooked food substances to swallowable consistency.

Starting in the glacial period before the most recent one, that is, over 200,000 years ago, the control of fire enabled people to become permanent inhabitants of the temperate zone. Part of that use of fire of course was to keep people warm. Unlike wolves, bears, horses, deer, and the like, people are restricted by the tropical physiology they have inherited from their primate ancestors, so survival in the temperate zone in the face of increasing glacial chill was only possible with the warmth provided by clothing and the hearth. As creatures de-pendent on the products of the chase, there was the added problem of eating something that was left over from a recent hunt when it had frozen solid. The Pleistocene cow, or auroch, was quite a large animal, and it was unlikely that a given band of human hunters could have consumed the whole thing at a sin-gle sitting. A day later, its icy remains would have defied mastication without some remedial treatment. The answer was the development of cooking.

While the control of fire had become a human universal well over 200,000 years ago, its use in the preparation of food was essential for survival in the northern stretches of human habitation (especially as glacial conditions in-tensified), in a fashion quite unlike that practiced farther south. This has been referred to as "obligatory cooking."[18] While this did indeed make it possible to eat what had previously been frozen, it had another incidental consequence. It meant that the food being eaten required less chewing before it could be swallowed, and this in turn meant that there was a reduction in the amount of tooth substance required to last a person throughout life. Relaxation in the selection maintaining tooth size meant that mutations affecting dental di-mensions could occur with impunity, and, since the average mutation inter-feres with the development of the structure it controls, that structure—simple tooth substance in this case—can be predicted to reduce in the course of time. The argument is the same as the argument for the reduction of skin pigment among those people who have longest resided in areas where the selective forces maintaining skin color are less than in those regions subjected to the maximum amount of ultraviolet radiation. Both skin color and tooth size re-duction are examples of evolution by entropy.

The maximum amount of dental reduction in the world, then, should occur in those areas where cooking has longest been used for the preparation of food. The archaeological record shows that this first occurred in a stretch running from the Middle East to the Atlantic shores of Europe, and it is not surprising to realize that the people in that area today, and their relatives just to the north, have the smallest teeth relative to body size of any of the peoples of the world. A simple version of the world distribution of human tooth size can be seen in Figure 16-2.[19]

Eventually the advantages of cooking spread elsewhere in the world. The spread to the south was not needed to thaw previously frozen food, but it was discovered that it made it possible to use as food something that had turned bad by being left out in the tropical heat for several days. It even made it possible to eat things that would have been indigestible raw: wheat, rice, yams, and the like, thus opening up a vast realm of potential foodstuffs that had previously been unavailable for human sustenance.

Cooking got into Australia last, and it is no surprise to discover that aboriginal Australian (non-European) teeth are closer to the size of the average human Pleistocene ancestor than are those of any other people in the world, and the farther south in Australia one goes, the less reduced are the teeth. Finally, the invention of pottery in the heart of those areas that first developed

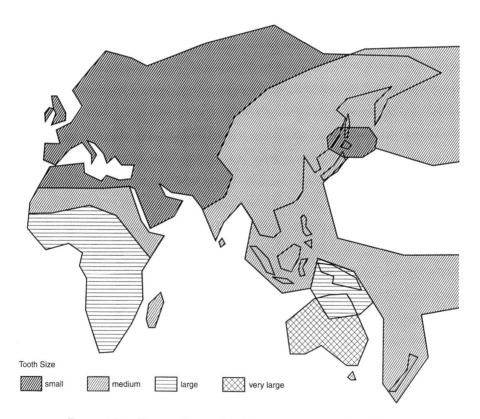

Tooth Size

small   medium   large   very large

FIGURE 16-2   HUMAN TOOTH SIZE DIFFERENCES IN THE OLD WORLD

agriculture completely eliminated the selective forces maintaining any tooth substance at all. Yes, it is nice to be able to chew what we refer to as "toothsome" morsels, but, in the absence of teeth, sustenance can be ingested in the form of soups that need no chewing whatsoever. The smallest teeth in the world today occur among those in the area where pottery was first invented and has been in use for the longest period of time—the Near East.

SICKLE-CELL ANEMIA

We can perceive differences in skin color and, to a lesser extent, tooth size, but there are many ways in which humans differ that we cannot see directly. Amongst these are differences in hemoglobin, a molecule whose principal function is delivering oxygen from the lungs to the tissues where it is used for metabolic purposes, and then taking the product of metabolism, carbon dioxide, back to the lungs where it is released into the atmosphere in exhaled breath. In addition to its primary role in oxygen transport, the hemoglobin molecule can affect the red blood cell that contains it.

One inherited hemoglobin variant, hemoglobin S, will tend to crystallize after it gives up its oxygen, and the crystals align themselves within the surrounding cytoplasm of the red blood cell as long stiff rods. These can change the shape of the softly rounded blood cell to an angular pointed affair that reminded microscopists early in the past century of miniature sickles: the famous "sickle-cells" of sickle-cell anemia. Those stiff, sickle-shaped cells get stuck in the capillaries at the peripheries of the circulatory system preventing blood from flowing through. The body, in response, dissolves the cells to restore circulation at the expense of the loss of those sickled cells, and the loss of red blood cells is what constitutes anemia—thus, sickle-cell anemia. The process also dumps immature malaria parasites into the plasma where they are sought out and destroyed by disease-fighting white blood cells before they can spread their infection to other red blood cells. This then reduces malaria although it does not eliminate it from the system.

The phenomenon of sickle-cell anemia was first identified by clinicians in the United States and noted to occur amongst Americans of African ancestry. Inevitably, sickle-cell anemia was regarded as an African disease and it is still thought of by many physicians and the public at large as an African "racial" marker. As it happens, although much of the sickle-cell anemia in America did come over with the Africans who were brought in as slaves, the genes that were responsible for the presence of that condition in Africa were not of African origin, ultimately having been brought in from the Middle East by traders down the African east coast or by caravan routes across the Sahara.[20]

Sickle-cell anemia is a single gene trait, and one needs to inherit the gene for hemoglobin S from each parent in order to show a full-scale manifestation of the phenomenon. Such a person is homozygous, which means having a double dose of the S gene (the SS condition), and that person has greatly reduced chances for survival. A person with one gene for normal hemoglobin and one gene for abnormal hemoglobin is a heterozygote exhibiting the AS condition. A homozygous normal is AA. In spite of the fact that the sufferers from sickle-cell anemia tend to have a sharply reduced life span and usually do not have children, the frequency of the gene is maintained from generation to generation in certain parts of the world. The reason is that the AS condition allows its possessors to survive attacks from a particularly mean kind of malaria. They are not immune to malaria, but they have a much greater chance of surviving it than do AA people.

As it happened, when West Africans adopted agriculture a couple of thousand years ago, the changes in settlement patterns and the hewing out of farm lands from what had been forest altered conditions to such an extent that that particularly noxious kind of malaria flourished and became a major threat to human survival. When hemoglobin S was introduced, then, it achieved relatively high frequencies in a relatively short period of time among the people who already lived there. Figure 16-3 shows the distribution of the gene for hemoglobin S in the middle of the twentieth century.[21] Like the distribution of skin color and tooth size, it follows the distribution of the selective force to which it represents an adaptation, but that selective force does not have the

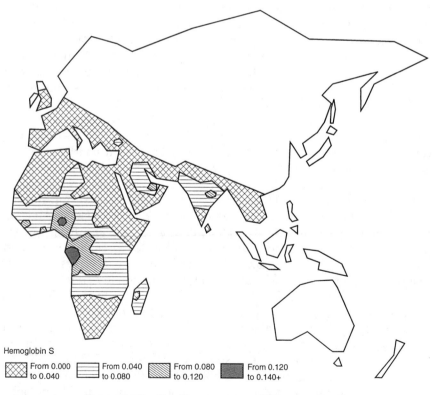

Hemoglobin S

From 0.000 to 0.040	From 0.040 to 0.080	From 0.080 to 0.120	From 0.120 to 0.140+

FIGURE 16-3   THE DISTRIBUTION OF HEMOGLOBIN S

same distribution as the selective forces that control those other traits, and none of them coincide with either a given locale or what constitutes "race" in the popular sense of the term. There are many other forms of abnormal hemoglobin, and some of them are systematically distributed in conjunction with the distribution of other kinds of malaria.

THE ABO BLOOD GROUP SYSTEM

The final clinally distributed trait I am going to consider is another one that we cannot see but which we all know about, namely the ABO blood group system. This is controlled by three genes at a single locus found on the long arm of chromosome 9. Every person inherits one gene from each parent. If one has an A from both parents or an A from one and an O from the other, one tests as A since O is recessive. Likewise, whether one is BB or BO, one tests as B since B is also dominant over O. If one has an A and a B, one tests as AB. To test as "O," one needs to be homozygous for the O gene, namely, OO. This is all very well known since it is vital information for blood transfusions. O is the universal donor and can be given to people with any of the other genes,

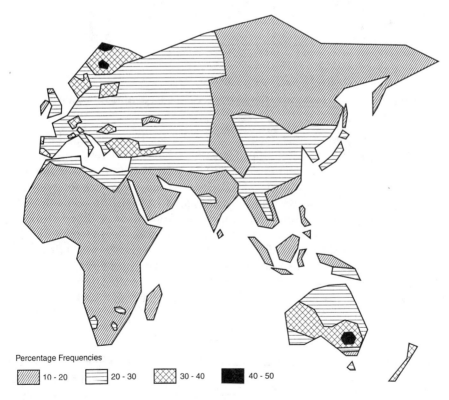

Percentage Frequencies

10 - 20   20 - 30   30 - 40   40 - 50

FIGURE 16-4 THE PERCENTAGE DISTRIBUTION
OF THE GENE FOR BLOOD GROUP A IN THE ABO SYSTEM

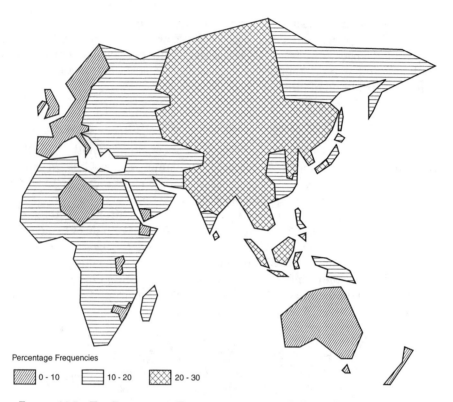

Percentage Frequencies

⬚ 0 - 10   ⬚ 10 - 20   ⬚ 20 - 30

FIGURE 16-5   THE PERCENTAGE DISTRIBUTION OF THE B GENE IN THE ABO SYSTEM

but neither A nor B can be given to an O individual. This is essential medical information, but there has been much less interest in why there are differences in the ABO system in the first place. There has been some suggestion that the different genes have something to do with the resistance or susceptibility to different diseases, but this is not well worked out. The system is inherited in simple and straightforward fashion, and the distributions of the A, B, and O alleles (i.e., genes that fit at the same locus on the chromosome) are well known, as shown in Figure 16-4 (on page 249), Figure 16-5, and Figure 16-6.[22] Once again, the distributions are evidently completely unrelated to the distributions of the traits plotted in Figures 16-1 through 16-3, and only confusion would result from having to force them all into a single interpretive framework.

REGIONAL FEATURES

One could present many more traits in the format offered earlier, and none of them would show the same kind of distribution. Likewise, none of them can be associated with a particular region of the world. Yes, there are latitudinal changes in features such as skin color, but that is not the same as restricting a given feature to a particular segment of geography. That is because the selective forces

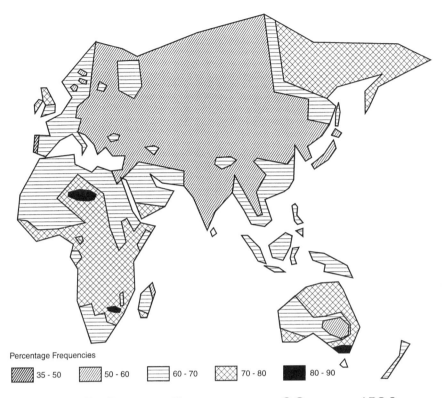

Percentage Frequencies

35 - 50   50 - 60   60 - 70   70 - 80   80 - 90

FIGURE 16-6   THE PERCENTAGE DISTRIBUTION OF THE O GENE IN THE ABO SYSTEM

that govern their distributions are not themselves restricted by local geography. However, there are human features that can be associated with particular regions. We can recognize particular nuances of cheek bone and eye opening formation as recalling the inhabitants of the Far East, or ear shape in Africa, or aspects in the shape of the nose as being peculiarly characteristic of Europe. Unlike the traits dealt with previously, however, there is no adaptive value in those nuances of eye, ear, and nose morphology. The only thing we can say about them is that they tend to resemble what can be seen in the regions from which the ancestors of those people came.

It seems evident that if traits can be identified with a particular region, then they have no adaptive significance, and no regional manifestation is either better or worse than any other. Clearly such regional traits are inherited, but they are just the inherited nuances of what was there and nothing else. At most this constitutes what I have labeled "family resemblance writ large."[23] As Marco Polo and Ibn Battuta recognized, those resemblances grade from one region to another without any break and are unrelated to survival capabilities. It is only when we see representatives out of context that we categorize them with "racial" labels, and these can only prevent us from a full understanding of the nature of human biological variation on a world-wide scale.

NOTES

1. Herodotus, *The Histories*, 4 vols., with an English translation by A. D. Godley (Cambridge: Loeb Classical Library, Harvard University Press, 1920).

2. Marco Polo, *The Travels of Marco Polo, the Venetian*, the translation of Marsden revised, with a selection of his notes, Thomas Wright, ed. (London: H. G. Bohm, 1854).

3. Mohammed, In Allah Ibn Battuta, *Travels in Asia and Africa*, translated by H. A. R. Gibb (New York: R. McBride, 1929).

4. C. Loring Brace and A. Russell Nelson, "The Peopling of the Americas: Anglo Stereotypes and Native American Realities," *General Anthropology* 5 (1999): 1–7.

5. C. Loring Brace, "The Roots of the Race Concept in American Physical Anthropology," in Frank Spencer, ed., *A History of American Physical Anthropology, 1930–1980* (New York: Academic Press, 1982), pp. 11–29; C. Loring Brace, "Region Does Not Mean Race: Reality vs. Convention in Forensic Identification," *Journal of Forensic Sciences* 40 (1995): 171–175.

6. Julian S. Huxley and Alfred C. Haddon, *We Europeans: A Survey of "Racial" Problems* (London: Jonathan Cape, 1935).

7. Ashley Montagu, *Man's Most Dangerous Myth: The Fallacy of Race* (New York: Columbia University Press, 1942).

8. Julian S. Huxley, "Clines: An Auxiliary Taxonomic Principle," *Nature* 142 (1948): 219–220.

9. E. O. Wilson and William L. Brown, Jr., "The Subspecies Concept and its Taxonomic Application," *Systematic Zoology* 2 (1953): 97–111.

10. Frank B. Livingstone, "On the Non-Existence of Human Races," *Current Anthropology* 3 (1962): 279.

11. Frank B. Livingstone, "Anthropological Implications of Sickle Cell Gene Distribution in West Africa," *American Anthropologist* 60 (1958): 533–562.

12. C. Loring Brace, "A Non-Racial Approach toward the Understanding of Human Diversity," in Ashley Montagu, ed., *The Concept of Race* (New York: The Free Press of Glencoe, 1964), pp. 103–152; C. Loring Brace, "A Four-Letter Word Called 'Race'," in Larry T. Reynolds and Leonard Lieberman, eds., *Race and Other Misadventures: Essays in Honor of Ashley Montagu in His Ninetieth Year* (Dix Hills, NY: General Hall, 1996), pp. 106–141.

13. Ashley H. Robins, *Biological Perspectives on Human Pigmentation* (Cambridge, England: Cambridge University Press, 1991); Nina Jablonski and George Chaplin, "The Evolution of Human Skin Coloration," *Journal of Human Evolution* 39 (2000): 57–106.

14. The Vitamin D argument is outlined in Jablonski and Chaplin, see Note 13. The effects of mutations under conditions of relaxed selection are presented by Brace in "A Four-Letter Word Called 'Race'," see Note 12.

15. Figure 16-1 is updated from Figure 3 in "A Four-Letter Word Called 'Race'," see Note 12.

16. Charles Higham, *The Archaeology of Mainland Southeast Asia: From 10,000 B.C. to the Fall of Angkor* (New York: Cambridge University Press, 1989); Matthew Spriggs, "The Dating of the Island Southeast Asian Neolithic: An Attempt at Chronometric Hygiene and Linguistic Correlation," *Antiquity* 63 (1989): 587–613.

17. Maciej Henneberg and C. Loring Brace, "Human Skin Color as a Measure of Time in situ," *American Journal of Physical Anthropology Supplement* 30 (2000): 177.

18. C. Loring Brace, *The Stages of Human Evolution*, 5th ed. (Englewood Cliffs, NJ: Prentice Hall, 1995).
19. A selection of the data used to construct Figure 16-2 is summarized in C. Loring Brace, Shelley L. Smith and Kevin D. Hunt, "What Big Teeth You Had Grandma! Human Tooth Size, Past and Present," in Marc A. Kelley and Clark S. Larsen, eds., *Advances in Dental Anthropology* (New York: Wiley-Liss, 1991), pp. 33–57.
20. Frank B. Livingstone, "Who Gave Whom Hemoglobin S: The Use of Restriction Site Haplotype Variation for the Interpretation of the Bs Gene," *American Journal of Human Biology* 3 (1989): 289–302.
21. The distribution pictured is adapted from Walter F. Bodmer and Luigi Lucca Cavalli-Sforza, *Genetics, Evolution and Man* (San Francisco: Freeman, 1976).
22. Figures 16-4, 16-5, and 16-6 are simplified from the information provided by A. E. Mourant, Ada Kopec, and Kazimiera Domaniewska-Sobczak, *The ABO Blood Groups: Comprehensive Tables and Maps of World Distribution* (Springfield, IL: C. C. Thomas, 1958).
23. In "A Four-Letter Word Called 'Race,'" in Note 12, p. 136, reprinted in C. Loring Brace, *Evolution in an Anthropological View* (Walnut Creek, CA: AltaMira Press, 2000), p. 320.

Suggested Readings

Brace, C. Loring. *The Stages of Human Evolution*, 5th ed. Englewood Cliffs, NJ: Prentice Hall, 1995.
Brace, C. Loring. *Evolution in an Anthropological View*. Walnut Creek, CA: AltaMira Press, 2000.
Hannaford, Ivan. *Race: The History of an Idea in the West*. Baltimore: Johns Hopkins University Press, 1996. The extraordinary recency and subjectivity of the concept of "race" is eloquently documented.
Montagu, Ashley. *Man's Most Dangerous Myth: The Fallacy of Race*, 6th ed. Walnut Creek, CA: AltaMira Press, 1997. An update of a classic in the field and the last word on the subject by its original author, also available in a college edition.

PALEOANTHROPOLOGY AND LIFE HISTORY, AND LIFE HISTORY OF A PALEOANTHROPOLOGIST

TIMOTHY G. BROMAGE

One of the few truly vivid childhood memories I have is being taken by my mother and father to hear a lecture by Louis S. B. Leakey in Riverside, California, in 1964. It took place in a gymnasium and we sat on the first row in the bleachers furthest from the lectern and the screen. My neck was getting tired from having to look up and to the left at what seemed to be an endless concatenation of images of stone tools that, to me, looked to be all the same and made out of the same stuff. These tools were part of the human story told from a place called Olduvai Gorge. Perhaps this memory remains because of the something like five dollar per person charge for tickets, compared to what was then a twenty-five-cent Saturday matinee. However, though they seemed so far away, the man and the images thrown up by the projector seemed bigger than life, and I stayed awake for the whole thing.

For thirty years the significance of this moment escaped me until just now. Why did my parents take me? What motivated them to make the long drive and spend all that money? I now know that my parents were unwitting partners in one of life's mysteries, the laying down of one more landmark by which we might see our way through life on a map already sighted, surveyed and drawn in our infancy. Is it a coincidence that I find myself at this writing moment at the Leakeys' dining table at the Olduvai Camp overlooking the gorge in the hues of a setting sun? That lecture thirty years ago was about me.

While the subsequent mapping out of a career can take many turns into many different subdisciplines, for me it would include a series of forays into the microscopic realm of bones and teeth as well as fieldwork on the role of habitat and geography during the early stages of human evolution. What kind of career is this? Like many careers in anthropology, it has no real name. If pushed to recognize my major field, I would have to say *paleoanthropology* because every thread, in one way or another, is stitched into this general interest. My interest was facilitated by an eclectic undergraduate preparation at the California State University at Sonoma that comprised a mixture of physical anthropology, biology, paleontology, and geology, and that engendered a certain interdisciplinary perspective—the stuff of which paleoanthropology is made.

Though attracted to paleoanthropology during my graduate career at the University of Toronto, I was not comfortable with traditional descriptive morphological approaches to early hominids (studies of their features, shapes and sizes, that is, *characters*). My supervisor, Becky Sigmon, helped me to approach problems that were more "process-oriented" and that required explanations about how a character developed during growth and development (ontogeny) and about how characters combined with other characters to reflect a specific habitat and niche for early hominids. For reasons unknown to me, but probably having to do with the preponderance of cranial and facial remains of early hominids, I concentrated my early studies on the growth and development of the early hominid face.

I wanted to know something about how these early ancestors grew up, their ontogeny. Specifically, I wanted to know how (and then later *why* in respect to ecological studies) the shape of their faces changed from infancy, through adolescence, and into adulthood. This was fantasy because the state of the art in morphology was not up to the task of providing mechanistic solutions to this problem. Frustration alternating with elation and failure alternating with success would characterize the next some years. This was treacherous and uncharted scientific inquiry and it meant that much background work would have to be undertaken to make possible the main task. But I wanted to contribute something of a dynamic nature to studies of early hominids. The one laboratory in the world up to this task was the Hard Tissue Research Unit at University College London, where Alan Boyde and Sheila Jones had the techniques and the experience to help me see this pioneering study through. Ultimately, I was able to uncover some of the dynamics of facial growth in our ancestors and I saw that many of our earliest forebears were much more ape-like than anthropologists had come to believe.

Bones grow and change shape through a combination of surface deposition and resorption processes. The jaws, for instance, may become more and more protruding (prognathic) during growth if bone deposition on the forward facing surfaces is combined with resorption on the opposite surfaces of the bone resulting in a drifting forward of the jaws. These processes—deposition and resorption—can be readily identified with the scanning electron microscope (SEM) by characteristic bone surface features. In principle, therefore, if you survey the surfaces of all the hominid youngsters' faces, you should be able to describe a species-specific *pattern* of areas of deposition and areas of resorption that occurs during the growth period. From this pattern you could then infer the directions of growth over the faces—those that are becoming more protruding, and those that are retreating. In practice, however, inferring the pattern is trickier than that.

For a year I worked on developing a non-destructive technique for making high resolution replicas (casts with surface detail to 0.0001 of 1 millimeter!) of large complex surfaces such as facial skeletons. A liquid rubber-like material is spread like cake frosting, allowed to harden, removed from the fossil, and sprayed with an epoxy. The epoxy dries into a thin hard shell, a perfect replica of the original, suitable for studying with the SEM.

However, the prospect loomed that these early hominid faces, having possibly been dragged around by scavengers, washed downstream to the lake's edge or the mouth of a cave, and then covered by tons of sediment, might have suffered a little damage over the millions of years! The combination of those processes threatened to remove, except in the most favorable of circumstances, all the subtle surface signs of bone resorption and deposition that I needed to see with the SEM. So it was time to find out. For one year I visited laboratories in South and East Africa, examining, photographing, cleaning and replicating all the immature hominid faces then available. These included the Taung child, the first early hominid found in Africa, named as *Australopithecus africanus* by Raymond Dart in 1925. Probably the most famous of all hominid specimens, the Taung child would eventually be the carrier of the unexpected message I would have for my anthropological colleagues.

The day finally arrived for my first peek at the surface remodeling of my hominid specimens. There I was, perched in front of the SEM, about to witness something of the actual development of a multimillion-year-old child's face. I looked, and I looked, and I saw nothing. The problem was not with my techniques. The problem, it seemed, was that I had replicated, to a very high resolution, nothing worth looking at! The bones were, as I had feared, damaged to the extent that none looked anything like what I had been trained to recognize as a developing fresh bone surface—those forming and resorbing. It was necessary to spend the next year experimenting with the many agents that might be obscuring the bone remodeling features I was looking for. This has been called microscopic taphonomy, looking for the patterns of possible *microscopic damage* caused by weathering and transport, being contained in a sediment, and fossil preparation techniques. Thus, in numerous controlled experiments, I abraded bone surfaces so that I might be able to look through the damage to see the biological information underneath. Gradually it was possible to separate damage from biology, and one year later I looked at the hominids again. To my great relief, I could see the remodeling and growth patterns clearly.

Interpretations of the earliest hominids—the australopithecines—have swung back and forth through the decades, sometimes emphasizing their ape-like characteristics, sometimes their humanlike characteristics. By the early 1980s the humanness interpretation was in full swing. Caught up in this, I expected to see something of the human facial remodeling pattern in Taung. Unexpectedly the remodeling pattern for Taung was typical of a monkey or ape—it was prognathic; that is, all the forwardly directed parts of the face were depositional, not partly resorptive as in modern humans, which encouraged the development of forward-jutting jaws in Taung. This was true for *Australopithecus afarensis,* the earliest recognized hominid, its descendant *Australopithecus africanus,* and even *Homo habilis.* The pattern of remodeling for the *Paranthropus* species (sometimes called the robust australopithecines), however, indicated areas of resorption over front parts of the jaws, and this meant that growth of the face of *Paranthropus* emphasized a more downward facial growth direction contributing to the flatter and more humanlike face observed for the paranthropines.

This work on bone was complemented by studies of the rate and pattern of tooth development because we knew that such studies could tell us much more about the developmental biology of early hominids. I teamed up with Chris Dean, also in Alan Boyde's lab at University College London, to look at growth lines in tooth enamel of several early hominid species and we were able to show that early hominid rates of development were more apelike. They had much shorter growth and development periods than those of modern humans, contrary to what had been previously thought. In addition, Holly Smith of the University of Michigan has recently drawn attention to the close relationships between life history variables for all primates (variables such as adult brain size, body size, and features of dental development). These relationships have independently demonstrated that the durations of life history periods must have been more apelike in early hominids than in modern humans. The response to this new paradigm was so powerful that we were motivated (away, in fact, from our real interests) to spend the next several years conducting further tests of our experimental assumptions.

One such assumption was that the lines in enamel called "cross-striations" formed in an incremental manner, that is, one per day, called a circadian rhythm, or periodicity. It was further assumed that an average of seven cross-striations accrued between adjacent Striae of Retzius (another incremental growth line in enamel that is much more pronounced than the cross-striations). These assumptions were useful because we noted that these Striae of Retzius of the internal enamel, being very robust in relation to cross-striations, regularly emerged to the incisor enamel surface as perikymata, a surface growth feature resembling a microscopic valley that courses around the tooth in a band (look closely at your two upper or lower central incisors and see the faint lines running around them). When these perikymata are counted their numbers could thus be used to calibrate crown formation times (that is, an estimate of the time it took to form the crown), other dental developmental events and the ages at death for some early hominid species. Despite substantial circumstantial evidence that the assumptions about enamel circadian rhythmicity were correct, critics noted a lack of experimental proof.

So our searches for answers to questions about the past would require experimental biology studies of the present. It happened that there was a collection of bones and teeth of pregnant pigtailed macaque (*Macaca nemestrina*) females and their infants that had been sequentially labeled at recorded intervals with fluorescent substances. If observed in thin sections of the bones and teeth with ultraviolet light by a conventional light microscope, these substances would reveal the developing surface (at the times of administration of the labels) by colored lines. (It is for this reason that children treated frequently with tetracycline antibiotics sometimes grow up with yellowed teeth.) In the meantime, many other colleagues began to work on related problems, and the paradigm continued to receive support. Studies verified that on average there were indeed seven or eight increments between each Stria of Retzius, and thus each perikymata. As it sometimes happens in science, while finally proving that enamel did indeed grow in a daily manner, we discovered that Japanese researchers had reported similar experimental work in the 1930s and 1940s.

Research in paleoanthropology often involves work in the laboratory. But when most people think of paleoanthropology, they think of the more romantic setting in the field where the hominid discoveries are made. So from the cool and dark room of the SEM my colleagues and I emerge once each year into the hot light of the African tropics and subtropics. Indeed, paleoanthropological research today is quite interdisciplinary. This means that all possible field and laboratory aspects of the geosphere and biosphere are examined in order to paint a more complete picture of the past. There are scientists who study the overall structure of the landscape or cave setting, how it formed, how sediments and fossils were accumulated, and how old these geological features and fossils may be. Others specialize in the anatomy and evolution of certain animals or plants, while others piece together the environmental setting. Archaeologists study any cultural evidence. These interdisciplinary studies of the past are often complemented by studies of contemporary geological and biological processes and by research on animal behavior and ecology.

In the early 1980s I teamed up with Friedemann Schrenk of the Hessisches Landesmuseum in Darmstadt, Germany, to do something a little different. By the vagaries of nature all of the early hominid discoveries have been made in either eastern or southern Africa, but not in between. The geographic center between them, along Lake Malawi, harbors Late Pliocene sediments called Chiwondo Beds. We had the idea that if one went to a place between the known early hominid localities then it should be possible to investigate how the two regions were related to one another. Research about such a place could then say something about *continental* Africa instead of only one site or one region. So, was this area in between, that is, southeast Africa, a unique region all unto itself, was it part of a continuous distribution of African faunas (animals) and floras (plants) from the south to the north, or was it like a Pony Express station whose stationmaster kept logs of which hominids and other animals went where and at what time?

This turns out to be a basic problem in ecology concerning habitats (the environment in which an organism lives) and niches (the biological roles that an organism has in its habitat). Relating back to our questions about southeast Africa, were the habitats of the region unique, were they continuously distributed around Africa, or did habitats change and were hominids and other animals forced to adapt and perhaps shift themselves to other parts of the continent? And how must early hominid niches have changed if their habitats changed? Thus one can potentially say a great deal about human evolution by studying things other than the hominid fossils themselves.

We hypothesized that the ecological zone of southeast Africa, called the Zambesian Ecozone, has most probably been the meeting point for faunas from the north and south since the continents have been in their current positions. The Zambesian Ecozone comprises the woodlands and grasslands of southern Zaire and Tanzania, Angola, Zambia, Malawi, and northern Mozambique and Zimbabwe. It is situated between the *temperate* ecological domain of southern Africa below, and the *tropical* ecological domain of eastern Africa above. We reasoned that while animals able to acquire their resources in more than one domain could have been happy in both eastern and southern Africa, those restricted to more specific habitats might have crossed over this region only when their appropriate vegetation zones shifted location. According to a general theory proposed by Elisabeth Vrba of Yale University, we thought that these vegetation zones were shifting their locations about 2.8 million years ago, at which time cooler and drier conditions prevailed around the world because of the growing polar ice caps. Thus, there should have been a shift of grassland and woodland vegetation zones northward toward the equator if Vrba's theory was correct.

To test these ideas we decided to do fieldwork in Malawi. It took us ten years to collect five hundred fossils. Most of these fossils were isolated teeth, not the whole skulls or partial skeletons of other paleoanthropological projects! But the stationmaster's log at our Pony Express station needs only a tooth to record the passing of the animal it once belonged to, and so after our ten years of surveying in Malawi we felt that our five hundred specimens were sufficient to begin testing our ideas.

When we compared the Chiwondo Beds faunas with those of eastern and southern Africa it was clear that the Malawi Rift belonged largely to the paleoecological domain of eastern Africa. That is, of the animals normally belonging only to eastern or only to southern Africa, the Malawi Rift was dominated by the animals characteristic of eastern Africa. The faunal sample included only a few southern African animals. But the presence of another group of animals had still to be explained. These were the animals shared between eastern and southern Africa. Were they shared because their habitats were shared, or because they could live in many different habitats, or could it be (as we thought) that many animals were recorded as shared because some populations had dispersed from their origins in southern Africa to eastern Africa 2.5 million years ago (consistent with Vrba's theory)? Sure enough, when we looked at the whole African record it was clear that many animals had dispersed from southern to eastern Africa about 2.5 million years ago, suggesting that the vegetation zones which the animals depended upon had drifted northward toward the equator during the Late Pliocene climate change.

Fortunately, after many years of scratching for fossils, we finally found an early hominid mandible to help tell our story. I led the team that day. Early in the morning, as always, I emerged from my tent and sat down on the mat in front to put on my boots. Usually I'm half asleep, but this particular morning I called out to my friends at the breakfast table (how they get up at 5:00 A.M. is beyond me), "This is going to be a great day! I don't know why yet, but it's going to be a great day." Hours later in the field we were finding one antelope tooth after another and, getting a little fed up, I said, "OK, we have enough bovids now ... find me a hominid!" At that moment one of our local survey-ors about ten feet away looked down and there, at his feet, was a beautiful ho-minid mandible. We have attributed this specimen to a species called *Homo rudolfensis*, known mainly from east of Lake Turkana in Kenya and including the famous skull KNM-ER 1470 that is a bit more robustly constructed than *Homo habilis* (which you may be more familiar with). As it turned out, not only do we have this species represented far to the south of its previously known distribution, it may also represent the oldest representative of early *Homo* yet discovered.

The biogeographic significance of this hominid species in the Malawi Rift lay in its association with the eastern African animal group. Remember that during the drying and cooling of global climates about 2.5 million years ago, the southern and more temperate African faunas followed their northward-drifting vegetation zones. But where should the tropical equatorial animals of eastern Africa, including the hominids, go? We think that these animal and ho-minid species stayed in the tropical African ecological domain and either suc-cumbed and became extinct or they became new species. Thus *Homo rudolfensis* may have emerged in tropical Africa as a result of the climatic cooling event that occurred about 2.5 million years ago, and remained there while other an-imals were busy dispersing northward toward the equator.

Furthermore, as it turns out, several anatomical characters of the Malawi mandible share their affinity with *Australopithecus afarensis*, the earliest known hominid species from eastern Africa. We thus have the basis for a scenario of hominid evolution rooted with *Australopithecus afarensis* and compliant with both Vrba's Habitat Theory and the known distributions of early hominids. This scenario is completely new in its approach because it *depends* largely upon what we know about the ecology and deals rather less upon studies of the anatomical characters themselves. Perhaps you can see if the morpholo-gy of early hominids taught to you from the classroom or the textbooks is compatible with the scenario we propose.

The scenario goes like this: The geographic distribution of ancestral pop-ulations of the proto-hominids was broadly constrained to tropical Africa and its tropical forests. Some populations found themselves at the edge of the species distribution to the east along the lush riparian habitats meandering across the rain shadow of the developing African Rift Valley (these *riparian habitats* are the typical tree-lined rivers crossing the more open landscapes in eastern Africa). *Australopithecus afarensis* arose in this *eastern* African tropical ecological domain by approximately four million years ago, maintaining a close connection to and remaining near the broad riparian habitats. Over time the riparian habitats connecting eastern and southern Africa permitted populations to migrate into southern Africa during relatively warm and humid times by three million years ago. This was facilitated by the birth of the ancient Lake Malawi and the penetration of the Malawi Rift and its associated rift habitats into temperate Africa. As *Australopithecus afarensis* dispersed southward it transformed into, first, a geographic variant and, subsequently, into *Australopithecus africanus*.

By approximately 2.8 million years ago cooler and drier conditions prevailed. During the interim between 2.8 and 2.5 million years ago these changing conditions created more extensive open habitats with arid-tolerant vegetation around the remaining relatively lush but narrowed "ribbons" of tree-lined riverine forest. The selective pressures of this habitat change increased the survival of more large-toothed varieties of animals and hominids capable of feeding on tougher fruit and open savanna food items. These pressures were sufficient to result in the evolutionary splitting of *Australopithecus afarensis* into *Paranthropus* (sometimes called robust australopithecines) and *Homo* lineages by about 2.5 million years ago.

The beginning of the *Paranthropus* lineage, represented by *Paranthropus (=Australopithecus) aethiopicus* (you may know this species by one of its more famous representative skulls, the "Black Skull" KNM-WT 17000), maintained a reliance on fruit resources in the riverine part of its habitat, particularly during the dry season, but it was equally adept at grinding on its molar teeth those tough and hard food items it now required from the open habitats. Over time this lineage adapted itself more fully to the open part of its habitat and became more facially robust and large-toothed in order to efficiently process the tougher, more durable vegetation of the savanna. This evolved taxon, *Paranthropus boisei*, probably never left its ancestral connection to the more closed features of its environment, however, as these habitats would continue to provide essential protection, sleeping localities, and some foods.

Homo rudolfensis shared with *Paranthropus* a number of cranial and dental adaptations to the tougher fruit and open savanna food items sought by early hominids. However, while *Paranthropus* was principally adapted by means of very robust jaws and teeth to its tough and abrasive diet, *Homo rudolfensis* exhibited an increased behavioral flexibility (including a larger and more provoking, inquiring, and capable brain) as its adaptation to the new climatic circumstances. However, judging by its teeth, *Homo rudolfensis* seems to have shifted to proportionately less abrasive foodstuffs and more omnivorous habits. Perhaps material culture, such as stone tools, ameliorated the effects of climate change to the degree that *Homo rudolfensis* could take advantage of other resources more efficiently than was ever possible before (stone tools have been found in East African deposits aged approximately 2.5 million years ago, though hominids have yet to be recovered in association with them).

Paranthropus boisei and *Homo rudolfensis* remained in the tropical latitudes during this time. The eastern African tropical faunas remained within their biogeographical domain rather than brave the deterioration of habitats south of the African Rift Valley. It would not be for another half a million years or so before *Paranthropus boisei*, at least, would disperse to more southern latitudes during an expansion of its biome sometime after two million years ago.

Waning of the forests and woodlands and the expansion of more open arid grasslands invigorated not only evolutionary adaptations to savanna life in tropical eastern Africa, but also resulted in the drift northward of faunas tracking the shift toward the equator of grassland and woodland biomes into eastern Africa about 2.5 million years ago The southern temperate zone experienced more seasonal extremes and many organisms maintained their preference for moderately seasonal climes and temperate vegetation by moving northward with the shrinking of their biome toward the equator. Amongst these migrants was *Australopithecus africanus* who, having been adapted to a very modest temperate ecology and having endured the continued drying and cooling of southern Africa for some half a million years or more, now found its suitable habitats shifted to the north toward the African Rift Valley.

During its time in southern Africa *Australopithecus africanus* experienced the pressures of climate change in much the same way as its ancestral cousin, *Australopithecus afarensis*, had done in eastern Africa. Some populations became pushed to the edge of their habitat and became adapted to more open habitats. Indeed, selection favored some of the trends similar to those of *Paranthropus* in eastern Africa. Other populations, however, endeavored to maintain their habitat preference for forested environments, so they dispersed northward along a riparian corridor connecting southern with eastern Africa. While dispersing toward the eastern African tropical domain, selection for increased behavioral flexibility was related to the diversity of non-vegetable food resources available in their new biome. This emerging taxon, *Homo habilis*, rapidly established itself as an omnivore and with its material culture was able to take advantage of more resources.

By approximately two million years ago, Africa began to rebound from its relatively cool and dry climate to return to slightly more warm and humid conditions. *Paranthropus boisei* now dispersed southward along re-established habitats into southern Africa, varied there as a geographic variant under more temperate conditions, and evolved into *Paranthropus robustus*. *Homo habilis* also expanded southward into the southern African temperate domain but it maintained a very much broader niche, increasing its distributional area as a single species. *Homo rudolfensis* remained endemic to the eastern African tropical domain due partly to its preference for more open habitats around the rain shadow of the African Rift Valley and partly, perhaps, because they were excluded from geographic realms already occupied by *Homo habilis.*

CONCLUSION

I have touched upon only a few of the laboratory and field pursuits concerned with the field of paleoanthropology that have touched my career. It is truly an interdisciplinary science, and while many of its participants may specialize in one subfield, they are nevertheless engaged in a number of fields. Being an interdisciplinary science, all of its parts necessarily combine to portray the richness and diversity of the human lineage and its evolutionary predicament. For instance, our field studies document the global climate change to cooler and drier conditions 2.5 million years ago. This favored a tougher savanna vegetation which all terrestrial vertebrates, including early hominids, had to deal with. Thus *Paranthropus* species evolved larger teeth and facial skeletons to support stronger muscles to chew the tougher roughage. In our laboratory we have documented the cellular changes in bone and tooth development which were required by the changing habitat. Thus, global climate change favored the cellular changes in the *Paranthropus* face, among other developments, in the evolution of hominids.

SUGGESTED READINGS

Bromage, T. G. "Faces from the Past." *New Scientist* (January 11, 1992): 38–41. This is a general description of bone and tooth development relevant to an understanding of early hominid growth and development. The ontogeny of the early hominid face is summarized and the ways in which faces are connected to the braincase are portrayed over the course of human evolution.

Shell, E. R. "Ways (Waves) of Creation." *Discover* (May 1993): 54–61. In an interview with Elisabeth Vrba, the Habitat Theory is described in terms of what is called the "turn-over pulse hypothesis." The interplay between global climate change, animal structure and behavior, and speciation or extinction are discussed for African horned animals (bovids) during the Late Pliocene.

THE EVOLUTION
OF A PHYSICAL ANTHROPOLOGIST

KATHARINE MILTON

Until recently, no one had to wonder what they would do when they grew up because the answer was simple: Individuals fortunate enough to survive to adulthood typically did whatever their mother or father had done and that was that. Today conditions are different. Now almost everyone must face the question of what career to pursue. Though a fortunate few seem born knowing they want to be brain surgeons or fashion designers, for most of us the question is not so simple. And indeed for some of us, the question of what career to pursue continues to preoccupy us for some years into adulthood. I was one of these rather slow starters. That is to say, I stumbled in and out of several different career trajectories before I finally fell backward into the right choice. I guess I represent a classic example of the fact that many of the best things in life aren't planned—at least not initially.

EARLY ATTEMPTS AT CHOOSING A CAREER

When I was growing up in Alabama, though good grades were emphatically encouraged, never once was the idea presented to me that one might study something just for fun—that it might be a real kick to use one's mind. Nor did anyone ever suggest entering a field such as biology, mathematics, or physics—anything in the sciences was neither mentioned nor conceived. Ditto for business. The notion of a "career" in terms of itself, of the joy and happiness that might come from one's work, simply wasn't an issue. Perhaps my parents thought it was obvious and I always have been slow at realizations. I do remember that at one point my father did say I should become a lawyer because I loved to argue. But that was about it for suggestions regarding my future career.

When I occasionally discussed the subject of college with my mother (my father being too busy to engage in such conversations), I dimly realized that while at college one was supposed to acquire a degree in "something"—from my mother's point of view, some practical thing that, "will help you earn a living if you lose your husband in an accident and have to support your children." That certainly didn't sound like much fun; in fact it sounded like something to avoid.

In any case, off I went to a college in Virginia, Sweet Briar, which far from being as saccharine as its name implies, turned out to be the most intellectually rewarding of all my by-now extensive encounters with higher education. The professors at Sweet Briar were terrific, they loved their subjects, they loved to teach, and I loved learning from them. It was only at this point that I began to realize that thinking was fun. Toward the close of my senior year, the fun turned to nervousness. I had taken considerable coursework in English literature prior to the twentieth century but hadn't managed to get to my own century, which I found of particular interest. My professors recommended graduate schools with good programs in twentieth century English literature. I made application to several of these programs, went through my graduation ceremony at Sweet Briar, and returned home to Alabama. That summer I just sat around in a daze—I didn't know what to do, what I would do, what day of the week it was. It was a shock to suddenly be out of college, the arena where my life had been totally focused for the past four years. I was a graduate, I had a B.A., I was supposed to be doing something but that something was not manifesting itself with any clarity.

I was saved by a phone call. The University of Iowa rang up to say that yes they would take me as a graduate student and yes they even had a job for me so that I could earn my tuition and living expenses. So off I went to graduate school in Iowa City, once again suffused with purpose, to study modern English literature and prepare for a career as a literary critic. I got my M.A. and moved to New York to seek a position as a literary critic. This was not so easy as such jobs seemed in remarkably short supply. I took a position at Time Inc. as an editorial assistant while I pondered my future—was journalism the answer to my career concerns?

During this period I also got married and my husband's job required that we move to Argentina. Buenos Aires was beautiful and sophisticated and once I got settled in, my life was perfect in every way except for just one little thing—I was bored to death within only a few weeks. There were no jobs for women in Buenos Aires for which I was qualified and I had very little to do. I worked at numerous small jobs—occasionally writing for the English language newspaper and such but basically these were stop-gap activities and realizing this, they only made me sad. In frustration, I began reading books in the English language library near my house. They had a biology section with books on animal behavior and I read through the entire shelf. Much of the work was ecological and I gradually decided that being a behavioral or ecological scientist would be an ideal thing to aspire to because then I would never again find myself with nothing to do. The literary careers I had initially been fumbling toward were always ones that required a formal setting and other people—their presence, their books, a formal working infrastructure—in order to be active. Being a scientist doesn't necessarily require a formal setting or the presence of other people in any type of routinized environment. You can do many types of science wherever, whenever—if there are no cats, monkeys, or earthworms around to observe, you can study plants or your fellow humans. The trick, or so it seemed to me, was to learn what problems were worth studying and how one would go about compiling information on these problems in a scientific manner.

So that is how I got into my career as a scientist—pure desperation, a handy library, a fortuitous shelf of books—and the idea that science would save me from boredom for the rest of my life. I hated being bored, I couldn't stand having nothing of real interest to do and I would have done anything to escape this boredom. People, particularly women raised in a conventional setting, often don't realize that they may have a mind that requires more than the daily routine and an occasional newspaper or magazine to be happy. I was lucky—being bored in Argentina while I was still quite young made this crystal clear and so off I went, back to the United States and back to school once more but this time to get my scientific education.

MONKEY BUSINESS AS A CAREER

Suffice it to say that it was very difficult for an English major to get into graduate school to study biological subject matter. Finally, I managed to get accepted into the newly created Anthropology Department at New York University to study physical anthropology—as it was a new program, it is likely that few students initially applied, giving me a better chance. In a program in physical anthropology, I would be able to study the ecology and behavior of non-human primates—prosimians, monkeys, and apes—as well as that of my own species and this seemed to offer sufficient scope for my scientific aspirations. Further, the city of New York, with its many colleges, universities, and museums gave me the opportunity to delve into a number of other courses and programs while enrolled in the Ph.D. program at NYU.

By 1973 I had managed to leap through all of the sticky academic hoops required for what is termed *advancement to candidacy*. This meant that now all that stood between me and the Ph.D. was my dissertation research—in other words, course work, exams, boring professors, and the like were behind me forever. But now, I needed a research topic for my thesis. In the early 1970s most field studies of wild primates were strongly focused on aspects of sociality. In particular, as primates were known to have a large number of different patterns of social organization, there was considerable interest in determining the factors that might underlie all of this variability. But at the time, relatively little attention was being paid to features of the environment—that is, to aspects of the ecology of the primates rather than only to aspects of their sociality. It seemed to me that this was trying to understand the cherry on the top of the sundae without looking at the composition of the sundae itself. Since most individuals then interested in primate behavior were, like me, in departments of anthropology, which tend to be dominated by social scientists, it is easy to see why they were pondering social behaviors rather than features of the environment. Perhaps they felt that examining patterns of food distribution, dietary quality, predator pressures, and the like would produce a type of environmental determinism at the monkey level. But I suspected that more attention needed to be paid to factors impinging on the monkeys from the outside rather than just determining that monkey A was dominant over monkey B or noting that some primate species lived in large groups and others in small ones.

I somehow had decided that a detailed examination of diet was likely to provide me with a key to understanding most aspects of primate behavior but it is difficult for me to be certain of just how I arrived at this dietary focus. Perhaps it was due, at least in part, to an article I had read in *American Anthropologist* in which Bartholomew and Birdsell gave a strikingly original, *ecological* overview of early human evolution in which they focused on potential environmental pressures placed on the earliest humans as a means of understanding key features of human morphology and behavior.[1] Also, some primatologists were beginning to explore aspects of diet in their fieldwork, which must have indicated to me that "this was what one was supposed to be doing." But I also knew, probably because even then I did not confine my reading to journals and books only about primates but rather read widely in the general ecological and evolutionary literature, that to understand diet, one had to do more than just describe what the monkeys were eating—make dietary laundry lists. Rather, one had to be able to document what foods were available in the forest and then determine why the monkeys were choosing certain foods rather than others. Thus from my earliest days as a researcher, I also had an interest in plants.

I came up with several dissertation topics that didn't work out. For example, first I wanted to study the ruffed lemur, *Varecia variegatas*, in Madagascar—it had an unusual loud call, gave birth to twins rather than a single infant, and had other striking characteristics that I felt must relate in some manner to dietary energetics, but political conditions in Madagascar made such research impossible. I then thought about studying a New World monkey, *Cebus apella*, unusual because it had such a wide geographical distribution relative to other members of its genus. I suspected its dentition (and therefore its diet) might explain its distribution—but there were so little data available in the early 1970s on members of the genus *Cebus* that even if I had obtained information on the diet of *C. apella*, I would have had almost nothing to compare it with—leaving me with a problem in a vacuum. If you want to understand how something is similar to or different from something else, you need information on the something else to compare with the material you compile.

OFF TO PANAMA

Finally, Alison Richard, a primatologist at Yale, suggested I go to Panama and work in the tropical forest there to gain some practical experience. I decided to focus my attention on mantled howler monkeys (*Alouatta palliata*). In fact, these howler monkeys had been the first primates studied in the natural environment—in the early 1930s. C. Ray Carpenter had observed howlers for a period of months and published an excellent monograph on features of their social organization, diet, and behavior.[2] Various other well-known primatologists had also examined aspects of howler behavior in the ensuing years but generally for only short periods of time. Thus I would be following in the footsteps of illustrious predecessors and could build on their earlier observations. The question was, what was it about howler monkeys that I was going to research? I felt that some aspect of the howler diet would be appropriate but in March of 1974 when I flew to Panama, I was still very uncertain as to what my study actually would consist of. It is clear, however, that my interests were always focused on diet, for in reading over an old letter I wrote in 1973 to request permission to come to Panama to begin my preliminary research, I state that one of my reasons for wanting to work on howler monkeys at a field station called Barro Colorado Island was the fact that the island had a *herbarium* (formal plant collection) that would permit me to identify the plant foods the monkeys were eating and learn the scientific names of the tree species.

When I arrived in Panama I must have presented an amusing and unpromising sight. I was rather plump and stuffed into somewhat inappropriate field clothes. I knew nothing about keeping off the myriad hoards of ticks and red bugs that make the researcher's life in this tropical forest a perpetual living hell and in fact during my first week on the island I actually went on a picnic and *sat on the ground*—tantamount to committing suicide in this bug-infested environment. I had no idea how one was supposed to carry out real field research, and toward this end I was burdened with an old blue American Tourister suitcase, giant sized, that must have weighed over one hundred pounds as it was crammed with every scientific article I owned to aid in planning my research assault. I was so out of shape that for first few weeks when walking on the trails, I had to stop and rest every twenty or thirty feet. Barro Colorado Island was created in the early part of this century by damming the nearby Chagras River to form a waterway for the Panama Canal. The rising water flooded most of the region, leaving only the steeper hilltops sticking up out of the new lake. Barro Colorado is a six-square mile island composed of these rolling hilltops and walking about on the island typically involves a considerable amount of climbing up and down steep trails in the hot muggy climate.

Back in the early 1970s tropical ecology had not yet become the popular research field it is today. There were few other scientists on the island my first months there and often I was the only person eating dinner in the large dining hall. But frankly, I didn't notice or care, a personality trait that has stood me in good stead over the course of my career—because I had an entire island full of exotic animals as my companions. The forest was loaded with howler monkeys, cebus monkeys, spider monkeys, tapirs, wild pigs, deer, coatis, sloths, agoutis, weird bugs, and neon-blue butterflies the size of dinner plates. I kept a little notebook and recorded all the animals that I saw, particularly noting information on where I saw howler monkeys and various details of their behavior as well as collecting samples of the plants they were eating.

I've always devoted considerable time to the observation of plants as well as animals. Understanding what trees are doing helps me to understand the behavior of the monkeys and vice versa. Plants face most of the same problems animals do—namely, how to obtain adequate nutrition, how to find the best mate, how to do the best one can for one's offspring, and how to avoid danger and illness. And they've had to solve these critical problems while rooted in one place in the ground. Working with trees and their fruits, seeds, flowers, and leaves has been an education in itself, since many of their solutions to these problems are subtle ones that can involve exotic chemicals, elaborate genetic mechanisms, and the like.

You might assume that a fruit is a fruit is a fruit. But scientists believe that the first primitive fruits were elaborated millions of years ago to help plants disperse their seeds, thereby improving their prospects for colonization and growth. The sweet juicy pulp surrounding the seeds is the plant's way of luring seed dispersal agents such as monkeys, bats, or birds into eating the fruit, simultaneously scattering or swallowing the seeds, which may then be defecated some distance from the parent tree. The solutions plants have evolved to their problems often in turn become primate problems; certainly we can assume that over evolutionary time natural selection has favored plant defenses that help them avoid the loss of their new leaves, nectar-filled flowers, unripe fruits, and edible seeds to hungry primates. How primates get around these plant defenses and solve their dietary problems are, in essence, what has made primates primates. The old adage, you are what you eat, is absolutely true. As Darwin noted, living matter possesses an almost infinite capacity to replicate itself. Yet at the same time, dietary resources available on the planet at any one time are always limited and always far lower than the potential mouths seeking to devour them. Thus selective processes have produced myriad ways of securing some portion of these always finite essential resources—and these different dietary battle plans in essence are the diverse array of living life forms present on the planet. With our overly well-stocked supermarkets and endless food at our fingertips, we often forget that obtaining adequate food and water is generally the single most compelling daily activity of most other living organisms. Indeed, even human societies that live in remote regions and lack our technological means of food preservation typically devote the greatest percentage of their daylight hours to activities directly involved in obtaining, cleaning, and preparing the food they eat.

HOWLER MONKEY ECONOMICS

I wasn't on Barro Colorado Island very long before finding a dissertation topic. I decided to study the interface between the components of the howler diet, howler digestive processes, and howler food acquisition activities (where and when different foods were available)—because what I observed in my first few weeks on the island did not tally with what I had expected from reading the literature. Howler monkeys were known to be arboreal herbivores—that is, they lived in the trees not on the ground and they obtained all of their foods from plant parts. But I could quickly see that howler monkeys were not just some type of arboreal cows that sat around stuffing themselves with the most convenient leafy foods all day—rather the monkeys were traveling all over the forest, eating many different species of leaves as well as considerable amounts of fruits and flowers—ten, twenty, or more species in some days. Clearly making a living as an arboreal herbivore was a far trickier business than I'd been led to believe. I wanted to figure out what was going on.

My viewpoint—the reality I saw in 1973—was simultaneously both the same and different from that seen by my scientific predecessors who had carried out earlier observations on howler monkeys in this same forest. As scientific knowledge is always advancing, many new things had been learned since these earlier howler monkey studies—new information about the chemical constituents of wild plants, about the often subtle mechanisms involved in food selection and, most importantly, about the deceptive nature of reality—the fact that though tropical forests looked as if they could provide an endless food supply for plant eaters, in truth most of this lush greenery was not of a quality to sustain life for mammals the size of howler monkeys. *Optimal foraging theory*[3] had also emerged, a theory that presented models that made predictions about how a given animal should behave when faced with different types of dietary situations. I had read all of this ecological literature and thus when I began to examine howler monkey behavior in 1974, though their behavior probably differed little if at all from that observed by my predecessors, I was mentally primed to view their foraging activities somewhat differently. In this way, each new generation of scientists builds on the scientific resource base passed on to them by their predecessors.

The approaches that I employed in the fieldwork and the results I obtained are presented in detail in my book on howler monkeys, which was my doctoral dissertation.[4] I spent approximately fourteen months carrying out my study, using two different groups of howler monkeys and collecting data in a systematic manner that made it highly amenable to statistical analyses. I carried out simple feeding trials to examine howler food choices and digestive processes. I also carried out work on different aspects of the forest, determining the density of different tree species, their spatial patterns, the production patterns of new leaves and fruits, and so on. I was able to integrate these botanical data successfully with the feeding and physiological data on the monkeys and come up with a novel synthesis—what I termed a study of *monkey economics*—that took food availability, food locations, dietary quality, howler energetics, and howler digestive abilities and integrated them into a solid overview of howler monkey dietary behavior. These same data also permitted me to understand a considerable amount about howler monkey social behavior. During these months of fieldwork, it was often hard for me to get up at 4 A.M. and walk out into the dark, frequently rainy forest for twelve hours of monkey observations, but I kept at it, confident that my results would make the momentary discomfort well worth the effort. And I believe that they were. Often researchers state that they are never satisfied with their research—indeed, some never publish anything because it isn't perfect. Well, nature isn't interested in perfection and neither am I. I'm interested in doing the best job possible with the facts known at the moment—and this is what I believe I did in my book. I've since moved on and learned considerably more and now of course I'd change some things to reflect what I've since learned; but at the time, I believe my book was state of the art and I was thrilled with my synthesis. My favorite story about my dissertation work and the book that resulted from it is one that was told to me by a colleague from Duke who was flying out to the West Coast. He noticed that the young woman sitting next to him was intently reading a book. On inspection it turned out not to be a hot new best-seller but rather my howler monkey book, being read by a prospective graduate student coming to visit the Berkeley campus. My friend was very impressed and of course once I heard that story, I thought the prospective student seemed unusually promising.

After obtaining the Ph.D. in Physical Anthropology, I went on to spend two more years on Barro Colorado Island working on questions my dissertation work had raised. In fact even now, twenty years later, I still travel to Panama each year to continue my research on howler monkeys. These visits, which generally occur around Christmas or during summer vacation, used to drive my parents in Alabama absolutely crazy. They could not believe that in a few years I hadn't answered every question worth asking about those pesky monkeys. But as I've tried to explain, scientific work generally leads from one question to another and one could spend several lifetimes studying howler monkeys on Barro Colorado Island and still have an eternity of interesting questions left over. Why, for example, over the past fifty years has average troop size for howler monkeys on this island remained at around nineteen individuals? Why, too, are there so few juvenile monkeys in the population when so many cute new babies are born every year? Clearly most of these baby monkeys must not make it to adulthood but why is this? Are predators eating them? Are they dying of disease? Are their mothers abandoning them and, if so, why? Or am I just off in my censusing work? I imagine I'll be working on questions like these until I'm too old to climb those steep hills. Then I'll probably sit in my laboratory at Berkeley and fiddle with my years of data on the computer. Few of my colleagues work on demographic questions—censusing monkeys at the same times year after year is tedious, there are many confounding variables and often years can pass before any population shifts occur to give insight into critical factors that warrant investigation. Right now, for example, I am studying the parasites of howler monkeys, trying to determine how parasites affect the health of an infested monkey and what the critical parasite load may be for monkeys of different ages. Examining these questions will take me four or five years—and as

I go along, I will add new questions. I'm not frustrated by the long time this type of population study takes, because I know that finding answers to complex questions about long-lived animals such as monkeys generally takes many years. Too, I have other research interests that provide me with more immediate feedback and intellectual gratification.

MORE MONKEY BUSINESS

Howler monkeys are my first love but I've also given away a large piece of my heart to another monkey, the woolly spider monkey *Brachyteles arachnoides*, a rare geographic isolate found only in one small area of southeastern Brazil. Woolly spider monkeys have long been almost mythical creatures to primatologists—they seem always to be described in terms of superlatives—the largest monkey in the New World, the most endangered monkey, the least known and little studied monkey, and so on. Even when I was in graduate school I dreamed about studying woolly spider monkeys. But because they were so rare there were few potential study sites and further, I thought that a Brazilian primatologist would certainly want to carry out the first study of their ecology since this species occurs only in Brazil. Years passed and yet no one had managed to get a study of this fabulous monkey under way. Given its highly endangered status, this was absurd. We needed to obtain all of the information we could on their ecology to try and implement an intelligent conservation program. But it never occurred to me that the someone who might do this would be me. I'd obtained my position at Berkeley and was busily trying to master the intricacies of teaching huge courses with five hundred or more students and handle all of my other new responsibilities. Any thoughts of monkey business were on hold for the moment when out of the blue I received a remarkable invitation. A private landowner in Brazil wrote to me inviting me to come and carry out a study of the woolly spider monkeys living in the forests on his ranch. As he'd heard I liked to live close to the monkeys I was studying, he offered to build me a small house in the forest and cut me a series of trails to facilitate my work.

Few people, I imagine, are fortunate enough to get invitations like this. I went to my department chair and told him about the letter. And he agreed that it was an amazing research opportunity and that I should take full advantage of it. One nice thing about my department at Berkeley is the fact that it both expects and encourages its professors to carry out original research and does not penalize them if they take a leave of absence for this purpose. No one pays my salary while I'm gone but at least when I return, my job is waiting for me. So I wrote back and said I was coming, obtained a small grant to cover a few expenses and off I went.

In this case, I had no central hypothesis to test—rather, since there had never been any long-term studies of this monkey species, anything I could learn about its ecology and behavior would be a benefit. Thus my objectives were to count the number of woolly spider monkeys on the ranch and to obtain as complete and detailed an account of their diet, ranging patterns, and social behavior as was possible. But interestingly enough, this study turned out to involve some dramatic and totally unexpected new insights. Some see what they think they should see—luckily, my formal academic training was so spotty that I've never suffered from a bad case of preconception. Perhaps just for this reason, I saw something very unexpected when I studied woolly spider monkeys, so unexpected in fact that it's taken a number of years for my point of view to be fully accepted.

Woolly spider monkeys are related to spider monkeys (genus *Ateles*) and closely resemble them in general appearance. In fact, to me woolly spider monkeys look like a blown-up version of spider monkeys and they even have the same type of whinnying call. There have been a number of excellent studies of wild spider monkeys at various sites in Central and South America and all of these studies have shown that spider monkeys take their diet almost exclusively from ripe fruit. In fact, spider monkeys are one of the most extreme examples of ripe fruit specialists in the primate order. I guess because of the close physical similarity between spider monkeys and woolly spider monkeys, people thought that fruit would also figure heavily in the woolly spider monkey diet. This "common sense" view was so prevalent that whenever woolly spider monkeys were captured and put in zoos, they were fed fruit. Apparently no one ever connected the short life span of captive woolly spider monkeys with the fact that perhaps, just perhaps, they were being fed the wrong food.

But there were some indications that woolly spider monkeys might not be all that frugivorous. For one thing, woolly spider monkeys were larger than spider monkeys. For reasons as yet imperfectly understood, in mammals larger body size results in lower energetic costs per unit of body weight. This relationship permits the larger animal to utilize foods lower in energy than those tolerated by their smaller counterparts. Large body size in woolly spider monkeys to me indicated lower quality foods—in other words, fibrous leaves, not sugary fruits. In addition, the teeth of woolly spider monkeys showed differences from those of spider monkeys and at least one expert in primate dentition had predicted that when woolly spider monkeys were studied, they would be found to eat large quantities of leaves. But given the striking similarity of spider and woolly spider monkeys in most other traits, these more subtle observations on their body size and dentition were generally ignored and fruit was regarded as the probable dietary foundation.

To make a long story short, my field study of woolly spider monkeys was a dream study in which everything went right. The monkeys seemed to realize that this was their chance to tell their story and though I'm not the sentimental type, it often seemed as if the monkeys were going out of their way to make sure I saw and understood what they were doing, even waiting at times for me to get my camera ready or repeating an action two or three times as if to say, "do you think she's finally figured out what's going on?" I believe that, ultimately, I did, though initially many behaviors of woolly spider monkeys were difficult for me to understand. First, my data showed that leaves, not fruit, made up the overwhelming percentage of the annual diet of woolly spider monkeys. Inspection of another group of woolly spider monkeys in a nearby forest likewise showed precisely the same leaf-eating pattern. At first I thought, well, maybe this is just a seasonal thing that will change in a few weeks. But it prevailed over all sample months but one, leaving no doubt that the foundation of the woolly spider monkey diet is leafy matter and that fruits (and flowers) are more limited, generally seasonal delicacies. Zoos, listen up—if you are ever fortunate enough to obtain a woolly spider monkey or two, be sure to give them leafy matter as their major dietary component, not ripe sugary fruits!

For a long time, too, I was totally puzzled by the fact that woolly spider monkeys didn't seem to have any type of permanent social grouping. Each female appeared to have a home range or core area in which she would generally be found. But various females often would come together at different points during the day or from day to day and forage for one or more hours as a group. I could find no consistent pattern to their fusioning and fissioning. Males were the oddest of all. Immature males often showed up alone and hung around with a particular female for days or even weeks. Then at other times smaller or larger groups of males would appear, foraging and associating with one or more of the females I was observing for a period of time and then off they would go, not to be seen again for days. In addition, these woolly spider monkey males had some very striking attributes in the form of the largest testes (and penis) I'd ever seen on a monkey. Indeed, when I first saw the testes of a fully adult male woolly spider monkey, I thought the animal had elephantiasis or was deformed. Why on earth, I thought, would an arboreal monkey, swinging through the trees with all those sharp sticks, branches, and thorns, need with those megatestes?

Woolly spider monkeys, ever the cooperative study subjects, were not long in letting me know why such testes might prove useful. One of my females became sexually receptive. She generally foraged only in the company of her juvenile offspring. Suddenly one day she increased her day range from the normal four hundred or so meters to almost a full kilometer (one thousand meters). Shortly thereafter, I noticed that male woolly spider monkeys suddenly began appearing out of nowhere in large numbers. These males showed up in groups of two or three until there were nine or ten males clustered around her. The coy female acted as if she didn't even see the males, moving about and attempting to feed but, at the same time, she emitted a ridiculous twittering vocalization I'd not heard before and that I later termed the "mating twitter." The males obviously found her twitter absolutely irresistible and one after another each male would attempt to copulate with her. Unlike many male primates, these males didn't fight or act aggressive toward one another in terms of gaining access to the female; rather, each waited until the one before had moved away from the female before approaching her. This lack of aggression was all the more impressive because it was obvious that the males were intensely excited, so much so that at times they almost fell out of the trees, often hugging one another in their enthusiasm. I decided the males must have a type of dominance hierarchy, perhaps worked out in their daily activities, that let them know more or less the correct order in the copulatory scheme and thus keep quarreling to a minimum. But where do the huge testes fit in? In my view, the arena for reproductive success in this monkey species has moved from overt fighting between the males for sexual access to receptive females into the interior of the female's reproductive tract. I speculate that the huge testes of the males provide copious quantities of sperm at each ejaculation and that males compete for reproductive success at least in part through sperm competition in which each male tries to wash out and dilute the sperm deposited by his predecessors and in this way father the infant.

To understand why selection may have favored sperm competition in this species, we need to consider its diet. Unlike fruits, leaves do not offer a rich source of readily digestible energy. As woolly spider monkeys eat diets composed largely of leaves, I would imagine that excess energy is generally in short supply. The fluid grouping patterns of the females appear to force males to travel extensively to monitor their reproductive condition. Such travel activities may leave little excess energy for male-male combat, favoring a less dramatic form of male competition. Perhaps in this species, owing to its generally limited energetic substrate, selection has favored sperm competition rather than energetically expensive and dangerous fighting between males for possession of a sexually receptive female. Too, many males in a mating aggregation may also be closely related, which would also tend to lower intermale aggression. If you don't father the infant, perhaps your brother will, passing on many of your own genes in the process.

Sperm competition may explain the huge testes in woolly spider monkey males, but there is still the huge penis to explain. Most primates are not noted for penis size. In fact the erect penis of the gorilla, the largest living primate, is only around one and a quarter inches in length while the human male has one of the largest penises in the primate order.[5] A scientist named William Eberhard has speculated that in many mammals, penis size may often relate to female choice—that is, to pleasing the female rather than to specific features related to sperm deposition.[6] In the case of woolly spider monkeys, the large penis may aid in depositing a large amount of sperm high in the female's reproductive tract, but its size is so large relative to the penis size in most other primates that I believe some further selective pressures are involved. Chimpanzees, for example, have unusually large testes and multi-male mating behavior, and sperm competition is also believed to occur in this species. But the erect penis of a male chimpanzee is only around three inches long, indicating that a large penis is not essential in sperm competition. Thus it may well be that penis size in woolly spider monkeys relates in some way to pleasing the female and to female choice—that is, it may be the female who has the ultimate say as to which male in the crowd will father her infant. Copulation in this species is unusually prolonged, lasting for four to eight minutes rather than the thirty seconds or less typical of most primates. This suggests that in some manner, female woolly spider monkeys may be judging individual males through features of penis size and copulatory competence, though this remains to be demonstrated.

All in all, with the leafy diet, the fluid pattern of social organization, and the dramatic and unexpected features of mating behavior, woolly spider monkeys gave me one surprise after another but finally I believe that I was able to make sense of what initially had seemed to be a totally confusing set of behaviors and morphological features. In terms of the contributions of my study to woolly spider monkey conservation, sad to say but even now, some ten years later, very little has been done to facilitate the conservation of this fabulous monkey. Indeed, conservation organizations have more or less ignored my findings and seem disinterested in factual information about the species. Due to this apparent disinterest, I am wary of large conservation foundations and their professed concern with "saving" particular species.

PROBLEMS IN HUMAN ECOLOGY

In 1979 I made my first trip to Brazil to compare several howler monkey species there with the mantled howlers I'd been studying in Panama. While carrying out this research, which often took me to very remote areas in the Amazon Basin, I began to notice something rather strange. In all large Brazilian cities there are dozens of newsstands, which always have well-stocked postcard racks. Many of these postcards depict indigenous peoples of the Brazilian rain forest; these beautiful people are shown lavishly painted in intricate patterns with natural dyes, wearing beautifully colored feathers and ornaments, and carrying out ceremonies or participating in daily activities. I'd hang around these newsstands, buying dozens of the beautiful cards to send to my friends. But it began to dawn on me that though I always saw these postcards in cities, when I was actually deep in the rain forest looking for howler monkeys, I never saw a single Indian. Where are these people, I asked myself, and why don't I ever see a village or meet an indigenous person? Finally, it is no exaggeration to say that I became absolutely obsessed with this discrepancy. I wanted to see the human inhabitants of these tropical forests and I began to realize too that when I found them, I wanted to live among them and observe how they were using their forest environment. I made a decision that my next fieldwork would be with humans in the tropical rain forest. I realized that human cultural practices could change greatly in even a single generation and that time was running out in terms of being able to document the ecological interactions of these forest peoples before they were heavily exposed to western technology. Indeed, at that point I wasn't even sure if there were indigenous groups in the rain forest that were still living in a traditional manner.

After returning to the United States, I began to research studies on tropical forest peoples and found, not surprisingly, that though some attention had been paid to cultural features of some of these societies—to kinship relations and the like—and that some attention had been paid to their material goods—to patterns on pottery or baskets—ecological work was very limited. I further determined, through travel, questioning, and interviews with Brazilian anthropologists, that there still were various indigenous groups deep in the rain forest that as yet had been largely unaffected by exposure to outside influences. Thus I decided that I would carry out a series of studies on indigenous peoples of the Brazilian rain forest to document features of their ecology before western technology intervened.

My reading of the literature showed that the behavior of forest-based peoples in Amazonia had been the object of considerable anthropological speculation in spite of the lack of ecological information. In particular, single-factor hypotheses related to diet had been used to try and explain many features of these forest-based cultures such as settlement size (generally small), nomadic and semi-nomadic behaviors (tropical forest peoples are reported to move about a great deal), lack of social stratification (such societies are often described as egalitarian and appear to largely lack stratification), and even behavioral traits such as aggression (some scholars had speculated that tropical forest peoples were aggressive and engaged in frequent warfare because protein dietary sources in the tropical forest were in short supply). Tropical forest peoples frequently were denigrated in these writings by being referred to as "marginal" peoples or "refugees"—terms suggesting that they would not want to live in the tropical forest if they hadn't been forced to. One especially insensitive paper actually compared them to street people, implying, I guess, that they were dysfunctional misfits in the modern world! Others referred to forest peoples as if they were relics of the Pleistocene, peoples without a history, whose customs never altered. Finally, there were views that ranged from the noble savage in the Garden of Eden to the other end of the spectrum in which tropical forest peoples were portrayed as cannibals and headhunters. Clearly there was a lot of work to be done if all of these often contradictory and confusing portrayals were ever to be reconciled into a coherent and factual account of the real lives of forest dwellers. And, as I've noted, the time remaining to actually gather information on peoples of the forest who were still living without shotguns, machetes, and the like was fast running out.

I wrote a grant proposal to test one of the hypotheses about Amazonian forest peoples then in the anthropological literature—namely, that forest dwellers living in upland regions well away from major rivers would suffer more from these postulated protein shortages than indigenous societies living near large rivers—ostensibly because the deep forest dwellers would lack access to fish, turtles, and other riverine protein sources. I selected an indigenous group called the Maku for this dietary work, who were ideal because they lived in upland forest regions with poor, sandy soil, regions noted for their paucity of game animals. I felt that if I could find no evidence of protein shortage in this extreme situation, the possibility of it occurring in richer areas of

Amazonia would be even more improbable. After eighteen months of petitioning for permission to do my study from various Brazilian agencies, permission was granted and with a grant from the National Geographic Society in hand, I set off for Brazil to study the dietary ecology of the Maku and test the protein limitation hypothesis.

After various delays and setbacks I managed to get to a small town called Sao Gabriel de Cachoeira, located in the northwest of the Brazilian state of Amazonas on the bank of the Rio Negro. I could then find no means of transport to go farther into the region where the Maku were reported to live. I went around looking for anyone with a canoe who might be willing to take me for some weeks along smaller rivers into the Maku area but could find no one. Finally, the Brazilian Air Force agreed to fly me in as they had to take supplies to a remote Catholic mission in the area They flew me in an old cargo plane dating from World War II. The plane landed on a dirt runway, sending up a huge dust cloud; the soldiers quickly threw the cargo, including all of my supplies for six months, into the dirt, they helped me out of the plane, waved goodbye, and off they flew—leaving me standing alone in the middle of the forest on a dirt runway with a large crowd of people racing toward me. This was truly a moment of intense fear on my part. I spoke not a word of any indigenous language, I was in the middle of the Amazon Basin totally out of contact with anyone or anything familiar to me, I had no idea what would transpire, and I was afraid. Immediately I was surrounded. These were not the Maku but rather were Tukanoans, riverine people who would know how I might find the forest-dwelling Maku. By sign language and using some words of Portuguese they let me know that I could stay in the headman's house and they helped me carry all my goods there. I rigged up my hammock in one corner of the mud house and stacked my goods along a wall, covering them with a large sheet of plastic to keep off falling dirt, palm thatch, and bugs. That night the Tukanoans had a huge ceremony that involved the drinking of much manioc beer and considerable noise and intoxication. Again, I was frightened, especially as small groups of very inebriated Tukanoans kept staggering into the hut to try and converse. All of this was totally strange—I longed for the tranquillity and relative simplicity of my monkey studies and rued the day I'd foolishly decided to try and work with members of my own species—scary, strange, and all too human.

Eventually I adjusted, eventually I did meet some Maku who let me accompany them back to the forest and live with them, and eventually I did compile the data required to test the protein-limitation hypothesis. I came to know many of the Maku and feel at home in their forest environment and eventually to understand some relatively rudimentary aspects of their ecology and their relationship with the Tukanoans. Suffice it to say that the Maku appeared to have less of a problem with protein resources than the Tukanoans—suggesting that the view of protein shortages in the upland forests may be inaccurate. Indeed, my data suggested that the main dietary problem of forest-based peoples such as the Maku may relate more to locating sufficient amounts of energy-rich carbohydrate foods than it does to protein.

Following this initial study, I've had the good fortune to live with four other indigenous groups in the Brazilian Amazon (the Arara, Parakana, Arawete, and Mayoruna) as well as the so-called "lost tribe" (the Hagahai) in Papua New Guinea, and have been able to collect the same data on dietary ecology and uses of the forest environment in each case. My strategy in terms of these human studies has been to try and document the ecological practices of as many different forest-based indigenous societies as possible, as soon all such societies will be brought into contact with the outside world on a more routine basis and many features of their ecology will be rapidly altered. Thus, I'm attempting to maximize the size of my data base while I can.

In the future, I hope to be able to visit several other recently contacted or as yet uncontacted indigenous groups in the Amazonian forests to collect similar data and, in addition, I also have a wealth of new questions about the societies among whom I've already had the privilege of living. The careful study of forest-based human ecology has been much neglected and I believe it is essential to gain a better understanding of human behavior and human management practices in this unique and complex ecosystem. Such studies offer insights into dietary practices and activity patterns that promote human health and well being, they offer us the chance to learn more about the myriad useful plants and animals which inhabit the forest environment and, by observing the ecological practices of the indigenous inhabitants, we can learn more about indigenous management practices that preserve rather than destroy the forest.

SATISFIED WITH SCIENCE

All in all then, it would appear that my decision to become a physical anthropologist has more than fulfilled my every expectation. Indeed, being a physical anthropologist, to my way of thinking, is one of the most wonderful things imaginable because, in essence, it means that you can look at, examine, and speculate on just about anything you find of interest in the natural world. By definition, physical anthropologists deal with any subject matter having to do with human evolution, human adaptation, human biology, and human behavior. There is little that, in one way or another, does not impinge in some manner on our own existence as a species and thus, in effect, my career has been a liberating experience that has set me free to explore wherever my thoughts lead and, at the same time, offers me excitement and discovery, continuous mental stimulation, interesting students and colleagues and, best of all, the opportunity to advance our understanding and appreciation of the myriad complexities and beauty of the natural world. Isn't that just about as close to having your cake and eating it too as anyone could ever hope? I think so!

Notes

1. G. A. Bartholomew Jr. and J. B. Birdsell, "Ecology and the Protohominids," *American Anthropologist* 55 (1953): 481–498.
2. C. R. Carpenter, "A Field Study of the Behavior and Social Relations of Howling Monkeys," *Comparative Psychological Monographs* 10 (1934): 1–168.
3. T. W. Schoener, "Theory of Feeding Strategies," *Annual Review of Ecology and Systematics* 2 (1971): 369–403.
4. K. Milton, *The Foraging Strategy of Howler Monkeys: A Study in Primate Economics* (New York: Columbia University Press, 1981).
5. R. J. Short, "Sexual Selection in Man and the Great Apes," in C. E. Graham, ed., *Reproductive Biology of the Great Apes* (New York: Academic Press, 1981), pp. 319–341.
6. W. G. Eberhard, *Sexual Selection and Animal Genitalia* (Cambridge, MA: Harvard University Press, 1985).

Suggested Readings

Milton, K. "Protein and Carbohydrate Resources of the Maku Indians of Northwestern Amazonia." *American Anthropologist* 86 (1984): 7–27. This paper discusses the study I carried out of the Maku diet and goes into detail about protein limitation and other factors involved in the ecology of forest dwellers in Amazonia.

_____. "Habitat, Diet, and Activity Patterns of Free-Ranging Woolly Spider Monkeys (*Brachyteles arachnoides*, E. Geoffroy 1806)." *International Journal of Primatology* 5 (1984): 491–514. For those interested in further information on the behavior of this fabulous monkey, this paper discusses in detail my study site, the diet of the monkey, and its ranging behavior.

_____. "Mating Patterns of Woolly Spider Monkeys, *Brachyteles arachnoides:* Implications for Female Choice." *Behavioral Ecology and Sociobiology* 17 (1985): 53–59. A more scientific accounting of the incredible sexual activities of woolly spider monkeys.

_____. "Primate Diets and Gut Morphology: Implications for Human Evolution." In M. Harris and E. B. Ross, eds., *Food and Evolution: Toward a Theory of Human Food Habits*. Philadelphia: Temple University Press, 1987, pp. 93–116. Why is the digestive tract important in understanding the food choices of an animal? Once you read this paper, the answer will be clear and the role played by diet in shaping the evolution of a given lineage, including our own, should be much easier to appreciate.

_____. "Foraging Behavior and the Evolution of Primate Cognition." In A. Whiten and R. Byrne, eds., *Machiavellian Intelligence: Social Expertise and the Evolution of Intellect in Monkeys, Apes, and Humans*. Oxford: Oxford University Press, 1988, pp. 285–305. This paper evaluates results of an earlier paper in which I first discussed the role played by diet in terms of the brain size of different primate lineages. I find my initial paper still relevant and update many earlier comments in terms of more recent research on aspects of brain size in mammals.

_____. "Comparative Aspects of Diet in Amazonian Forest Dwellers." *Philosophical Transactions of the Royal Society, Series B* 334 (1991): 253–263. My study of four indigenous groups in the Brazilian Amazon proved surprising. Not only did each group have its own distinctive dietary focus, but different groups often appeared to taboo the foods most favored by their closest neighbors.